CW00471294

THE CREATION OF POVERTY AND INEQUALITY IN INDIA

Exclusion, Isolation, Domination and Extraction

Parthasarathi Shome

First published in Great Britain in 2023 by

Bristol University Press
University of Bristol
1–9 Old Park Hill
Bristol
BS2 8BB
UK
t: +44 (0)117 374 6645
e: bup-info@bristol.ac.uk

Details of international sales and distribution partners are available at bristoluniversitypress.co.uk

British Library Cataloguing in Publication Data
A catalogue record for this book is available from the British Library

ISBN 978-1-5292-3038-3 hardcover
ISBN 978-1-5292-3039-0 ePub
ISBN 978-1-5292-3040-6 ePdf

Cover design: Lyn Davies Design
Front cover image: Alamy/Stock Illustrations Ltd
Bristol University Press use environmentally responsible print partners.
Printed and bound in CPI Group (UK) Ltd, Croydon, CR0 4YY

No one is more equal than me.
I am no more equal than anyone.

Contents

List of Figures and Tables

Figures

Tables

Preface

Undertaking a study of the poor is fraught with the danger of exposing one's foolhardiness in attempting to deconstruct an intensely discussed yet unresolved area of human concern. Examining global poverty and poverty in India, it is clear that it is imperative to expand the understanding beyond a traditional economic approach and bring together diverse streams of thought and analyses, perhaps resulting in a Gordian's knot. For, when one broadens the investigative approach usually confined to a focus on micro- or macro-economics to one that embraces anthropology, history and sociology in a geopolitical context, then the complexity of analysis intensifies. Analyses from various social sciences fields have to be employed, for confinement to a single approach would lead to misidentification of the genesis and incomplete or inadequate policy solutions. The knot has to be untangled to see what is found as the crux of the challenge of poverty and inequality so that commensurate policy interventions may be made.

This volume reveals what I found in my search. It reflects my attempt to pin down the prevalence of poverty and inequality, track them through time, and carry out a diagnostic of its genesis. I found the genesis in different bases or foundations in different societies. Only correct identification would lead to meaningful policy prescriptions and commensurate solutions for the eradication of poverty and redressal of inequality. While I make a series of international comparisons, the analysis, as it progresses, narrows down on India. The policy prescriptions for India should be relevant for developing countries generally.

Travel through the vast expanses of the globe leads an observer to encounter extreme poverty and its squalor and dehumanization in public places and to conclude that poverty has to be the deepest failure of humankind. This malaise has perverted India's development in particular. That poverty and extreme poverty continue to exist and are tightening their grip in significant pockets of the globe – in fact in every corner – in the twenty-first century is testimony to the persistence of that failure.

The challenging nature of any study on poverty and inequality has been succinctly expressed by investigators such as Gayatri Chakravorty Spivak and Partha Chatterjee who hypothesized that subalterns or the poorest are not heard for themselves because their voices tend to be represented by scholars, politicians or lawyers. Such professionals, even as they speak on behalf of the poor, actually drown out the latter's voices. This was termed 'epistemic violence' – a violence through discourse rather than physical violence – concluding that the question of self-representation is a problem and remains a challenge. This is a humbling caution for someone who plans to undertake research in the field.

This book hypothesizes that socio-economic policy strategies to confront poverty that have been employed in India have not had final success mainly due to the failure to attack the problem at its genesis which, in the case of India, is the prevalence and operation of its caste structure. Using the latest available statistical evidence of the trajectory of poverty and inequality, traversing through the incidence of caste and its ramifications, and finding comparable generators of poverty in the historical incidence of slavery in the United States – a mere example being the condition of the African American prior to, and after, the Tulsa Massacre – and in global colonialism – gleaned from studies of pre-colonial and post-colonial societies – I argue that policies of redressal have to hit at the root causes. Otherwise, there will be little final success as post-colonial experience has already revealed from across the world.

Narrowing down on caste in India, a question that arises relates to the ramifications of assigning caste at birth and the automatic separation that follows through the span of life. In turn, it affects not only earning capacities for life but also the wellbeing of the living. Inequality and poverty associated with low castes are, therefore, created at birth without a significant likelihood of redemption. This comprises the crux of the book's hypothesis.

The weight and ramifications of colonialism on India's prevailing pervasive poverty cannot be over-emphasized as the work of many investigators has revealed. This may be viewed as a supplementary factor to caste as the prime explanations of poverty. Thus, in India's case, both international reparations to correct for colonial wrongs as well as a strong-handed eradication of caste – not merely through a constitutional provision – with its long reach through millennia are both essential to rid itself of poverty.

Unless the potential 'capability' of every member of society – to borrow Amartya Sen's term – is achieved, neither will a fulfilling life nor the full production possibility of its economy. Yet, elites in almost every historically recorded society appear to have benefitted from exclusion through birth rights, land rights, rights to collect revenue and rights to enter religious edifices while excluding others. Ignoring the obvious diminution of economic good by curtailing human productivity through multiple barriers on physical movement, the freedom to choose one's profession, or to choose a life partner, could perhaps be explained through a perverse, yet pervasive acceptance of a status quo that ensures domination, thus disproportionately benefitting only a segment of society. Occasional outbursts in the form of social revolution have failed and have even robbed members of some societies of basic dignity.

Only policies of human radicalism could hit successfully at such barriers that, in turn, could target poverty at its roots. Hannah Arendt has argued that society can accept the atrocities that policymakers wreak on fellow citizens as long as they themselves remain unaffected. To implement such policies, supportive bureaucracies act in an inimical manner against society as a whole. She termed this characteristic 'banality' – callousness or opacity of the members of society – as was manifested in Nazi Germany. Ironically, this has relevance in today's democracies in which the more common pattern has been reduced to structures that rule with a compliant group of cabinet members supported by a bureaucracy that plays the role of supplicant and provides succour to political leaders to advance their own careers. Arendt's argument also applies to the behaviour of the upper tiers in caste ridden societies and in those effectively separated along racial lines in both of which large portions of society not only find themselves in poverty but are unable to pull themselves out of it.

In light of the failure of the state to solve the challenge of caste, lower castes have consolidated existing caste structures using caste codifications and gained economic, social and political advantage. Yet, this cannot comprise a long-term solution. Indeed, in post-colonial India, caste fissures have deepened in political and social life with a growing incidence of lynching, arson, rape and murder. The only way to get rid of the malaise, not just theoretically in law but in practical and effective ways, is to identify policy action that would cut through the very existence of caste, however bitter a pill that would be to swallow for the beneficiaries of caste.

The field of poverty and inequality is widely analysed though the investigations have been carried out mainly in separated branches of the social sciences. This volume breaks from that approach by including analysis based in various social sciences, thus widening its scope to a wider range of perspectives. Nevertheless, given the ever-expanding analytical scope of poverty and inequality, I remain fretful that, though I have attempted to be comprehensive, I am likely to have overlooked some aspects and associated works. Second, I must caution the reader that my analyses, views expressed, and comments made on colonialism, slavery and caste pertain mainly to institutions and to those individuals who were responsible for their implementation and perpetration. Thus my positions should not be attributed to, or be taken as representative of, all individuals in a society. Indeed, many instances of individuals from colonial societies exist of those who fought to reform the condition of the sufferers. Unfortunately, it has taken centuries for the institutions to be modified or reformed. Lamentably, strong perverse elements linger and continue to reappear in the new millennium.

I am indebted to several individuals for suggesting readings and ideas for my research though I desist from attempting to draw up a list lest I should leave anyone out in whose debt I remain. However, I must mention Professor Kunal Chakraborty for illuminating me on various sources on the history of caste. International colleagues broadened my knowledge of the concepts of banality, radical humanism and other emerging conceptual and analytical premises while I was apprising myself of the historical and sociological tenets of colonization and decolonization. That included not only the continuing exclusions of African Americans in the United States but also Black Asian and Minority Ethnic Groups (BAME) in the United Kingdom through a vast array of research material. I remain grateful to them. I also benefitted from the comments of four reviewers in the proposal stage and in my formulation of the final manuscript.

I completed the work while I was visiting the International Inequalities Institute at the London School of Economics between 2019–23. Together with the familiar perusal of books and reports, ironically, the onset of the pandemic drew me towards using the internet as a reliable source of information enabling access to an array of scholarly works. In addition, I ventured to selectively use sources including print media such as newspapers and visual media such as documentaries that, if missed, would possibly leave a gap in my analysis. I found confidence from authors in particular fields of the social sciences that use such media. I appreciate the discussions I had with Mimi Chaudhury and her perusal of early drafts of my proposal before it took final shape. Rohitash Chaudhary provided technical support, formatting tables and figures. Mary Hilna Paul provided office support towards the end of the project. I appreciate the team at Bristol University Press for the ease with which I could work with them since my submittal in January 2022. No institution or individual is, however, responsible for the findings or views expressed in this volume – they are entirely mine.

Partho Shome
London, UK

1

Introduction

> No fellow should be richer than another, no man should exploit another, each person has value and dignity.
>
> Kenneth Kaunda, founding President of Zambia[1]

Undertaking a study of the poor

The objective of this volume is to identify the sources of poverty and inequality in India, to draw instances from the global experience, to analyse their manifestations and ramifications and to explore solutions for eradicating poverty and alleviating inequality. Poverty is found not to be a condition for which subsidies and the provision of work would suffice. Global examples, including India, reveal that the genesis is more fundamental, more intrinsic, more embedded, indeed, generated by deliberate events that occurred and can be traced in recorded history. Those events separated some population groups from others through identifiable means and, sometimes, by imposing conditions by decree. Identifiable sources include enslavement, racial and gender differences, as well as discrimination against the indigenous, sexual minorities if identified, religions other than that of the majority and other differences. An example of non-identifiable means that stands out is caste determined at birth which is the particular case of the Indian subcontinent. There appears to be no universal scholarly agreement whether the establishment of caste came about from the segregation of an indigenous or settled population by an invading population, its extreme manifestation being the untouchability of one person by another.

After millennia of contiguous existence, there remains little physical difference among castes. Therefore, the prevailing practice of caste is ensured by identity markers such as surnames, birthplace, or assigned occupation

[1] See Meebelo (1973) for a detailed discussion of Zambian humanism taught by Kenneth Kaunda.

(see Chapter 6). Similar instances occurred in history during periods of colonialism and slavery and post-abolition periods in other societies (see Chapter 5). In every case, the process that occurred and continues to occur comprises exclusion, isolation, domination and perpetration of social and economic differences. It leads naturally to inequality and to poverty by predetermining occupations, thus curtailing the freedom to choose a profession according to one's ability or desire. In turn, this gives rise to distortions in the natural choices that would be otherwise made by the members of a society. These distortions are found to be of varied intensities and tend to lead to a society's production outcomes that are well below its potential or what economists term the 'production possibility frontier'.[2]

Redressal of poverty and inequality has been attempted through economic and socio-economic policy but, from their limited effects on prevailing conditions, it would not be erroneous to conclude that they cannot be, respectively, eradicated or alleviated without sweeping away their foundations. Independent India, through its 1950 constitution, attempted to abolish untouchability and provided protection in public sector jobs and education for *Dalits* – essentially the untouchables – and, later, for all backward classes. Nevertheless, as will be seen, caste differences continue to play important roles in society, particularly in rural India. Indeed, the lack of success in the eradication of caste has led lower castes to strategize and acquire positions as kingmakers and even rulers in Indian politics. Yet the deleterious effects of caste continue for the vast powerless majority and, in particular, for those groups who are not even considered as belonging to any caste. The latter are considered low and polluted at their very birth – the lowliest of the untouchables – who remove nightsoil and dead animals or cremate dead bodies, occupations that they are born into. As they are identified by birth into a condition that remains unchangeable through life, they suffer poverty as a natural consequence of life itself, until their death.

Studying the unequal and the poor in India may usefully begin with noting the inequality among income cohorts or deciles and by tracking the extent of poverty reduction (see Chapters 2–4). It has to proceed by examining counter measures that have enabled the acquisition of economic and political rights. These have taken the form of education and public sector job guarantees that can confront the ability to earn income by one group or many groups through their domination – through unjustifiable rule setting – over another group or groups. In India, reflecting the much worse condition of women than men in society as well as in economic participation, special attention must be paid to the condition of women and children, in particular, girls. Their education is especially important for achieving equality with boys

[2] For an exposition, see Shome (2021), pp 63–73.

(see Chapter 9). Another evidence of inequality and poverty is between rural and urban areas. Arguments in favour of rural-to-urban migration as an economy grows reflect the thinking of several economists; yet there is evidence that rural inhabitants are willing to sacrifice up to one-third of their urban incomes if work options in rural areas are offered, for example, in public works projects or through transfers of productive assets. In light of this, it may be expected that the provision of appropriate socio-economic infrastructure in rural India would diminish migration successfully. These concerns comprise another fertile area for examination in the context of poverty and inequality (see Chapter 7). Often, the poor are, in effect, excluded from being able to access public sector provisions for health, nutrition, sanitation and clean water; these aspects need to be examined carefully (see Chapter 10).

However, a question remains as to whether such measures are sufficient to eradicate poverty or alleviate inequality, or whether the continual monitoring of untouchability and caste practices should occupy the prime place in policy. It is clear that the provision for public services has not been sufficient. Doing away with caste is more challenging reflecting how the power of caste differentiation has emerged to buttress Indian politics. Nevertheless, it will be argued why eradicating caste and its deleterious ramifications should be the central focus for helping to achieve India's future prosperity in full. The sequence of inequality and poverty – tracing the genesis, through the practice and ramifications, to policy actions taken and further needed – is shown in Figure 1.1. It illustrates the primary hypothesis of this volume, that inequality and poverty as they occur, are phenomena that are not merely the description of a condition but are created through exclusion, isolation, domination and perpetration of social and economic differences by one group over another.

The genesis can be found in historical practices such as colonialism, slavery, racism and caste, all of which enabled the removal of human and economic rights from one group of individuals. They reflect a power to extract output by imposing extraordinary burdens on work conditions, usurpation of property and tax terrorism. Therefore, the exclusive treatment of poverty and inequality employed by economists as observed conditions is not sufficient. Historians have tended to take the issue forward in terms of historical perspectives while anthropologists and sociologists have tended to use observation of identifiable groups as a technique of analysis. These approaches have to be considered as a holistic whole in order to get a grip on the matter of poverty and inequality.

Partial compensatory policies such as cash and asset transfers and enhancements in primary health and education provision are well-intended socio-economic policies though they are inadequate in significantly reducing the gap of inequality or eradicating poverty. Only when the original sources

Figure 1.1: Theme

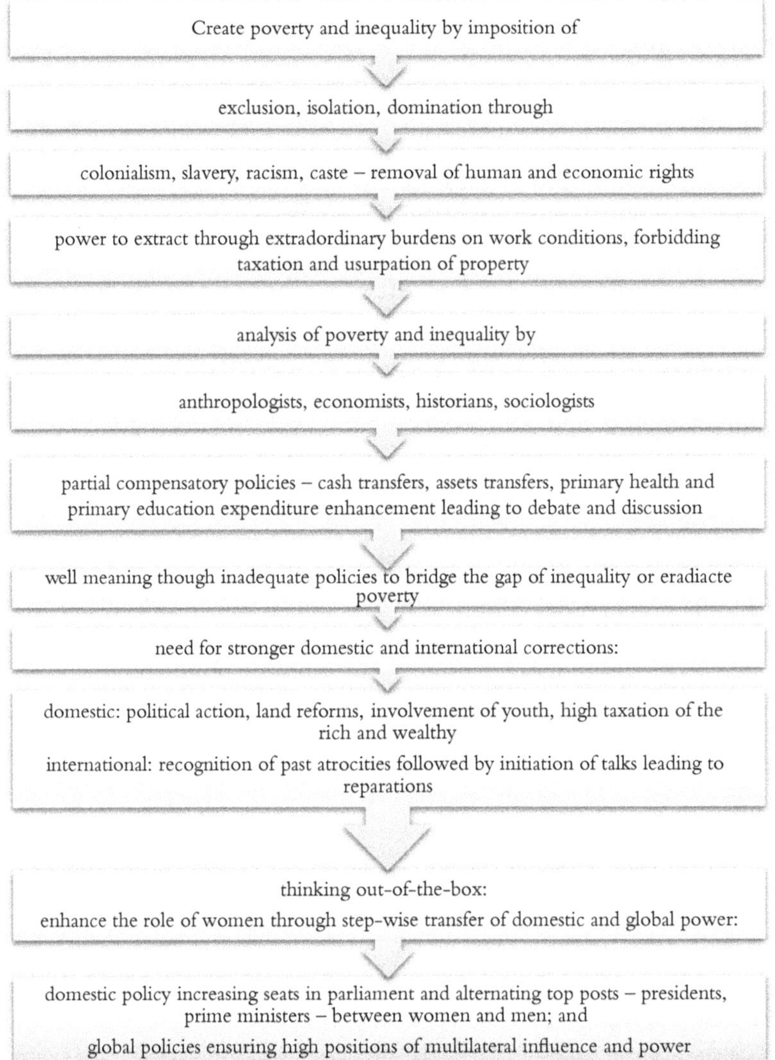

of inequality and poverty are recognized by governments can the actions that can really solve the phenomena be put in place and implemented. Such actions relate to both domestic and international spheres. The former includes political action, land reform, enhancement of the position of women and, last but not least, participation of youth – without exception – after the higher school years in *shramdaan*, or contribution of effort, in the form of service to rural education and in urban slums, and for university degree holders as well as doctors and nurses to serve along similar lines in more advanced or complex functions. Indeed, this is not unique in that lessons may be drawn from several international experiences historically. Reflecting the harrowing lives of women in India, and recognizing the evidence of their leadership in the past and continued achievement in the present despite all odds, their role needs to be speedily enhanced through reserving the number of top public posts such as in the national parliament, state-level legislatures and local governments and all public sector jobs to represent their proportion in total population.

Internationally, reflecting the extremities of past injustice, reparations must be designed from the ex-colonial powers to the ex-colonies. Despite extreme reluctance, if not refusal to do so thus far, a few countries are indeed coming forward with partial apologies and minimal compensation. But both the international effort and the extent of transfers need to be intensified and broadened. This is occurring to some extent at the United Nations (UN). However, its overall soft-touch approach through the sponsorship of events and reports needs to be sharpened through an international commission chaired and managed by sufferer countries. The latter's findings would be put on record for posterity while, hopefully, they will finally draw adequate attention of ex-colonial countries with obligations to take meaningful and adequate actions. The recognition that global equality can be achieved only if the original sources of global inequality and poverty are removed from their roots, is crucial for enabling stepped-up reparations and transfers. Otherwise, poverty will continue to be addressed with a bandage and antiseptic rather than through the major surgery that is called for.

Dreze and Sen's (1995) conceptualization of capability deprivation represents the manifestation of poverty. To quote,

> Poverty of a life … lies not merely in the impoverished state in which a person actually lives, but also in the lack of real opportunity – given by social constraints as well as personal circumstances – to choose other types of living. The relevance of low incomes … relates … to their role in curtailing capabilities … . Poverty is, thus, ultimately a matter of 'capability deprivation'. (p 11)

The attempt in this volume is to take a step back in an effort to identify the cause of the lack of opportunity they speak of, and proposes that opportunity is actually stolen by the happenstance of birth which is then followed by exclusion. Sen (1995) articulated the contours of capability and re-emphasized it in Sen (2009). The capability premise is centred on his question, 'the equality of what?'. Sen attempted to synthesize previous works on inequality that verged on the inequality of incomes, wealth, opportunities, rights or liberty into a composite whole, that is, the capability or capacity to secure basic needs, life satisfaction, empowerment and agency or ownership. Thus, merely a pursuit of growth of a country's gross domestic product (GDP) or increase in its per-capita GDP could not safeguard health, education, gender equality or subjective wellbeing. Rather, the application of the criterion of capability enhancement would enable their achievement. Even these, though they are important instruments of poverty reduction, by themselves may not suffice since they do not reveal how they combine in a particular population to enhance capability.[3] It was in this context that Sen and Haq formulated a concept of the Human Development Index (HDI) comprising incomes, life expectancy and education that, later, expanded into a more complex index, the Multi-Dimensional Poverty Measure (MDPM)[4] (see Chapter 4).

Tomlinson (1988) studied the economic and social history of the sub-continent. He pointed to a growth in the relevant literature since the 1960s leading to a voluminous corpus of research. He pointed to one survey of empirical work by Charlesworth (1982) since 1800 that listed over 150 titles, more than half of which were published in the 1970s. In his words, such works had grown into a cottage industry. Considering their influence and knowledge base, however, it should, therefore, be explicable why the present author concluded that any analysis of poverty eradication and inequality reduction in India would be incomplete unless its treatment of the issue was opened to, and inclusive of, as many fields as possible under one umbrella.

This volume takes a holistic approach to the analysis of poverty and inequality rather than adhering to a single instrument of analysis. It thus embraces anthropogenic, economic, historical and sociological instruments wherever these are relevant and concludes with policy prescriptions for change adopting 'human radicalism' as an instrument. While it addresses issues from a global perspective, it narrows down on India as a case study where sectoral issues are discussed while considering India's experience in a cross-country context. It uses international and country-sourced data and employs secondary as well as primary sources of information. In attempting such an approach, it has kept in mind Piketty's (2021) criticism of the narrowness of the purely economic approach, pointing to the need for widening the scope of analysis. To quote,

> it is (a) recurrent temptation on the part of professional economists, whether in the university or the marketplace, to claim a monopoly of expertise and analytic capacity they do not possess. In reality, it is only

---

3 To reiterate, the question posed in this volume is to ask what produced the incapability in the first place; the answer, in turn, is found from various instances in human history.

4 See Alkire and Foster (2011).

> by combining economic, historical, sociological, cultural, and political approaches that progress in our understanding of socioeconomic phenomena become possible. This is true, of course, for the study of inequalities between social classes – and their transformations throughout history, but the lesson seems to me far more general … . Another factor behind the excessive autonomization of economics is that historians, sociologists, political scientists, and philosophers too often abandon the study of economic questions to economists. All social scientists should try to include socioeconomic trends in their analysis, gather quantitative and historical data whenever useful, and should rely on other methods and sources when necessary. (p 149)

That is, it can only be more illuminating to give the issue at hand a 360-degree examination from as many perspectives as possible than from a narrow perspective of a single social science. And the analysis should also allow for subjectivity to be recognized and included as Levinas (2006), an ethical meta-physicist, challenged, 'the dehumanisation perpetrated by all the "social sciences" that seek to explain away human subjectivity in the name of abstract principles … . wherein subjectivity would have no internal finality' (p ix). Accordingly, this volume uses an inter-disciplinary approach by taking up a range of social science disciplines. It attempts to engage a 'deconstructionist' approach, in the manner of decolonization[5] as its tool of analysis. A basis of argument is attempted to be reconstructed for the cause of the subaltern, and corrective actions recommended fearlessly, however unusual some of them may appear from a more conventional perspective.

Exclusion, isolation, domination, extraction and perpetration: caste, slavery and colonialism

The question that remains in Dreze and Sen's exposition is what factors or constraints might generate the limitation on capability in India. What appears as a likely answer that differentiates India from its cohorts in East Asia is its characteristic and practice of caste. It is the enablement of exclusion, isolation, domination, extraction and perpetration through caste practices that stands out. First, groups are assigned roles by virtue of their birth on the basis of which they can be excluded from selected aspects of leading a free life;[6] second, in India where the caste structure and its ramifications have been felt for centuries or even millennia, such groups have only recently – since India's independence – been selected to receive compensatory benefits for

5 See Mignolo and Walsh (2018).

6 Indian village practice has tended to exclude lower castes from the village boundary and to live, instead, outside it, immediately raising their costs of conducting life.

redressal of their imposed characterization. Such compensatory government action, or even making caste-based untouchability unconstitutional, has not helped to a sufficient extent, however, to remove barriers altogether or free individuals to enhance capability reflecting Sen's fundamental criterion, that of individual choice.

Overt exclusion of population segments from their basic rights such as through divisions by caste or pigmentation or covert exclusion through discriminatory practices in the workplace or by other exclusionary domination curtailing freedoms to choose lifestyles or earn a living, has, perhaps, been the most potent source of poverty and inequality.[7] The origin of caste is curious. A religious explanation, perhaps comforting to those who practise caste, is that it emanated from Brahma, the creator of the Universe, the first among the Hindu Trinity, the others being Vishnu, the preserver, and Shiva, the destroyer. Of the castes, Brahmans emerged from Brahma's head, Kshatriyas from his arms, Vaisyas from his thighs and Sudras from his feet.[8] Their roles in society were accordingly assigned in a descending order, from cerebral to menial. Another interpretation indicates that the system appeared with the arrival in India of fairer-skinned Aryans from southern Europe and northern Asia around 1500 BCE. The original inhabitants of India were dominated, separated and consolidated into society along unbreachable, occupational lines at a lower rung. Centuries later, the *Manu-smriti* – its received text dates from circa 100 CE – put it in fine print.[9] An emerging manifestation in India's prevailing political environment is an exacerbation of the subjugation of lower castes within

---

7 This is indeed an area that has appeared in the works of authors from different genres, examples being Mistry (1997); Rao (2009); Lieven (2011); and Wilkerson (2020) among others.

8 In the *Rigveda*, the oldest literary document of India, it is found that the four castes are only mentioned once, in a hymn which belongs to the latest chronological stratum of the *Vedas*. In that hymn the Brahmana, the Rajanya, the Vaisya and the Sudra are described as having been created from the head, arms, thighs and feet respectively of the primeval male. But in the rest of the Rigveda, the great bulk of which is undoubtedly much older than the hymn in question, neither any mention of a four-tiered division nor any indication of the existence of the caste system is found. A steady development of the complex from the simple would have followed in the later *Vedas*. See Macdonell (1914).

9 The *Manu-smriti* prescribed to Hindus their *dharma* – that is that set of obligations incumbent on each as a member of one of four main *varnas* or social classes. It has since carried weight reflecting its wide coverage that includes 12 chapters of stanzas, which total a formidable 2,694. It deals with cosmogony; the definition of dharma; the sacraments (*samskaras*); initiation (*upanayana*) and the study of the *Vedas* (the sacred texts of Hinduism); marriage, hospitality, funeral rites, dietary restrictions, pollution and means of purification; the conduct of women and wives and the law of kings. The last leads to a consideration of matters of juridical interest, divided under 18 heads, after which the text returns to

the Hindu hierarchy through lynching and other means. This is being achieved through increasingly successful injections of religious divisionism in different Indian states.

If caste is a fundamental obstacle, it nevertheless lies within the comfort zone of the Indian psyche. Here exclusion and domination can be comfortably practised and the setting free of the potential in every human in Indian society has to remain partially unattainable. Indeed, the basis of such a comfort zone may lie in a lack of awareness or consciousness in many cases, Indian society is so glued in its structure. For example, the continuance of surnames that are actually caste and sub-caste names, determines and charts the course of one's economic and social life from birth to death in vast swathes of India. No other society can be cited whose fundamental premise is based on the identification of, and exclusion by, caste at birth. Deshpande (2001) used 1992–93 data to analyse the impact of the 'caste at birth' phenomenon on the standards of living of three major caste/tribe groups deriving therefrom a 'caste deprivation index' and concluding that caste is an essential ingredient in the stratification pattern of the Indian population.

China eradicated class differentiation through extreme measures taken by its communist party during its cultural revolution of the 1960s–1970s. Indeed, it appears that only China has been able to wield ruthlessness to the extent that it has during vast sweeps of its modern history.[10] Viewing that experience, it is an extraordinary challenge to develop an appropriate framework for the eradication of poverty and alleviation of inequality without such extreme societal pain; yet an alternative route has to be found. The enhancement of capabilities is crucially linked with the pace of reducing exclusion structures that have been set up by societies from ancient times and have continued into the modern day.

Through history, socio-economic exclusion has comprised not only caste but also rights by heredity, rights obtained by gender, rights of invaders versus original inhabitants, exclusion of the rights of minority sexual orientations or religious preferences, sufferers from particular diseases such as leprosy or tuberculosis and many others that do not receive compassionate treatment in many societies. They have existed through millennia, through the application of vagrancy laws in Victorian England for begging that led to incarceration

religious topics such as charity, rites of reparation, the doctrine of karma, the soul and hell. The text makes no categorical distinction between religious law and practices and secular law. Its influence on all aspects of Hindu thought, particularly the justification of the caste system, has been profound. See Britannica (2015).

10 Dreze and Sen (1995), however, appear to have taken a view that China's path to economic growth occurred before its cultural revolution or its later market-led reforms, reflecting its early focus on education and nutrition, a premise that will be addressed in Chapter 3.

and exclusion from regular society,[11] isolating religious minorities to 're-educate' them with national customs and language imposed not by custom but by government as in China, or the forceful location of African Americans 'south of the railway tracks' away from whites, or in barren 'Homelands' in apartheid South Africa, or the re-transport of Black citizens back to the Caribbean in the UK's Windrush action. The list is unending.

Throughout its history, the US has used a distinction of race to classify access by Blacks to education, health services, housing markets and loans. Exclusion may be purely economic or social or, more likely, both.[12] Where attempts have been made in modern times to remove obstacles, extreme hatred has been manifested by significant portions of its white society against equalization. The ruthlessness of exclusion including the annihilation of Jews, gypsies and homosexuals and physical experiments on the human body in Nazi Germany to enhance perceived economic and social wellbeing of one portion – so-called Aryans – of the population at the cost of all others is yet another example. Wilkerson (2020) brought India's caste system, the US's race structures and Nazi atrocities of mass annihilation, under the same titular consideration. The veracity and power of exclusion by caste is thus seen as one of the harshest of socio-economic practices prevalent today. Poverty and inequality are direct results of that.

The complexity of the story of colonialism emerges from a long-standing debate over its pros and cons. This discussion was presented by Gardner and Roy (2020) in a survey and analysis of the relevant literature. One strand that did not perceive any net benefit from colonialism to the imperial states – colonial home economies – was of the view that it affected overall economic growth adversely, with high costs to the exchequer for operations, maintenance and upkeep of colonies, while primarily benefitting a political and financial elite in those economies. French analysts also argued about the preponderance of benefits accruing to a small coterie of colonialists in the name of the French people. Belgium could also be cited, where expenditures

11 The Vagrancy Act of 1824 was enacted 'for the more effectual suppression of vagrancy and punishment of idle and disorderly persons' in England. It retained the traditional vagrancy offences adding loitering with intent to commit an arrestable offence and offences against public decency and morality (for example, prostitution, indecent exposure and homosexual behaviour). Repeat offenders, deemed incorrigible rogues, could be whipped and incarcerated. Street beggars were regularly pursued including destitute children (see www.southernafricalitigationcentre.org/wp-content/uploads/2017/08/04_SALC-NoJustice-Report_A-Short-History-of-English-Vagrancy-Laws.pdf). Aspects of that law began to be dismantled in Britain one and a half centuries later. Similar laws were introduced in Britain's colonies and many remain in place even after their independence, often for the new rulers' convenience, if not misuse.

12 See Boushey (2019) for a comprehensive survey of the literature on the US linking poverty with race.

of the Congo Free State area had to be initially assumed by the king from his personal funds reflecting the unpopularity of the project. But the king's expenditures turned out to be high and, compounded by atrocities in tax collection, the government eventually took over the region's governance.

The opposite strand argued that the export markets that colonies provided benefitted the home countries so that, if colonies were to be abandoned, any vacuum created would be filled by other imperial states. Indeed, others such as Belgium, France and Germany did not compare with the colonial power and reach of Britain but nevertheless strove for comparable presence. All in all, in reviewing the rates of growth of selected colonized countries, Gardner and Roy (2020) concluded that, as far back as the sixteenth century, the per capita GDPs of the subsequently colonized countries such as China and India were comparable to those of European colonizers. Through the colonization period, however, both China and India suffered declining per capita GDP until the departure of the colonizers.

Focusing on India, many studies such as by Sen (1981); Mukerjee (2010); and Dalrymple (2019) to name a few, established this fact so that, in the final analysis, it is difficult to identify many researchers in present times who could sing the praises of a colonial era that wrought benefits for the colonized.[13] Even though a few colonies gained, in particular in Latin America such as Mexico that compared well with Spain, by and large such gains accrued mainly to the colonial owners and the locally created gentry who ruled on their behalf at the cost of the vast majority of the colonies' populations.

Roy's (2020) analysis indicated that British colonialism in India made some livelihoods rich and left others poor. To note, at the time of India's independence in 1947, the British left behind infrastructure comprising ports, canals, sanitation, medical care, urban waterworks, universities, postal system, courts of law, railways, the telegraph, meteorological office, statistical systems and scientific research laboratories. Roy (2020) clarified that these were built with British knowhow with Indian assistance and were built to assist governance directly or indirectly. They also helped private enterprise and improved the quality of life. Nevertheless, the fact remained that there was scant development in the interiors whose governance was left to the local landlords whose role was mainly to collect land revenue from the rural poor. Given that the rural agricultural population comprised almost three-quarters of the country's population, inequality increased and exacerbated regional differences in incomes. It is not surprising that the not so well-known Bengal famine of 1943–44 took the lives of some three million Bengalis even during the final period of British rule.

[13] Sen's contribution to this literature is voluminous. In many ways, it is inter-related, yet with fresh ideas and concepts. It may be worthwhile, perhaps, to read them sequentially (see Sen, 1995, 2000, 2009).

Gardner and Roy (2020) found that inequality increased in most colonized economies. Studies of African colonies, for example, have indicated that the average height and weight of local populations in Kenya and Ghana decreased though the conditions of some ethnic groups improved, revealing differences in the effects of colonial rule among regions. In this context, Roy (2020) questioned whether there indeed was any deep-seated colonial legacy in the form of colonial institutions that the ephemeral European presence might have left behind. Here the available literature reveals that, in India, despite the provision of socio-economic infrastructure by the British in cities and towns, indigenous institutions under the princely states of India that ruled as British protectorates provided better health, education and roads than did those regions that the British ruled directly. Gardner and Roy (2020) concluded that, despite the European colonial presence being minimal in terms of numbers, during the colonial period, income distributed between colonies worsened.

The role of colonialism in the generation of exclusion came under serious discussion also by Piketty (2020) who effectively assigned the source of inequality to internecine genocide in Europe. Bhambra (2021) and Reddy (2021) expressed doubt over such an exclusive premise that eschewed the role of colonial extraction by those powers that fuelled extreme inequalities. Piketty's statement that 'The US Civil War put an end to slavery in the US in 1865 and it took enormous African American mobilization to end racial discrimination in 1964–65', stands out as an assertive statement that concluded racial discrimination to have ended. The world is well aware of the nature and intensity of racial discrimination in the US even today giving rise, in turn, to poverty and inequality.

Piketty (2021) appears to view the entire matter as an ideological struggle without considering any element as an outcome of colonial extraction. 'It is ideological differences that drive the replacement of a prevailing balance of power during a period of crisis' (p 142). Citing Reddy's work, Piketty insisted that he did not consider all ideologies on the same scale. For example, in his view, tax progressivity was less effective for equality than education was.[14] Citing Paidipaty and Ramos-Pinto (2021) who pointed out that, in the post-war era, dominant economic powers would not accept the establishment of a multilateral institution such as an international trade organization due to fears that that could give too much voice to countries such as Brazil and India, Piketty elaborated how Western powers injected 'shock trade liberalization' in the 1980s–90s

[14] Here Piketty intersperses societal ideologies with country policies which appears to be a unique transposition.

that had deleterious ramifications for domestic tax revenue as well as the availability of public funds for state building in the Global South. He viewed financial liberalization including cross-border capital movements and a commensurate rise in international tax avoidance since the 1990s as having been propelled by Europe.[15]

Bhambra's (2021) fundamental disagreement with Piketty lay in her central thesis that colonialism generated inequality which, she believed, Piketty bypassed. To quote,

> we acknowledge … (and that which we do not) affects political understandings in the present, for example, of how global inequality is configured. If we imagine our past to be determined by national boundaries, we are likely to think that contemporary inequalities are shaped by national processes, including the ideologies that percolate within borders. If, instead, we understand our past as a colonial past, then, our understanding of inequality in the present will be different. In part, because our understanding of the state – which is regarded as the key locus for the shaping of inequalities and the ideologies that justify them – will also be different. ... Along with many social scientists, Piketty posits a 'postcolonial state' contrasted to the modern nation without addressing the processes of colonization that were themselves part of state formation. (p 73)

Bhambra considered France and Haiti to be part of the same conceptual universe and, similarly, Britain and India as another. In terms of inequality between the colonizer and the colonized, coercion and forceful extraction led to rapid wealth accumulation of colonial powers versus a sharp slide into poverty of the colonized. This matter is considered further in Chapter 5. Wilder (2015) explained how eminent anti-colonial thinkers, poets and political leaders such as Aime Césaire, Leopold Senghor and others sought to remake France by advocating for colonial self-determination and fuller racial and cultural integration within the French empire. Bhambra (2021) quoted Wilder (2015) thus, 'If colonization was taken seriously, however, then the modern nation state would only be seen to emerge in the period of decolonization as previous states would be more appropriately understood as *imperial* or colonial states'.[16] The ramifications of colonialism and its variants on inequality and poverty comprise the subject matter of Chapter 5.

---

[15] Why Piketty perceived that sometimes this occurred during labour, social-democrat and socialist regimes was not too clear, however.

[16] See Bhambra (2021), p 74.

Economic growth and poverty

Market economics takes, as an unquestioned premise, the initial possession or 'endowment' of assets or wealth that an individual possesses when entering the market with his plan to supply or exercise demand.[17] The reason behind differences in initial endowments, however unequal, was not questioned for a long time, when economists tended not to worry about inequality as much as they did about the efficiency in the allocation of resources and maximizing production in the economy. A concept of 'optimality' was enunciated by the Italian economist Vilfredo Pareto in 1896. As an economy functioned, as long as someone gained without anyone becoming worse off than in the initial position, it was 'optimal'. All economic theory was based on the efficacy of the perfect market. The so-called 'natural law' of the market assured increased benefit to all – from their initial endowment points – as economies grew. Essentially, there was no recognition of directly uplifting the position of the poor at higher rates than that of the non-poor.[18] For example, development economists such as Little (1982) and others confined their view of development economics as a field that focused on the rise in per capita incomes without worrying about its distribution; though, later, they expanded that to a more inclusive view.[19]

Inequality in income and wealth exacerbated as the rate of return to capital exceeded the rate of economic growth. Worse, some of the stock of wealth comprising money, property, stocks, bonds and other capital, could be hidden and not counted. Solow (2017), the growth economist, recognized this. To quote,

> From the very beginning of national accounting, it has been understood that the focus on gross investment and gross product is a standing temptation to error. If GDP increases from one year to the next only because there is a bigger charge for depreciation of fixed capital, it is obvious that nothing has really gotten better … . A useful and substantial extension of the standard statistical picture of the economy would be the regular publication of distributional information. I would want to go well beyond the familiar Gini coefficient, which hides more than it reveals. For starters, I would

---

17 Note that the gender-neutral pronoun 'he' has been used throughout the book reflecting usual practice.

18 This was obvious even to Shome (1973), as expressed in his Master's thesis.

19 Little (1977, 1982). Similarly, in Agarwala and Singh's (1958) esteemed edited volume of papers on economic development, poverty was mentioned only three times in passing.

> urge the regular calculation of the distribution of personal income by size, say by income deciles.[20]

More economists picked up on the matter. Basu and Subramanian (2020) elaborated on the concepts of achieving economic growth, poverty alleviation, and inequality mitigation as separable goals of development, pointing out that

> the pursuit of any one of them does not necessarily secure the ends of either or both of the other two. Such engagement requires a measure of conceptual clarity, an identification of normative priorities, and the deployment of carefully crafted policies that accommodate trade-offs among competing goals. In particular, policies such as the single-minded pursuit of growth as a panacea for all the difficulties of development appear to be misguided, and based on a faulty application of deductive reasoning to past experience. (p 352)

They then proceeded to decompose the changes in poverty into effects that are attributable to economic growth and those attributable to distributional changes. In light of this, it is noteworthy that India's recent spurt in economic growth to the second position after China (see Chapter 2) did not usher in a more equal economy.

Ghatak (2021) reiterated the point thus,

> The problem with the growth-centred narrative is that while growth is necessary for poverty alleviation, it is not sufficient. For example, suppose we ignore the pandemic and contraction in GDP, and assume a dream annual growth rate of 10%. It will take 22 years of sustained 10% growth per year in incomes to bring an individual who is now right on the rural poverty line up to merely the level of per capita income (which is low by global standards to start with). For an individual on the urban poverty line, this would take 18 years. And, no country in history has had two decades of sustained double-digit growth! (p 6)

From a comparison of India's performance in inequality and poverty reduction with selected international cohorts, what is revealed is that the rise in India's inequality has been internationally the highest in recent years, with inequality increasing in both income and wealth (see Chapter 4, Tables 4.1

[20] Robert Solow (2017). Available at: https://equitablegrowth.org/improving-the-measurement-and-understanding-of-economic-inequality-in-the-united-states/. Accessed August 31, 2021.

and 4.4 of this volume). The question remains whether India, languishing in extreme poverty and despite high growth, is losing the battle to subjugate it.

One impact of growing inequality has been the state of people's happiness measured by selected criteria as explained in Chapter 3. Brockman et al. (2009) found that, during 1990–2000, happiness declined in China even as material living standards improved significantly. It revealed that a rise in income inequality negated the salient impact of economic growth on happiness. Lakshmanasamy and Maya (2020) investigated the link between happiness and income in India for 12 Indian states between 1990–2014. They found a flat happiness response to income change as income inequality rose. Conducting daily life by the poor can be made extremely challenging when rising inequality burrows into the standard of living.

Over and above that, the financing of India's democracy has been well-known to be based on unaccounted-for monies accumulated through tax evasion and money laundering. Eradication of the black economy has been pursued by successive governments to little avail. The last attempt, in 2016, was a brutal governmental exercise in demonetization of the Rupee that resulted in unnecessary deaths, greatly inconvenienced the poor in particular in the small retail sector, and very likely exacerbated poverty and inequality as the poor use disproportionately more cash in conducting daily life. In the final analysis, it did not reduce the cash circulating in the economy as per a statement of the then central bank governor who later resigned.

Not surprisingly, in the face of extreme challenges in conducting daily life, Indians have expressed themselves as unhappy and finding it difficult to cope. The international indices of happiness have revealed India to be a very unhappy country in a cross-country comparison. This is despite a culture of extended families and presumed village support systems that should provide societal support in emergencies and in daily life. The reality, as expressed, turned out to be that Indians did not experience the existence of adequate social support to make themselves happy. Indices related to happiness are covered in Chapter 3.

Poverty and its attributes require a more powerful lens to be analysed than a macro-economic lens alone. In their analysis of the economics of poverty, Banerjee and Duflo (2011) attempted a more micro-economic approach by addressing the economic and psychological complexities in the lives of the poor. They used randomized control trials, social experiments and field observations. They proposed that successful policies comprised those that are small and can be carried out at the margin. Ravallion (2012) commented that they provided some interesting insights but questioned how far that approach could be used to fight global poverty. Indeed, while not opposing micro steps to alleviate poverty, this volume argues in Chapter 11 in favour of massive societal action if poverty eradication is the goal. This is based on the argument, as enunciated previously, that poverty is the consequence of artificially constructed and imposed conditions such as race and caste differences to exclude, isolate and extract disproportionate benefits by powerful groups from dominated groups which can be removed only with the aid of deep and wide policy action.

Dreze and Sen (1995) pointed out that early economic philosophers and investigators such as Adam Smith (1790), John Stuart Mill (1848) and others were cognizant of the links between the ability to do things that were valued and the 'freedom to lead valuable lives', on the one hand, and economic policies that generated income and wealth, on the other. Sen (2000) viewed such freedom in its many aspects as the driving force behind development. In the context of this volume, the absence of that freedom in India has emanated from an exclusion of some of its citizens, and a domination by others, that have limited the productivity of certain groups in society and created an impossibility to lead valuable lives. If that is agreed, certainly the excluded may be expected to be intrinsically unhappy in life.

Socio-anthropogenic accounts

The natural question that might follow is whether the poor would like to be more entrepreneurial if given the opportunity. Banerjee and Duflo (2008) posed a counter-question as to whether public service delivery in the form of microcredit and small business promotion actually comprised the desire of the recipients. Using cross-country evidence, they concluded that there was no evidence that the median poor entrepreneur wanted to expand his or her existing businesses; instead, owning a business may represent a survival strategy rather than something they wanted to do. They also evaluated a programme in India that attempted to involve poor rural parents in improving local public schools. Even when they possessed the right to intervene and access funds and despite knowing that the children were not learning much, the parents opted out from intervening. Banerjee and Duflo's (2008) finding may be revealing of a condition that, left to themselves, the poor may not be able to assert, or speak for, themselves in a formal setup or environment.

On the basis of reportage of individual case studies, glimpses may be obtained regarding the aspirations of the poor for their children. Kumar (2021), for example, reported on cases as early as 1880–1920. Even then, parents were found to aspire for their children's educational and social progress. Citing Coombes' (1920) work, he related the experience of a mother going through extraordinary vicissitudes travelling by foot and train, to borrow a meagre amount of money for her son's education and, later, saving all his letters and taking pride in how he had progressed with his studies. Coombes reported another instance of a father who visited his son in school and exhorted him to focus on reading, writing and to like the English language, instead of merely acquiring a trade. He expressed his hope that his son would become a village officer rather than an artisan. From such instances, Kumar (2021) concluded that,

> [a] section of the labouring poor valued education. Even though they served the reformatory punishment, they (the student) attempted to use education in order to transform their life, escape the life of manual labour and gain knowledge … . With education, they wrote letters, read books, and dreamt about, along with their parents, a gentleman's life. (p 249)

It is likely, however, that the poor could also suffer from a steadfast conviction of a societal status quo represented by socio-economic constraints of caste. Despite this, some individuals would have attempted to overcome the system through sheer perseverance. The outcomes of such efforts are usually not known, however, since often there was a pervasive fixity in a labourer's grinding daily life that consumed all his time and effort. Das (2015) reported that an urban manual labourer expressed to her, his sickly physical condition when given the opportunity to do so at an individual level. Recounting the interview in front of his home, she reported,

> [an] encounter I had with Z, a young man who was sitting outside his house and greeted me … I asked him why he had not gone to work. He said, 'My mind is not okay today – I get such disturbing thoughts, I am feeling so angry, I have pain in my hand – I have to go and get some medicine.' At this point, he held his head between the two palms of his hands and bent his head as if in despair. …' Madam Ji, people do not understand. Every day, I have to lift such heavy weights. I feel my body collapsing. If I do not take some drink, I will collapse. Now I get these tensions, these terrible headaches … . I have to find some way of getting relief. Just as I have to drink some to make my body fit for work.'
>
> In such cases, the question of what is normal is mediated by the questions, what is illness and what is treatment under conditions of poverty? I heard the expression 'as long as my hands and feet are moving' as the trope through which Z represented the labouring body. (p 41)

An underlying helplessness, an acceptance perhaps and, above all, a deep unhappiness with his prevailing status is revealed in the statement of the labourer.

Yet, in an apparently curious stance, Das and Das (2010) surveyed available studies of caste-based feudal systems of rural structures, concluding on a positivist rather than a normative note, indicating that some had doubted whether the caste system was purely discriminatory. They discussed the *jajmani* system which was an economic system found in Indian villages in which lower castes performed various functions for upper castes and received grain or other goods in return. To quote,

> The discussion on the *jajmani* system was anchored to the wider question of the characteristics of the caste system, and its relevance for understanding the operation of a moral economy as distinct from the market economy in India. Thus, for instance, Louis Dumont, the foremost interpreter of the caste system for Western, especially French, audiences, argued that the relations between different castes were hierarchical but non-antagonistic, since the system was holistic. He contrasted the logic of hierarchical inclusion with that of the ethos of competition and exclusion in the Western system. It is not our intention to provide a full discussion of the sophisticated analysis of the emergence of economic ideas in European societies that Dumont undertook. We only wish to point out that as far as the discussion on the caste system in India was concerned, the focus on the *jajmani* system led to debates about whether the system was exploitative – Marxist interpreters of Indian society were much more likely to think of feudal or semi-feudal elements of agrarian relations, while the 'culturalist' or 'structuralist' interpretations emphasized the importance of the *jajmani* system in offering some protection to those who were lower in the social hierarchy through customary practices ensuring that members of these castes would not be deprived of their subsistence needs. As an example of the former stance, Beidelman argued in 1959 that the source of the *jajaman*'s power was not ritual superiority but landownership, while the foremost proponent of the latter view was Louis Dumont. We should point out, though, that even anthropologists such as Kathleen Gough, who was otherwise inclined to emphasize the feudal elements in rural social relations, thought that subsistence rights of the poor were assured in the traditional moral economy, but that they had been disrupted by forces of modernization in general and colonialism in particular. (p 6)

Thus, Das and Das, while presenting the views of several authors, seemed reticent in proffering their own view, based on a fine-toothed comb analysis, of the rights and wrongs of the matter.

When caste and women are combined, the deleterious effects are intensified. Examining violence against women, Kapadia (ed) (2003) investigated the contemporary cultural, social, political and economic situation of women in India. The argument was that the position of women could not be said to have changed despite apparently positive progress in education and paid employment. Not only through a declining sex ratio but also through a complex system of male biases, patriarchal norms and values across all castes and classes, they suggested an institutionalized bias against the female child in parts of India. North and South India were contrasted.

Kapadia (2018) studied two subordinated groups of untouchable women in a village in the state of Tamil Nadu in southern India. Their lives and work provided a clarification of the 'three axes' of identity – gender, caste and class. The author argued that subordinated groups did not internalize the values of their masters; instead, they subtly rejected them. Elites held economic but not the dominant symbolic power over the low castes. The latter's rituals, cultural values and discourses rejected the norms of Brahmin elites. It was concluded that caste and class processes could be addressed only through their interrelationship with gender.

Yet another aspect that has to be of interest is the marginalized condition of the child. Das (2015) provided a subtle insight into it. To quote,

> Mukesh was on the edges of conversation in the house; he was aware of his father's transgressions and fearful of what this might mean for his mother and himself, but all he could do was to inform his mother about what he saw and try to protect her from the dangers of the illness and the dangers of a world he barely understood. In taking the role of her protector, he worked with bits and pieces of information that came his way – guessing at what are the consequences of adult desires, such as that of his father for another woman. (p 65)

The precarious role of the child in an adult world of low castes appears to get worse due to the prevalence of extreme poverty. It is in these vignettes that the fault lines of the Indian state in its less-than-adequate effectiveness in eradicating extreme poverty gets exposed to full view. To emphasize, as is the hypothesis of this volume, without the removal of caste from the veins and arteries of the Indian psyche, essentially poverty will be persistent and is likely to remain a permanent feature of Indian society.

Selected international comparisons

Comparisons between China, India and South-East Asian economies are of relevance here.

China and India

At least since its 1991 economic liberalization, India's growing inequality has been of increasing concern to every fair-minded social scientist. Piketty (2014), the author of *Capital*, a globally recognized volume explaining inequality and its forebears with a sweep over centuries, co-authored another study, Chancel and Piketty (2017), issued from the World Inequality Lab (WIL), an international research institution, that is highly embarrassing for India. They used a Forbes indicator of Indian billionaires owning 2 per cent of total wealth in the 1990s, growing to 10 per cent by 2015, pointing to the stark rise in income inequality. Income concentration of the top 10 percent grew rapidly since the early 1980s. The remaining 90 per cent suffered significant declines in income shares. The indicators are discussed in some detail in Chapter 4. A wide range of international comparisons are undertaken to examine what various cohort groups of countries have achieved to enhance capability. Contrasting India with China has been in vogue reflecting that they were, by and large, at comparable stages of development around 1980 after which they diverged, and the difference became more pronounced with time. Chancel and Piketty compared the rates of per-capita income growth for China and India (and other countries) during 1980–2014, being 187 per cent for India and 659 per cent for China or three and a half times higher, as well as the skews when different income deciles and sub-deciles were compared. Clearly the trajectories of economic growth took different directions in the two countries. Further cross-country comparisons have also been carried out in Chapter 4.

The reason for such a stark divergence must be explored, that is, are there any lessons to be learnt not merely in economic terms but also from the perspective of the freedom that Sen (2000) talked about, 'The use of democratic prerogatives – both political liberties and civil rights – is a crucial part of the exercise of economic policy making itself. In a freedom-oriented approach, the participatory freedoms cannot but be central to public policy analysis' (p 110). Interestingly, Dreze and Sen (1995) went to some length to make the point that basic education in China had been achieved well before its market-based rapid economic growth which they cite as its main enabler. They contrasted this with India's failure to provide the same. This varies from the view that China's extreme autocracy helped it to control runaway population growth and to employ forced labour which, by all accounts, it continues to do at least among the ethnic minority of the Uyghurs if not others. In the prevailing circumstances and reflecting increasingly emergent information from its regions, it is important to reflect what impact they may have had on China's economic take-off. In the ordinary circumstances, could it be surmised that those policies would have contributed to population growth being severely controlled and to economic output taking off? Dreze and Sen made their argument based on the Indian state of Kerala which achieved similar or better socio-economic progress than China without China's draconian policy methods. The extreme differences in geographical size in these two entities cannot, however, be ignored.

Currently, many of China's economic and socio-economic indicators are even three times higher or better placed than India's.[21] An exploration of the causes and an assessment of the continuation of China's draconian human rights curbs would be insightful. Reflecting the speed of China's rise,[22] a question that lingers is whether India should have adopted China's growth trajectory by denying the 'freedom' of expression and associated human rights. That would be despite Sen's assertion that these were integral components of the freedom to lead valuable lives. In light of India's much slower growth and socio-economic performance, the role – beneficial or reductive – of India's democracy stands out especially in reflection of Sen's emphasis of the role of democracy in the freedom component of capability.

Both China and India are large in terms of their geographical dimensions. An essential difference is China's relative homogeneity with a limited number of languages, religions and uniformity in social practices in contrast to India's diversity. This may have given rise to a larger manifestation of regionality in India with the south-western state of Kerala having occupied the top position in socio-economic indicators among all states over the years of independence. This reflects, to no small extent, Kerala's successful and, to some extent, historical assimilation of the different religious practices – Hindu, Muslim, Christian – of its population.[23] A contrast could also be made between the southern Indian states[24] as a group vis-a-vis the so-called northern *Bimaru*[25] states that reveals consistently better achievement in lowering the poverty headcount in the south than in the north (see Chapter 8).

East Asian economies

If the preceding discussion imparts any fear regarding whether certain assurances falling under the concept of freedom may be eschewed if socio-economic development is the goal, then such foreboding should be nipped in the bud. Those emerging societies that have achieved and maintained freedoms to do things they value, have done so with a remarkable array of alternative political frameworks that have accompanied their socio-economic development. For example, East Asian economies such as Singapore, South Korea, Taiwan and Thailand have essentially adopted market principles with a relatively autocratic stance during the initial decades of their post-colonial

[21] World Development Report, various years.

[22] Gave and Gave (2019) portray China vis-a-vis Europe and the United States in *Clash of Empires*.

[23] Nevertheless, news reports of several cases of deaths of young brides in Kerala in 2021 have dented Kerala's reputation.

[24] Andhra Pradesh, Karnataka, Kerala and Tamil Nadu.

[25] Bihar, Madhya Pradesh, Rajasthan and Uttar Pradesh.

growth that achieved both high incomes and the provision of socio-economic services. Others such as Cuba and Vietnam imposed socialist regimes that put socio-economic services ahead of income growth while allowing society to share fairly in the benefits of whatever growth was achieved. Costa Rica and Sri Lanka could be said to have adopted mixed systems that also achieved noteworthy socio-economic outcomes.[26]

Vietnam has since moved more towards a market orientation while keeping socialist guidance in place, achieving both high growth rates based on rapid adoption of modern technologies and continued socio-economic stability. And Sri Lanka remained much ahead of its sub-continental neighbours in all internationally measured socio-economic indices until its economic collapse in 2022. All these countries were able to reduce capability deprivation irrespective of the forms of economic arrangements or political frameworks that they adopted. One experience that they have not shared, by and large, is India's oppression through caste. Further, the East Asian countries are culturally Buddhist, the Western countries have descended from a Christian background, while India's experience has been predominantly Hindu Brahmanism; and, though Buddhism reigned over centuries in India, Hinduism regained its foothold. The deleterious impact of this aspect will be considered in Chapter 6 in some detail.[27]

Selected socio-economic indicators

Indicators that enhance the freedom to lead valuable lives should comprise primary education, primary health, women's emancipation, access to water and electricity, assurance of privacy at least in basic functions such as bathing and relieving oneself, land and forest rights of *adivasis* or the original inhabitants of India, and the tolerance of political, caste and religious freedoms or sexual orientation, rather than oppression and violence towards minorities. The nature and extent of their prevalence indicate a sense of overall happiness or unhappiness.[28] Importantly, the often-precarious condition of women and the girl child has to be considered by examining their education, treatment at home and in society and marital imposition through child marriage often accompanied by a condition of perpetual

[26] Sri Lanka's economic collapse in 2022 was not merely a result of economic mismanagement but of a family's sequestering of massive economic resources that broke from the country's socialistic-economic practices of the past.

[27] However, caste or religious oppression is also present in Myanmar, Pakistan and Sri Lanka (see Chapter 6).

[28] The effect of violence is also of importance and is being studied in some detail today. See, for example, Kunnath (2017).

pregnancy. The condition of childhood itself has been studied in depth by social anthropologists that provides valuable insights for any economic study.[29]

Numerical indicators can also be utilized to buttress analysis. Comparisons of socio-economic indicators are carried out in Chapter 3 for a group of countries that reveal India's international position in such indicators. Brazil, China and India are sometimes compared reflecting their position as a part of the Brazil, Russia, India, China and South Africa (BRICS) group of nations.[30] Another is the group of countries that belong in the Indian sub-continent that are compared where appropriate. Occasional comparisons with other countries are also made. The intention is to employ a range of reliable statistical information that points to the state of poverty and inequality as expressed through selected socio-economic indicators in different cross-country groupings. For example, the life of a child may be chronicled on the basis of statistics on under-five mortality, malnutrition causing stunting, exclusion and discontinuation from primary and secondary school, and reasons thereof, female-male enrolment for education, child labour in adult roles, the percentage of girls married or in union, and births by adolescents and the percentage of displacement through conflict or victims of homicide (see Chapters 3 and 8). The impact of poverty on children's stunting is being examined using econometric modelling by Deshpande (2022). Quite revealing for the condition of women are the statistics on major crimes committed against women on the one hand and the incidence of female political representation on the other, thus imparting a contrast in their life conditions.

Focusing on education per se, in a recent volume of collected papers, Gupta et al. (2021) correctly traverse beyond statistical indicators to cover issues of quality, exclusion and marginalization in the way education is imparted, the carryover of practices established under colonial rule to the modern era, raising issue with the meaning and purpose of education, questioning whether education as imparted carries the potential for transforming the oppressive conditions of human living or for emancipation. This is why it is important to bring in different approaches – both qualitative and quantitative and from different social sciences – to come to grips with prevailing incidence, practices and avenues to improve education. This approach is needed to analyse socio-economic conditions in general.

Policies

Policies including traditional tax and expenditure policies buttressed by socio-economic and anthropogenic policies together with the removal of

---

29 See Das (2015); Kapadia (2018) and others.

30 Brazil, Russia, India, China and South Africa.

administrative constraints would comprise an appropriate policy package. In addition, without the mandated participation of youth and international reparations to correct past wrongs, no amount of effort would achieve the goal of eradicating poverty and redressing inequality.

Administrative constraints

Bureaucracy in a country could throttle society's progress and hinder economic growth. One of the earliest critical revelations of the detrimental impact of bureaucracy on diminishing the Indian economy's productivity was by Bhagwati and Desai (1970) with more instances provided by others through subsequent decades.[31] To use Dreze and Sen's (1995) classifications of 'market excluding and market complementary policy' (p 21), Indian policy interventions were often market-excluding rather than market-complementary, in that they comprised, by and large, ways and means to nip enterprise and enthusiasm in private productive activity. During the erstwhile 'License Raj', productive activity could take place only on the basis of licenses issued by a regime of bureaucrats occupying line ministries, rather than by professionals with knowledge in a subject area. The weight of such a counter-entrepreneurial policy stance was likely to have fallen heavily on the poor and the lower castes since overall employment was adversely affected. Only in 1991 the economy began to be liberalized and the chains of hierarchical decision making in production was dented. It occurred under a financial assistance programme of the International Monetary Fund as a consequence of India approaching it for a loan. That was at a time of severe diminution in India's foreign exchange reserves to less than a month's worth of imports. It was unlikely that India would have liberalized in the absence of multilateral pressure, a fact that appears to have been expunged from its economic history books.[32]

In any event, much of the bureaucracy has continued relatively unperturbed with its essential structure, job guarantees and perks remaining in place such is its might, while preserving its vested interests intact. This edifice of the colonial era that the colonialists set up have long been discarded from their own administrative systems. China, by contrast, was successful in doing away

[31] To take another example, see Mukhopadhyay (2008), who elaborated on India's often inverted and, therefore, irrational customs tariffs schedule running to hundreds of pages. The inversion emanates from inputs being subjected to higher tariff rates than the outputs leading to economic distortions.

[32] In this India is not alone as many countries exclude embarrassing portions from their recorded history, not the least of which are ex-colonial countries that refrain from including in their history books in schools and colleges the deleterious ramifications of their colonial past on colonial populations.

with the major fault lines of bureaucracy with commensurate freeing up of economic and social decision making and achievement.

The negative ramifications of the license-based approach on productivity have been severe in the long term. Well-intentioned policy makers and reform commissions set up by consecutive governments have, by and large, been unsuccessful in altering prevailing bureaucratic structures in any fundamental way. Worse, bureaucracy has established itself with renewed vigour at lower levels – state, municipal, *panchayat* – of government as well. Rent seeking and an objective of perpetuation rather than reform have exacerbated poverty since their negative impact trickles down to the lowest levels where the interlocutors could be low-level government agents. Administrative reform elements will be put forward in Chapter 11.

Socio-economic policies

With that backdrop, this volume concludes with a mix of policy prescriptions beyond the design of cash and food redistributive programmes, the need for which is, of course, not to be minimized. The policy mix, described in some detail in Chapter 11, bears on fiscal policies including rationalized transfers of assets and incomes. They also include tax policies that are distributive in nature while keeping in mind any deleterious impact on the efficiency of resource allocation. Social policy interventions are recommended in the form of actions for services to be provided by recruited youth. They would be given specific assignments, prior to completing their education process, to ensure standards in schools and health centres, to monitor the implementation of ongoing sanitation projects, to undertake assignments to examine the account books of banks and other tasks depending on their prior training. Such a policy would be akin to practices in many countries regarding military draft except that, in this case, it would be services by private individuals to the disadvantaged communities. Many instances of such a manner of service provision exist in the recent socio-economic history of many countries including in India's past.

Policy action must ensure the provision of goods and services that the poor lack. In a broader sense, that would comprise food, cash and assets. Dreze and Sen linked market reforms – 'removal of unproductive government controls – with a radical shift in public policy in education and health' (p 16). An essential mix is that of a market-propelled growth in industry and trade complemented by the public provision of basic education and primary health. Last but not least, the provision of education and health services should be complemented with structural measures including the availability of credit, transfer of productive assets such as milch cows, small machinery for asset building as well as land in particular where government has considerable fallow land in its possession.

Ensuring access to public services including health, nutrition, sanitation and clean water to the poor is another policy area in public service provision that needs to be speeded up. India's provisions in these sectors have been, at best, lacklustre, even in urban areas. Tap water cannot be drunk safely any longer. Sanitation has improved though not at the same pace as in many comparable countries. A 2014 World Health Organization-UNICEF cross-country comparison revealed the top ten countries that achieved the highest reduction in open defecation since 1990 as a percentage of population. In the Indian sub-continent, it showed a rapid decline in open defecation in Bangladesh, Pakistan and Nepal. Reflecting its numbers on the use of open fields, India did not feature in comparative improvement, while Sri Lanka also did not feature but for the opposite reason; that there was little open defecation there. Ethiopia's reduction was most striking, while Bangladesh, Peru and Vietnam rapidly reduced their incidence as well (see Chapter 10). Little can be said regarding the ongoing *swatch bhaarat* – clean India – programme other than to rely exclusively on government reports.

The dearth of hospital beds stood out starkly during the worst of the 2020 COVID-19 pandemic even in New Delhi, the country's capital. Little reliable accounts could be drawn from rural or mufassil areas. International reports indicated the total number of deaths to be five-to-nine times the official estimates.[33] Even earlier, the condition of public hospitals in major cities such as Kolkata was repeatedly reported to be shocking, including accounts of cats found devouring new-borns lying in the corridors. Public health centres in the *bimaru* states were appalling, with regular reports of sudden deaths of cohorts of new-borns, or multiple deaths of adults due to lack of oxygen canisters. Child wellbeing remains low as revealed from ample statistical evidence in Chapter 9.

How are expenditure policies to be financed? The source will have to be through the generation of tax revenue for which there is ample scope. The government has rationalized parts of the tax structure but has remained reticent in carrying out taxation measures to correct its inequity that, if corrected, could generate considerable revenue. Carrying out tax reform along those lines would be a win-win proposition in that it will improve the equity in the tax system while yielding needed revenue to finance services for the poor that are currently lacking. Chapter 11 will go in detail into the recommended tax policy package.

---

[33] The *Economist* newspaper regularly reported on COVID-19 in India including on 13 March, 2021, 24 April 24, 2021, 8 May, 2021, 19 February, 2022 and at other times.

Socio-anthropogenic policies

Socio-economic policies are necessary but not sufficient. To fulfil a sufficiency condition, socio-anthropogenic policies must be employed. For a long-run solution to subjugate inequality and poverty, they will need to be fundamental. The position of women must be enhanced as already elaborated through legislation without delay, mainly in the form of equal representation as men in economic and political participation in the workplace and in society. And the condition of vulnerability of poor children must remain under close examination and, wherever and whenever found, resources allocated for its rapid alleviation. For example, can the transportation of busloads of impoverished children who are taken away from – sold by – their parents for a pittance be tolerated by a civilized society? Could there be any excuse not to allocate the required resources to constantly monitor and put an end to such ongoing practices engendered by abject poverty? To confront some of these realities, youth must be employed to contribute a couple of years as they complete school and college education in social service as already elaborated.

Last, but not the least, caste has to be removed from the Indian's consciousness. It militates against any practice found elsewhere in the world in which the journey of life can be determined through a mere name from birth to death (see Chapters 6 and 7). There are arguments in favour of caste empowerment through which lower castes have been successful to garner political representation and economic empowerment, but perhaps that reflects government's slowness in doing the right thing in the first place. A pernicious feature such as a caste surname continues to play a central role in politics and in daily life in much of India. India has to look into this infirmity with deep concern and correct for it in effective terms – and the sooner the better.

Conclusion

The secret to India's poverty eradication lies in matters of caste, politics and bureaucracy that cause market failures and create a sitting population of subalterns more so than merely inappropriate redistributive policy design for cash and food transfers. It is apparent that the poverty problem cannot be transcended without a holistic approach that combines economic and social policies in a nuanced manner. The alleviation of inequality will depend on India's ability to forcefully undertake redistributive tax policy complemented by adequate allocation of public resources in education, health and nutrition including water. But most of all, the abolition of caste and caste surnames, equalization of women's status to men, and obligatory social work by youth are needed to ensure enablement of the eradication of poverty and alleviation of inequality.

References

Agarwala, Amar Narain and Sampat Pal Singh (eds). (1958) *The Economics of Underdevelopment*. New York: Oxford University Press.

Alkire, Sabina and James Foster. (2011) 'Understandings and misunderstandings of multidimensional poverty measurement', *Journal of Economic Inequality*, 9: 289–314.

Banerjee, Abhijit and Esther Duflo. (2008) 'Mandated empowerment: handing antipoverty policy back to the poor?' *Annals of the New York Academy Sciences*, 1136(1): 333–41. Available at https://doi.org/10.1196/annals.1425.019, accessed 22 June 2021.

Banerjee, Abhijit and Esther Duflo. (2011) *Poor Economics: A Radical Rethinking of the Way to Fight Global Poverty*. New York: Public Affairs.

Basu, Kaushik and S. Subramanian. (2020) 'Inequality, growth, poverty and lunar eclipses: policy and arithmetic', *Development and Change*, 51(2): 352–70. Available at https://doi.org/10.1111/dech.12512, accessed 22 June 2021.

Bhagwati, N. Jagdish and Padma Desai. (1970) *India: Planning for Industrialization, Industrialization and Trade Policies since 1951*. Delhi: Oxford University Press.

Bhambra, Gurminder K. (2021) 'Narrating inequality, eliding empire', *The British Journal of Sociology*, 72(1): 69–78. Available at https://doi.org/10.1111/1468-4446.12804, accessed 1 May 2021.

Boushey, Heather. (2019) *UnBound: How Inequality Constricts Our Economy and What We Can Do About It*. Cambridge: Harvard University Press.

Britannica. (2015) The Editors of Encyclopaedia. 'Manu-smriti'. *Encyclopedia Britannica*, 4 Feb. Available at www.britannica.com/topic/Manu-smriti, accessed 6 April 2021.

Chancel, Lucas and Piketty, Thomas. (2017) 'Indian Income Inequality, 1922–2015: from British Raj to Billionaire Raj?', WID.world Working Paper 2017/1. Available at https://wid.world/document/chancelpiketty2017widworld/, accessed 1 May 2021.

Charlesworth, Neil. (1982) *British Rule and the Indian Economy, 1800–1914*. London: The Macmillan Press Ltd.

Coombes, J. W. (1920) *The Making of Men*. London: Seeley, Service & Co. Limited.

Dalrymple, William. (2019) *The Anarchy – The Relentless Rise of the East India Company*. London: Bloomsbury Publishing.

Das, Veena. (2015) *Affliction – Health, Disease, Poverty*. New York: Fordham University Press.

Das, Veena and Ranendra K. Das. (2010) *Sociology and Anthropology of Economic Life I: The Moral Embedding of Economic Action*, Vol. 1. New Delhi: Oxford University Press.

Deshpande, Ashwini. (2001) 'Caste at birth? Redefining disparity in India'. *Review of Development Economics*, 5(1): 130–44. Hoboken: Blackwell Publishing Ltd.

Deshpande, Ashwini. (2022) 'The impact of caste and untouchability: a missing link in the literature on stunting in India.' Working Paper, Centre for Economic Data and Analysis (CEDA), Ashoka University, India.

Dreze, Jean and Amartya Sen. (1995) *Economic Development and Social Opportunity*. Delhi: Oxford University Press.

Gardner, Leigh and Tirthankar Roy. (2020) *The Economic History of Colonialism*. Bristol: Bristol University Press.

Ghatak, Maitreesh. (2021) 'India's Inequality Problem', *The India Forum*, 2 July. Available at www.theindiaforum.in/article/does-india-have-inequality-problem, accessed 2 July 2021.

Gupta, Vikas, Rama Kant Agnihotri and Minati Panda (eds) (2021) *Education and Inequality: Historical and Contemporary Trajectories*. Hyderabad: Orient BlackSwan.

Kapadia, Karin. (ed) (2003) *The Violence of Development: The Politics of Identity, Gender & Social Inequalities in India*. London: Zed Books.

Kapadia, Karin. (2018) *Siva and Her Sisters: Gender, Caste, And Class in Rural South India*. New York: Routledge.

Kumar, Arun. (2021) 'Rethinking inequality and education: crime, labour, and the school curriculum in Indian reformatory schools (1880s–1920s)', in Vikas Gupta, Rama Kant Agnihotri and Minati Panda (eds) *Education and Inequality: Historical and Contemporary Trajectories*. Hyderabad: Orient BlackSwan.

Kunnath, George J. (2017) *Rebels from the Mud Houses: Dalits and the Making of the Maoist Revolution in Bihar* (1st edn) London: Routledge. Available at https://doi.org/10.4324/9780203740798, accessed 1 May 2021.

Lakshmanasamy, T. and K. Maya. (2020) 'The effect of income inequality on happiness inequality in India: a recentered influence function regression estimation and life satisfaction inequality decomposition', *Indian Journal of Human Development*, 14(2): 161–181. Available at https://doi.org/10.1177/0973703020948468, accessed 1 May 2021.

Levinas, Emmanuel. (2006) *Humanism and the Other*. Urbana: University of Illinois Press. (First published in French in 1972.)

Lieven, Anatol. (2011) *Pakistan: A Hard Country*. London: Penguin Books.

Little, Ian M. D. (1982) *Economic Development*, New York: Basic Books.

Macdonell, A. A. (1914) 'The early history of caste', *The American Historical Review*, 19(2): 230–44. Available at doi:10.2307/1862285, accessed 23 April 2021.

Meebelo, Henry S. (1973) 'The concept of man-centredness in Zambian humanism', *The African Review: A Journal of African Politics, Development and International Affairs*, 3(4): 559–75.

Mignolo, Walter D. and Catherine E. Walsh. (2018) *On Decoloniality – Concepts, Analytics, Praxis*. Durham: Duke University Press.

Mill, John Stuart. (1848) *Principles of Political Economy*. London: J. W. Parker, West Strand.

Mistry, Rohinton. (1997) *A Fine Balance*. Toronto: McClelland & Stewart.

Mukerjee, Madhusree. (2010) *Churchill's Secret War – The British Empire and the Ravaging of India During World War II*. New Delhi: Tranquebar Press, Westland Ltd.

Mukhopadhyay, Sukumar. (2008) *Essays in Indirect Taxation*. New Delhi: Manupatra.

Paidipaty, Poornima and Pedro Ramos Pinto. (2021) 'Revisiting the "Great Levelling": The limits of Piketty's Capital and Ideology for understanding the rise of late 20th century inequality', *The British Journal of Sociology*, 72(1): 52–68. Available at https://doi.org/10.1111/1468-4446.12840, accessed 30 April 2021.

Piketty, Thomas. (2014) *Capital in the Twenty-First Century*. Translated by Arthur Goldhammer. Cambridge/London: The Belknap Press of Harvard University Press.

Piketty, Thomas. (2020) *Capital and Ideology*. Translated by Arthur Goldhammer. Cambridge: Harvard University Press.

Piketty, Thomas. (2021) 'Capital and ideology: a global perspective on inequality regimes', *The British Journal of Sociology*, 72(1): 139–150. Available at https://doi.org/10.1111/1468-4446.12836, accessed 30 April 2021.

Rao, Anupama. (2009) *The Caste Question – Dalits and the Politics of Modern India*. Ranikhet / New Delhi: Permanent Black / Orient Blackswan.

Ravallion, Martin. (2012) 'Fighting poverty one experiment at a time: A review of Abhijit Banerjee and Esther Duflo's "Poor Economics: a radical rethinking of the way to fight global poverty"', *Journal of Economic Literature*, 50(1): 103–14. Available at www.jstor.org/stable/23269972, accessed 22 June 2021.

Reddy, Sanjay G. (2021) 'Beyond property or beyond Piketty?' *The British Journal of Sociology*, 72(1): 8–25. Available at https://doi.org/10.1111/1468-4446.12822, accessed 1 May 2021.

Roy, Thirthankar. (2020) *The Economic History of India, 1857–2010*. Fourth Edn, New Delhi: Oxford University Press.

Sen, Amartya. (1981) *Poverty and Famines: An Essay on Entitlement and Deprivation*. Oxford: Oxford University Press.

Sen, Amartya. (1995) *Inequality Reexamined*. Oxford: Oxford University Press.

Sen, Amartya. (2000) *Development as Freedom*. New Delhi: Oxford University Press.

Sen, Amartya. (2009) *The Idea of Justice*. London: Allen Lane.

Shome, Parthasarathi. (1973) 'Non-Ethical Distribution and Failure of Markets', Master's Thesis, University of Rochester, Department of Economics.

Shome, Parthasarathi. (2021) *Taxation History, Theory, Law and Administration. Springer Texts in Business and Economics*. Cham: Springer. Available at https://doi.org/10.1007/978-3-030-68214-9, Accessed 22 May 2021.

Smith, Adam. (1790) *The Theory of Moral Sentiments*. London: A. Millar.

Solow, Robert. (2017) 'Improving the measurement and understanding of economic inequality in the United States', Washington Centre for Equitable Growth, Washington, DC, 12 July. Available at https://equitablegrowth.org/improving-the-measurement-and-understanding-of-economic-inequality-in-the-united-states/, accessed 31 August 2021.

Stutzer, Alois and Bruno S. Frey. (2010) 'Recent advances in the economics of individual subjective wellbeing', IZA Discussion Paper, No. 4850:1–33. Available at www.iza.org, accessed 7 January 2023.

Tomlinson, Brian Roger. (1988) 'The historical roots of Indian poverty: issues in the economic and social history of modern South Asia: 1880–1960', *Modern Asian Studies*, 22(1): 123–40. Available at www.jstor.org/stable/312494, accessed 22 June 2021.

Wilder, Gary. (2015) *Freedom Time: Negritude, Decolonization, and the Future of the World*. Durham: Duke University Press. Available at https://doi.org/10.1515/9780822375791, accessed 1 May 2021.

Wilkerson, Isabel. (2020) *Caste: The Lies that Divide Us*. London: Allen Lane, Penguin Random House.

PART I

Macro-Economy and Human Development

> In Capital and Ideology, I attempt to illustrate the complementarity between natural language and the language of mathematics and statistics. ... The neglect of quantitative and statistical sources by many social scientists is unfortunate, particularly since critical examinations of the sources and the conditions under which they are socially, historically, and politically constructed are (sic) necessary to make proper use of them.
>
> Thomas Piketty[1]

[1] Piketty (2021), p 149.

2

Macro-Economic Indicators: A Backdrop

Introduction

This chapter discusses selected economic indicators to place India in perspective, in particular in a comparison with China and, selectively, with Brazil. This reflects the premise that, in order to assess the state of poverty and inequality and their alleviation, an understanding of the basic macro-economic conditions of their economies can be helpful. That is the objective of this chapter. Brazil, China and India are large economies, members of the Group of 20 (G20) countries, and are often brought up together in international forums. Thus, some comparisons and contrasts among them are inevitable.

To begin, should the performance of the macro-economy and economic growth be of relevance in poverty alleviation? The answer to this is in the affirmative as has been shown by Srinivasan (2001) in which he finds that 'there is a robust association between reduction in absolute poverty and sustained and significant growth in aggregate income' (p iv). Further, as an economy liberalizes, changing terms of trade and barriers to trade could increase inequality in the short run as some may be better positioned to benefit from the more open economic policies than others. Both China and India have experienced a similar phase. Therefore, complementary policies have to be in place to ensure that any increase in inequality is only temporary. Fourth, keeping in mind the caveats against causal interpretations of associations, some policies and factors seem to promote growth and reduction in poverty. On the whole, macro-economic stability, a disciplined labour force, public and private investment in education and health, high rapid development of economic infrastructure – power, transport, communications, roads and port facilities as provided in Chinese special economic zones (SEZs) – and the ease of doing business are believed to enable growth and associated with it, poverty reduction.

There are strong historical contrasts between India and China, the foremost being the political evolution in the two countries. China has experienced a dearth of fundamental human rights where economic and socio-economic decisions are the subject of a monolithic system, a framework that continues to this day and has decidedly worsened recently after a short interim period of improvement. Policy implementation occurs without much debate, earlier through a Marxist-Leninist regime, followed by state capitalism more recently.[1] Indeed, today, as China's international clout has deepened and spread, it has been promoting this philosophy in its global reach and not merely in its immediate geographical neighbourhood, except in India where a primarily adverse relationship reflects a historical indeterminacy of their international borders. By contrast, India adopted democratic principles in its 1950 constitution and, though struggling with challenging political dimensions in which complexities arise constantly, by and large has adhered to it thus far, though India's policymaking and its implementation are, as a result, much more laborious, perhaps even lugubrious. Nevertheless, that can no longer remain an explanation for India's relative slowness in solving its poverty problem. Indeed, India has voted in a majoritarian regime that is at its helm at present which should make policy implementation quicker and easier so that any explanation for slowness appears increasingly to be an excuse for failure. Conspicuous government consumption expenditure in building edifices and monumental urban facades after demolishing well-functioning ones has become a glaring feature rather than prominent poverty eradication programmes that are sustained. On the other hand, China's indicators on poverty have made impressive strides, and it recently declared that any remnants of absolute poverty have been eliminated. Brazil has flitted between unpredictable democratic leaders and a long military dictatorship (1964–85) during its post-independence period since 1822 and has suffered deep-seated inequality despite its much higher per-capita income.

Advanced and emerging economies alike have incurred significantly higher public expenditure during the COVID-19 pandemic in 2020 that continued in 2021 than could have been anticipated before the pandemic. Resultantly, they have reached unprecedented fiscal deficit ratios of 10–16 per cent of gross domestic product (GDP) in the face of a heightened need, in particular, for socio-economic expenditure. The International Monetary Fund (IMF) estimated that India's general government[2] fiscal deficit would reach 12.3 per cent of GDP in financial year (FY) 2020–21, primarily due

[1] The phraseology may be considered somewhat loose by some; nevertheless, they should convey the intent of China's evolved policy mixes over time.

[2] General government comprises all – central, state and local – levels of government.

Table 2.1: Real GDP growth (annual per cent change)

Year	India	China
1995	7.6	10.9
2000	4.0	8.5
2005	9.3	11.4
2010	10.3	10.6
2015	8.0	6.9
2019	4.2	6.1
2020*	–8.0	2.3
2021**	12.5	8.6
2022**	6.9	6.0

* Estimate.

** Projections. For 2022, the IMF's projections were subsequently reduced to 6.6 per cent reflecting escalating international oil prices due, to no small extent, to the ongoing Russo-Ukrainian war.

Note: For India, figures are presented on FY (1 April–31 March) basis. Based on the calendar year, India's growth is estimated at –7.1 per cent for 2020 and projected at 11.3 per cent for 2021.

Source: IMF Database and World Economic Outlook, IMF, 23 March 2021

to weak revenue collection from a depressed economy. This deficit level was higher than during the 2008–09 global economic crisis.

In the last two decades, India's GDP growth rates increased until 2010 but steadily declined after that (see Table 2.1). The year 2020 was estimated as a significantly negative growth year reflecting both an already declining trend and the deleterious economic ramifications of the COVID-19 pandemic.[3] A high GDP growth rate projected for 2021 mainly reflected a high rate on the low 2020 GDP base.

Macro-economic indicators

In a comparison of India with China, it may be observed that, though both India and China have enjoyed high growth rates, China's GDP growth rate

[3] Goldman Sachs, a bank, has estimated the severity of the lockdown as a result of the pandemic by interpreting the extent of school closures and tracking smart phone data as proxies for drop in economic activity. Out of 100, it gave India a score of 87, the US 57 and UK 74 at the peaks of their crises, implying that the negative impact on the rate of growth could be relatively the highest for India (*The Economist*, 2021).

has been above that of India for most of the past four decades. Interestingly, India's GDP growth rate in 2016 stood slightly above China's though, in 2018, this trend reversed back to the usual trend, with India's GDP growth rate standing lower at 4.2 per cent compared to China's 6.1 per cent in 2019. Also, both countries lost quite a few points in GDP growth since 2010 (see Table A2.3 in Appendix 2.2). In what follows, what emerges is a stark contrast in the macro-economic indicators of China and India exposing considerably more stringent constraints on India to address poverty alleviation and adopt equality enhancing policies.[4] Indeed, Datt and Ravallion (2002) found that India just about maintained its 1980s rate of poverty reduction in the 1990s rather than any acceleration since the 1991 economic liberalization, with poverty having declined at a little less than one percentage point per year over the main post-reform period, with any acceleration in poverty reduction remaining 'contentious'.

India faced more challenges in terms of per capita GDP growth while China's one-child policy until recently – though it relaxed it to a two-child policy in 2016 and to a three-child policy in 2021 – would have helped its per-capita statistics.[5] India abandoned any population targets after a foray into it that was considered to have been a political disaster due to its manner of implementation. This was proven in the parliamentary elections that followed in 1977 when the incumbent prime minister suffered a resounding defeat.[6]

In their 2019 GDP break-up, China's high industry share continues as per cent of GDP (39) in contrast to India's (25). India's higher services share (59) than China's (54) is reflective of a higher residual that perforce has to absorb new labour. The trends reveal the higher and deeper global links of China which has become the manufacturing hub of the world compared to India's relatively fledgling links. Gross capital formation (GCF) is considered a good indicator of economic growth inasmuch as the investment of capital leads to higher production. India's GCF was 30 per cent of GDP during

4 See Shome (2012) for details on India's macro-economic – fiscal and exchange rate – imbalances that existed even after the 1991 economic liberalization.

5 China's transition from a one-child policy to a three-child policy, occurring in a span of six years, reflects an effort to arrest and reverse its rapidly aging population.

6 By contrast China continues to use population as a social control tool even today, for example in the Xinjiang region. Birth rates in the mostly Muslim Uighur ethnic group of Hotan and Kashgar plunged by more than 60 per cent from 2015 to 2018, the latest year available in government statistics. Across the Xinjiang region, birth rates continue to plummet, falling nearly 24 per cent last year alone, compared to 4.2 per cent nationwide. To cite Kashgar, a prefecture in southern Xinjiang which is almost entirely Uyghur, the birth rate averaged 19 per thousand in 2014, 13 per thousand in 2018 and 4.15 per thousand in 2019. The authorities' explanation that the goal is to control excessive population growth is matched by encouragement of majority Chinese to increase family size through various material incentives.

2010–19 while China's hovered just below 50 per cent though it declined to 43 per cent in 2019 (see Table A2.3 in Appendix 2.2).

Some contrasts with Brazil may also be instructive here. Brazil's economic decline in the last decade has been revealing in terms of failed economic policies unable to cross any milestone in an adverse political structure that has acted more as a millstone around Brazil's neck. The foundation for growth had been laid at the end of Brazil's dictatorship with the signing of a new constitution in 1988 that created independent institutions and a new currency in 1994 that eradicated hyper-inflation. A commodity boom led by hydrocarbons in the 2000s resulted in an annual growth rate of 4 per cent, new jobs, a decline in poverty by 40 per cent, climate talks and Brazil's playing a leading international role through BRICS (an emerging economy grouping comprising Brazil, Russia, India, China and South Africa). In 2009, Brazil's happiness index was ranked 17 out of 144 countries.[7]

In the 2010s, the boom ended, and the authorities apparently hid the size of the fiscal deficit caused by excessive public expenditure, leading to the impeachment of Brazil's president in 2016. The subsequent president narrowly escaped impeachment for corruption, who was followed by another during whose care the economy collapsed, the annual growth rate declining to less than 1 per cent and, during the pandemic, to negative levels in 2021. People sank back into poverty, school attendance dropped, inequality jumped, with the top 1 per cent of the population becoming phenomenally richer than the poorest 50 per cent, recorded at the bottom among comparable countries. And the climate issue was ignored with the president encouraging deforestation, the outcome being that the Amazon emits more carbon dioxide today than it absorbs, a condition that had never existed earlier.

Curiously, in 2019, military expenditure in terms of GDP was noticeably higher in India – 2.4 per cent – than in China or Brazil but in India, their numbers have steadily decreased over time. By contrast, it has remained the same in China at 1.9 per cent during 2010–19 raising serious doubts about the reliability of this information in reflection of its public arms displays in recent years (see Table A2.3 in Appendix 2.2).

There is little doubt that, to recuperate its GDP, India needs significant injections of investment, including foreign direct investment (FDI). Though India's FDI increased from $27 billion to $51 billion during the 2010–19 period, its scale was a quarter that of China's (see Table A2.3 in the Appendix 2.2). Even Brazil's FDI was around one-and-a-half times that of India in 2019. It is not impossible to speculate on the reasons for such a difference, important factors comprising India's substandard government-provided

7 See Neri (2015).

economic infrastructure, a thin supply of what may be considered modern labour, slow improvement in the ease of doing business in particular the ease of paying taxes, lethargic reform in the tax structure and its application by the tax administration and many other such constraints.

The 2019 difference in their international debt service as a per cent of exports of goods, services and primary income[8] was stark – 53, 10 and 9 for Brazil, China, and India (see Table A2.3 in Appendix 2.2) respectively. Brazil is a highly indebted economy, explaining the economic doldrums it faces intermittently, while China's growth strategy has rested on an export push through a long-term policy of undervalued currency and maintaining tight control on imports that has generated a secularly large trade surplus with the rest of the world. In fact, its trading partners are all indebted to it today. India has relied more on domestic debt than on foreign debt. Its currency was historically overvalued thus restricting export growth and enabling little import substitution except through government licenses and subsidies.

China's undervalued currency began to unravel only recently under international pressure. Nevertheless, even after effective appreciation of its currency in 2019, China's exports remained 18 per cent of GDP, the same as India's. On the imports side, they were 21 per cent and 17 per cent of GDP for India and China respectively, revealing India's relatively higher import dependence (see Table A2.3 in Appendix 2.2). Thus, overall, India suffered a trade deficit of 3 per cent of GDP while China enjoyed a trade surplus of 1 per cent of GDP. Nevertheless, as percentages of GDP, both countries suffered significant losses in exports and imports during the pandemic, reflecting setbacks in global trade. There is little doubt that the gulf between the two economies has grown, and is continuing to grow rapidly enough that it appears it would be almost impossible for India to catch up with China even in the medium term.

Ironically, however, if exogenous external shocks such as the 2002 international financial and economic meltdown or unanticipated war are to affect domestic growth adversely, India's structural nature and composition of international trade have tended to give it a vantage position and cushion it against the impact of such shocks (Goel, 2022). Thus, while the conditions unraveled by the Russo-Ukrainian war have led to an inevitable escalation in domestic oil prices and, commensurately, in inflation, India's dependence on Russian crude oil is less than China's dependence. Further, though India imports commodities such as fertilizers, precious stones, nuclear power and other items from Russia whose curtailment is bound to hurt India's economy adversely, India has had the opportunity to step into the vacuum created in

8 Total debt service is the sum of principal repayments and interest actually paid in currency, goods, or services on long-term debt, interest paid on short-term debt and repayments (repurchases and charges) to the IMF.

international markets in commodity sectors such as, for example, wheat, confectionary, nuts, fruits and pulses before other economies were able to take comparable action (Anbumozhi, 2022). Thus, admittedly, while India's GDP growth rate was revised down from 7.2 per cent to 6.6 per cent in 2022 by the IMF, this deceleration was lower than in many comparable economies.

Despite such macro-economic vignettes, however, India's continuing poor, developing country status is confirmed by its net official development assistance and official aid in dollars. India's (US $2.5 billion) receipts were almost six times higher than that of Brazil (US $0.4 billion) in 2018 while a net outflow had already begun from China. This indicator is a crucial one revealing their relative economic status. In terms of management of their economies, a single policy instrument provides illuminating evidence. India struggled to provide ultra-modern economic infrastructure through instruments such as special economic zones. It introduced SEZs through an Act of Parliament in 2006, but performance has trailed that of China's SEZs. While the latter are mammoth but less than 20 in number, India approved some 160 of them, even some single buildings being designated as an independent SEZ, reflecting an intrinsic failure in its SEZ policy and systemic corruption in the allotment of land by government to private operators. Indeed, it became well-known that it spawned a real estate market for, after allotments were made, there was little subsequent government monitoring of SEZs being actually set up.

Another limitation on FDI is India's overall stance on its international taxation policy. To expect FDI to occur on a large scale while a regime of retrospective application of tax law rages on multinational enterprises (MNEs) has been folly. Until this policy was reined in after a decade of its 2012 introduction through changes in the law and only prospective application of tax changes was assured, the tax regime dampened GDP, rather than tax collection being the outcome of GDP and GDP growth. While government introduced a change in the law on retrospective application, there are nevertheless pre-conditions attached to it that may continue to make potential foreign investors cautious about investing in India.[9]

In terms of non-tax policy, China attracts foreign investors because of its disciplined labour force, among other things, that India has not been able to guarantee. Foreign investors continue to go to China despite stringent pre-conditions such as technology transfer and a minimum length of stay for established enterprises. Despite an increasing politicized environment and a demand that sensitive technologies used in China by foreign firms be controllable by the authorities, foreign investment continues to flock

[9] See Shome (2021), pp. 340–47, for a discussion of why retrospective taxation makes it 'impossible to perform' for businesses.

there. Such long-term strategic benefits that China enjoys have not accrued to India.

Selected technology modernization indicators

Selected micro-indicators regarding relative technology orientation reflect the extent of modernization. Mobile cellular subscription per 100 persons increased rapidly in all three countries and, in 2016, India's number (85) was competitive with China (97) and Brazil (118) (see Table A2.4 in Appendix 2.2). However, the number of subscribers reduced both in Brazil (99) and India (84) in 2019. In India, where 90 per cent of mobile subscriptions are with private providers, the scaling back could be the result of winding up of businesses by many private telecom companies and increases in spectrum usage cost.[10] With a smaller number of service providers and tariff hike for various plans, it was likely that affordability declined for the poor to own mobile phones. However, this could be temporary as explained next.

The Indian telecom sector is approaching a duopoly state if Vodafone-Idea doesn't survive the competition posed by two other major players. Government also decided to shut down or privatize existing public sector telecom companies due to their swelled losses and subscribers shifting to private telecom service providers.[11]

Government decided not to shut down Bharat Sanchar Nigam Limited (BSNL) and Mahanagar Telephone Nigam Limited (MTNL), two public sector telecom companies, and announced a revival package of around Rs 690 billion in October 2019.[12] Therefore, the anticipation that price hikes would not be controllable in the future have dissipated somewhat.

Individuals using the internet as a percentage of population in India (22) was behind China (53) and Brazil (61) in 2016:[13] in 2019, the usage of internet services by individuals in India increased by 57 per cent – increasing from 22 per cent of the population to 34.5 per cent – (see Table A2.4 in Appendix 2.2). This could have been the result of cheap data availability, free data packs and better speed provided by private players to lure subscribers to consume more data. Broadband – optical fibre cable for the internet – however, has been slow in coming though it is picking up speed over the past two years. India's lower education levels may not yet enable its wider population to use the internet while it is rapidly becoming familiar with the

---

[10] See Sharma (2021).

[11] BSNL's loss swelled to Rs 155 billion from Rs 149 billion, and that of MTNL increased to Rs 38.11 billion from Rs 33.98 billion between 2019–20 and 2018–19.

[12] *Times of India* (2021), 3 February.

[13] Also, high technology exports as a per cent of manufactured exports were 13, 31 and 10, respectively, for Brazil, China and India in 2019.

rudimentary functions of a mobile phone. Nevertheless, positive changes are occurring. However, with the emergence of lower-priced smart phones, and low-cost data availability and data usage, the use of internet services is showing a rising trend. Voice call charges have approached nil with different packs or plans. Internet speed has also increased. An increase in the number of over-the-top (OTT) platforms offers services directly to viewers over the internet. And, as the number of applications available on smart phones that use data increases, data consumption is also going up.

To conclude, trends reveal India to have made progress in its economic indicators, though an international comparison indicates that progress has not been rapid enough, and that India needs to speed up the changes if it has to catch up with China. While mobile phone and internet use have increased with positive signs of progress, the falling behind of the poor can, at least partially, be explained by India's growing inequality (see Chapter 4).

Impact of demonetization on the poor

The danger that government policy, intended to be corrective for a particular economic objective, can be detrimental to the lives of the poor is an ever-present danger. This section provides an example of a government policy that affected the poor and vulnerable adversely. The Indian government demonetized 86 per cent of its currency in circulation – all Rs 500 and Rs 1,000 notes – without prior announcement on 8 November 2016. Its stated objectives were to seize undeclared income, destroy 'black' – or counterfeit – money and thus expand the formal portion of the economy, thereby enhancing the tax base. Evidence has suggested that demonetization had appreciable costs in terms of lost jobs and output. Though some of it may have been temporary,[14] its societal costs would have to be immeasurable in particular if wellbeing and happiness are factored in.

At the macro-economic level, whatever was the amount of black money coming into banks by 31 December 2016, the date until when their legality was extended, and into the Reserve Bank of India (RBI), the central bank, by 31 March 2017, the end of the financial year, would have been estimated by the RBI – what has come in and what has not – in comparison with the cash earlier issued by it. The RBI would have thus arrived at a calculation of change in its liabilities, and quantify mismatched assets and liabilities in its balance sheet. It would have then returned some government bonds it held thus enabling government to increase spending and, in turn, restoring GDP to normal. Also, there was an expectation that cash holders would be reticent to deposit large amounts of cash in banks prior to the cut-off date

---

[14] Lahiri (2020a).

and, instead, buy gold with the tax-evaded cash that they were holding. However, the view that black money holders would find refuge in gold was based on the assumption that merchants would be willing to sell gold in exchange for cash, albeit at premium prices, and thus assume any amount of tax evaders' risk by increasing their own cash holdings.

The impact of demonetization on the poor was explained away by the parliamentary majority with the assertion that farmers could, after all, put their money into banks. This argument was reminiscent of a policymaker of the previous government asserting that there must be a ration shop every 50 yards where the poor could access government-subsidized cereals which of course was absurdly inaccurate.[15]

The reality of the status of the informal sector has been analysed by Chakraborty (2021) using 2017–18 data, indicating that,

> Formal employment has stagnated and paid employment as a share of total employment has fallen. Among the poorest consumption class, nine out of ten are in informal employment … . Workers who have either no education or have completed only primary education … are (more) likely to be in informal employment.
>
> Two-thirds of women workers are still employed in agriculture. In particular, women's unpaid work and care responsibilities … tend to invisibilise their economic contributions … . A major difference between men and women in informal employment (is the) percentage of the population employed as contributing family workers – it is more than four times higher among women in informal employment relative to men. (Chakraborty, 2021, pp 4–5)

Demonetization affected informal sector employment more adversely than the formal sector as the informal workers – more than formal sector workers – as access to, and availability of, the new currency bills were more restricted for the informal sector. The COVID-19 pandemic worsened their condition as they were sent to their home villages overnight without warning. Based on a sample study of 176 women between 23 and 30 April 2020, it was gleaned by Chakraborty (2020) that 83 per cent of women witnessed a severe income drop and 97 per cent of street venders reported nil income during the pandemic with a switching of chores to the elderly and child-care issues ensuing.

Even women waste pickers faced restrictions, thus leading to a disappearance of incomes of the poorest of the poor.

---

[15] This is merely to point out, shorn of all superstructure, the callousness of policymakers towards the poor or their livelihood (2020b).

If comprehensive government surveys were conducted in India's interiors to understand the concerns of the rural sector, they would have realized that policy making failed to address the crucial dependence of rural workers and farmers on the use of cash. They should have assessed the banking infrastructure in rural India before making their policy decision deeply adverse to the wellbeing of the poor. Even if all farmers could access a bank, how far was their nearest bank? A mere statistic regarding the total number of new bank accounts was abjectly insufficient. Policymakers should have realized that not just tax evaders, smugglers or terrorists used cash but, significantly, the poor. Neither did they see fit to observe the queues for banking services of the urban commoner.

Informal work in the urban sector may be said to comprise domestic work, street vending, waste picking, home-based work and construction work. To cite an example, reports indicated that daily venders in Kolkata's vegetable and fish markets experienced a crash in sales since purchasers commonly used Rs 500 notes to do their shopping which had been demonetized. The sufferer was not the buyer as much as the seller whose daily earnings fed the family. Such examples abounded. Suffering of the poor and the sick could have been averted if government had readied counter-measures through appropriate instructions to ensure that the poor did not go unfed or the sick received treatment in an emergency, for example, when they collapsed standing in queues in front of banks causing some deaths. It was ironic, therefore, for policymakers to claim that the entire country was with them, that is, was in favour of demonetization.

Kohli (2018) estimated that cash returned to the public at a much faster pace than anticipated. Table 2.2 shows cash use before and after the 2016 demonetization.[16] It shows cash use was declining before, but increased after, demonetization. In China, cash use declined throughout the period. In Brazil the changes were very small. Kohli also asserted that there was an attempt to spin estimates to claim some degree of success as much as a belabouring of attempts to substantiate more formalization of the economy and job creation. In the end, the RBI admitted that, in its estimation, almost 99 per cent of the demonetized currency had returned to the RBI. Hence, in effect, the entire quantum of black money circulating earlier could be surmised to have been deposited in the banking system which, in turn, was returned to the RBI. Lahiri (2020b) estimated that, post-demonetization, tax base and tax revenue expansion and digitized payments continued as per trend.[17]

Aggarwal and Narayanan (2017) estimated the impact of demonetization on domestic trade in agricultural commodities. Using data on arrivals

---

[16] See Appendix 2.1 for a discussion of the use of cash in India.

[17] Lahiri (2020b).

Table 2.2: Cross-country: cash in circulation,[1] 2014–18

	Value (% of GDP)			Growth (%)			Growth (%) per-capita[2]		
	2014	**2016**	**2018**	**2014–16**	**2016–18**	**2014–18**	**2014–16**	**2016–18**	**2014–18**
Brazil	3.8	3.7	3.8	-2.6	2.7	0.0	-15.7	-6.0	-20.8
China	10.4	10.0	8.9	-3.8	-11.0	-14.4	-1.4	5.8	4.3
India	11.6	8.7	11.3	-25.0	29.9	-2.6	-16.6	53.0	27.6

Note: [1] Banknotes and coins in circulation reported in US dollars using the end-of-year exchange rate. [2] Value per-capita (USD) = [Value in USD]/[Population].

Source: Bank of International Settlements (Red Book of Statistics), March 2021

and prices from close to 3000 regulated markets in India for 35 major agricultural commodities during 2011–17, they examined post-demonetization short term impact and recovery effects of a period of 3 months.[18] They employed difference-in-difference and synthetic control techniques for pre- and post-monetization periods to identify the impact of demonetization. They found 15 per cent of domestic agricultural trade was lost in the short run and 7 per cent at the end of the three-month period after demonetization. Trade in perishables was lost by 23 per cent and 18 per cent respectively. The immediate monetary contraction affected both the supply and prices adversely, though the price impacts lingered longer.

This points towards demonetization's adverse impact on GDP growth. The findings also provide a clue to the growing farmer discontent that escalated to a full-fledged revolt in 2020 in the face of new national legislation regarding agriculture that was pushed through parliament without debate.[19] Other analyses have revealed that, post-demonetization, there were marked declines in the 2017–18 kharif sowing season.[20]

To conclude on the demonetization experience, even if it is accepted that the government's action had to be kept secret for an effective outcome, there were news flashes that appeared to contradict such a premise. For example, Rs 30 million were reported to have been deposited in old Rs 500 and 1,000 bills by government's own political party just before the demonetization announcement. The use of new Rs 2,000 bills prior to demonetization was also reported. Government failed to provide explanations for such

[18] The 35 commodities are representative of agriculture inasmuch as they represented significant shares of land and production value.

[19] Several states witnessed continuing farmer protests – including in Madhya Pradesh, Tamil Nadu, Rajasthan and Maharashtra, thereby exhibiting extraordinary resilience in adhering to their cause.

[20] Chand and Singh (2016).

infractions which, if they were true, would lead to strong doubts regarding the motivations behind the entire exercise. Instead, government could have used other policies such as a re-instatement of the bank cash transactions tax (BCTT) that had been introduced by the previous government in 2006 but also withdrawn by them in 2009. This had been done despite BCTT's success in limiting the high velocity of bank transactions that would illegally convert black money into white. No such sensible policy was carried out.

Comparing Indian governments

In the 21st century, India's governments have undergone significant changes in their philosophical stance. The 2000–03 period was one governed by the National Democratic Alliance (NDA), a coalition with the Bharatiya Janata Party (BJP) as the majority party, followed by two United Progressive Alliance (UPA) governments between 2004–08 (UPA-I) and 2008–13 (UPA-II), a coalition in which the Indian National Congress (INC) party had the majority, followed again by an NDA coalition (NDA-II) with a strong BJP majority between 2014 and 2019 followed by a BJP government to the present. While the UPA's thrust was on secularism and all the benefits and challenges that come with it, the NDA and BJP have attempted to veer society towards a nationalist ethic that has been manifested in *Hindutva*, a markedly non-secular stance moving the country away from the earlier conceived and practised secularism of any post-independence era government since India's 1950 constitution was introduced.

It appears that India's macro-economic indicators have, by and large, fared worse during NDA-BJP rule. This is visible from a perusal of Table 2.3 which shows the rates of change of major indicators during their regimes. While the UPA-I years suffered high inflation but brought it down in UPA-II, the NDA-II years again suffered high inflation. In per cent of GDP, the NDA-II years suffered declines in the growth of agriculture and industry's shares which, in India, implies obligatory absorption in the services sector of excess informal labour. In per cent of GDP, growth in trade – imports and exports of goods and services – together with gross capital formation, all worsened during the NDA-II years. Growth in foreign remittances worsened as did net inflows of FDI when compared to UPA-I. Though changes in external debt stocks and debt service (in terms of per cent of exports of goods, services and primary income) improved, they also point towards lower inflows of FDI. Improvement occurred only in the growth in revenue, and tax revenue, in terms of GDP, reportedly reflecting the introduction of information technology in the filing and processing of tax returns, while the pace of reduction in military expenditure slowed in terms of GDP. In technology use, the increase in mobile and internet use slowed during the NDA-II years.

Table 2.3: India: performance of consecutive administrations in macro-economic indicators

Percentage change in indicator				
Indicator	**NDA-I**	**UPA-I**	**UPA-II**	**NDA-II**
	2000–03	**2004–08**	**2009–13**	**2014–18**
Inflation, GDP deflator (annual %)	6.1	60.6	-12.1	36.7
Agriculture, forestry and fishing, value added (% of GDP)	-9.4	-5.7	2.4	-8.2
Industry (including construction), value added (% of GDP)	0.5	6.6	-8.7	-5.5
Exports of goods and services (% of GDP)	15.0	34.9	24.7	-13.6
Imports of goods and services (% of GDP)	12.5	49.0	9.8	-9.3
Gross capital formation (% of GDP)	10.6	4.9	-15.2	-7.5
Personal remittances, received (current US$) (millions)	63.0	166.5	42.2	11.9
Foreign direct investment, net inflows (balance of payments (BoP), current US$) (billions)	2.7	699.5	-20.9	21.8
External debt stocks, total (Debt Outstanding and Disbursed (DOD), current US$) (billions)	17.6	83.7	66.7	13.9
Total debt service (% of exports of goods, services and primary income)	70.8	-33.4	34.2	-38.8
Revenue, excluding grants (% of GDP)	1.3	5.6	10.4	13.7
Tax revenue (% of GDP)	3.4	14.7	12.2	19.9
Military expenditure (% of GDP)	-9.2	-9.8	-14.5	-4.6
Mobile cellular subscriptions (per 100 persons)	795.3	525.0	60.5	19.3
Individuals using the Internet (% of population)	219.7	121.6	194.9	64.0

Source: World Development Indicators, 2020, World Bank (last updated on 16 December, 2020)

Socio-economic indicators that are usually associated with development and the alleviation of inequality and poverty also fared worse during the NDA-II years (see Table 2.4). The changes in population growth rate, life expectancy at birth, undernourishment, immunization, secondary school enrolment and urban population growth worsened, while environmental statistics on forest area, energy use, CO_2 emission and electric power went unreported in the NDA-II years. In fact, the statistical capacity scores worsened during those years. It is of some concern, therefore, in what light the current government views socio-economic development and redressal of poverty when juxtaposed with its nationalist political agenda. India may continue to face a future of

Table 2.4: India: performance of consecutive administrations in socio-economic indicators

Percentage change in indicator

Indicator	**NDA-I 2000–03**	**UPA-I 2004–08**	**UPA-II 2009–13**	**NDA-II 2014–18**
Population growth (annual %)	-6.6	-9.3	-16.1	-9.5
Life expectancy at birth, total (years)	1.9	2.7	2.5	1.7
Prevalence of undernourishment (% of population)	..	-24.8	-3.0	-8.5
Immunization, measles (% of children ages 12–23 months)	7.1	12.5	6.4	9.4
School enrolment, secondary (% gross)	10.6	17.5	15.3	0.3
Urban population growth (annual %)	10.3	-6.2	-7.5	-0.9
Forest area (sq km) (thousands)	2.1	2.5	1.4	..
Energy use (kg of oil equivalent per capita)	1.7	14.1	11.2	..
CO2 emissions (metric tons per capita)	1.3	27.8	11.1	..
Electric power consumption (kWh per capita)	9.4	24.3	27.7	..
Statistical Capacity score (overall average)	..	1.4	-2.9	-4.1

India: Performance of consecutive administrations in socio-economic indicators

Percentage change in indicator

Source: World Development Indicators, 2020, World Bank (last updated on 16 December, 2020)

exclusion and thwarted socio-economic development unless the current government more successfully explains and makes changes in its course of action in fundamental ways.

Where the performance of different governments is being discussed, it is pertinent to mention the latest escalation of inequality in India – 'the super-rich get richer and everyone else gets poorer'.[21] It was reported that the fortunes of the country's two richest persons have compounded to astounding levels while millions have lost paid work or have sunk into poverty during the pandemic. The share of the incomes of the top 1 per cent has risen rapidly by more than 20 per cent last year, owning almost 40 per cent of total wealth, much higher than in China or the US. This has

[21] *The Economist*, 5 December 2020, p 53.

resulted as much from political influence and impact on share prices as from productivity or technology advancements. A decade back during UPA, the 20 most profitable firms generated less than a third of the profits. During the current regime, they generate 70 per cent. Competition within industry decreased with more smaller companies being ousted.

Thus, the market shares of giant firms have gained during the last decade and much of the US $36 billion increase in foreign investment has been from Facebook and Google into the enterprises of the two largest Indian conglomerates. This clearly reveals that a primary motive of MNEs comprises profits and they have little concern regarding issues of equality. This emulates a dangerous emerging pattern in global development that has witnessed a rapid emergence of concentration of wealth and incomes among mutually hand-holding global corporations. Such gaming the system has adversely affected global equality and poverty with the abatement of malnutrition and stunting ostensibly sliding back.

Clearly the contrasting performances of the two Indian regimes stand out. What is noteworthy is that, during the pandemic, Latin America has also suffered a rise of populations dropping into poverty and suffering hunger, including Brazil. During the 2003–11 presidency, its National Council for Food and Nutritional Security (CONSEA) had been able to remove Brazil from the list of undernourished countries in the World Food Programme's Hunger Map in 2014. This was achieved through a policy mix of school meals, a rise in the minimum wage and family grants. The subsequent regime's eschewing such programmes together with the impact of the pandemic – during which the daily death count rose to 4,000 at its peak – precipitated many Brazilians from being able to afford food.[22]

Mehrotra and Parida (2021) provided some explanations for the exacerbation of poverty in India from the time of demonetization which he has termed a 'monumental blunder … followed by a poorly planned and hurriedly introduced Goods and Services Tax (GST). Both delivered body blows to the unorganized sector and micro, small and medium enterprises (MSME) sector' in the manner in which they were implemented. The decline in economic growth carried with it household savings, private investment and public expenditure limited by a fiscal crisis. Exports fell below the 2013–14 level ($315 billion) for five years, a decline in absolute dollar terms for the first time since the 1991 economic liberalization. Joblessness increased to a 45-year high by 2017–18, youth (15–29 years of age) unemployment tripled from 6 to 18 per cent between 2012 and 2018, and joblessness reached a

[22] In Latin America as a whole, gross domestic product (GDP) fell by 7 per cent during the pandemic against 3 per cent for the world. India was worse, at a GDP decline of 8 per cent.

45-year high. It is not surprising that poverty and inequality were expected to rise in the aftermath of the COVID-19 crisis with the contraction of the economy, more so than comparable cohorts in a cross-country comparison.

References

Aggarwal, Nidhi and Sudha Narayanan. (2017) 'Impact of India's demonetization on domestic agricultural markets', WP-2017–023, Indira Gandhi Institute of Development Research (IGIDR), November. Available at www.igidr.ac.in/pdf/publication/WP-2017-023.pdf, accessed 4 May 2021.

Anbumozhi, Venkatachalam. (2022) 'How the Ukraine Conflict Is Impacting India's Economy', Conversations and insights from the edge of global business, Research Strategy and Innovations at Economic Research Institute for ASEAN and East Asia, Jakarta, 11 May, accessed 24 September 2022.

Chakraborty, Shiney. (2020) 'Impact of COVID-19 National Lockdown on Women Informal Workers in Delhi,' Institute of Social Studies Trust (ISST), New Delhi, May. Available at http://pub_compressed_ISST_-_Final_Impact_of_COVID_19_Lockdown_on_Women_Informal_Workers_Delhi.pdf, accessed 20 May 2022.

Chakraborty, Shiney. (2021) 'Women in the Indian Informal Economy,' *Brief*, Institute of Social Studies Trust (ISST), New Delhi, February.

Chand, Ramesh and Jaspal Singh. (2016) 'Agricultural growth after demonetization'. NITI Aayog. Available at https://niti.gov.in/writereaddata/files/document_publication/Demonetisation_Agriculture_Blog.pdf, accessed 11 May 2021.

Datt, Gaurav and Martin Ravallion. (2002) 'Is India's economic growth leaving the poor behind?', *Journal of Economic Perspectives*, 16(3): 89–108. Available at doi: 10.1257/089533002760278730, accessed 21 June 2021.

IMF. (2021) World Economic Outlook, April 2021: Managing Divergent Recoveries. Available at www.imf.org/en/Publications/WEO/Issues/2021/03/23/world-economic-outlook-april-2021, accessed 3 May 2021.

Goel, Manjusha. (2022) 'A study of impact of Russia-Ukraine war on the Indian economy', *International Journal of Scientific Engineering and Research*, 10(5) May: 12–15. Available at www.ijser.in, accessed 24 May 2022.

Kohli, Renu. (2018) 'Demonetisation's multiple failures', *Ideas for India*, 12 October. Available at www.ideasforindia.in/topics/macroeconomics/demonetisation-s-multiple-failures.html, accessed 7 May 2021.

Lahiri, Amartya. (2020a) 'The great Indian demonetization', *Journal of Economic Perspectives*, 34(1): 55–74. Available at doi: 10.1257/jep.34.1.55, accessed 5 May 2021.

Lahiri, Amartya. (2020b) 'Deposits after demonetisation rose by Rs 6 trillion and yet bank credit fell, study shows', *The Print*, 5 March. Available at https://theprint.in/opinion/deposits-after-demonetisation-rose-by-rs-6-trillion-and-yet-bank-credit-fell-study-shows/375880/, accessed 7 May 2021.

Mehrotra, Santosh and Jajati Keshari Parida. (2021) Poverty in India is on the rise again, *The Hindu*, 4 August. Available at https://www.thehindu.com/opinion/lead/poverty-in-india-is-on-the-rise-again/article35709263.ece, accessed 4 August 2021.

Neri, Marcelo. (2015) 'Brazil's new middle classes: the bright side of the poor', in Dayton-Johnson J. (eds) *Latin America's Emerging Middle Classes*. International Political Economy Series. London: Palgrave Macmillan. Available at https://doi.org/10.1057/9781137320797_4, accessed 1 May 2021.

Piketty, Thomas. (2021) 'Capital and ideology: a global perspective on inequality regimes', *The British Journal of Sociology*, 72(1): 139–150. Available at https://doi.org/10.1111/1468-4446.12836, accessed 30 April 2021.

Sharma, Kanuj. (2021) 'Telecom subscribers and operator wise market share of telecom companies in India (2020–21)', *CANDYTECH*, 22 January. Available at https://candytech.in/mobile-subs-and-operator-wise-market-share-of-telecom-companies-in-india/, accessed 23 March 2021.

Shome, Parthasarathi. (2012) 'Rebalancing and structural policies – an Indian perspective', *Oxford Review of Economic Policy*, 28 (3): 587–602.

Shome, Parthasarathi. (2021) *Taxation History, Theory, Law and Administration. Springer Texts in Business and Economics*. Cham: Springer. Available at https://doi.org/10.1007/978-3-030-68214-9, accessed 5 May 2021.

Srinivasan, T. N. (2001) 'Growth and Poverty Alleviation: Lessons from Development Experience', DBI Research Paper Series, No. 17, Asian Development Bank Institute (ADBI), Tokyo. Available at http://hdl.handle.net/11540/4122, accessed 21 June 2021.

The Economist. (2021) 'Lights, power, inaction', 1 May, p 66. Available at https://www.economist.com/finance-and-economics/2021/05/01/tracking-the-economic-impact-of-indias-second-COVID-wave, accessed 20 May 2021.

Times of India. (2021) 'Government has no plan to close down BSNL, MTNL', 3 February. Available at https://timesofindia.indiatimes.com/business/india-business/government-has-no-plan-to-close-down-bsnl-mtnl-dhotre/articleshow/80674702.cms, accessed 7 May 2021.

World Bank. (2020) *World Development Indicators*. Washington D.C.

3

Population, Poverty and Happiness

Introduction

The primary motivation of this chapter is to draw attention to the deleterious ramifications of uncontrolled population growth on poverty and the happiness of a society. There was a short period in the 1960s during which the link between rapid population growth and famine and pestilence was pointed out by citing Malthus's (1798) early work,[1] as well as of others. Recalling Bacaër (2011),

> In 1798 Malthus published *An Essay on the Principle of Population*, in which he argued that the supply of food could not follow for a long period of time the natural tendency of human populations to grow

[1] To quote Malthus from his 6th edition: 'Whatever was the original number of British emigrants which increased so fast in North America, let us ask, Why does not an equal number produce an equal increase in the same time in Great Britain? The obvious reason to be assigned is the want of food; and that this want is the most efficient cause of the three immediate checks to population, which have been observed to prevail in all societies, is evident from the rapidity with which even old states recover from the desolations of war, pestilence, famine, and the convulsions of nature. They are then for a short time placed a little in the situation of new colonies; and the effect is always answerable to what might be expected. If the industry of the inhabitants be not destroyed, subsistence will soon increase beyond the wants of the reduced numbers; and the invariable consequence will be that population, which before perhaps was nearly stationary, will begin immediately to increase, and will continue its progress till the former population is recovered.

The traces of the most destructive famines in China, Indostan, Egypt, and other countries, are by all accounts very soon obliterated; and the most tremendous convulsions of nature, such as volcanic eruptions and earthquakes, if they do not happen so frequently as to drive away the inhabitants or destroy their spirit of industry, have been found to produce but a trifling effect on the average population of any state' (pp 519–20).

Malthus also provided examples from warring Flanders, the 1666 London plague, Lithuania, Prussia, Egypt and Turkey to buttress his argument.

> exponentially. If the population remained relatively constant, this was because a great part of mankind was suffering from food shortage. Malthus saw the 'principle of population' as an argument against the writings of Godwin and Condorcet, which emphasized progress in human societies. Malthus' essay influenced the theory of evolution of Darwin and Wallace and was criticized by Marx, but was put into practice with the Chinese one-child policy. (p 1)

Advancement of society and an economy was linked to the ability of a country to control population growth. Multilateral institutions strongly encouraged population control for developing countries. Following this policy route, China opted in favour of a one-child policy with severe consequences for those who failed to adhere to it. India too had a population policy encouraging a two to three children family but abandoned it later.

With global advancements in crop production, disease control, education levels, and rapid improvements in per-capita gross domestic product (GDP) often accompanied by enhancements in the economic standard of living, the earlier emphasis on the need for population control receded. Two factors seemed to play a part. First, economic advancements seemed to have imparted a sense of confidence to advanced and developing economies alike that a high rate of population growth could not only be managed but used for further advancements of individual economies. This was termed the 'demographic dividend'. Second, there was a reappearance of a major influence of the declared Western religions to re-emphasize the abrogation of the use of population control methods across the globe and that influence appears to have come to stay. During the present millennium, admitting the negative effects of rapidly growing populations, India has resumed the discouragement of population growth though China, having overtly pursued strict population control earlier, recently loosened its grip on draconian population control measures and, instead, encouraging larger families. This chapter presents the reality in the form of deleterious impacts of uncontrolled population growth on economies and societies including the underlying unhappiness of highly populated societies such as India.

Population, GDP and poverty

We begin by comparing selected population and education statistics of Brazil, China and India. Their population growth rates in 2019 were 0.8, 0.4 and 1.0 respectively. While India has made progress in containing its population growth rate, it is clear that it needs to achieve lower rates (Table 3.1), in particular since, even in 2019, the mortality for under-fives remained 34 for 1,000 births in India in contrast to 14 in Brazil and eight in China. Education statistics also reveal differences. School enrolments in India lagged behind

Table 3.1: Cross-country: socio-economic indicators

Indicator	Brazil				China				India				
	2010	**2016**	**2018**	**2019**	**2010**	**2016**	**2018**	**2019**	**1990**	**2010**	**2016**	**2018**	**2019**
Population growth (annual %)	0.9	0.8	0.8	0.8	0.5	0.5	0.5	0.4	2.1	1.4	1.1	1.0	1.0
Urban population growth (annual %)	1.3	1.1	1.1	1.0	3.3	2.7	2.5	2.3	3.0	2.5	2.3	2.3	2.3
Mortality rate, under-5 (per 1,000 live births)	19	16	14	14	16	10	9	8	126	58	41	36	34
School enrolment, primary (% gross)[1]	103.5*	..	..	..	99.0	98.3	100	101.9	91.4	109.1	114.5	..	96.8
Primary completion rate, total (% of relevant age group)[2]	..	..	..	..	98.29#	..	..	..	..	95.75#	96.23	94.37#	91.66
School enrolment, secondary (% gross)	95.3*	..	..	..	88.2	..	..	..	..	63.1	75.1	74.4	73.8

*Last reported numbers are available for year 2011.

Values reported in Table 3.1 are from the preceding years of 2009 and 2017 for India and from year 2009 for China.

Note: [1] 'Gross enrolment ratios indicate the capacity of each level of the education system, but a high ratio may reflect a substantial number of overage children enrolled in each grade because of repetition or late entry rather than a successful education system. The net enrollment rate excludes overage and underage students and more accurately captures the system's coverage and internal efficiency. Differences between the gross enrollment ratio and the net enrollment rate show the incidence of overage and underage enrolments' (WDI, World Bank). [2] Primary completion rate, or gross intake ratio to the last grade of primary education, is the number of new entrants (enrolments minus repeaters) in the last grade of primary education, regardless of age, divided by the population at the entrance age for the last grade of primary education.

Source: World Development Indicators, 2020, World Bank (last updated on 16 December 2020)

those of Brazil and China. Comparing China and India, Table 3.1 shows that, for primary education, China had 99 per cent enrolment in 2010 and 100 per cent in 2019.[2] India's numbers were 100 per cent and 97 per cent respectively. Why it fell in 2019 is not known. Nevertheless, both China and India achieved high primary school enrolment. Regarding secondary education, enrolment in China was 88 per cent in 2010 but the 2019 figure is not reported. India's numbers were 63 per cent and 74 per cent respectively. It reveals that, even in 2019, India remained below China's 2010 level of secondary school entrance.[3] Brazil's numbers were 100 per cent for primary school enrolment and 95 per cent for secondary school enrolment in 2010 itself. Its 2019 numbers are not reported. Thus, India has to speed up its achievement in secondary school enrolment compared to Brazil and China.

In emerging economies, urban population growth is often a result of poor absorptive capacity of the rural sector, in particular agriculture, and therefore of involuntary rural-to-urban migration. Urban population growth is a reflection of it. In all three countries the rate has declined which is a good sign. However, the urban population growth rate continues to remain high both in China and India, despite bringing it down in recent years. It is difficult to agree with the view that economic growth should necessarily lead to the growth in urban population together with the growth in services while agriculture contracts. In India this argument is falsifiable since the nature of many of the services that have grown in urban areas are absorptive and not innovative, that have absorbed excess rural labour at low wage rates, the quality of life not having improved in this transition. Chapter 8 addresses this point further.

In analyses presented by Ravallion (2009); Sarkar and Mehta (2010) and others, some explanations for the differences in the performance of Brazil,

---

[2] Gross enrolment ratio for primary school is calculated by dividing the number of students enrolled in primary education regardless of age by the population of the age group which officially corresponds to primary education and multiplying by 100. Primary education provides children with basic reading, writing, and mathematics skills along with an elementary understanding of such subjects as history, geography, natural science, social science, art and music (WDI, World Bank, 2020).

[3] It may not widely known that, in the 1970s–early 80s, India routinely shared knowledge with China in education and training. Even in the mid-1990s, China regularly sent members of its populace to India's research institutions to learn and emulate what India had achieved. It is not known what China has shared in return even as its economic indicators have tripled India's. While Japan has come forward with several aid projects to India, China has created barriers, a stance that is unlikely to change direction in the foreseeable future. Globally, China cannot be perceived or assessed in a vacuum; rather, going forward, that has to be in a perspective of its revealed geopolitical and politico-historical stance, role and in the context of expanding interest in its own geographical neighbourhood, with far-reaching regional and global ramifications.

China and India in their efforts at poverty reduction related to population and its impact on per-capita indicators, emerge. Ravallion's view is that, though all three countries experienced declines in poverty during periods of economic reform – and he refers to macro-economic stability in this context – the extent of their poverty reduction has differed, and the reasons for that are different. He finds that China's market led growth led to rapid poverty reduction. Also, China's inequality was less than in Brazil and India to begin with (though, with rapid growth, inequality increased later). By contrast, by continuing to focus on the access to various types of opportunities in the hands of the better off, Brazil and India limited their success in poverty reduction. Sarkar and Mehta arrived at a comparable conclusion regarding India's pre- and post-reform inequality situation in that income inequality widened when economic growth took off post-reform (1993–94 to 2004–05). They pointed to two indicators of rising inequality in urban areas: (i) as per capita consumption growth doubled in the post-reform decade, poverty declined by less than a quarter of the pre-reform decade; and (ii) post-reform, the growth in post-reform wage rate of regular workers was negative up to the 50th percentile of wage earnings; beyond that point, it turned positive; and it rose sharply, reaching 5% per annum in the highest quintile of wage earnings.

Ravallion's (2009) conclusion, in particular for India, was that it needed to do more to ensure that its poor were able to access and participate in the country's growth process and its social policies. He did not provide an explanation where he would fit India's efforts at reserving public sector education, jobs and legislative seats for lower castes and backward groups that should have implied, to a certain extent, a spreading of access to opportunities. Thus, an explanation for India's relative lack of success had to emanate from other sources as well such as population pressure.

The relationship between population, GDP and poverty may be perceived to be linked in two directions. The first is generally accepted by social scientists in that, if the poverty rate declines *pari passu* with the rise in per capita GDP, the population growth will decline. The reverse is not that obvious: as population growth is controlled, per capita GDP growth should improve; and the poverty rate should diminish. However, the associations of the three variables indeed appear to be in both directions. This issue is crucial for India at this stage since two facts have emerged over the last four decades, that 'multi-dimensional poverty' has emerged to be a tough nut to crack just as the population number skyrockets despite its diminishing growth rate. By contrast, China's poverty has almost disappeared even as it used a tight population policy, an aspect that has been loosened only recently.

The World Bank's World Development Indicators (WDI) for 1950–2100 projected that India would overtake China's population in the 2020s, thus

Figure 3.1: Total population, 1950–2100

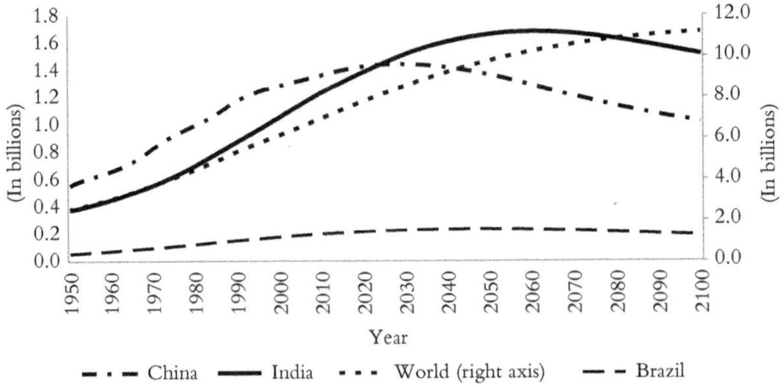

Note: Figures show estimates for period 1950–2015 and the 2015–2100 projections are based on the probabilistic projections of medium variant fertility.

Source: World Population Prospects: the 2017 Revision, United Nations Population Division

becoming the most populated country in the world. It is at that cusp at this moment and will remain so, cresting at 1.6 billion in subsequent decades. Figure 3.1 shows the total population from 1950 projected to 2100 (using polynomials to obtain the best fit). It can be seen that, in the 2020s, India would overtake China's population (at a time when the latter's population would crest) and remain so to the end of the century.

Figure 3.2 shows what was behind this phenomenon. In the 1960s, from a higher rate of population growth than India's, China began to reduce it stringently. From the beginning of the 1970s, China's population growth rate fell below India's and remained so thereafter. Thus, even though India was on a steadily declining trend throughout, China's population growth rate crashed to below that of India and that difference increased. Only in the last few years, China's population growth rate has picked up again as a deliberate policy, nevertheless remaining below India's. Behind this is the fact that, from a higher rate of population growth in the 1960s, China lowered it as a strict policy and took it below India's from the beginning of the 1970s. Thus, even though India has been on a slowly declining trend throughout, China's reduction was much steeper. Recently, in a reversal of policy, China's rate has picked up, nevertheless remaining considerably below India's.

Population growth is explained by the fertility rate or the average number of live births per woman. Fertility differences explain the different population trends. Currently, India's rate of decrease in the fertility rate parallels that of Brazil but India's base fertility levels have been much higher, implying higher population growth in India (Figures 3.2 and 3.3). And China kept

Figure 3.2: Population growth rate

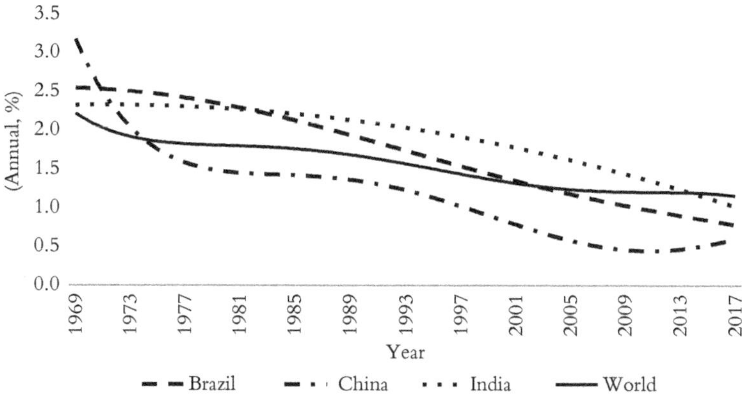

Note: The lines are polynomial.

Source: World Development Indicators (WDI), World Bank

down its fertility rate at much lower levels than both Brazil and India. These differences took China to newer heights over India in the subsequent decades in all economic and socio-economic indicators.[4]

Figure 3.3 reveals that China kept down its fertility rate which remained much lower than both Brazil and India. Interestingly, moving forward, all three countries will have lower fertility rates compared to the world average (which will be higher to no small extent due to the higher fertility rate of Nigeria). Nevertheless, India's base population being high, its population will crest at some 1.6 billion in the 2060s as indicated earlier. Herein lies India's fundamental challenge for, certainly, this could not represent a demographic dividend without significant accompanying improvements in reducing inequality and control of poverty through a successful provision of adequate nutrition, health and education, aspects that will be addressed in Chapters 8 and 9.

As GDP growth rates increased in both China and India, China's lower population growth rate assisted it to pull its per capita GDP growth rate up, thus rapidly raising its population to a higher plane of individual incomes altogether, together with eradicating absolute poverty and making it increasingly productive. By contrast, India's abandonment of any population

---

[4] While this argument is sometimes circumvented by observing that a high population has a 'demographic dividend' since it represents a young working population with higher productivity than that of an older population, it has little overall merit in a population of low nutrition, health and education.

Figure 3.3: Total fertility, 1950–2100

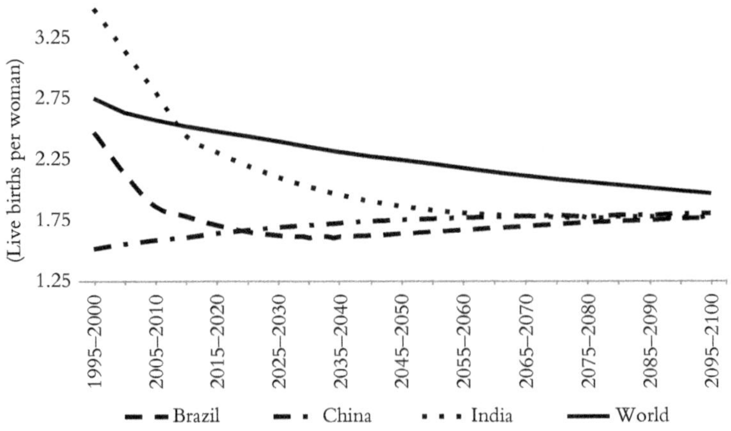

Note: Figures show total fertility estimates for period 1995–2015 and probabilistic projections of total fertility (medium variant) for the period 2015–2100.

Source: World Population Prospects: The 2017 Revision, United Nations Population Division

policy led to a ballooning of population 'left behind' and much lower catching-up in per capita GDP growth.[5]

As an illustration of the association of population growth with income growth, Figure 3.4 depicts the cross-country growth rates of per-capita GDP for 1968–69 to 2016–17. China's per capita GDP growth remained significantly above that of India though, in the last couple of years, India crossed China ephemerally. This reflects China's recent relaxation of its population policy after half-a-century of control while India abandoned it much earlier to a bellicose absence of policy. In sum, it emerges that population growth and per-capita GDP growth are closely associated. As India's GDP growth steadily increased, the rate crossed over the slowly declining population growth rate from the beginning of the 2000s (not graphed)[6].

[5] After losing parliamentary elections in 1977 due to poorly implemented population control that included forcible vasectomies and other extreme means, the ruling Congress Party essentially abandoned population policy. All political parties, instead, converted population into vote banks. The outcome can be perceived through cross-country figures. What may be deciphered is the direction of the association between population growth and GDP per capita, and its link to the poverty rate.

[6] Note, however, that both India and China's per capita GDP growth rates have been higher than the global trend while Brazil's has oscillated considerably around the global trend reflecting its historical economic instability.

Figure 3.4: GDP per-capita growth rate (in constant 2010, US$)

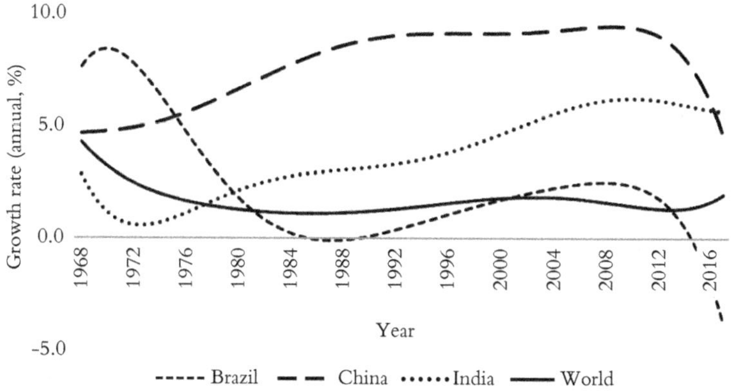

Note: The lines are polynomial.

Source: World Development Indicators (WDI), World Bank

Revival of policy to reduce poverty

Figure 3.5 shows GDP growth rate over population growth rate and examines its behaviour. In a fashion, this variable reflects the upward pull (or downward push) of GDP growth as population is controlled (or remains unattended). The visual impact is immediate: while India has had a slightly upward – little better than horizontal – trend in the five decades covering 1969–2017, China's upward pull had been phenomenal until about 2010. After 2010, China's trend declined, due to loosened population policy. Clearly, a deliberate and meaningful population policy would assist India to thrust upward its per capita GDP growth.

Another population-reflecting indicator is depicted in Figure 3.6, that of the Extreme Poverty Headcount Ratio (EPHR) – per cent of population living below $1.90 per day, for 1980–2015.[7]

In 1981, 88 per cent of Chinese were living below this mark, as opposed to 57 per cent Indians, the global average being 42 per cent. Brazil, at 21 per cent, was way better than the average. The drastic improvement of China – crossing India by 2000 – is phenomenal. By 2015, the EPHR indicators had changed to 13.4 per cent for India, 3.4 per cent for Brazil and 0.7 per cent for China, the world average being 10 per cent. Thus, India remained worse than the global average while China's EPHR almost disappeared.

[7] EPHR is income based. It yields numbers lower than Multi-dimensional Poverty or Severe Multi-dimensional Poverty indices. The difference reflects their inclusion of more dimensions, than income alone, of poverty.

Figure 3.5: GDP growth rate/population growth rate

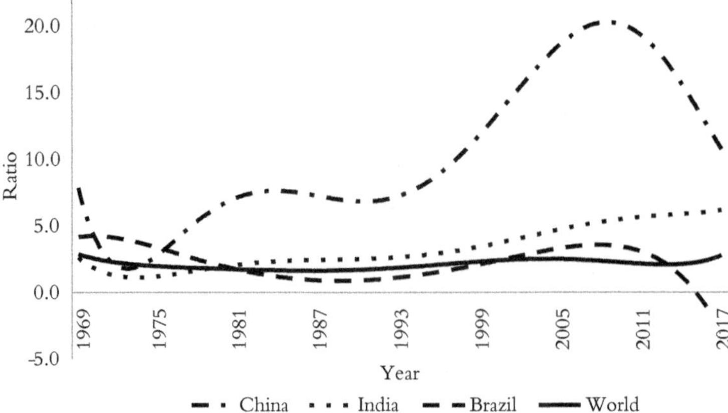

Note: The lines are polynomial.

Source: World Development Indicators (WDI), World Bank

Figure 3.6: Extreme Poverty Headcount Ratio (EPHR)

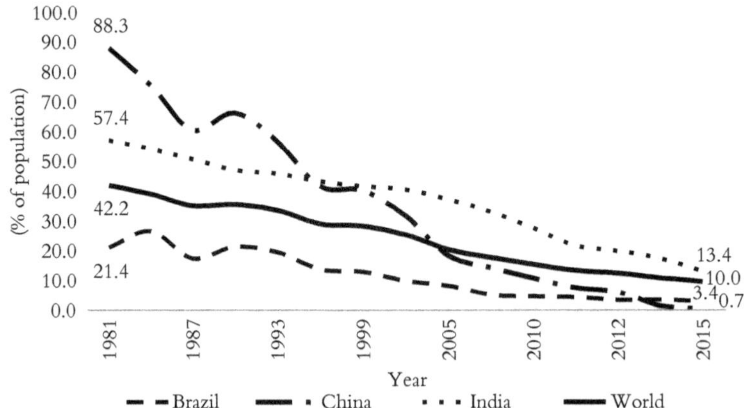

Note: EPHR is the per cent of population living below $1.90 a day (2011 PPP), where PPP is purchasing power parity.

Source: http://iresearch.worldbank.org/PovcalNet/

The reversal of trends was driven by China's economic effort as much as its harnessing population growth.

Figure 3.7 amplifies cross-country headcount magnitudes under EPHR during 1981–2015. Globally, there were 1.9 billion extremely poor (EPHR) in 1981 which reduced to 736 million in 2015, or a reduction of 61 per cent in 35 years. China reduced it from 878 million to 10 million – a

Figure 3.7: Extreme Poverty Headcount (EPH)

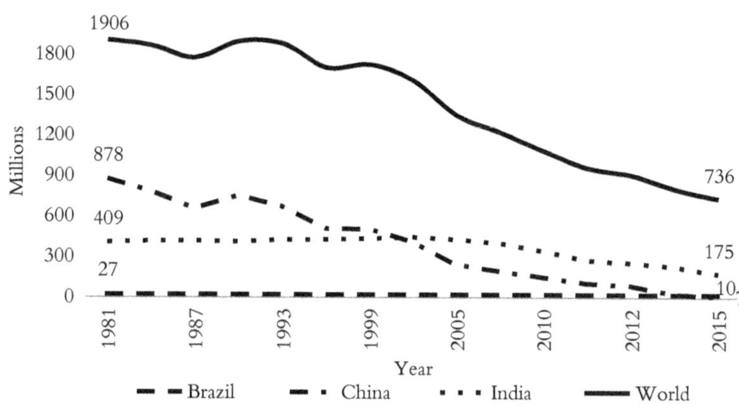

Source: http://iresearch.worldbank.org/PovcalNet/

reduction of 99 per cent, and India from 409 million to 175 million – a reduction of 57 per cent, or below average reduction. Brazil reduced it from 36 million to 7 million – a reduction of 74 per cent, or above average. It is indicative that, among the three, only India's effort was below even the world average.[8]

What explains India's lack of success in reaching global comparability in diminishing extreme poverty? The answer lies at least partly in its inability to address population growth meaningfully.

Ghatak (2021) reported,

> India's share of the world's extreme poor is higher than its share of the world population. India accounted for 139 million of the total 689 million people (20.17%) living in extreme poverty in 2017 (World Bank 2020), with its population being 17.8% of the world population. (World Bank 2019)
>
> The fact that there are many Indians who are rich and many who are poor, however, does not necessarily mean that there is greater inequality in India compared to other countries ... hence, we need to dig deeper to see what the story with inequality in India is. (pp 1–2)

[8] One question to ponder at the end of this discussion of the poor (per capita consumption of US $2.16 per day) and the extremely poor (US $1.08 per day) is how then do they actually live? Banerjee and Duflo (2007) examined the economic lives of the extremely poor – their choices, their constraints, their challenges – in 13 countries of Africa, Asia and Latin America, including India.

To bring light to reality, while improvement in economic conditions at the individual level would lead to lower birth rates, in reverse, lower birth rates should also contribute to economic prosperity and poverty reduction. There is cross-country research evidence of this two-directional relationship. For example, East Asia and South-East Asia – including Thailand, Indonesia and the countries of Indochina – experienced impressive declines in their fertility rates during the last 25 years. Sinding (2009) confirmed that their 'decline in poverty and improvement in living standards are attributable at least in part to (their) very successful fertility reduction policies'. Evidence offered by other researchers is appearing from Africa as well.

In sum, while improvement in economic conditions at the individual level leads to lower birth rates, in reverse, lower birth rates should also contribute to economic prosperity and poverty reduction. Looking at it from an economic viewpoint, India's ultimate escape from poverty could occur only through significantly deeper reductions in the fertility rate than currently achieved buttressed by growth oriented economic policies. However, India possesses perhaps an even more egregious obstacle through its practices of societal exclusions of various sorts, in particular its caste system (see Chapter 6), that have to be eradicated more successfully than at present, together with more dynamic economic policies and not merely consumption subsidies that, in combination, could be expected to have a perceptible positive impact on its well-being and happiness.

The 15th Finance Commission, a quinquennial constitutional body that suggests to parliament, revenue sharing arrangements from the central government to individual state governments, would have included population growth rate as a negative criterion for centre-state revenue sharing. In this light, for the 2024 parliamentary elections, party manifestos should include explicit population policies to reduce the fertility rate including through a mix of incentives and disincentives. Or India would possibly have to wring its hands at more babies being born into slavery, the evidence for which is cited in Chapter 11, footnote 2.

The 'happiness' of a population

The earliest recognition of happiness appears in the *Ramayana*, King Rama's instruction for reigning with justice to Bharata, his brother, before Rama withdrew to the forest and, subsequently, in the *Bhagawat Gita*, the omnipotent Krishna's song sung to Arjuna. The *Gita* makes a short appearance in the *Mahabharata*, India's mammoth epic, claimed to be the longest written account across the globe to this day. Later came discourses of Western philosophers such as Aristotle, Plato, Jeremey Bentham, John Stuart Mill and Immanuel Kant just to name a few. In more recent times, psychologists and sociologists have joined the fray, investigating the link between unhappiness and depression or identifying which societies, if any, had achieved happiness. Poets have taken up happiness as a favourite topic, including the Romantic poets of Britain, Indian poets whose poetry are replete with happiness, and those in Latin America whose quintessential emphasis on sadness (*rancheros*) juxtaposed a fulfillment of happiness.

Life, liberty and the pursuit of happiness comprised the Declaration of Independence of the US as far back as 1776. Since 1972, the miniscule Himalayan kingdom of Bhutan has drawn the attention of the world by pursuing Gross National Happiness (GNH) as its central objective of development over GDP. Other societies have attached increasing importance to happiness and wellbeing including a Canadian venture to construct an Index of Wellbeing and a French initiative to measure its wellbeing. Thus 'the greatest happiness of the greatest number', as Bentham (1907) proclaimed, continues to remain a well-cherished goal in any society.

Nevertheless, the question, 'what is happiness?' remains debatable, usually drawing an uncertain answer, 'I wonder'. Economists, confident that intricate psychological and sociological questions can be answered on the basis of quantitative measures and qualitative indices, entered the field of happiness research. Initial work by Easterlin (1974) was taken up by Sen (1995) who brought in the concept of inequality into that of unhappiness for India. Extensions of the analysis were made by Majumdar and Gupta (2015) who conceived of happiness as not only a subjective measure of the quality of life but also emphasized that it represented different things to different people. Nandy (2012) brought in quantitative aspects, representative of economists who began linking happiness to income, employment, health, religion, marriage, education and workplace satisfaction, though unemployment, poverty, literacy rate, life expectancy, inflation rate, crime rate and political stability also began to be included as variables that affected happiness. Indeed, the idea of happiness was perceived as a measurable, objectified variable signifying the quality of life and the sense of well-being of a mentally healthy person (Nandy, 2012).

Multilateral efforts through the World Happiness Index (WHI) are currently being made to measure a society's happiness by realistically simplifying its components, while nevertheless combining qualitative – emotional spot reactions to freedom, corruption and societal support – responses, as well as quantitative – income, longevity – indicators. Thus, based on the work of several investigators through the early 2000s, happiness has transcended the individual and has reached a societal level, focusing on underlying factors that could determine its happiness. The distribution of happiness in a population has also been of concern. Emerging data sets from surveys over several decades have included queries regarding the level of happiness in four categories on an ordinal scale – 'Very Happy' to 'Not Too Happy'. Typically, therefore, data on happiness come in an ordinal scale. While 'Very

Happy' may be ranked higher than 'Not Too Happy', it is not known by how much, or by what distance, it is ranked higher. This may be somewhat problematic from an economist's point of view inasmuch as the 'spread of a distribution' may interest them, but it may not represent a crucial concern to other social scientists. Easterlin and O'Connor (2020) have revisited the issue of happiness and have been taking the literature forward most recently.

Peiró (2006) examined the relationships between socio-economic conditions and happiness in 15 countries. He found age, health and marital status to be closely associated with happiness as did some of his predecessors. In the more recent linkage, Zagórski et al. (2010) found economic growth and happiness were closely related. They estimated the effect of education and income on happiness using large national samples from 32 nations at various stages of economic development. They found that the higher was the average education in a society, the smaller was the (marginal) gain in happiness to be reaped from advanced education (that is, from additional units of education) on an individual's happiness. Similarly, the richer was a society, the less was the gain in happiness from additional household income. However, the authors found that a nation's level of economic development appeared to have a strong positive effect on well-being.

More recently, Lakshmanasamy and Maya (2020) addressed the link between happiness and income in the context of India using World Value Survey data for 12 Indian states from 1990 to 2014. They adapted the Easterlin Paradox[9] to their work, delinking any increase in the happiness level from growth in income. They found a flat happiness response to income change. Indeed, growth in income increased income inequality, as well as the inequality in well-being. They specified a functional relationship between material aspirations and life satisfaction and showed that it could have an impact on raising inequality in life satisfaction. They concluded that reducing income inequality and improving trust, sociability, health, education and employment could reduce inequality in life satisfaction and improve happiness levels in India.

---

[9] The Easterlin Paradox states that at a point in time happiness varies directly with income, both among and within nations, but over time the long-term growth rates of happiness and income are not significantly related. The principal reason for the contradiction is social comparison. At a point in time, those with higher income are happier because they are comparing their income to that of others who are less fortunate, and conversely for those with lower income. Over time, however, as incomes rise throughout the population, the incomes of one's comparison group rise along with one's own income and vitiates the otherwise positive effect of own-income growth on happiness. Critics of the Paradox mistakenly present the positive relation of happiness to income in cross-section data or in short-term time fluctuations as contradicting the nil relation of long-term trends. See Easterlin and O'Connor (2020).

Interestingly, Brockmann et al. (2009) found that, during 1990–2000, happiness declined in China even as material living standards improved significantly. The authors explained this paradoxical finding by drawing on the concept of frustrated achievers who felt deprived as income inequality became skewed in favour of the upper income groups, so that the financial position of most Chinese worsened relative to the average. In turn, they speculated that this could be a phenomenon applicable to other transition economies under certain conditions.

Nevertheless, some social scientists in the fields of sociology and anthropology have taken the view that currently, though happiness is a 'multidimensional, trans-disciplinary, multifaceted discipline', it remains 'incomplete' (Moreno-Leguizamon and Spigner, 2011). And happiness has taken on 'public policy change and political action to minimize objective reality harmful to individual, family, community or social wellbeing' (McNaught and Knight, 2011). In this context, the criticism, 'economists whose philosophical ancestry is logical empiricism still write as if the old positivist fact/value dichotomy were beyond challenge' (Helliwell and Putnam, 2005), has been assuaged by the recent development of the concept of subjective wellbeing (SWB). SWB incorporates both an individual's feelings as well as the outcomes of interactions with others in a socio-economic, cultural and political environment. Data sources such as the World Values Survey, Physical Quality of Life Index, Happy Planet Index, Gallup World Poll, Gallup-Healthways Wellbeing Index, Human Development Index and others have produced numerous usable data sets.

Perhaps the existence of a fertile field prompted a 2009 UK Commission (Stiglitz-Sen-Fitoussi, 2009), set up to recommend which measures of SWB should be included for policymaking, to comment, 'it is possible to collect meaningful and reliable data on subjective and objective wellbeing. SWB encompasses cognitive evaluations of one's life, happiness, satisfaction, positive emotions such as joy and pride, and negative emotions such as pain and worry'. Nevertheless, specific or narrower senses of inequality – rate of growth of income inequality, employment, deteriorating ecology, climate change, ethnicity, condoning gender-related provocations, nature or intensity of disability, exclusions from and placement in the life cycle, religious location – marginal, minority, majority – and sexual orientation that affect SWB, have yet to be adequately incorporated in SWB or WHI estimates.

In a comprehensive review of different methodologies, Clark et al. (2018) included the WHI methodology. The 2019 World Happiness Report (WHR) elaborates. WHI is a good beginning to assess cross-country (un)happiness. Different sample sizes are used for different countries – over 150 countries every year. India's sample size has been 3,000 individuals and that of China 5,000 for the last several years. WHI is based on only six explanatory variables – GDP per capita, healthy life expectation, social support in times of trouble, freedom to choose, altruism or charitableness and sense of societal corruption. The first two are positivist indicators obtained from economic data while the last four are collected on the basis of binary (yes/no) responses. By incorporating the last four, the WHI traverses a distance from pure positivism towards inclusion of values.

Three dependent variables are as follows. (a) Sample individuals are asked to give an overall life evaluation on a 0–10 scale (Cantril Ladder, Variable V1). (b) A positive 'affect' variable is generated as the average frequency (for each sample individual) of happiness, laughter and enjoyment on the previous day (V2); and (c) a negative 'affect' variable is the average frequency of worry, sadness and anger on the previous day (V3). Both V2 and V3 are calculated from binary responses.[10]

Results appear in WHR's Table 2.1, p 20. Three quarters of the variation in life evaluation V1 were explained by the independent variables. Of the latter, per-capita income and healthy life expectancy had significant effects on V1. On the other hand, social support, freedom and generosity had larger influences on positive affect V2 than on V1. The negative affect V3 was much less explained by the six variables.

In an extension, a further question was explored by adding V2 and V3 to the explanatory variables list with V1 as the dependent variable. In other words, more possibilities to explain life evaluation were included in the analysis. This exercise revealed that positive affect V2 had a highly significant impact on V1 while negative affect V3 had no influence. Thus, positive affect experienced the previous day influenced life evaluation, but negative affect did not. Humans appeared to be an optimistic lot.

After measurement, how is SWB to be used? Paul Dolan et al. (2011) delineated the use of SWB for public policy. They pointed to the need for theoretical rigour, policy relevance and empirical robustness in the use of SWB in policy design and appraisal. They listed different categories of questions that should be asked for policy design and appraisal. For wellbeing projects in particular, Moreno-Leguizamon et al. (2011) pointed to possible alternatives of results-based and outcome mapping approaches. The former attempted the improvement of wellbeing, while the latter targeted fundamental human change. A sequence of project development, and monitoring and evaluation (M&E), was specified in significant detail, signalling that wellbeing projects were here to stay.

In conclusion, happiness is absolute and relative. It comes from within; but it is also influenced or determined by others. As Cicero, Roman orator, advocate and senator, commented about Julius Caesar and Gnaeus Pompeius Magnus (Pompey), two of Rome's greatest generals, 'Do you think there is

---

[10] See WHR Technical Box 1 and statistical Appendix 1.

no understanding between them, that no agreement has ever been possible? Today there is a possibility. But neither of them has our happiness as their aim. They both want to be kings' (Cawthorne, 2005).

Unhappiness of Indians

Indians emerged as one of the unhappiest peoples on earth in the UN's 2021 World Happiness Report. And their unhappiness has been worsening in recent years. This comes on top of the distressing record on poverty and income inequality. Indians from the upper economic groups are believed to usually express confidence in strong social/family support and may find the survey results surprising. The report comprises 149 countries, and the range of findings is wide and deep. The case of India is discussed next.

A sample of individuals[11] is taken every year in each country and they are asked to score their happiness on a 1–10 scale. The variation in country scores is then attempted to be explained statistically with six variables comprising social support, freedom, absence of corruption, generosity, per-capita GDP and life expectancy. The first four variables are measured through binary (yes/no) responses to questions such as: do you have relatives you can count on whenever you need them? Are you satisfied with the freedom to choose what you do with your life? Is corruption widespread in government? And have you donated money last month? Per capita GDP is in Purchasing Power Parity (PPP) $ terms. Life expectancy weights itself with disability to reflect a 'healthy' life picture. The six variables may not explain the reported happiness score fully – for other aspects of life also affect happiness – but they perhaps are somewhat representative. At least the investigators believe so.

Table 3.2 ranks selected countries pertinent to India for happiness and its underlying factors. Note that the 2021 reported information reflects 2018–20 average data (a procedure common to every annual report). Examining India, first, it ranks itself at 139 in happiness out of 149 countries or at the bottom 90th per centile. Thus, India is at the bottom 10 per cent of all countries in unhappiness. In terms of its components, it is even worse for social support, which appears to be the driving force behind India's extreme unhappiness. India is just at the 50 per cent rank for corruption, and at the bottom 58 per cent for generosity. It ranks better for freedom, being within the top 21 per cent. It is not surprising that it is at the bottom 25 per cent for per-capita GDP and longevity.

Second, India's unhappiness is considerably worse in the ranking than other countries of South Asia, China and South Africa, and far worse than

[11] Sample sizes are found in the Report's ch. 2, Appendix 1, Table 1.

Table 3.2: Selected countries: ranking happiness and components, 2021

Country[1]	Happiness rank	Social support	Freedom	Corruption	Generosity	Longevity	GDP per capita
Finland	1	5	5	137	55	27	19
Brazil	35	53	74	79	81	73	71
China	84	92	27	–	110	36	64
Nepal	87	105	83	91	38	93	117
South Africa	103	63	100	29	87	121	81
Bangladesh	112	126	39	102	102	88	112
Sri Lanka	129*	80	59	28	36	61	76
India	139	141	31	75	44	104	102

Note: The number of countries varies between 140 and 149 for components ranking in 2021 report. [1] 149 countries' ranking figures are based on the three-year average of life evaluation 2018–2020. *No survey information exists for 2020, averages are based on the 2018–19 surveys.

Source: World Happiness Report, 2021, United Nations

Latin America, similar to the results of the 2019 report. A revelation is which countries are closest to India's rankings. India is slightly happier than Zambia and Sierra Leone, and slightly unhappier than Burundi and Yemen (not shown).

Table 3.3 moves from ranking the countries on their self-declared scale as described previously, to ranking their statistically derived happiness scores. Again, India comes out at the bottom in South Asia in the 2021 report (average of 2018–20 data). Table 3.3 also shows change in the happiness score over 2015–21; again, India's score deteriorated the most in South Asia. An examination of Table 3.4 further reveals that there has been a steady deterioration in Indians' happiness scores in recent years (with a slight improvement in 2021).

Table 3.3: Selected countries: change in happiness

Country	Happiness score			Change in happiness score	
	2015	2019	2021[1]	(2015–19)[2]	(2015–21)[3]
Finland	7.41	7.77	7.84	0.36	0.43
Brazil	6.98	6.30	6.33	-0.68	-0.65
China	5.14	5.19	5.34	0.05	0.20
Bhutan	5.25	5.08	–	-0.17	–
Nepal	4.51	4.91	5.27	0.40	0.76
South Africa	4.64	4.72	4.96	0.08	0.32
Bangladesh	4.69	4.46	5.02	-0.23	0.33
Sri Lanka	4.27	4.37	4.32	0.10	0.05
India	**4.57**	**4.02**	**3.82**	**-0.55**	**-0.75**

Note: [1] 2021 Report presents happiness score as averaged over 2018–20. [2] Each entry shows the difference in average scores reported in 2015 and 2019 reports (that is between 2012–14 and 2016–18 average data). [3] Each entry shows the difference in average scores reported in 2015 and 2021 reports (that is between 2012–14 and 2018–20 average data).

Source: World Happiness Report, 2021, United Nations

Table 3.4: India: happiness ranking and scores, 2013–21

Year of report	2013	2015	2016	2017	2018	2019	2020	2021
Happiness rank	111	117	118	122	133	140	144	139
Happiness score[1]	4.77	4.57	4.51	4.32	4.19	4.02	3.57	3.82

Note: No report was issued in 2014. [1] In the 2021 report, happiest was Finland at 7.84 and least happy was Afghanistan at 2.52.

The determinants of happiness in the exercise reveal why Indians are so unhappy in a global comparison. Table 3.2 indicates India's ranking at the bottom layer on the criterion of social support, much worse than how it fares on the other criteria. It does not require much speculation that if health, nutrition and quality education were available to the majority of the population, there would be less need for social support, less poverty and a higher score. Indeed, the early 2021 months of the COVID-19 pandemic bared to the world Indians' predicament and vicissitudes on these counts, in effect, the condition of even the middle classes being ground down to the bottom.

References

Bacaër, Nicolas. (2011) 'Malthus and the obstacles to geometric growth (1798)', in *A Short History of Mathematical Population Dynamics*. Reprinted by London: Springer. Available at https://doi.org/10.1007/978-0-85729-115-8_5, accessed 30 December 2022.

Banerjee, Abhijit V. and Esther Duflo. (2007) 'The economic lives of the poor', *Journal of Economic Perspectives*, 21(1): 141–168. Available at doi: 10.1257/jep.21.1.141, accessed 22 June 2021.

Bentham, Jeremy. (1907) *An Introduction to the Principles of Morals and Legislation*. London: Oxford Clarendon Press. (Reprint of 1823 edition. First printed 1780.)

Brockmann, Hilke, Jan Delhey, Christian Welzel and Hao Yuan. (2009) 'The China puzzle: falling happiness in a rising economy', *Journal of Happiness Studies*, 10: 387–405. Available at https://doi.org/10.1007/s10902-008-9095-4, accessed 30 December 2022.

Cawthorne, Nigel. (2000) *History's Greatest Battles: Masterstrokes of War*. United Kingdom: Arcturus Publishing.

Clark, Andrew E., Sarah Flèche, Richard Layard, Nattavudh Powdthavee and George Ward. (2018) *The Origins of Happiness: The Science of Well-being Over the Life Course*. Princeton: Princeton University Press.

Dolan, Paul, Richard Layard and Robert Metcalfe. (2011) 'Measuring Subjective Well-Being for Public Policy: Recommendation on Measures', Special Paper No. 23, Centre for Economic Performance, London School of Economic and Political Science. Available at https://cep.lse.ac.uk/pubs/download/special/cepsp23.pdf, accessed 30 December 2022.

Easterlin, Richard. (1974) 'Does economic growth improve the human lot? Some empirical evidence', in Paul A. David, Melvin W. Reder (eds) *Nations and Households in Economic Growth – Essays in Honor of Moses Abramovitz*. New York: Academic Press, Inc., pp 89–125.

Easterlin, Richard A. and Kelsey J. O'Connor. (2020) 'The Easterlin Paradox', IZA DP No. 13923, IZA Institute of Labor Economics. Available at http://ftp.iza.org/dp13923.pdf, accessed 21 May 2021.

Ghatak, Maitreesh. (2021) 'India's inequality problem', *The India Forum*, 2 July. Available at https://www.theindiaforum.in/article/does-india-have-inequality-problem, accessed 2 July 2021.

Helliwell, John F. and Robert D. Putnam. (2005) 'The social context of well-being', in F. A. Huppert, N. Baylis and B. Kevern (eds) *The Science of Well-Being*. Oxford: Oxford University Press, pp 435–60.

Lakshmanasamy, T. and K. Maya. (2020) 'The effect of income inequality on happiness inequality in India: a recentered influence function regression estimation and life satisfaction inequality decomposition', *Indian Journal of Human Development*, 14(2): 161–181. Available at https://doi.org/10.1177/0973703020948468, accessed 30 December 2022.

Majumdar, Chirodip and Gautam Gupta. (2015) 'Don't worry, be happy: a survey of the economics of happiness', *Economic and Political Weekly*, 50(40): 50–62. Available at doi:10.2307/24482627, accessed 1 May 2021.

Malthus, Thomas Robert. (1798[1826]) *An Essay on the Principle of Population*, 6th edn, Vol. I. London: John Murray.

McNaught, Allan and Anneyce Knight (eds) (2011) *Understanding Wellbeing: An Introduction for Students and Practitioners of Health and Social Care*. Banbury: Lantern Publishing / Scion Publishing.

Moreno-Leguizamon, Carlos and Clarence Spigner. (2011) 'Monitoring and evaluating wellbeing projects', in Knight, Anneyce and McNaught, Allan (eds) *Understanding Wellbeing: An Introduction for Students and Practitioners of Health and Social Care*. Banbury: Lantern Publishing / Scion Publishing, pp 50–66.

Nandy, Ashis. (2012) 'The idea of happiness', *Economic and Political Weekly*, 47(2): 45–48. Available at http://www.jstor.org/stable/23065608, accessed 31 March 2021.

Peiró, Amado. (2006) 'Happiness, satisfaction and socio-economic conditions: some international evidence', *The Journal of Socio-Economics*, 35(2): 348–65. Available at https://doi.org/10.1016/j.socec.2005.11.042, accessed 30 March 2021.

Ravallion, Martin. (2009) 'A comparative perspective on poverty reduction in Brazil, China, and India', *World Bank Research Observer*. Available at https://documents1.worldbank.org/curated/en/751951468181726134/pdf/770070JRN0wbro0Box0 377291B00PUBLIC0.pdf, accessed 21 June 2021.

Sarkar, Sandip and Balwant Singh Mehta. (2010) 'Income inequality in India: pre- and post-reform periods', *Economic and Political Weekly*, 45(37): 45–55. Available at www.jstor.org/stable/25742070, accessed 22 June 2021.

Sen, Amartya. (1995) *Inequality Reexamined*. Oxford: Oxford University Press.

Sinding, Steven. (2009) 'Population, poverty and economic development', *Philosophical Transactions of The Royal Society*, 364: 3023–30.

Stiglitz, Joseph E., Amartya Sen and Jean-Paul Fitoussi. (2009) 'Report by The Commission on The Measurement of Economic Performance and Social Progress', Paris. Available at www.economie.gouv.fr/files/finances/presse/dossiers_de_presse/090914mesure_perf_eco_progres_social/synthese_ang.pdf, accessed 30 December 2022.

United Nations. (2021) *World Happiness Report*, New York.

World Bank. (2020) *World Development Indictors*, Washington D.C.

Zagórski, Krzysztof, Jonathan Kelley and Mariah D. R. Evans. (2010) 'Economic development and happiness: evidence from 32 nations', *Polish Sociological Review*, 169: 3–19. Available at www.jstor.org/stable/41275132, accessed 30 March 2021.

4

National Income, Human Development and Inequality

Introduction

India's growing inequality since economic liberalization and even earlier has been of increasing concern to fair-minded social scientists. Chancel and Piketty (2017) authored an analysis drawing attention to the issue.[1] Drawing on this and subsequent and previous research carried out by various researchers, as well as the Human Development Report (HDR) published annually since 1990, this chapter examines the state and trajectory of inequality in India. It notes that, though India has made progress in the dimensions or components of the HDI, it has fallen behind comparable countries. It, therefore, needs to speed up if it were to achieve the United Nations' Sustainable Development Goal (SDG) of 'leaving no one behind' by 2030 to which it is signatory.

Inequality indicators in India

India has experienced some success in its story of income growth, but a question remains as to the extent to which its income inequality has been addressed. Available data focuses on the above-20 age group as the income-generating section of the population. That comprised 351 million in 1980–81, 778 million in 2013–14, 810 million in 2015–16 and 872 million in 2019–20 reflecting the last available population data. What may be concluded from analysis is that there has been consistently worsening inequality when the averages of annual growth rates of group incomes for 1980–2016 are examined.

---

[1] They issued their findings from the World Inequality Database (WID) of the World Inequality Lab (WIL), a globally recognized research institution. See also Piketty (2014), that took on the status of a global bestseller.

From the state of the 'bottom' 50 per cent of this group, and even the next 40 per cent, that is, all but the top 10 per cent, there is little doubt that controlling income inequality remains the most intractable prevailing challenge for Indian society. Indeed, based on sporadic reports reflecting indirect indicators, the situation has been worsening and consistent updated data are eagerly awaited by domestic and international analysts alike.

Table 4.1 dissects income inequality over time. Between 1980–81 and 2015–16 (36 years), the share of national income declined significantly for the bottom 50 per cent population – from 23 per cent to 15 per cent – and for the next 40 per cent population – from 45 per cent to 29 per cent. Contrarily, it increased significantly for the top 10 per cent – from 7 per cent to 21 per cent– – as well as its component groups. However, interestingly, the numbers reveal that the degree of inequality on account of the top 1 per cent dipped between 2013–14 and 2015–16. The last two columns of Table 4.1 confirm these results through positive or negative growth rates of the shares themselves. The first column shows at what rate the shares changed between 1980–16, revealing worse rates as the incomes of groups decrease. Yet, the final 2014–16 period reveals that the shares deteriorated for all groups other than 9 per cent (of the top 10 per cent) which experienced a positive rate of growth.

From the information in Table 4.1, it may be hypothesized as to who comprised India's middle class in 2015-16. Table 4.1, Column 1 shows that the average adult annual income of the bottom 50 per cent was Rs 0.045 million (Rs 45,000) and for the next 40 per cent it was Rs 0.113 million

Table 4.1: India: income distribution over time

Income group[1]	**Average income**[2, 3]	**% of national income**			**Growth in national income share**[4]	
	2015–16	**1980–81**	**2013–14**	**2015–16**	**1980–16**	**2014–16**
Bottom 50%	0.045	23.3	15.0	14.7	-37	-2
Middle 40%	0.113	45.2	29.8	29.2	-35	-2
Next 9%	0.597	24.2	33.6	34.8	44	3
Top 1%, of which	3.300	7.3	21.6	21.3	191	-1
Top 0.1%	12.674	2.0	8.5	8.2	311	-4
Top 0.01%	52.674	0.6	3.8	3.4	498	-10
Top 0.001%	2,10.628	0.2	1.8	1.4	612	-25

Note: [1] Distribution of per-adult pre-tax national income. [2] In Rs million. Average income for full population Rs 0.155 million. [3] Correction for inflation using national income deflator (base 2017). [4] [(Final Year-First Year)/First Year] *100.

Source: World Inequality Database

(Rs 113,000) approximately. It would be a fallacy to term them middle class by globally acceptable standards. For the next 9 per cent, it was about Rs 0.6 million (Rs 600,000), or Rs 0.05 million (Rs 50,000) per month. If we categorize them as middle class, it would leave 90 per cent of the above-20 age group of India as below middle class.

Table 4.2 examines average adult incomes by income groups in ratio of average national income. Note that the first row is unity (as it should be for the full population). We divide unity into component groups. Looking at 1980–81, the bottom 50 per cent earned half the national average, and the next 40 per cent 1.1 times the average. Thus, even in 1980–81, 90 per cent of the population barely reached or lay much below the average income of the population. By 2013–14 (and 2015–16), their shares had deteriorated to 30 per cent and 70 per cent, respectively, of the national average. The top 9 per cent moved from 2.7 times to 3.9 times the average, and the very top 1 per cent from 7.3 to 21.3 times. It is obvious how, over three- and-a-half decades, the average group incomes of the top 10 per cent rose significantly in terms of the national average, while those of the 'bottom' 90 per cent languished or declined.

Looking within the very top 1 per cent, for the top 0.1 per cent component within it, their average compared to the national average rose from 20 to 82 times, for the top 0.01 per cent from 57 to 341 times and, for the topmost 0.001 per cent, from 191 to 1,362 times. Thus, the scale of increase itself increased with higher income groups over the period. The last column of Table 4.2 takes the sum of each year's income growth rate and presents the

Table 4.2: India: average group income – ratio of average national income

Income group	**Ratio**				**Average of annual income growth rates per adult**[1]
	1980–81	**1991–92**	**2013–14**	**2015–16**	**(1980–16)**
Full population	1.0	1.0	1.0	1.0	3.4
Bottom 50%	0.5	0.4	0.3	0.3	2.0
Middle 40%	1.1	1.1	0.7	0.7	2.1
Next 9%	2.7	2.7	3.7	3.9	4.5
Top 1%, of which	7.3	10.2	21.6	21.3	7.2
Top 0.1%	20.0	27.5	85.4	82.0	8.5
Top 0.01%	56.9	88.9	378.1	340.7	10.7
Top 0.001%	191.3	293.2	1822.5	1362.2	14.3

Note: [1] (Sum of per year growth rates)/36.

Source: World Inequality Database

average. Again, it reveals more rapid growth rates – from a low of 2 per cent to a high of 14.3 per cent – as we move up the income scale. Clearly income inequality worsened between 1980–81 and 2015–16. Specifically, the growth rates rose from 2 per cent for the bottom 90 per cent of the population, to 4.5 per cent for the top 9 per cent and 7 per cent for the top 1 per cent. Of the top 1 per cent of the population, the top 0.1 per cent of the population experienced 8.5 per cent growth, the top 0.01 per cent experienced 10.7 per cent growth and the top 0.001 per cent experienced 14.3 per cent growth. This series reveals secularly rising inequality in the country, worsening as one moves down from the top to the bottom.[2,3]

Reflecting the focus on income disparity between the richest 1 per cent (or 0.01 per cent) and the bottom 50 per cent following the argument of Chancel and Piketty (2017) that the rapid growth of income at the top end of millionaires and billionaires is a by-product of economic growth, Kulkarni and Gaiha (2018) used the India Human Development Survey 2012 (a nationwide panel survey)[4] to examine the links between poverty and income inequality, especially the top 1 per cent versus the bottom 50 per cent. They found negative growth elasticities with respect to poverty. Greater was the disparity between the income share of the top 1 per cent and the share of the bottom 50 per cent, greater was poverty. Among various experiments they conducted, the highest negative impact that they found was one in which a 1 per cent greater income disparity was associated with a 1.24 per cent higher value in the poverty variable. Thus, they concluded that 'the consequences of even a small increase in income disparity between the richest 1 per cent and the bottom 50 per cent are alarming for the poorest' (p 22).

Comparing India with China and Russia

How does India compare with China? Table 4.3 addresses this question and also brings in the Russian Federation into the picture for a reason. As

2 India's income inequality estimates reflect Chancel and Piketty (2020) who extended and updated Banerjee and Piketty (2005). For the detailed methodology of estimates available on the WID between 1922 and 2015, researchers may refer to the Chancel and Piketty paper.

3 Nevertheless, it emerges from a comparison of the columns (Table 4.2) for 2013–14 and 2015–16 that, between these years, the average income growth of the top 1 per cent and their components in ratio of the national average declined, however slightly. This could be an accidental measurement blip since subsequent sporadic reports indicate that income concentration has been increasing in favour of the very top groups. The averages increased for the next 9 per cent while remaining the same for the bottom 90 per cent.

4 The nation-wide human development panel survey was released in two rounds in 2005 and 2012.

Table 4.3: India, China and Russia: real income growth per adult (%)

	1980–16[1]		
Income group	**India**	**China**	**Russia**
Full population	214	776	23
Bottom 50%	98	386	-33
Middle 40%	103	732	-4
Next 9%	352	1057	77
Top 1%, of which	815	1800	622
Top 0.1%	1191	2271	2343
Top 0.01%	1781	2921	7555
Top 0.001%	2139	3524	23187

Note: [1] [(Final Year-First Year)/First Year] *100

Source: World Inequality Database

it reveals, all groups in India have experienced real income growth, though the rate goes up rapidly as incomes increase. China has experienced more rapid growth, with much higher numbers as incomes go up. In Russia, unbelievably, the 'bottom' 90 per cent population have actually experienced a decline in their real incomes while the top 0.1 per cent has experienced even higher growth than in China. This is a case of an extreme exacerbation of income inequality.

What is significant is that the World Inequality Database (WID) of the World Inequality Lab (WIL) which provides a pretax income inequality series, has now reported g-percentile[5] shares, up to 2019. Indian data are not reported after 2015; therefore, from then on, they are depicted just as a horizontal line indicating nil change. In an addendum, the authors of WIL expressed critical concern regarding the absence of data reporting by India even where international participation had become common practice. They indicated that 'we assume that the distribution of pretax income is unchanged between 2015 and 2019 and that all income g-percentiles grow at the average per-adult national income growth rate'.[6]

Differences across regions and states in India also have had an impact on the overall scores. Work by Datt and Ravallion (2002), for example, revealed

[5] 'G-percentile files use 127 rows: 99 for the bottom 99 percentiles, 9 for the bottom 9 tenth-of-percentiles of the top percentile, 9 for the bottom 9 one-hundredth-of-percentiles of top tenth-of-percentile, and 10 for the 10 one-thousandth-of-percentile of the top one-hundredth-of-percentile.' See Alvaredo et al. (2016), p 15.

[6] Chancel (2020).

that the diversity in performance across Indian states provided 'important clues for understanding why economic growth has not done more for India's poor' (p 106). They found that the sectoral and regional imbalance of growth impeded poverty reduction considerably.[7] Deaton and Dreze (2002) also arrived at comparable conclusions from examining data for 1987–88, 1993–94 and 1999–2000 in that, while poverty did decline in the 1990s, it proceeded in line with earlier trends. They showed that regional disparities increased post-1991 reform, with the southern and western regions performing better than the northern and eastern regions. Economic inequality increased within states, between rural and urban areas, and within urban areas. Health and education indicators improved in the 1990s, but with diverse performance. Therefore, on the whole, they found no support for sweeping claims that the nineties had been a period of 'unprecedented improvement' (p 3729), with Deaton and Kozel (2005) commenting that, though poverty declined, 'the official estimates of poverty reduction (were) too optimistic, particularly for rural India' (p 177).

Chauhan, Mohanty, Subramanian et al. (2015) examined the variations in 81 regions of India between 1993 and 2012. They found that the poverty headcount ratio declined in 70 regions, increased in seven, and remained similar in four. The southern regions of Odisha and Chhattisgarh suffered most from persistent poverty. The spread in poverty headcount ratio among regions increased from 0.38 in 1993–1994 to 0.64 in 2011–2012. Thus, regional disparity increased significantly, and income inequality worsened. The Gini index measuring inequality decreased in 20 regions and increased in 61 regions.

Coming to country differences, Ghosh (2010), by comparing China and India, provided explanations as to the differences in their performance in poverty reduction. She pointed out that economic growth was less important than the nature of that growth, that is,

> the extent to which the growth is associated with growing inequalities that do not allow the benefits of growth to reach the poor; the extent to which the structural change involved in the growth process generates sufficient opportunities for productive non-agricultural employment; the extent to which markets and states function in ways that ensure the provision of basic needs and universal access to essential social services are provided. All this also means that government mediation

[7] India's rapid population growth, in particular in lower-income deciles and in the 'Bimaru' states (Bihar, Madhya Pradesh, Rajasthan and Uttar Pradesh) could explain a 'thinning' of per-capita incomes as one moves down income deciles.

> of the process of global economic integration matters in affecting the processes that will ultimately determine the extent to which economic growth delivers better conditions for the poor. (p 22)

The author was of the view that, reflecting the Chinese revolution, the substantial state ownership of and investment in capital assets, and an unchanging financial structure and system, China integrated with the global economy under different conditions than India whose integration was by means of economic liberalization. China had already ensured adequate food supply and universal primary education so that it could move rapidly towards high levels of investment and growth. India had not ensured such socio-economic expenditure and continued to struggle to bring down the rate of poverty reduction as found by other authors mentioned previously.

While Ghosh continued to mention China's 'export-oriented industrialization, which became the next engine of growth' (p 22), it has to be recalled that, during its high growth period, China persistently pursued an artificially devalued currency policy and began correcting it only under international pressure (Shome, 2012). In contrast, India's currency remained overvalued during the same period. Ghosh remained critical of India's lack of success in poverty reduction. She concluded,

> Clearly, macroeconomic flexibility in a market driven environment is not the best recipe either for growth and stability or for poverty reduction. India's growth experience, while higher than for many other developing countries, was still less than the rapid growth experienced by China and other East and Southeast Asian economies. And more fundamentally, it could not deliver the desired structural change in terms of the composition of output and employment that would have ensured substantial poverty reduction. (p 23)[8]

The impact of macro-economic performance on inequality was investigated by Ganaie et al. (2018). They arrived at conclusions regarding the relationship between income inequality and its selected macroeconomic determinants using data between 1963–2007. They used the income share of the top 1 per cent of the population as an alternative measure of inequality. They found that real per-capita gross domestic product (GDP) was negatively associated with overall inequality, and positively associated with the income share of

---

8 Also see Bardhan (2007) who arrived at a midway conclusion. Anand et al. (2014), however, analysed India's period of rapid growth, 2004–09, and arrived at the conclusion that robust economic growth was 'a major driver of poverty reduction and inclusiveness in India' (p 1).

the top 1 per cent. They estimated that government expenditure and trade openness had a positive impact on the distribution of income while an increase in the price level led to an increase in inequality. Further, as the share of agriculture in GDP increased, the distribution of income improved.

Subramanian and Jayaraj (2015) assessed the evolution of inequality in the distribution of consumption expenditure in India from 1983 to 2009–10 using National Sample Survey data and adjusting them for plausibility. Their conclusions were closer to Ghosh's in that inequality in the distribution of consumption expenditure widened over time,

> which is at odds with the impression of more or less unchanging inequality conveyed in some of the literature available on the subject in India. (p 0)[9]

> the outcome of statistical analysis coincides with the common perception that India, in recent years, has indeed been a country of widening economic inequality, with little evidence of either inter-personal or inter-caste inclusiveness in growth. (p 16)

The trend in the investigative literature points in the direction that, while poverty and inequality in India might have improved from the 1980s, they did not perform any better after the 1991 economic liberalization than before it. Income concentration at the top increased and, despite some improvement in income rise in different income groups, fell short of progress in China. Certainly, India should have done better.

Wealth inequality

There is ample emerging evidence on wealth inequality globally and in India. Chancel et al. (2021) in the 2022 World Inequality Report, examining the global state of inequality, indicated that

> Income and wealth inequalities have been on the rise nearly everywhere since the 1980s, following a series of deregulation and liberalization programs which took different forms in different countries. The rise has not been uniform: certain countries have experienced spectacular increases in inequality (including the US, Russia and India) while others (European countries and China) have experienced relatively smaller rises… confirm that inequality is not inevitable, it is a political choice. Contemporary global inequalities are close to early 20th century levels, at the peak of Western imperialism. (p 11)

---

9 This part of the quotation pertains to the abstract of their paper.

Banerjee and Duflo (2021), in their 'Foreword' to the same Report, brought up the US and UK as harbingers of inequality that impacted on emerging economies such as China and India,

> the slowdown of growth in the US and UK in the 1970s that led to the conviction that a big part of the problem was that the institutions that kept inequality low (minimum wage, unions, taxes, regulation, etc.) were to blame, and that what we needed was to unleash an entrepreneurial culture that celebrates the unabashed accumulation of private wealth. We now know that the Reagan-Thatcher revolution … was the starting point of a dizzying rise in inequality within countries that continues to this day. When state control was (successfully) loosened in countries like China and India to allow private sector led growth, the same ideology got trotted out to justify not worrying about inequality, with the consequence that India is now among the most unequal countries in the world (based on this report) and China risks getting there soon. (p 3)

Narrowing down on India, Ghatak (2021) worked on the inequality of wealth in India. Using the WID developed by Piketty and his colleagues, he concluded that there had been an alarming rise in wealth inequality in India. To quote,

> The share of total wealth of the top 1% of the population was fairly constant around 12% from 1961, the earliest year for which we have numbers, to 1981. Since 1991, the year of liberalisation, it has steadily increased and reached 42.5% in 2020. The share of total wealth of the bottom 50% fell marginally to 10.9% from 12.3% between 1961 and 1981, and then started declining sharply and stood at a mere 2.8% in 2020. The share of total wealth of the middle 40% follows a similar pattern, hovering around 45% till 1981 and then falling steadily to 22.9% in 2020. (p 2)

The following conclusions may be drawn from Table 4.4. There was negative growth in the share of wealth of the bottom 50 per cent during 1961–91 as well as for the next 40 per cent (though to a lesser degree) while there was positive growth in the share for the top 10 per cent and the highest for the top 1 per cent of wealth owners. The situation worsened even further during 1991–2020 when there was a deepening of the negative growth not only for the first 90 per cent, but the next 9 per cent also experienced negative growth in its share of wealth. Only the top 1 per cent experienced positive growth in the share of wealth and that rate accelerated phenomenally.

Table 4.4: India: wealth inequality

Wealth group[1]	**Share of net personal wealth**[2] **(%)**					**Growth in net personal wealth share**	
	1961	**1981**	**1991**	**2012**	**2020**[3]	**1961–91**	**1991–20**
Bottom 50%	12.3	10.9	8.8	6.4	2.8	-29	-68
Middle 40%	44.5	44.1	40.7	30.8	22.9	-9	-44
Next 9%	31.3	32.5	34.4	32.1	31.8	10	-8
Top 1%, of which	11.9	12.5	16.1	30.7	42.5	36	164
Top 0.1%	2.8	2.7	4.4	18.4	–	58	–
Top 0.01%	0.6	0.5	0.9	12.4	–	42	–
Top 0.001%	0.1	0.1	0.1	8.1	–	8	–

Note: [1] Distribution of per-adult net personal wealth. [2] Net personal wealth share held by a given percentile group. Net personal wealth is the total value of non-financial and financial assets (housing, land, deposits, bonds, equities and so on) held by households, minus their debts. The personal or household sector – in the national accounts sense – includes all households and private individuals as well as unincorporated enterprises whose accounts are not separated from those of the households who own them. The population comprises individuals over age 20. The base unit is the individual (rather than the household). This is equivalent to assuming no sharing of resources within couples. [3] Values for 2020 are obtained from Ghatak (2021) which are reported to be from Oxfam.

Source: Wealth Inequality Database (WID)

Table 4.5 compares wealth inequality in China, India and Russia as was attempted for their income inequality (see Table 4.3). Despite some incomparability of years of available data, useful insights may be drawn from the table. What is observed is that the rate of growth in the share of wealth for all groups was negative in all three countries between 2012–15, the exception being the top 1 per cent that gained in share. In other words, there was an acceleration of wealth transfer to the top 1 per cent from the other 99 per cent of wealth owners. Data are not available for India for a breakdown of the top 1 per cent but it is clear that, for China and Russia, within the top 1 per cent itself, the growth was higher as wealth ownership share went up right to the top 0.001 per cent of wealth owners. This is a situation of extreme worsening of wealth distribution in the 21st century which has accelerated with time.

Human Development Index

Since 1990, the United Nations Development Programme (UNDP) has published an annual HDR in which a defined HDI is computed for a large

Table 4.5: Wealth inequality: India, China and Russia

Wealth group	Share of net personal wealth (%)						Growth in share		
	2012			2015		2020	2012–15		2012–20
	India	China	Russia	China	Russia	India	China	Russia	India
Bottom 50%	6.4	6.6	3.7	6.4	3.5	2.8	-3	-5	-56
Middle 40%	30.8	26.9	28.4	26.2	25.2	22.9	-3	-11	-26
Next 9%	32.1	39.3	32.5	37.8	28.7	31.8	-4	-11	-1
Top 1%, of which	30.7	27.3	35.5	29.6	42.6	42.5	9	20	38
Top 0.1%	18.4	13.1	19.6	16.4	26.3	–	25	34	–
Top 0.01%	12.4	8.0	11.8	11.0	16.9	–	37	43	–
Top 0.001%	8.1	3.9	6.7	5.8	9.8	–	49	48	–

Note: The latest data available for India are for 2012 and for China and Russia it is for 2015. The 2020 data for India were sourced from Oxfam as indicated by Ghatak (2021).

Source: Wealth Inequality Database and Ghatak (2021)

cross-section of countries. Currently, the HDI represents an alternative to the GDP as a singular measure of development. Although the HDI has faced recent critique from some authors in its failure to include wider dimensions of development – such as ecology (Sagar and Najam, 1998) – than it currently does, there is little doubt that the HDI has broadened the discussion and assessment of development.

Emergence of the HDI

The HDI is attributable to Sen and Huq as elaborated by Sen (2020).[10]

> Even though I feel honoured by the fact that I sometimes get credit for the Human Development Index (HDI), I must emphasize that the HDI was driven entirely by Mahbub's vision, and (I must add here) also by his cunning about practical use. The simple HDI never tried to represent all that we wanted to capture in the indicator system, but it had much more to say about quality of life than GDP. (p xi)

And the concept has been taken forward by several authors, the most recent being the authors of the HDR who use the HDI and incorporate a

[10] See 'Introduction', Human Development Report (HDR), 2020, p xi.

methodology enunciated by Atkinson (1970) in the broadening of inequality dimensions. Sen (1973) raised some conceptual and measurement issues of poverty and inequality and suggested a framework for inequality and an alternative measure of poverty. Atkinson (1987) re-examined some issues in measuring poverty – the choice of the poverty line, the poverty index, and the relation between poverty and inequality, pointing to a diversity of views regarding not only the choice of poverty line but also its level and structure.

It is not as if the HDI has not been the subject of criticism in particular from social scientists from fields other than economics. Sagar and Najam (1998), for example, critiqued the HDI for its failure to incorporate ecological aspects, having become stagnant and failing to reflect the world it originally sought to portray or to enhance the development debate. According to them, the HDI narrows down on country rankings while ignoring global aspects crucial to development including ecological concerns. In the same vein, Ranis et al. (2006) pointed to the insufficiency of the three dimensions of the HDI, proposing additional components as indicators, totalling 31. Their motivation was based on a view that a full assessment of human development required a broader set of indicators than the HDI alone. They went further, finding that the under-five mortality rates performed as well as the HDI itself, and that per-capita income was not highly representative of various dimensions of human development. Indeed, an entire history of the HDI was undertaken by Stanton (2007) beginning with the history of economic thought to Sen's (1995) human capabilities approach and the HDI.

Construction of the HDI

Currently, the construction of the HDI uses a framework of minimum and maximum values for various components of human development. The rationale for the setting of minimum and maximum is explained in the 2020 HDR.[11] For life expectancy, no country in the 20th century had a life expectancy of less than the minimum set at age 20; the maximum was set at 85 as an aspirational goal since some countries are close to achieving it (Hong Kong with 84.9 years and Japan with 84.6 years). The education minimum was set at 0 years since societies could exist without formal education; a projected maximum for 2025 was set at 15 years noting that even a Master's degree was obtainable in 18 years. The minimum for gross national income (GNI) per capita per annum was set at $100 reflecting that considerable subsistence and nonmarket production existed near the minimum, which was not captured in the official data. The maximum was

[11] See Technical Note 2, p 2.

Table 4.6: Minimum and maximum values of indicators

Dimension	Indicator	Minimum	Maximum
Health	Life expectancy (years)	20	85
Education	Expected years of schooling (years)	0	18
	Mean years of schooling (years)	0	15
Standard of living	GNI per capita (2017 PPP$)	100	75,000

Source: 2020 HDR, Technical Note 2, pp 2–6

set at $75,000 per capita following Kahneman and Deaton (2010) who had shown that there was little gain in human development and wellbeing from above $75,000 per capita per annum.

Table 4.6 may be used to derive the value of each dimension (left hand column) that comprises the HDI. Thus,

$$\text{Dimension Index} = \frac{\text{Actual value} - \text{minimum value}}{\text{Maximum value} - \text{minimum value}}$$

The dimension indices combine to yield the HDI. Thus,

$$\text{HDI} = (I_{\text{Health}} * I_{\text{Education}} * I_{\text{Income}})^{1/3}$$

HDI being the geometric mean of the three indices, where I_{Health} is the index of health dimension, $I_{\text{Education}}$ is the index of education dimension, and I_{Income} is the index of income dimension.

An additional aspect, that of gender-related intersectionality, was introduced in the United Nations' 1995 HDR comprising two measures of wellbeing, namely a Gender-related Development Index (GDI) and a Gender Empowerment Measure (GEM) to address gender inequality. Potentially this could advance the HDI one step further as a meaningfully applicable index to ordinally measure human and gender development. To take one example among a number of such exercises, Charmes and Wieringa (2003) explained the introduction of GEM incorporating gender and power concepts in Africa, attempting to link socio-cultural, religious, political, legal and economic spheres into them while pointing to the challenges involved in carrying out the task. Schuler (2006) surveyed how the two indices have been used in the publications of the UNDP as well as in academic studies. The finding was that GDI had been misinterpreted as a gender inequality measure and that the policy impact of both GDI and GEM had been limited.

HDI in India

Pari passu with the worsening of inequality in income and wealth and the inability of 90 per cent of India's population to reach middle-class status, as argued earlier, India has signed the United Nations' 17 sustainable development goals to be achieved by 2030 to lift its citizens from 'extreme poverty' and 'hunger' and to 'leave no one behind'. This indicates that India recognizes that a good portion of its citizens continues to suffer from basic deprivation and that there are substantial barriers to human development which could be removed through strong and feasible policy options. Therefore, the question naturally arises regarding its HDI.

The HDI is an index incorporating ten indicators under the broad criteria of education, health and living standard as shown in Table 4.7 and Table 4.8. An examination of India's HDI component indicators is revealing. Comparing the recent HDI data sets of 2015 and 2019, India's HDI rank remained at 131 between 2015–19 (Table 4.7), thus showing no comparative improvement. Its HDI – the maximum being 1 – went from 0.62 to 0.65. HDI components, life expectancy at birth, went from 68.6 to 69.7, average school years from 6.2 to 6.5, and per capita GNP from $5,391 to $6,681 (at 2017 Purchasing Power Parity) (Table 4.7). Even though India made slight improvements in the components, other countries made at least as much improvement so that India's relative ranking remained the same at 131. Over the same years, China's HDI

Table 4.7: Selected countries: Human Development Index (HDI)[1]

HDI rank			**HDI value**		**Life expectancy**		**Average school years**		**Per capita GNI ($)**[2]	
2015	**2019**		**2015**	**2019**	**2015**	**2019**	**2015**	**2019**	**2015**	**2019**
1	1	Norway	0.95	0.96	82.0	82.4	12.5	12.9	64,683	66,494
10	17	US	0.92	0.93	78.9	78.9	13.3	13.4	59,559	63,826
16	13	UK	0.92	0.93	81.1	81.3	12.8	13.2	43,885	46,071
49	54	Russia	0.81	0.82	71.5	72.6	11.8	12.2	24,847`	26,157
79	84	Brazil	0.76	0.77	75.0	75.9	7.6	8.0	14,775	14,263
90	85	China	0.74	0.76	75.9	76.9	7.7	8.1	12,644	16,057
119	114	South Africa	0.70	0.71	62.6	64.1	10.1	10.2	12,528	12,129
131	131	India	0.62	0.65	68.6	69.7	6.2	6.5	5,391	6,681

Note: [1] 188 countries in 2015, 189 in 2019. [2] Per capita GNI (constant 2017 PPP terms).
Source: Human Development Report, 2016 and 2020, and Appendix Table A4.1

Table 4.8: Selected countries: changes in HDI

2015–19	Change in HDI rank	CHI[1]		IHDI[2]		HDI-IHDI (% loss)[3]	
		2015	2019	2015	2019	2015	2019
Norway	0	5.4	6.0	0.90	0.90	5.5	6.1
US	-5	12.9	12.1	0.80	0.81	13.6	12.7
UK	3	7.8	7.9	0.85	0.86	8.0	8.2
Russia	-5	9.6	10.0	0.73	0.74	9.8	10.2
Brazil	-5	25.0	24.4	0.56	0.57	25.5	25.5
China	5	–	15.7	–	0.64	–	16.0
South Africa	5	32.0	31.2	0.46	0.47	34.7	34.0
India	0	26.5	25.7	0.46	0.48	27.1	26.4

Note: [1] Coefficient of human inequality. [2] Inequality-adjusted HDI. [3] Loss (%) = [(HDI – IHDI) / HDI] *100. For India (2019), 26.4 = [(0.65 – 0.48) / 0.65] *100.

Source: Human Development Report, 2016 and 2020, and Appendix Table A4.2

rank, which was already higher than India's in 2015 (90), improved to 85 in 2019. Also noteworthy is that, while India's HDI component indicators improved slightly, its per capita GNP increased by 24 per cent, a telltale sign of income growth becoming more concentrated on high deciles. The improvements in India's HDI were thus insignificant compared to the strides several countries were able to make. These comprise hard lessons for India.

Table 4.8 takes two time points – 2015 and 2019 – to examine any improvement or the lack of it. Between 2015–19, in contrast to zero upward movement in India's HDI rank, China's rank improved by five and South Africa's rank improved by five. Brazil's rank declined by five, the same as for the United States and Russia, as revealed in the first column.

Introducing inequality into HDI

HDI can be nuanced by incorporating the degree of inequality in each of the three HDI dimensions for the derivation of the Inequality-adjusted Human Development Index (IHDI). To quote,

> The IHDI adjusts the HDI for inequality in the distribution of each dimension across the population. It is based on a distribution-sensitive class of composite indices proposed by Foster, Lopez-Calva and Szekely (2005), which draws on the Atkinson (1970) family of inequality

> measures … . The IHDI accounts for inequalities in HDI dimensions by 'discounting' each dimension's average value according to its level of inequality … . [T]he IHDI measures the level of human development when inequality is accounted for. (p 4)[12]

An unweighted average of inequalities in health, education and income is denoted as the coefficient of human inequality (CHI). It averages these inequalities using the arithmetic mean. Thus,

$$CHI = \frac{A_{Health} + A_{Education} + A_{Income}}{3}$$

where

$$A_x = 1 - = \frac{\sqrt[n]{X_1 \ldots X_n}}{X}$$

A_X, or the 'Atkinson measure', is obtained for each dimension – life expectancy, mean years of schooling and disposable household income or consumption per capita. $\{X_1, \ldots, X_n\}$ denotes the underlying distribution in each dimension. CHI is shown in Table 4.8.

Next, each inequality-adjusted dimension index is derived from its corresponding HDI dimension index, I_X, by multiplying it by $(1 - A_X)$. Thus,

$$I_X^{\star} = (1 - A_X) \star I_X$$

where $I_{Income}^{\star}$ is the inequality-adjusted index for income. Once the three inequality-adjusted dimension indices are derived, the IHDI is derived as their geometric mean. Thus,

$$\begin{aligned} IHDI &= \left(I_{Health}^{\star} \star I_{Education}^{\star} \star I_{Income}^{\star}\right)^{1/3} \\ &= \left[(1 - A_{Health}) \star (1 - A_{Education}) \star (1 - A_{Income})^{1/3}\right] \star HDI \end{aligned}$$

IHDI values are depicted in Table 4.8. And the loss in HDI value due to inequality can be written as:

---

12 Technical Note 2, HDR (2020).

$$\text{Loss} = 1 - [1 - A_{\text{Health}}) \star (1 - A_{\text{Education}}) \star (1 - A_{\text{Income}})^{1/3}$$

In essence, the inclusion of CHI into HDI yields IHDI. When there is no inequality present, HDI = IHDI. Since inequality is invariably present, the two may be expected to be different as is evident from a comparison of Table 4.7 and Table 4.8. The loss in the value of HDI due to the presence of inequality is shown in the last two columns of Table 4.8 (HDI-IHDI).

The percentage loss between HDI and IHDI is highest for India (26.4) other than South Africa (34), again revealing that inequality continues to have frustrating ramifications for India's human development in a cross-country lineup.

Multidimensional poverty index

Cross-country comparisons can be sharpened through the UNDP concept of 'Multi-dimensional Poverty Index' (MPI) that inserts 'deprivation cutoffs' on the previously mentioned components of human development. It uses micro data from household surveys, and – unlike the Inequality-adjusted Human Development Index – all the indicators needed to construct the measure come from the same survey.

More details about the general methodology can be found in Alkire and Jahan (2018); Alkire and Kanagaratnam (2018) and Alkire et al. (2021).[13] Deprivation in various indicators is used in the concept of Multi-dimensional Poverty (MDP). To quote Alkire et al. (2021),

> The global MPI specifies that a person is identified as **MPI poor** if he or she is deprived in at least one-third of the weighted indicators. In addition, the measure also identifies those who are close to the one-third threshold, that is, individuals are **vulnerable** to multidimensional poverty if they are deprived in 20% to 33.33% of weighted indicators. The measure also specifies a higher poverty cutoff to identify those in **severe** poverty, that is, those deprived in 50% or more of the dimensions. (p 7)

Table 4.9 focuses on 2020 and reveals that 27.9 per cent of the Indian population were in MDP, and 8.8 per cent in Severe MDP (SMDP). These

[13] For example, if all individuals in the household are in an age group where they should have formally completed six or more years of schooling, but none has been able to so complete, then the household is deprived in years of schooling (Alkire et al., 2020). Deprivation cutoff points are also set for child mortality, nutrition, sanitation, electricity, drinking water, housing, cooking fuel and assets ownership.

figures were far smaller in Brazil, China and South Africa. While some authors including Aaberge and Brandolini (2014) have raised issue with the indicators used to measure MDP and SMDP and the procedures for weighting them, and have questioned if they could be meaningfully used to measure poverty, nevertheless they are considered to be useful tools until greater sophistication could be incorporated in their construction. To conclude, even the MDP and SMDP point to the same conclusion for India as do the HDI and IHDI. Though India has made progress in reducing MDP and SMDP, speed is of the essence for comparable gains that other countries have made so that India could achieve the UN Sustainable Development's 2030 Goal of 'leaving no one behind' in severe poverty to which India is signatory.

Figures for 2021 for India's national MPI related measures were developed by the Oxford Poverty and Human Development Initiative (OPHI) and UNDP under the auspices of Niti Aayog, Government of India. This new Indian national version of the MPI complements the ten indicators of the global MPI with metrics on maternal health and bank account under the dimensions of health and standard of living, respectively. Cross-country comparisons were not provided, however. India's 2021 information is shown in parentheses in Table 4.9. The proportion of population in MDP improved, declining from 27.9 per cent to 25.1 per cent, while the intensity of deprivation worsened from 43.9 to 47.9. Nevertheless, the MPI which is an index obtained by multiplying the two (see Table 4.9, Footnote 3), improved, declining from 0.123 to 0.118. What this implies is that the

Table 4.9: Selected countries: Multi-dimensional Poverty (MDP)

	PMDP[1]	**Intensity of deprivation**[2]	**MPI**[3] **(2020)**	**SMDP**[4]	**Number of poor in MDP**[5]
	(Reported 2020, %)			**(2020, %)**	**(2018, mn)**
Brazil	3.8	42.5	0.016	0.9	8.0
China	3.9	41.4	0.016	0.3	55.5
India	27.9 (25.01)	43.9 (47.13)	0.123 (0.118)	8.8[6]	377.5[6]
South Africa	6.3	39.8	0.025	0.9	3.6

Note: [1] Proportion of population in MDP. [2] Intensity is the average share of indicators in which poor people are deprived. [3] MPI = PMDP x Intensity. For India, [MPI India (0.123) = 27.9 ★ 43.9] = 0.123. [4] Severe MDP (see section 4.6 for definition). [5] 2018 figures comprise the last year reported in MPI Report 2020. [6] Updated figures were not provided.

Source: Global Multi-dimensional Poverty Index (MPI) Report 2020, Appendix Table A4.3 and India National MPI Baseline Report, 2021

improvement in Population under Multi-dimensional Poverty (PMDP) overwhelmed the worsening in intensity, thus yielding an improvement in the multiplicative index (MPI).

References

Aaberge, Rolf and Andrea Brandolini. (2014) 'Multidimensional poverty and inequality', Discussion Papers, No. 792, Statistics Norway, Research Department, Oslo. Available at https://www.econstor.eu/bitstream/10419/192774/1/dp792.pdf, accessed 3 June 2021.

Alkire, Sabina and Selim Jahan. (2018) 'The New Global MPI 2018: Aligning with the Sustainable Development Goals'. HDRO Occasional Paper, United Nations Development Programme (UNDP). Available at http://hdr.undp.org/en/content/new-global-mpi-2018-aligning-sustainable-development-goals, accessed 1 May 2021.

Alkire, Sabina and Usha Kanagaratnam. (2018) 'Multidimensional Poverty Index – Winter 2017–18: brief methodological note and results', *OPHI MPI Methodological Notes No. 45*, Oxford Poverty and Human Development Initiative, University of Oxford. Available at https://www.ophi.org.uk/wp-content/uploads/OPHIMethNote_45_Winter_2017-18_FINAL.pdf, accessed 1 May 2021.

Alkire, Sabina, Usha Kanagaratnam and Nicolai Suppa. (2021) 'The Global Multidimensional Poverty Index (MPI) 2021', *OPHI MPI Methodological Notes 49*, Oxford Poverty and Human Development Initiative, University of Oxford. Available at www.ophi.org.uk/wp-content/uploads/OPHI_MPI_MN_49_2020.pdf, accessed 30 December 2022.

Alvaredo, Facundo, Anthony B. Atkinson, Lucas Chancel, Thomas Piketty, Emmanuel Saez and Gabriel Zucman. (2016) 'Distributional National Accounts (DINA) Guidelines: Concepts and Methods used in WID.world', WID.world Working Paper 2016/02 (revised April 2018). Available at https://wid.world/document/dinaguidelines-v1/. An updated and extended version of the guidelines was published in September 2020 and is available at https://wid.world/document/distributional-national-accounts-guidelines-2020-concepts-and- methods-used-in-the-world-inequality-database/, accessed 18 June 2021.

Anand, Rahul, Volodymyr Tulin and Naresh Kumar. (2014) 'India: Defining and Explaining Inclusive Growth and Poverty Reduction', IMF Working Paper No. 14/63, International Monetary Fund. Available at https://www.imf.org/en/Publications/WP/Issues/2016/12/31/India-Defining-and-Explaining-Inclusive-Growth-and-Poverty-Reduction-41486, accessed 21 June 2021.

Atkinson, A. B. (1970) 'On the measurement of economic inequality', *Journal of Economic Theory*, 2(3): 244–63.

Atkinson, A. B. (1987) 'On the measurement of poverty', *Econometrica*, 55(4): 749–64, accessed 3 June 2021. Available at doi:10.2307/1911028

Banerjee, Abhijit and Esther Duflo. (2021) 'Foreword', World Inequality Report 2022, World Inequality Lab. Available at https://wir2022.wid.world/www-site/uploads/2021/12/WorldInequalityReport2022_Full_Report.pdf, accessed 15 December 2021.

Bardhan, Pranab. (2007) 'Poverty and Inequality in China and India: elusive link with globalisation', *Economic and Political Weekly*, 42(38): 3849–52. Available at http://www.jstor.org/stable/40276420, accessed 21 June 2021.

Chancel, Lucas. (2020) 'Indian inequality updates (2015–2019)', World Inequality Lab Technical Note 2020/09. Available at https://wid.world/document/indian-inequality-updates-2015-2019-world-inequality-lab-technical-note-2020-09/, accessed 18 June 2021.

Chancel, Lucas and Thomas Piketty. (2017) 'Indian Income Inequality, 1922–2015: from British Raj to Billionaire Raj?', WID.world Working Paper 2017/11. Available at https://wid.world/document/chancelpiketty2017widworld/, accessed 18 June 2021.

Chancel, Lucas, Thomas Piketty, Emmanuel Saez and Gabriel Zucman. (2021) 'World Inequality Report 2022', World Inequality Lab. Available at https://wir2022.wid.world/www-site/uploads/2021/12/WorldInequalityReport2022_Full_Report.pdf, accessed 15 December 2021.

Charmes, Jacques and Saskia Wieringa. (2003) 'Measuring women's empowerment: an assessment of the gender-related development index and the gender empowerment measure', *Journal of Human Development*, 4(3): 419–35. https://doi.org/10.1080/1464988032000125773, accessed 30 December 2022.

Chauhan, Rajesh K., Sanjay K. Mohanty, Subu V. Subramanian, Jajati K. Parida and Balakrushna Padhi. (2015) 'Regional estimates of poverty and inequality in India, 1993–2012', *Social Indicators Research*, 127: 1249–96. Available at https://doi.org/10.1007/s11205-015-1006-6, accessed 21 June 2021.

Deaton, Angus and Jean Dreze. (2002) 'Poverty and inequality in India: a re-examination', *Economic and Political Weekly*, 37(36): 3729–748. Available at http://www.jstor.org/stable/4412578, accessed 22 June 2021.

Deaton, Angus and Valerie Kozel. (2005) 'Data and dogma: the great Indian poverty debate', *World Bank Research Observer*, 20(2): 177–200. Available at https://elibrary.worldbank.org/doi/10.1093/wbro/lki009#, accessed 21 June 2021.

Datt, Gaurav and Martin Ravallion. (2002) 'Is India's economic growth leaving the poor behind?', *Journal of Economic Perspectives*, 16(3): 89–108. Available at doi: 10.1257/089533002760278730, accessed 21 June 2021.

Foster, James E., Luis F. Lopez-Calva and Miguel Szekely. (2005) 'Measuring the distribution of human development methodology and an application to Mexico', *Journal of Human Development*, 6(1): 5–25.

Ganaie, Aadil Ahmad, Sajad Ahmad Bhat and Bandi Kamaiah. (2018) 'Macro-determinants of income inequality: an empirical analysis in case of India', *Economics Bulletin*, 38(1): 309–25. Available at www.accessecon.com/Pubs/EB/2018/Volume38/EB-18-V38-I1-P30.pdf, accessed 22 June 2021.

Ghatak, Maitreesh. (2021) 'India's inequality problem'. *The India Forum*, 2 July. Available at www.theindiaforum.in/article/does-india-have-inequality-problem, accessed 2 July 2021.

Ghosh, Jayati. (2010) 'Poverty reduction in China and India: policy implications of recent trends', DESA Working Paper No. 92. Available at www.un.org/esa/desa/papers/2010/wp92_2010.pdf, accessed 21 June 2021.

Global Multidimensional Poverty Index (MPI). (2020) 'Charting pathways out of multidimensional poverty: Achieving the SDGs', Human Development Reports, New York: United Nations Development Programme.

Government of India. (2021) 'National Multidimensional Poverty Index: Baseline Report based on NFHS-4 (2015–16)', NITI Aayog, OPHI and UNDP. Available at www.niti.gov.in/sites/default/files/2021-11/National_MPI_India-11242021.pdf, accessed 2 December 2021.

Human Development Report. (2013) New York: United Nations Development Programme.

Human Development Report. (2016) New York: United Nations Development Programme.

Human Development Report. (2018) New York: United Nations Development Programme.

Human Development Report. (2020) New York: United Nations Development Programme.

Human Development Report, Technical Note 2. (2020) New York: United Nations Development Programme.

Human Development Survey. (2012) New Delhi: Springer Nature.

Kahneman, Daniel and Angus Deaton. (2010) 'High income improves evaluation of life but not emotional well-being', *Proceedings of National Academy of Sciences*, 107(38): 16489–493.

Kulkarni, Varsha S. and Raghav Gaiha. (2018) 'Beyond Piketty: a new perspective on poverty and inequality in India', GDI Working Paper 2018–033. Manchester: The University of Manchester.

Piketty, Thomas. (2014) *Capital in the Twenty-First Century*. Cambridge MA: The Belknap Press of Harvard University Press.

Piketty, Thomas and Abhijit Banerjee. (2005) 'Top Indian incomes, 1922–2000', *World Bank Economic Review*, 19(1): 1–20. Available at http://piketty.pse.ens.fr/fichiers/public/BanerjeePiketty2005.pdf, accessed 20 August 2021.

Ranis, Gustav, Frances Stewart and Emma Samman. (2006) 'Human development: beyond the Human Development Index', *Journal of Human Development*, 7(3): 323–58. Available at https://doi.org/10.1080/14649880600815917, accessed 20 August 2021.

Sagar, Ambuj D. and Adil Najam. (1998) 'The human development index: a critical review', *Ecological Economics*, 25(3): 249–64. Available at https://doi.org/10.1016/S0921-8009(97)00168-7, accessed 2 June 2021.

Schuler, Dana. (2006) 'The uses and misuses of the gender-related development index and gender empowerment measure: a review of the literature', *Journal of Human Development*, 7(2): 161–81. Available at https://doi.org/10.1080/14649880600768496, accessed 1 May 2021.

Sen, Amartya. (1973) 'Poverty, inequality and unemployment: some conceptual issues in measurement', *Economic and Political Weekly*, August. Available at https://kharagpurcollege.ac.in/studyMaterial/1244poverty_inequality_and_unemployment-Sem-6.pdf, accessed 3 June 2021.

Sen, Amartya. (1995) *Inequality Reexamined*. Oxford: Oxford University Press.

Sen, Amartya. (2020) 'Special Contribution – Human Development and Mahbub ul Haq', Human Development Report, UNDP. Available at http://hdr.undp.org/en/2020-report, accessed 9 July 2021.

Shome, Parthasarathi. (2012) 'Rebalancing and structural policies – an Indian perspective', *Oxford Review of Economic Policy*, 28(3): 587–602. Available at http://www.jstor.org/stable/43741314, accessed 23 June 2021.

Stanton, Elizabeth A. (2007) 'The Human Development Index: A History', Working Paperswp127, Political Economy Research Institute, University of Massachusetts at Amherst. Available at https://scholarworks.umass.edu/cgi/viewcontent.cgi?article=1101&context=peri_workingpapers, accessed 2 June 2021.

Subramanian, S. and D. Jayaraj. (2015) 'Growth and Inequality in The Distribution of India's Consumption Expenditure: 1983 to 2009–10'. WIDER Working Paper 2015/025, UNU-WIDER. Available at https://www.wider.unu.edu/sites/default/files/wp2015-025.pdf, accessed 22 June 2021.

PART II

Sources of Inequality and Poverty

> There is no substitute for natural language when it comes to expressing social identities or defining political ideologies ... (or) when it comes to doing research in social science or thinking about the just society. Those who believe that we will one day be able to rely on a mathematical formula, algorithm, or economic model to determine the 'socially optimal' level of inequality are destined to be disappointed.
>
> Thomas Piketty[1]

[1] Piketty (2021), p 149.

5

Racism, Colonialism and Slavery as International Practices

Introduction

This chapter attempts to reveal how racism and colonialism have comprised important factors in the genesis of poverty and inequality across the world. It would be pertinent to begin with a quote from Gilroy (2019):

> Du Bois had learned about the world's 'race problems' by placing colonial rule, the Third Reich and the US racial order in historical, moral and conceptual relation. (p 3) The widespread appeal of racialised group identity and racism, often conveyed obliquely with a knowing wink, has been instrumental in delivering us to a situation in which our conceptions of truth, law and government have been placed in jeopardy. (p 1)
>
> The attractiveness of generic racial identities is part of a psycho-political shift that has encouraged fascination with ossified culture: lacking vitality but easily regulated. The invocations to whiteness now circulating in Europe are freighted with notions of victimage and vulnerability. (p 2)

This chapter will pursue arguments along the earlier-mentioned lines in an attempt to establish their roles in perpetrating poverty and inequality.

Genesis of poverty and inequality

A reflection on the incidence of poverty and inequality globally leads to an inevitable conclusion, that they are not self-generated but are constructed, imposed and often perpetuated.

The genesis of inequality and, consequently, of poverty is a timeless phenomenon of societies. Indeed, the very nature of Man in its ability to remain in a state of opacity regarding the phenomenon, has to be pondered. In that vein, poverty and inequality must reflect certain societal beliefs and actions that must generate and elevate them. They comprise,

- first, to *exclude*, a portion of society from the rest. Exclusion can be specified in various ways. The more the exclusion is layered, the higher is the number of exclusion criteria and excluded categories generated;
- second, to *isolate* the excluded categories preferably into non-intersecting groups, more often than not by locating their residences apart and prohibiting any social interaction between them except for well-defined economic functions for which the input of a particular category may be needed by another category;
- third, to *dominate* them in as many ways as possible thus ensuring that the *economic return diminishes* per unit of work as the order of categories is descended even if those occupying the bottom categories approach extreme poverty;
- fourth, to remain oblivious of social ostracization and stark economic *differences that are likely to emerge and become acceptable* in society with little recognition of the tenets of natural justice; and
- fifth, to then *justify* class or racial differences that emerge in society at large led by dominant groups.

And, once the system is in place and is stable:

- to become *aware of the injustices* of the past and to *contemplate compensation* in pecuniary or non-pecuniary terms of the bottom categories; and
- to actually *introduce usually inadequate schemes of compensation* that may, nevertheless, remain circumvented or ignored.

Every attempt at such compensation across the world has failed to adequately redress the accumulated impact of exclusion, isolation, domination, and extraction.

Inequalities derived from whimsical exogenous criteria include the happenstance of the category of birth leading to wage differentials, and the acceptance of those practices over millennia. What economists working in this field generally do is to design and check the success of economic compensation schemes that have been attempted for the redressal of past practices. Using the nature of limited entitlements in societies in a search for their redressal, they study the most appropriate packages of compensation that may be designed including through inter-country reparation.

In this chapter we study the source or genesis of exclusion practices, whether through centuries of caste- or class-based societal structures or colonialism based on slave trade and indentured servitude, or random extractions from a conquered population. We address the role of exclusion as it has been constructed by selected 'advanced' societies. Romans took slaves when they conquered an area and isolated its population. In later millennia, Europeans finessed the slave trade or indentured servitude through which populations were transported across continents, died in millions, sold in marketplaces and made to serve without wage as they became property owned by their owner. Later some were allowed to buy their freedom by compensating their masters monetarily that often took most of their lives if not life itself. A few centuries back, white Australians decimated the first continental occupants – the aborigines – including complete annihilation of the original Tasmanians,[1] Chilean immigrants did the same on their own soil, and several other migrants in an endless series of similar behaviour patterns through history. In the last century, perhaps the worst annihilation episode in human history occurred when Germans excluded, isolated, dominated and annihilated some 6 million fellow humans[2] that they did not consider human. Britain's actions in the Second World War caused 3 million deaths in the province of Bengal in India by isolating mainly farmers and diverting, through domination, their produce to the war effort – a matter that is buried in British history until an increasing number of historians – both English and Bengali – began to author scholarly works on the issue over the last decade.[3] Croatians, in an emulation of the Third Reich, exterminated Serbs during the Second World War, while the Serbs exterminated Bosnian compatriots during the 1992–95 civil war that engulfed and dismembered the erstwhile Yugoslavia.[4]

---

1 Australia and New Zealand were places to send 'surplus people' (Crosby, 2004, p 249). The original white Australians comprised convicted criminals of British society who were punished to 'transportation' and sent to Australia. Even sailors arrived in New Zealand 'malnourished, poorly clothed, with no possibility of family life – tuberculosis, venereal disease just considered occupational diseases, but infecting the Maori' (p 232).

2 This comprised perhaps 3 million Jews, other races exterminated being East Europeans, as well as gypsies and homosexuals, altogether adding up to, arguably, some 6 million.

3 Dismembering a society with the objective of domination has reared its head in colonial history, more so than others by colonial Britain when it dismembered Bengal in 1905, India in 1947, Ireland in 1920, Malaysia in 1965 and others. These chapters in its taught colonial history have, by and large, disappeared or been given a sugar-coated interpretation.

4 Ironically the Germanic province of Slovenia declared independence from Yugoslavia first and Germany recognized it immediately together with other Western nations. The province of Croatia followed, and the West recognized it too. The legitimacy of their declaration and subsequent recognition has never been questioned. Only the fallout between the Serbs of Serbia and Bosnians of Bosnia-Herzegovina was condemned while ignoring the source of the initial provocations. A racial Germanic tone to the entire affair and the compliance of the rest of the European community were not to be missed, however. See Wintz (2010).

The formula in all of them, despite being spread across centuries, was to exclude, isolate, dominate and exterminate or, in the more benign cases, ostracize and then abandon.

In what follows, we take two of the most egregious continuations of exclusion, isolation and domination and half-hearted attempts at compensation. They are, first, the incidence of slavery in the American experience and its Black reverberations today and, second, the adoption of the colonial extractive systems of Britain, France and other colonial powers based on extraction through slavery in Haiti, and colonial occupation and indentured servitude in India, and comparable policies implemented by other European colonizers. We reserve an exposition of the effects of the caste system, India's domestically generated source of poverty and inequality, to Chapter 6.

Exclusion through slavery in the United States

Roughly 12.5 million Africans were shipped to the Americas, beginning in 1525 and finally abolished, individually by different countries, in the second half of the 19th century. Approximately 2 million, or 16 per cent, were estimated to have perished during transportation. Documentation has revealed that they were transported across the Atlantic in subhuman conditions even by the standards of Western societies in that era, sometimes being made to stand through the transcontinental journey to enable fitting in as many slave-hands as possible in the ship's bunker, with bodily functions performed in that position.[5] Britain, Portugal, Spain, France, the Netherlands, Denmark-Norway, Sweden, Courland (in today's Latvia), Brandenburg-Prussia and various Italian states and traders from Brazil and the United States took part in the trade. The Africans were sourced in Senegambia, Upper Guinea, Windward Coast, Gold Coast, Benin, Biafra and Angola.[6] It is not easy to imagine the extent of not just the robbing of human dignity, but of the transfer of human resources and incentive to produce, from Africa to Western colonial powers over a period of over three centuries during which slavery prospered. Chapter 11 calls for reparations and reimbursement not in infrequent spurts by individual Western leaders with ephemeral guilt and fancies but through concerted multilateral efforts and sustained pressure.

[5] See Fleming and Benjamin (2011); Rawley and Behrendt (2009); and Thomas (2006) for a glimpse of the literature.

[6] The destination of slaves reveals a few surprises. For example, in total, approximately 5 per cent were shipped to North America and 40 per cent to Brazil. Thus, slavery was not just a North American phenomenon.

Certain themes emerge from the existing literature on the institution of slavery.[7] Slaves of African origin were excluded from ordinary societal access or functions where they were deposited. Once on shore, they were sold at auctions usually on the quay and became property of the purchasers, their families separated from one another for ever. Isolated into crowded living quarters, their only interaction with their owners was when they tilled their fields during which horsemen used whips to push them to increase productivity, slaughtered livestock or entered owners' homes – mainly female slaves – for domestic duties. The children of female slaves fathered by masters were not recognized by the birth fathers, leave alone by society.

Compensation programmes have been absent in modern US society except for a few instances of transporting Black children to white schools and a few experimental cash or benefit programmes for Blacks.[8] By contrast, post-independence India introduced laws to reserve public sector education and government positions for untouchables though it has not been able to thoroughly protect them from the receiving end of violence. This aspect will be examined in Chapter 6.

Residents of the US who have travelled across its vast geography and observed its socio-anthropogenic inheritance tend to view America's racial prejudice as probably being embedded in a large segment of the population from its very foundation. Thomas Jefferson who authored the US Declaration of Independence emphasizing, 'All men are born free', also wrote, 'slaves should be returned to Africa or the Caribbean'. But he considered 'such massive deportation a logistical and economic impossibility (thus) ending it (slavery) was inconceivable'. When he died, he freed barely seven slaves of the hundreds he owned.[9]

Jefferson, who became the third US president (1801–09), made derogatory notes on the physique of 'negroes' that are not quoted here, yet, ironically, had a sustained personal relationship with Sally Hemmings, a Black slave who bore him several children. Interestingly, their descendants comprise an identifiable extended family today though not formally recognized by the US authorities, reflecting a continuing ingrained streak in that society of a deep fear of its blood-stained past. The opinions, attitudes, treatments and

---

7 See Wilkerson (2020) for a recent comparative treatment of American slavery that compares it with India's caste system.

8 African American is, more often than not, used in current American parlance (until the emergence of the Black Lives Matter movement in 2020) while, across the Atlantic, Black has continued to represent the more prevalent usage. The latter is used here without any particular driving force, or lack of it, in its favour.

9 Jefferson owned, on average, about 200 slaves at any point in time, and slightly over 600 over his lifetime. See Thomas Jefferson in *Encyclopaedia Britannica*, www.britannica.com/biography/Thomas-Jefferson/Slavery-and-racism.

comments of slave owners towards their Black slaves can be deciphered from ample extractions from historical accounts. These aspects are eschewed and seldom taught as a part of the regular syllabus in American schools.

It is as if the perception of the intelligentsia in most societies suffers from an opaque looking glass through which inequality is viewed. Would it be justified to blame only a nation's founding fathers who declared independence from Britain in 1776? For some years after the 1861–65 civil war and abolition of slavery, the Blacks improved their condition through entrepreneurial and agrarian skills. A review of the post-civil war period is instructive. Abraham Lincoln, a Republican American President is usually linked to the abolition of slavery to which he is known to have had an aversion. However, his objective was not the abolition of slavery but the preservation of the American Union. He wrote in 1862,

> If I could save the Union without freeing any slave I would do it, and if I could save it by freeing all the slaves I would do it. What I do about slavery, and the coloured race, I do because I believe it helps to save the Union.[10]

Indeed, Lincoln had contemplated transporting Blacks to Liberia in Africa, the Caribbean or Central America though such a project failed to take off. In the event, abolition through his Emancipation Proclamation enabled Lincoln to recruit Blacks in the Union army with 180,000 of them having served by the end of the civil war. In contrast to this relatively benign position, Alexander Stephens, Vice President of the southern Confederacy, had declared that slavery was a 'normal condition of the Negro (who) is not equal to the white man'. Contrastingly, Frederick Douglas, a Black abolitionist, wrote that the civil war was 'a contest between civilisation and barbarism'. Nevertheless, after their defeat, through a Proclamation of Amnesty and Reconstruction, the seceded southern states were allowed to claw back into the Union even if only 10 per cent of their voters were in favour of abolition. Thus, the fundamental underlying premise in favour of slavery in effect remained intact by a large majority. Further, there was no mention of Black suffrage or compensation.

After 1867, radical Republicans who were of the view that the fabric of southern society needed to be changed, took charge of reconstruction policy. It required states to adopt the 14th Amendment – granting citizenship to those born on American soil and allowing Blacks to vote – of the Union constitution. It was a short period when Black vigilance grew, with 90 per

10 Excerpted from Lincoln's letter to Horace Greely, a publisher, *The Economist*, December 2020, p 118.

cent of southern Blacks voting in elections, electing over 2,000 local and 185 federal (central) representatives including Black senators and a Black governor of the state of Mississippi. Some states introduced a wife's divorce and property rights, and provisions for state-run schools and orphanages, though little attempt was made to integrate schools for Black and white pupils. By the time their tenures were completed, Blacks in high-level elected representations vanished and their presence would not emerge for almost a century thereafter. The reasons for such a short-lived era of Black representation is elaborated next.

Economic redressals did not follow abolition. Freed slaves who wanted to buy land – having tilled the soil for their masters – were thwarted because small plots were not made available for purchase except in a couple of states. Conditions such as 'worthy and intelligent' in a jury were introduced that enabled the passive exclusion of Blacks from many walks of life and, therefore, from avenues to earn equivalent returns to work and life as whites. New 'Black Codes' incarcerated Blacks for the slightest infractions under 'vagrancy' and 'malicious mischief' rules that barred them from freedom and work. Such policies came into being with the tacit collaboration of southern Republicans and northern non-radical, moderate Democrats. Thus, the southerners were successful in finding their way back to their avowed policy adherence of exclusion, isolation and domination. Proposed laws would disallow Blacks to work in any job other than as servants or farmers forbidding them from leaving any job before a year, failing which a tax of US $1,600 (today's) would be levied. However, its passage was avoided by counter-interest groups. Soon campaigns of racial terrorism began to emerge which local authorities refused to retaliate against.

Though the Republicans won in the 1872 elections, radicalism had gone out of vogue since any federal support for reconstruction was absent. Thus, the equality project, if there had been one, for Blacks and whites, had a short life of about a decade. The southern whites saw the end of reconstruction as their 'Redemption'. Though the 13th Amendment had abolished slavery, enslavement crept in through the burden of heavy debt imposed on Blacks incurred for the slightest infringements who, therefore, remained chained to southern masters. Black-owned banks were systematically closed in the southern Richmond-Atlanta belt, Black businesses were obliterated in thriving Black communities in Oklahoma and western states, the socio-economic programmes were gutted including refusal of mortgage loans to Blacks in Baltimore and the eastern belt and the encouragement of owner-occupied housing became declared government policy, disabling Blacks from ownership.

Mention must be made of the Tulsa Massacre in Oklahoma on 31 May–1 June, 1921. A thriving Black community had achieved economic success in the Greenwood district of Tulsa comprising 35 city blocks. It had become a repository of Black businesses and came to be called the Black Wall Street despite stringent racial segregation laws that challenged Black lives and living. Trumped up charges reported in the *Tulsa Tribune* against Dick Rowland, a Black teenager, for assaulting a white teenager triggered a pogrom of the entire neighbourhood leaving some 300 dead and 300,000 displaced. The annals of US racial history reveal the removal of photographic evidence by the Tulsa police and the silence of the remaining Black population in the area for fear of a backlash (Messer, 2021; Ellsworth 1992 and 2021). This is a feature of society that has not vanished from sporadic practices in today's US society. To quote Gilroy (2019), 'News can be faked and spun, and truth held hostage, not by the politics of knowledge but by the political machinery that assembles carefully-managed ignorance, a curated ignorance' (p 2). It took a century for the US to set up an inquiry commission on the Tulsa Massacre and issue a report in 2021. The fact remains that this single event possibly ended Black entrepreneurship for the better part of a century that followed even as mortgages and business loans to Blacks essentially disappeared as the grip of segregation, isolation and extraction based on a racial ideology, unchanging at its core, tightened around Black communities across the country. It is in this context that Rhodes (2021) asked, '2021 marks the hundredth anniversary of the 1921 race massacre in Tulsa, Oklahoma. Will it take another hundred years before our nation has full and complete clarity about what happened?' (p 44). Such policies and events crested with the emergence of the Ku Klux Klan in the southern belt of Alabama and Louisiana, where total racial segregation was imposed, and Blacks were lynched regularly, hung head down, and burnt alive with impunity. To check some of the continuing mayhem, the US Congress passed on powers to the southern states with the apparent objective of better control of such extreme events but, ironically, it allowed southerners to solidify discrimination against Blacks in various forms. From 90 per cent during reconstruction, by the mid-20th century, only 7 per cent of Blacks remained registered to vote in southern states such as Mississippi. With the decline in the Black voter rolls, Black representation in elected offices also vanished. Most shockingly, historians regularly blamed southern Blacks for their ills, for Black southerners 'exercised an influence in political affairs out of all relation to their intelligence'.[11]

Others opposed this view including Du Bois (1935) who found that southern whites were firm believers and adherents to racist society and rule, and violence against Blacks had led to the failure of reconstruction. In an influential anthropological analysis of selected Black individuals in a poor

[11] 'The Dunning School', William Dunning, early 20th century. See Smith and Lowery (2013).

Washington DC neighbourhood, Liebow (1967), using interviews of Blacks found in street corners, demonstrated that Blacks had ordinary middle-class hopes. Yet, due to social barriers and obstacles, in every case study, they were cowed down into non-aspirational roles and states of existence. Later, Moreno-Leguizamon (1995), in a series of complex interviews of two parties, a Black ex-drug user and his white counsellor, demonstrated the divergence in communication between them despite apparent interest in a solution, buttressing his analysis with citations from television commercials on the dangers of drug use in which users were always Black and counsels were white.[12]

Martin Luther King, the activist and orator had declared, 'I have a Dream', and gave speed to the Civil Rights Movement in the US in the 1960s. At his death in mid-2020, Joseph Lowery, a firebrand pacifist preacher and an associate of King, as many other associates perhaps realized, expressed that King's 'Dream' of equality had been frustrated. Ironically, John Fitzgerald Kennedy, a northern US president (1961–63) from Massachusetts was sceptical about the entire Civil Rights matter and felt that he was being dragged into it. Lyndon B. Johnson, a southern president from Texas who followed as president after Kennedy was assassinated, was less ambivalent.

In prevailing times, there are pockets of phenomenal Black success including biracial president Barack Obama, the first female vice-president Kamala Harris of mixed race, recent Secretaries of State and Defence, a handful of US Senators, professionals who live along 16th Street directly north of the White House in Washington DC, or Atlanta, the capital of the southern state of Georgia, who have, by and large, all ascended the career ladder entirely on their own merit rather than through any comprehensive support policy or programme of the state. But deterioration in the condition of US Blacks at societal level has not changed and has been a centuries-long dilemma, the question being, what proportion of the US population, actually thinks so. The continuing occurrences culminated in the 2020 Black Lives Matter movement that started after the death by asphyxiation in broad daylight of George Floyd, a Black individual, on the roadside by a white policeman buttressed by his protective colleagues. These kinds of events were, and are, commonplace. It was happenstance that a Black woman recorded on her mobile phone the entire nine minutes of Floyd's asphyxiation until his breathing stopped.

---

[12] Liebow and Moreno-Leguizamon carried out their work at universities in Washington DC, the former at The Catholic University of America and the latter at Howard University that had been established as a premier Black institution in an era of racial segregation and racism.

America's treatment of excluding, isolating and dominating Blacks even after the abolition of slavery essentially explains the latter's inability to earn incomes and an irretrievable income and wealth gap during the past one and a half centuries that, in fact, worsened over the past 50 years. Most recently, it became even worse during the COVID-19 pandemic. The resultant rage was waiting to boil over. George Floyd's murder, in the worst display of police brutality of asphyxiation of a Black man by a white policeman's knees pressed on the former's neck, witnessed by the public, was the catalyst of what grew into global rage. As Prideaux (2021) recently said, 'the first thing to understand is why it was Mr. Chauvin's knee that was on Mr. Floyd's throat, and not the other way around'. The previous description of the history of slavery and its continuing manifestations perhaps gives a clue to the explanation of that mystery.

Dissecting race

What is mysterious in the US's race war is that, while whites in history could have perceived Blacks as fundamentally different due to their appearance, the fact of overt similarity of all races has become increasingly clearer to the modern human over the last century; yet discrimination continues oblivious to that knowledge. In a demolition of race difference, Shipman (1994) analysed race differences and provided certain facts,

> Anthropologists generally agree that the oldest known evidence of our genus and species comes from Africa. As Christopher Stringer (1993), one of the main protagonists in ongoing debates, says, 'We are all Africans under the skin.' … . Negroid peoples of the world may well have been the first to achieve anatomical modernity. (p 267)
>
> Drawing a line around an ephemeral entity like a human race is an exercise in futility and idiocy. The apartheid former government of South Africa foundered in its attempts to define racial categories and created a system rife with inconsistencies. (p 263)[13]

Shipman listed three hypotheses on the origin of race,

[13] See Tobias (1972). Nevertheless, the National Party introduced apartheid in 1948 in which different races could not socialize, leave alone marry. Geographical locations for ownership of property and workplace were pre-assigned. In 1970, Blacks were shorn of their citizenship and were designated to live in homelands, termed Bantustans, comprising mainly arid pockets in the hinterland.

(i) 'the multi regionalism hypothesis that has a markedly inclusive, rather than exclusive … regional groups of human ancestors evolved into modern humans – not instantaneously, but simultaneously over a prolonged period of time – in various parts of the world, evolving from the species *Homo erectus* to *Homo sapiens*;[14]

(ii) the Out of Africa hypothesis that "emphasizes that all modern humans share a recent common ancestry that makes racial distinctions recent and biologically trivial" (p 268); and

(iii) the Mitochondrial DNA (or mtDNA) indicator believed to be inherited solely through the maternal line (leading to) a complexity of defining races due to extensive inbreeding among various populations'. (p 269)

The author continued,

> The most universally accepted conclusion is this: that humans are closely related to chimpanzees – over 99 percent of our genes are held in common with the chimpanzee – that the differences among the human races are swamped by the tremendous genetic unity among them … . (Thus) less than one percent of our genes can possibly differ from one another. How can the differences be anything but trivial …? (p 269)

It is noteworthy that whether a person is formally categorized as Black or white depends on the 'Blood quantum' law of a particular US state. Thus, in Louisiana, a southern state, sufficiency of being Black until 1983 was arithmetically specified as anyone having one thirty-second or more of 'Negro blood' should be designated as Black by Louisiana state officials. This led to many a surprise for persons who applied for a passport and found out for the first time that he or she was Black. It took a long court case and much financial resources to be spent for the law to change. Indeed, several states had adopted a 'one drop' of blood rule for Black classification though the federal government did not ratify it.

This volume is not intended to be on US race history but one case from 1923 that stands out and is useful to cite is that of Bhagat Singh Thind who, to halt a second revocation of his application for citizenship, argued that technically he was both Caucasian and Aryan and should, therefore, be considered white and be granted citizenship. The US Supreme Court

---

14 It is currently known that all archaic humans including *Homo erectus*, *Homo floresiensis*, *Homo heidelbergensis*, *Homo neanderthalensis*, *Homo denisova*, *Homo sapiens* and others if any, emanated in Africa, and migrated through the Horn of Africa to the Levant, and populated the globe. Shipman mocks the use of *sapiens* – which means 'wise' – for humans, as audacious (p 268).

admitted that he may be technically Caucasian but ruled unanimously that common knowledge did not equate Caucasian to being white and thus Singh was not white.[15] Retrospectively all Indians were classified as non-white and stripped of US citizenship and land rights. So much for India's own fixation over race – Aryan-Dravidian – caste and untouchability despite the Indian constitution having abolished it in 1950 (see Chapter 6). It is hardly surprising that Shipman expressed the view that the matter of classification of races is idiocy.

Statistical evidence from the US

Evidence from the Pew Research Center, known for surveys and statistics, is drawn, beginning with inequality and then injecting racial inequality into the picture.[16] Figure 5.1 demonstrates unequal income growth over the past 50 years across groups. Between 1970–2018, median middle-class income increased from $58,100 to $86,600, or 40 per cent.[17] Nevertheless, for upper-income households, the increase was from $126,100 to $207,400, or 64 per cent. Lower-income households experienced an increase from $20,000 to $28,700, or 28 per cent. Over the time period specified, therefore, income inequality worsened significantly.

The incomes of the top 5 per cent grew at the fastest rate. Blacks are scarce at the top and crowd the bottom, with only four Blacks in Fortune 500's chief executive officers earning above US $14.5 million in 2018.[18] If a Black individual earns $60,000 annually, he or she gets to the top 10 per cent Black decile. It is $118,000 for whites and $135,000 for Asians.[19]

Figure 5.2 reveals a similar trend for wealth. The median wealth of middle-income households increased in the 1983–2001 period from $102,000 to $144,600, or by 42 per cent, for lower-income families from $12,300 to

---

15 United States versus Bhagat Singh Thind, 261 US 204 (1923). See JUSTIA, US Supreme Court. Available at https://supreme.justia.com/cases/federal/us/261/204/, accessed 28 June 2021.

16 The middle-income category comprises households with 2/3 to 2 times the overall median family income in 2018. The range comprises $40,100 to $120,400 for a three-person household. Those above and below comprise high income and low-income categories respectively. Median is where most families are clustered.

17 The original data source for these estimates is Current Population Survey, Annual Social and Economic Supplement for 1971 to 2019. In the survey, respondents provide household income data for the previous calendar year. Thus, income data refer to the 1970–2018 period.

18 Henceforth $ refers to US$.

19 This reveals that the top white decile earns twice, and the top Asian 2.25 times, as much as the top Black decile.

Figure 5.1: US median income (2018 $)

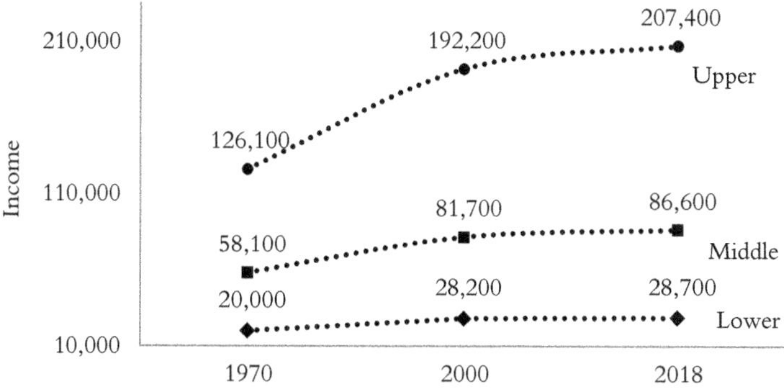

Source: Pew Research Report, Pew Research Center

Figure 5.2: US median wealth (2018 $)

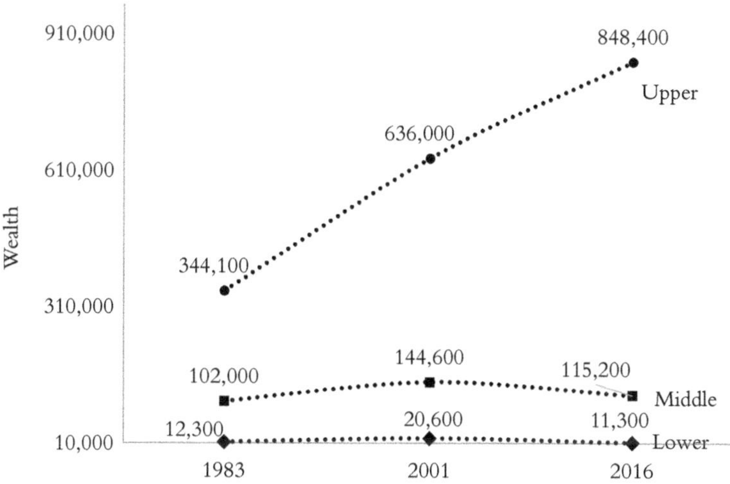

Source: Pew Research Center

$20,600 or by 67 per cent[20] and for upper-income families from $344,100 to $636,000, or by 85 per cent. The wealth gap between upper-income and lower- and middle-income families grew wider during 2001–16 when upper income households were 7.4 times more wealthy than middle-income ones, and 75 times wealthier than lower-income households. These proportions

[20] Though the percentage increase for lower income households is higher than for middle income households, their absolute difference remained very wide.

Figure 5.3: US racial wealth divide (2019 $)

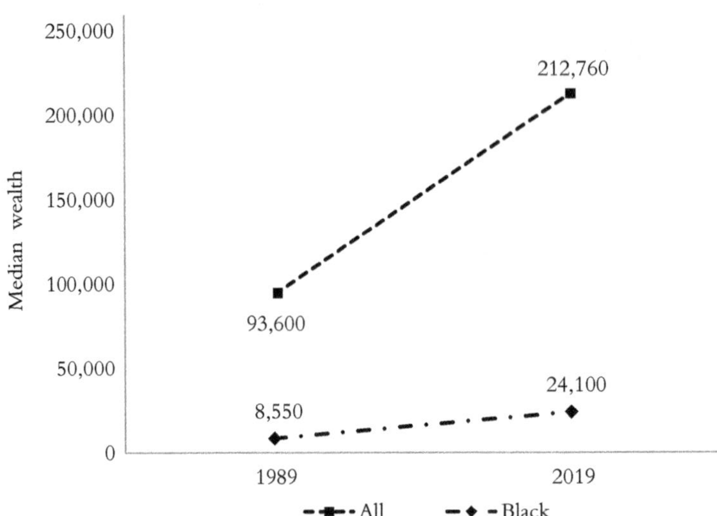

Source: Survey of Consumer Finances (inequality.org)

were 3.4 and 28 in 1983, respectively, revealing phenomenal worsening of wealth ownership over five decades.[21]

Figure 5.3 shows that the racial wealth divide has grown over the past three decades. The median Black family's wealth increased from $8,550 in 1989 to $24,100 in 2019, the overall median (including whites and Asians) increasing from $93,600 to $212,760. Between 2010 (15.5 per cent) and 2020 (9.9 per cent), the Black unemployment rate remained more than twice that of the whites.

A second dimension is to ask: can the situation change? An insight is the starkly opposing opinions of the Republicans and Democrats in a Pew survey of 6,878 adults of September 2019. While 60 per cent of Americans agree there is too much inequality, that figure hides the underlying story – only 40 per cent of Republicans in contrast to 80 per cent of Democrats do so. The Republicans feel personal factors explain inequality more – life choices, working less hard or crowding by immigrants – while Democrats emphasize racial discrimination, initial imbalance in opportunities, the educational system, the tax system, and the absence of corporate regulation. Republicans assign much less responsibility than Democrats to federal and state governments, corporations, wealthy individuals or churches for

[21] Counterintuitively, most of the economic progress of Blacks occurred before the civil rights legislation of the 1960s.

reducing inequality. Thus, attitudes to incomes and, associated with it, to race, remain deeply divided.

Measures such as ensuring acquisition of skills, increasing taxes on the wealthiest and transfers to the poor, eliminating college tuition and college debt, expanding medical benefits, increasing the minimum wage, and breaking up large corporations are viewed as significantly less important by Republicans than by Democrats; instead, Republicans consider illegal immigration much more detrimental than Democrats. Finally, three-fourths of the Republicans say that 'the poor have it easy because they can get government benefits without doing anything in return' as against one-fourth of the Democrats. Avarice seems tilted on one side.

There is a voluminous contemporary literature on inequality in the US, its ramifications, and experiments to alleviate it, much of it emanating as the long-term lingering effects of the institution of slavery. Some of this literature is summarized in Appendix 5.1.

The previously described trends are amplified when the COVID-19 pandemic is injected into the picture. According to the APM Research Lab, Black Americans have mortality rates that are significantly higher than all other race and ethnic groups except for Indigenous Americans. For each 100,000 Americans (of their respective group), 256 Indigenous Americans, 179 Blacks, 176 Pacific Islanders and 147 Latin people died from COVID-19, compared to 150 whites and 96 Asians, as of March 2021. Thus, as the pandemic proceeded, Indigenous Americans and Blacks suffered the highest actual COVID-19 mortality rates.[22] The higher death rate of Blacks reflects their continuation, despite health risks, in low-wage work in food-processing plants, grocery outlets and suchlike. The even higher death rate among the Indigenous Americans reflects the same reasons exacerbated by scarce health services in the Indian reservations.

A silver lining was the protests across the world by all races alike that 'Black Lives Matter' etched into the global social consciousness, and the final conviction of the policeman who asphyxiated George Floyd. This appeared to avenge the centuries long frustration with racism, if only symbolically. The election of Democrat Joseph Robinette Biden Jr, commonly known as Joe Biden, as president in 2021, buttressed by Vice President Kamala Harris of Indian and Black extraction, and a Democratic majority House of Representatives led by Nancy Pelosi, Speaker, who introduced a 'transformative structural change' programme, gave renewed hope. A Justice

[22] 'The colour of coronavirus: COVID-19 deaths by race and ethnicity in the U. S.', APM Research Lab, 5 March 2021. www.apmresearchlab.org/COVID/deaths-by-race, accessed 17 May 2021.

in Policing Act of 2020 was introduced by Pelosi and Senate Majority Leader Chuck Schumer with the support of a strong Congressional Black Caucus. As she unveiled the bill, Pelosi read out the names of Black men and women who died at the hands of police in recent years.[23] Cheered on by President Joe Biden, this was the most ambitious effort in decades by House Democrats to overhaul policing nationwide. The proposed Act was approved 220–212 on Wednesday, 3 March 2021.[24] It is astonishing then that the incidence of loss of Black lives at the hands of American police continues to occur even after the passage of the Act.

Donald Trump, the president prior to Joe Biden, left an indelible wound on the American psyche by regurgitating and intensifying the existing racial divide. Yet there was a ray of hope when there was denouncement of Trump's actions by Trump's defense secretary and army chief of staff and by Republican senators such as Mitt Romney, and apologies by a serving four-star general, all of whom expressed disagreement with the serving president. Only the election of Joe Biden as president revived expectation of a serious challenge to exclusion, isolation and domination of Blacks moving forward.[25] Nevertheless, a foreboding looms in the air as strong indications are that of a backlash gathering strength from Trump supporters in the proximate US presidential elections. Clearly the race war in the US is far from won.

Global colonialism

The complexity of the story of colonialism emerges from a long-standing debate over its pros and cons. This discussion was comprehensively presented by Gardner and Roy (2020) in a survey and analysis of the relevant literature. One strand that did not perceive any net benefit from colonialism to the imperial states – colonial home economies – was of the view that it affected overall economic growth adversely, with high costs to the exchequer for operations, maintenance and upkeep, while primarily benefitting a political and financial elite in those economies. French analysts also argued about the preponderance of benefits accruing to a small coterie of colonialists in the name of the French people. Belgium could also be cited where expenditures

---

[23] BBC (2020a), US Democrats introduce sweeping legislation to reform police, BBC News, 9 June 2020, www.bbc.com/news/world-us-canada-52969375, accessed 6 May 2021.

[24] With Biden's backing, Democrats revive George Floyd police reform bill, 3 March 2021, www.mprnews.org/story/2021/03/03/with-bidens-backing-dems-revive-george-floyd-police-reform-bill, accessed 6 May 2021.

[25] To this day, however, the question of reparations has not had any serious take-up though selected towns and academia including Asheville in North Carolina, Evanston in Illinois and Georgetown University have moved towards acknowledging moral responsibility for slavery and segregation.

of the Congo Free State area had to be initially assumed by the king from his personal funds reflecting the unpopularity of the project. Subsequently, expenditures turned out to be very high and, compounded by atrocities in tax collection, the government took over the region's governance from the monarchy.

The opposite strand argued that the export markets that colonies provided benefitted the home countries so that, if colonies were to be abandoned, the vacuum created would be filled by other imperial states. Indeed, the colonial power and reach of Britain could not be equaled by others such as Belgium, France or Germany that nevertheless strove for comparable presence. In reviewing the rates of growth of selected colonies, Gardner and Roy (2020) concluded that, in the sixteenth century, the per-capita gross domestic products (GDPs) of China and India were comparable to those of the later European colonizers. Through the colonization period, however, both China and India suffered declining per-capita GDP until the departure of the colonizers.

Focusing on India, several studies such as by Sen (1981); Mukerjee (2010); and Dalrymple (2019) to name a few, established this fact so that, in the final analysis, it is difficult to identify many researchers in present times who could sing the praises of a colonial era that favoured the colonized. Even though a few colonies gained in particular in Latin America such as Mexico that compared well with Spain, by and large such gains accrued mainly to the colonial owners and the locally created gentry who ruled on their behalf at the cost of the vast majority of the colonies' populations.

Roy's (2020) analysis indicated that, though the average rate of growth of per-capita national income was low, those of industry and services – in the deltaic and seaboard regions in particular where cities grew – were higher, while that of agriculture in the hinterland and drylands was lower where rural activities predominated. Thus, British colonialism in India made some livelihoods rich and left some others poor. To note, at the time of India's independence in 1947, the British left behind infrastructure comprising ports, canals, sanitation, medical care, urban waterworks, universities, a postal system, courts of law, railways, the telegraph, meteorological office, statistical systems and scientific research laboratories. Roy (2020) clarified that these were built with British knowhow and Indian assistance and were built to assist governance directly or indirectly. They also helped private enterprise and improved the quality of life. Nevertheless, the fact remained that there was scant development in the interiors whose governance was left to the local landlords whose role was mainly to collect land revenue from the rural poor. Given that the rural agricultural population comprised almost three-quarters of the country's population, inequality increased and exacerbated regional differences in incomes. It is not surprising that the not so well-known Bengal famine of 1943–44 killed some 3 million Bengalis even during the final period of British rule.

Gardner and Roy (2020) found that inequality increased in most colonized economies. Studies of African colonies, for example, have indicated that the average height and weight of local populations in Kenya and Ghana decreased though the conditions of some ethnic groups improved, revealing differences in the effects of colonial rule among regions. In this context, Roy (2020) questioned whether there indeed was any deep-seated colonial legacy in the form of colonial institutions that the lean and ephemeral European presence might have left behind. Here the available literature reveals that, in India, despite the provision of socio-economic infrastructure by the British in cities and towns, indigenous institutions under the princely states of India that ruled as British protectorates provided better health, education and roads than did those regions that the British ruled directly. Also, the indigenous commercial class suffered. For example, though industrialization in India was not banned, there is evidence that within textiles for example, India made yarn while cloth manufacture was essentially transferred to Britain; thus, India was relegated to the role of supplier of intermediate products and raw materials. The production of cloth and clothing was supplied back to India for their consumption.

Gardner and Roy (2020) concluded that, despite the European colonial presence being minimal in terms of numbers, during the colonial period, income distributed to colonies worsened. In what follows, the experiences in the colonies owned and governed by most European imperial states and their impact on exclusion and extraction and, in turn, on inequality and poverty, are discussed.

Exclusion practices of colonial Britain

In the case of Britain, as mentioned earlier, the British appear to have written off the reality of their colonial history other than a regular litany of contributions to colonial development if not to civilization itself. Their role in the extraction of resources by their forceful transfer from the colonies as well as their widespread practice of the slave trade and indentured servitude involving trans-continental mass transportation are all but written off from textbooks.

A seminal work on British rule and its link to Indian poverty was authored by Naoroji (1901–02)[26] who, in his *Poverty and un-British Rule*,

[26] Dadabhai Naoroji (1825–1917) was the first Asian to be a Member of Parliament (1892–95) in Britain, a founding member of the Indian National Congress, being elected thrice in 1886, 1893 and 1906, an unstoppable correspondent with the British government, and an author of many books. See Patel (2021).

his magnum opus of more than 500 pages of small print, brought to attention the impact of British presence in India on the precipitation and ramifications of poverty and the breaking of solemn pledges made earlier by Britain. That presence and role resulted in a wealth drain which he called 'destructive and despotic' (p iii) and clarified thus, 'owing to the enhanced demand for the produce of … the increased industry of the subjects of the State … there is reason to conclude that the benefits are more than counterbalanced by the evils inseparable from the system of a remote foreign dominion' (p iv).

Almost a century later, Sen (1981) commented,

> A capitalist economy will not only *permit* the private ownership of means of production; that is indeed one of its main *foundations*. On the other hand, a capitalist economy – like a socialist one – will not permit ownership of one human being by another, as a slave economy will. A socialist economy may restrict the employment of one person by another for production purposes, i.e. constrain the possibility of private trading of labour power for productive use. A capitalist economy will not, of course, do this, but may impose restrictions on binding contracts involving labour-power obligations over long periods of time. This, however, is the standard system under some feudal practices involving bonded labour, and also in some cases of colonial plantations. (p 3)

The use of indentured servitude by Britain was pervasive across its East Asian and Caribbean colonies allowing it to transport masses of labour across continents mainly to grow sugarcane in Fiji, British Guyana, Mauritius and other remote places where the transported populations were subjected to the most heinous conditions unfathomable under acceptable standards today. Sugar was of such high value reflecting growing demand in Britain and Europe that local populations in its colonies were used under the most stringent conditions for growing sugarcane. One example was Malaysia where, even after India, Myanmar, Pakistan and Sri Lanka had gained independence by the end of the 1940s, Britain refused to accede independence and carried out a violent 12-year war in the name of combatting communism. The reality was that Malaysia was one of the rapidly dwindling direct sources of low-cost sugar as colonies were slipping out of its grasp one by one. It was not uncommon for the colonial rulers to shoot every farmer in a plantation if there was any suspicion that they were communist sympathizers. Indeed, Malaysia could be viewed as Britain's colonial Vietnam.

Remarkably, just as Britain's colonial role has been obliterated from British school and college curricula to the extent that British youth could be said to possess nil knowledge of that three-century long chapter of their history, so the deleterious practices of caste established in India's ancient texts are still being perpetuated by Indians on their compatriots. The difference is that post-independence, successive Indian governments have attempted to ameliorate centuries of caste discrimination with equalization policies against caste differences. This was to be achieved through reserving, for lower castes, guaranteed school entry, public sector jobs and political positions such as for members of parliament hailing from untouchable castes who, post-independence, were renamed as 'scheduled castes' and 'scheduled tribes' (SC/ST). No such equalization programme or truth commission such as in South Africa after the demise of its apartheid regime has been attempted in British society. On the contrary, on the back of its history built on the shoulders of slavery, indentured servitude and racial laws, the UK governments of prevailing era have attempted to transport back selectively identified Black populations to their original countries, a recent example being what has been infamously termed the Windrush episode of 2019–20. In a final blow, a 2021 government report concluded that there was no 'systemic racism' in Britain, implying that any racism that might exist had nothing to do with its societal arrangements or government policies and practices.[27]

In recent terminology, Britain has set aside any idea or consideration of the existence of 'otherness'.

To quote Ashcroft et al. (2007) describing Spivak's (1987) concept, 'The process by which imperial discourse creates its 'others' … the other is the excluded or "mastered" subject created by the discourse of power. Othering describes the various ways in which colonial discourse produces its subjects' (p 156). Writing from the corner of the indigenous Maori in New Zealand, Tuhiwai Smith (2021) wrote,

> They are views which invite a comparison with 'something/someone else' which exists on the outside, such as the oriental, the 'Negro', the 'Jew', the 'Indian', the 'Aborigine'. (p 33)
>
> We believe that history is also about justice, that understanding history will enlighten our decisions about the future. *Wrong*. History is also about power. In fact, history is mostly about power. It is the story of the powerful and how they became powerful, and then how they use

[27] It is ironic that, in 1999, a UK government report entitled the Macpherson Report 'dubbed the police institutionally racist'. *The Economist*, 19 June 2021. Yet, within just two decades, a commission set up by the ruling government could not find any instance of systemic – implying institutional – racism in British society.

> their power to keep them in positions in which they can continue to dominate others. (p 35)

Britain's interest in the recognition of 'others', leave alone significant compensation or reparations for them, appears to have been put on the back burner at the behest of powerful sections of society for government to have issued the above-cited 2021 report regarding racism in Britain.

Bhambra (2021) pointed out an opacity that Piketty's (2020) work suffered from in that the latter interpreted the two world wars of the twentieth century as 'genocidal self-destruction' between the European powers (2020, p 19) while ignoring their colonial subjects who died fighting for them (not to mention the genocidal violence associated with colonialism itself). She pointed out that Piketty erroneously compressed the sources of inequality to 'the two world wars, the Bolshevik Revolution of 1917, and the Great Depression of 1929' (2020, p 30), but not the processes of decolonization that transformed the world and Europe with it, from the time of independence of Ireland in 1922. In 2020, when the statue of Edward Colston, a slave trader, was brought down by Black Lives Matter activists in Bristol, four were charged by the Crown Prosecution Service (CPS) with suspected criminal damage over the toppling of the statue.[28] It would not be too out of place to ask if it would not have been more appropriate for government to draw up a resolution to remove all statues of persons associated with the slave trade from public view and place them, for example, in a museum display – in a basement perhaps – where they would not continue to draw public ire while researchers could continue to have access to them.

Indeed, this has occurred with the Bristol statue but zero progress has been reported with respect to statues of other slave traders including Cecil Rhodes (1853–1902) in whose name the well-known Rhodes Scholarship has brought scores of Commonwealth students to study in the University of Oxford. Indeed, Oriel College on whose façade a statue of Rhodes is lodged, refused to take it down despite 150 Oxford dons publishing an open letter threatening to boycott the college, stop teaching its students and attending its seminars. Instead, the deification of the fruits of slavery – exclusion, isolation, domination and extraction – was effectively accommodated and perhaps consolidated and perpetuated into UK history. That does not, of course, mean that a future government will not veer away from that course for history can, and has been, rewritten. Neither has it meant that all Britons are party to such policies. A significant number strategize and participate in the Black Lives Matter movement, or carry out research and

[28] BBC (2020b), 'Edward Colston statue: Cases sent to Crown Prosecution Service', BBC News, 17 September 2020. Available at www.bbc.com/news/uk-england-bristol-54191039.

write, and regularly demonstrate against any policy that smacks of a racial tone or content.

Thus, first, it is the historical role of Britain in extracting from its colonies, a role that was ardently pointed out by Naoroji (1901–02) and revived with some intensity by Bhambra (2021); Dalrymple (2019); Mukerjee (2010); Sen (1992); Reddy (2021); Shome (2021) and others, that is so important to keep in view. In addition, second, it is the continuation of exclusion, isolation, domination, and a continued proffering of justification of its past and present policies that protect Britain from itself under a shroud. And Britain continues to sharpen this policy by its unwillingness to touch the issue in schools, universities, private clubs, literary discussions, or the wider establishment with which it is replete.

The meticulous research of Naoroji (1901–02) brought forward the matter of 'colonial drain' – that the British empire extracted much more from India than it ever gave back – up front. Later, Sen (1992) made detailed calculations of the extent of it. Recently, Bhambra (2021) took up extensively the issue of colonial drain from India that took place during British colonial rule through obligatory tribute, taxation and remittances. Shome (2021) described the nature of extractive taxes in some detail, for example, of boastful reports in the British parliament of enhancement of land revenue even during famine and despite abandonment of their land by farmers and the flight of labour under excruciating circumstances. Taxes on basic necessities such as salt, fines for extracting salt from the sea, and other impositions continued unabated. To recall Sen (1992),

> For the colonial administration the most important objectives with regard to the functioning of the Indian economy were: (i) to maintain the Indian market for British manufactures; (ii) to ensure the remittance on government account to meet the disbursements in Britain; and (iii) to ensure the remittance of returns on British investment in India. (p 137)

By the 1850's – a century following Robert Clive's 1757 victory in the War of Plassey – land revenue from India increased at a lower rate than prices, but that was more than compensated by an absolute and relative increase in indirect taxation.[29] Non-tax factors including deindustrialization[30] and a steep rise in agricultural indebtedness together with stagnated agricultural

[29] Moosvi (2008), p 24.

[30] The period 1840–1900 experienced import value of cloth increasing rapidly compared to that of yarn. Yet, cloth had to be imported rather than be produced in India from imported yarn (Table 1.18, Moosvi [2008], p 27).

wages exacerbated the depleted human condition in India. Real wages declined significantly between Akbar, the Mughal Emperor's reign (1556–1605) and the end of the nineteenth century, that is, well into the British period. Indeed, per capita income declined over the three centuries 1600–1900,[31] the structure of GDP remaining unchanged rather than moving in favour of industry. Under such stagnant conditions, extraction of taxes must have overburdened all producers – agricultural and non-agricultural – in the economy.

Britain was able to intensify its extractive policies by suppressing the 'Great Uprising of 1857' with the last Mughal Emperor, the uprising's token leader, being banished to Burma, and his sons executed (Ali, 2021). Nothing less than a mayhem of slavery-like poverty generation through extraction of revenue and crops irrespective of prevailing economic conditions, ensued. It reduced the earlier, fertile and prosperous regions of Bengal and Madras to famine and penury. While the German Nazis focused and concentrated their annihilation policies in a capsule of time, the British dragged isolation, extraction and reductive policies across centuries. In its long-term aspects, Britain remained unmatched in the policies it sculpted and implemented.

The diversion of production to Britain coupled with the extraordinary extraction through taxation and other means led to an excruciating burden on India's poor, continuing unabated until India's independence. Between 1860 and 1880 when severe production shortfalls in agriculture were experienced due to famines with resultant shortages in supply and deaths, marketed surplus was attempted to be maintained 'in part (through) compulsory extraction in the form of land revenue, rent and interest'.[32] Agricultural exports did not diminish in any significant scale, thus causing a severe imbalance between population and food availability; even industry was affected. Only export oriented industry was allowed – yarn, jute textiles, plantations and coal – that were the 'chosen fields of investment of British India'.[33]

India's accumulated reserves transferred and held in Britain – the Gold Standard Reserve – continued to grow, implying 'lost opportunities for reduction of taxes, or of immediate reduction of external debt', despite India paying higher interest on this debt compared to the interest it was earning from Britain on its reserves. Nevertheless, Britain's Royal Commission refused to recommend 'any upward limit on the accumulation in this reserve, and the reserve-to-import ratio went on rising'.[34] And taxes were not reduced either.

31 See Moosvi (2008), p 33.
32 Sen (1992), p 136.
33 Sen (1992), p 136.
34 Sen (1992), p 149.

Patnaik and Chakrabarti (2017) calculated that Britain drained an equivalent of $45 trillion from India during the period from the Battle of Plassey (1757) to the outbreak of the Second World War (1939) (Bhambra, 2021). Piketty did not bring into his consideration the impact of this on Britain's economy or to what extent the source of India's relative poverty today could be found in those colonial extractions that made Britain wealthy. Basically, Piketty failed to connect Britain or France's economic growth during the colonial period with their usurpation of the wealth of their colonies. Bhambra commented,

> Piketty's failure to acknowledge the common frame of empire as the condition from which nations subsequently emerged distorts his analysis of inequality on a global scale. By only comparing nations in the present and assessing the inequalities between them as consequent of their internal inequality regimes is to misunderstand the processes that have generated inequality globally … rather than an examination of the ways in which inequality has been produced through historically entangled colonial processes.
>
> European empires – such as those of Britain and France, or Germany – did not only have access to colonial 'treasure,' but also to populations to mobilize in their wars. Competition among them gave rise to wars which were rendered 'world wars' precisely because of the status of the respective powers as empires. Casualties and deaths among the colonized fighting on behalf of the metropole often exceeded those among the domestic population, especially in World War II. These wars were justified locally in 'nationalistic terms' binding populations to the imperial project of the nation, as part of the legitimation of their social and political structures. (p 77)

Only in 2021 did Britain finally recognize the deaths of soldiers from its colonies in the First World War. An independent inquiry commissioned by the UK Commonwealth War Graves Commission (CWGC) found that between 45,000 and 54,000 casualties of predominantly Indian, Egyptian, Somali and East and West African origins had occurred and that they had been commemorated 'unequally'. As many as 350,000 casualties, predominantly from East Africa and Egypt, were not commemorated by name or possibly not at all. Ben Wallace, the UK Defence Secretary, apologized for the lack of commemoration of those 350,000 First World War troops who had been buried in lumpy dumps in fields in the vicinity of manicured lawns with headstones for white casualties.

To continue with Bhambra's observation,

> It makes no sense to compare the economies of Britain and India over the long durée when for the two centuries prior to 1947 the wealth of India was siphoned off to the benefit of the British economy. What was true of Britain was also true of other European colonial powers. Not accounting for the historical processes and legacies of colonialism in the construction of inequalities both within and across countries is a fatal flaw in Piketty's analysis and undercuts the possibility of constructing a politics that could address the problems of our time. What is needed, instead, is a reconstructive postcolonial sociology that acknowledges the connected histories that have produced the present and seeks to address those inequalities through a commitment to global redistributive justice. (pp 77–78)

In continuation, Bhambra and Holmwood (2021) used a wider and deeper brush perhaps to paint a picture of the spoils of colonialism and its bequests in the development of modern Western society. Their attempt has been to decolonize contemporary social thought.

A mention must be made of Britain's differentiated product of exclusion, isolation and domination that it practised in South Africa after defeating Cetshwayo, the Zulu king, in the Anglo-Zulu War of 1879, under an 'apartheid' regime in its joint administration with Afrikaners of Dutch origin. Apartheid[35] policy comprised separating and isolating Black skin from white, from Indians, and from the coloureds of mixed race. Each group was separately housed, educated, and differently benefitted from any government expenditure. If they worked in white areas, they had to obtain passes and leave at night. Soweto, the sprawling main Black urban community, had no access to the highways that skirted all around it and served only the white population. Rural Black populations were sequestered in 'Homelands' that were carved out of the worst grade of land, more often than not uncultivable, so that many could not farm at all and were obliged to depend on canned food available in corner shops in their areas. It was not surprising that dissatisfaction burgeoned as poverty and inequality worsened and clashes between Blacks and the ruling regime took ominous form. What was even more revealing was that, even when Pieter Willem Botha, the last president of the apartheid regime, unleashed dogs and bullets on protesting Blacks in Soweto in the open view of a global television audience, Margaret Thatcher, then UK Prime Minister, and Ronald Reagan, then US President, refrained from condemning Botha.[36]

---

[35] Apartheid is an Afrikaans word meaning separateness, or 'apart-hood'. It could perhaps be interpreted as keeping hides apart.

[36] Thatcher was given a ceremonial funeral in 2013 attended by the British monarchy.

Nelson Mandela, the most revered post-war global statesman who became the first president of post-apartheid South Africa in 1994 after nearly three decades of incarceration for his movement for independence, appropriately expressed the view that, 'It would have been immoral to keep quiet while a racist tyranny sought to reduce an entire people into a status worse than that of beasts of the forest'.[37] Yet, was it the largeness of the heart of a person who was perhaps larger than life to take a post-apartheid view that could essentially be summarized as saying, let bygones be bygones? There was a Truth Commission in which all parties were invited to confess and assimilate into a racially integrated society but, again, there was no systematic redressal of poverty or inequality that had been generated through the application of the apartheid policy of exclusion, isolation and domination. By contrast, when neighbouring Rhodesia became independent assuming the name of Zimbabwe in 1980, and Robert Mugabe became its first president, he initiated land reform by transferring excess land in the hands of whites in favour of Blacks; the Western world condemned his actions, converting Zimbabwe effectively into a pariah state.[38]

Britain's sacking of Africa was not confined to southern Africa. Four thousand pieces of sculpture – the Benin bronzes – were seized in 1897 after sacking Benin, an ancient city in modern-day Nigeria. It was the year of the diamond jubilee of Victoria, queen of Britain. Dutch travellers two centuries earlier had observed Benin's main road as being seven to eight times wider than the widest in Amsterdam, with 30 very broad streets, the royal palace as large as the town of Haarlem itself and bedecked with long galleries decorated from top to bottom with cast copper, and the people as sincere and inoffensive. The error the *oba*, or ruler, made was to ask for a few weeks' postponement of a British regiment's visit to Benin so that he could spend some time in ritual contemplation. This was perhaps found to be an overbearing position. What followed was mindless slaughter of the same people by the regiment, its wholesale looting, the banishment of the *oba*, and public execution of his chiefs. The episode remains inexplicable to this day in academic circles (Phillips, 2021). Official institutions such as the British Museum have refused to return any of the bronzes, indeed, even to lend any of them for a short occasion (Hicks, 2020).[39] The prevailing

[37] See Chen (1990).

[38] The fact that Mugabe later became a despot was easy fodder to justify the view of the West.

[39] A request was made by Nigeria in 1977 to borrow an ivory mask showing Idia, a 16th century queen, to mark the Second World Black and African Festival of Arts and Culture in Lagos. It was refused by the British Museum, a position that it has basically not altered since. Smaller British museums, universities and the Church of England housing fewer Benin bronzes have, however, been open to the idea of repatriation of their bronzes.

British attitude has to be contrasted with an evolving corrective attitude of France and Germany that have begun reimbursement for their past colonial atrocities though in small amounts, a matter that is taken up next.

Complicity has been recently demonstrated not just with respect to private traders in slavery but by the state as well. Though the abolition of slavery by Britain was inevitable, Brown (2021), in a review of Rogers (2020) and Taylor (2020), pointed out that it was slow in coming with government conceding to gradual abolition – in four years, then seven years – revealing an 'inclination to concede the principle but postpone its application, perhaps indefinitely until 1833 … leaving a substantial record of government evasion, moderation, hesitance and deflection'[40] (p 25). Rogers described the anguish of an unnamed African woman slave left to die on board by the captain of a ship, Kimber; nevertheless, the High Court of Admiralty exonerated him in 1792. While some members of parliament found slavery loathsome, abolishing it was quite another matter. A few famous social reformers – such as Thomas Paine in 1774 – even left Britain out of disgust,[41] but they were few and far between. The slave trade grew rapidly over the next decade, with some 50,000 African slaves exported to the Americas per annum. Despite 519 petitions with 390,000 signatures to abolish the slave trade, it was ignored. With a revolt in the French slave colony of Saint Domingue (currently Haiti), the British establishment became anchored into a position of expanding its 'empire of slavery' (Brown, 2021, p 25).

Taylor revealed that investment in human property involved members of parliament, peers, civil servants, businessmen, financiers, landowners, clergymen, intellectuals, journalists, publishers, sailors and judges who, together, were responsible for protecting and preserving colonial slavery. In 1831, after an uprising by Jamaican slaves, an 'orgy of executions followed and for a year, Church of England vigilantes roamed the island terrorizing the Baptist clergy whom they blamed for inciting the revolt' (Brown, 2021, p 28). Thus, Taylor reminded the reader that slavery was not only done *to* people but that it was also done *by* people. It is not entirely surprising that the dithering by the modern British State is an unabashed policy veil that enables politicians to express abhorrence of racism yet find no institutional racism in their society.

[40] A project entitled Legacies of British Slave Ownership, conceived and executed by Catherine Hall and others of University College, London, has been successful in exposing the full extent of British investment in human bondage.

[41] In *Common Sense* (1776), Paine explained why. He found heredity on which Britain established a loathsome practice perpetuated by idiocy – the artificial noble sinking into a dwarf before the noble of nature.

French colonial extraction

The French colonial turpitude was no less by any measure. The works of Bhambra (2021) and Piketty (2020) are the most recent commentaries on its manifestations. France's treatment of Algerian soldiers with extreme brutality, its burdening Haiti with an unrepayable debt burden after granting Haiti its freedom from slavery, its daily manner of living such as converting hand-pulled rickshaws that were used in British colonies to hand-pushed rickshaws in the French Indian colonies such as Pondicherry, to avoid the sight of natives labouring to transport them, comprise a microcosm of their colonial behaviour from less than a century ago. Bhambra (2021) described France's treatment of Haiti in some detail. At the time of the French Revolution (1787–99), slave labour in Haiti produced raw materials including sugar, coffee and cotton, thus making it the most profitable French colony. They were turned into manufactured products in France, most of which were exported. Bhambra accepted Piketty's views that that era was 'an extreme and well-documented example of egregious colonial extraction' (2020, p 218) but pointed out that Piketty mistook the regime as merely proprietarian and viewed colonialism as an 'external' challenge to ownership societies, rather than viewing ownership societies as being formed through colonialism. She objected to his 'national' interpretation of history as opposed to a more 'colonial' interpretation.

Slavery had to be abolished in Haiti in 1793 when Haitian rebels obliged colonial commissioners to abolish slavery that initiated a thirteen year process termed the Haitian Revolution. It is remarkable that, nevertheless, slave property was turned into public debt that the new state of Haiti was forced to pay to compensate the erstwhile French slaveowners. This intrinsic colonial economic relationship that led to the stability of French interests through 'cultures that preferred to make their money through colonialism and slavery rather than through honest industry' (p 75) was entirely ignored by Piketty in Bhambra's assessment. Revealingly, after slavery was abolished, Indian labour was indentured for shipment to French plantations in Reunion and Mauritius who, thus, quickly replaced the enslaved. Bhambra critiqued that, beyond the mention of indentured servitude, 'there is no further discussion by Piketty on the use of indentured labour within European colonial plantations or how they contributed to the wealth of Europe and the poverty of the places from which human beings were taken' (p 75).

It should be recounted that the US too had an intrinsic interest in the subjugation of Haiti, employing the most ruthless actions there. While in their 1791–1804 revolutionary battles, Haitian slaves defeated the British, Spanish and French, thus becoming a hopeful symbol for abolitionists. Indeed, immigration from Haiti to the US took place and Chicago, a major US metropolis, was founded by Jean Baptiste Point du Sable, a Haitian immigrant. It was a foreboding for slaveowners. Even the celebrated US President Jefferson was on the latter's side. In the 20th century, Haiti's gold reserves were taken away with US interests introducing their own banks there. US Marines occupied Haiti in 1915 for two decades and ran it with extreme cruelty. The resistance fighter Charlemagne Peralite, for example, was spread-eagled on a cross like those lynched in the American South. Post-war US governments continued to buttress dictatorial governments led by the Duvaliers from whom the population fled abroad for three decades to the 1980s. It would not be wrong to recall that, in 1994, prior to another US interference, Joe Biden, currently US President, stated that Americans would not notice if Haiti sank into the sea.[42] Jovenel Moise, the last Haitian president who was strongly pro-Donald Trump, another US president, was assassinated on 7 July 2021 by his compatriots.

Returning to the role of France, its involvement in Africa took many forms of atrocities and extractions from Algeria as well as the ruthless use of one race against another such as in Rwanda. Two official reports were issued in 2021 on France's role in Africa and its actions during the Rwandan genocide of hundreds of thousands of Rwandans. The almost 1,000-page report on Rwanda exposed France's dismissive pooh-poohing during the presidency of Francois Mitterrand of accounts by reporters, academicians, officials and workers regarding Hutu atrocities.[43]

On 27 May 2021, during a visit to Kigali, Rwanda's capital, Emmanuel Macron, President of France, read out that 'France must look history in the face and recognise the share of suffering that it inflicted on the Rwandan people'. He continued, 'In ignoring the warnings of the most clear-sighted observers, France bore damning responsibility in a chain of events that led to the worst' and, without apologizing directly, expressed the hope that survivors of the 1994 genocide might 'perhaps forgive' France. He was referring to France's support of the majority French speaking Hutus who were responsible for the slaughter of minority English-speaking Tutsis.[44] It was not as if ex-colonial Britain had no interest in this (Carr [2015] and Cameron [2013]).

To understand Rwandan history in the context of colonial rule, Germans, who colonized Rwanda in 1899 had used a two-race policy for their own colonial benefit favouring mainly Tutsis and, thus, establishing a strong sense of separation between the minority Tutsis and majority Hutus. However, a 1916 League of Nations mandate at the end of the First World War passed

---

[42] Interview at the Public Broadcasting Service (PBS) on 9 December 1994, when he was US senator for the state of Delaware.

[43] See Kosicki (2007), Caplan (2008) and Wallis (2006).

[44] Hutus and Tutsis are two ethnically distinct tribal groupings. Eventually, an insurgency by the much smaller numbered Tutsis led themselves to come out on top.

on the administration of a portion of Rwanda to Belgium, the other portion getting merged with British Tanganyika (today's Tanzania). In 1928–29 and 1943–44, severe famines dispersed Rwandans to the neighbouring Congo and Uganda. Such travails, nonetheless, it was not surprising that there emerged two languages – French and English – that divided the population between Hutus and Tutsis respectively. Not only that, during the emergence of a period of eugenics or distinction among races, Europeans arrived in Rwanda to measure to differentiate the two races through skull and other body measurements. It may not be an exaggeration to observe that such European policies and field action enthused the minority Tutsis to develop a feeling of racial superiority over the Hutus and for the majority Hutus to harbour a strong sense of hatred against the Tutsis. It can only be hoped that the path President Macron began charting will not only compensate Rwanda in financial terms but also help progress to re-establish peace and harmony between the two groups.

German colonialism

Germany is usually recalled in the context of its Third Reich or the Nazi regime during the 1930s to 1945, when the end of the Second World War brought it to its knees. But its colonialism goes a long way back, for example in southern Africa, in particular, Namibia, where it carried out a genocide between 1904–08 on 75,000 of the Herero and Nama peoples. They were slain in battle, executed, starved in the Omaheke desert or worked unto death in labour camps. Germany did accept genocide as the appropriate word for what happened with reparations to be paid in the form of development aid. This is an admission of its past African colonialism that included economic exploitation, stolen treasures and immeasurable misery. Despite all its calls for human rights in other countries and how they may improve themselves, Britain has not apologized for any of its three centuries of slavery and colonialism combined. It could consider beginning by emulating Germany and admitting that 3 million Bengal inhabitants died through starvation by its diversion of cultivated crops to the war effort during 1940–43.[45] The peak of the famine was in 1943 though its aftershocks of cholera and typhoid led to further deaths and went beyond the end of the war.

During the Third Reich of Adolf Hitler, German Chancellor, some 6 million human beings from all over Europe – comprising mainly Jews but also other religious minorities, those considered racially inferior such as gypsies, and homosexuals – were annihilated. It is not a subject that is taken up elaborately in this volume – the episode is globally known, and

---

[45] See Sen (1981), Mukerjee (2010) and Dalrymple (2019) among others.

the story has been kept alive as it should be. At its side, one counter-fact should not be overlooked or ever forgotten though, by and large, history tends to de-emphasize it. To elaborate, Germany was not the only country that perpetrated Nazi policies during the war. Other countries such as the Croatian region, France and others that collaborated with the Nazis, did the same. France's Vichy regime that was in control during its Nazi occupation, collected and dispersed the same groups to concentration camps where they perished. To quote Ali (2021), 'It's a sordid history that the Gaullists and their successors (of most political persuasions) effectively covered up for decades. The reintegrated fascists played a horrific role during the Algerian war in both colony and metropolis' (p 11).

Netherlands' slavery and Belgium's colonialism

That the Netherlands used slavery as a primary tool of its economic progress has remained ensconced under its quilts to protect its brand as a small, peaceful country. The central element of its system of slavery was the economics of it, that is, the associated financial incentives. The reach of Dutch colonial plantations of coffee, spices and sugar included the Ganges Delta, Indonesia, Surinam, Curacao and the Caribbean into the mid-twentieth century. To take one example, in 1621, Pieterszoon Coen slaughtered 14,000 of the 15,000 inhabitants of Great Banda, a Moluccan island, and planted slaves there to grow nutmeg whose trade fetched multiple times the investment cost. Lukka (2020) narrates the record of Belgium:

> From 1908 onward, Belgium's occupation of Congo was a horrific regime and included massive expropriation of assets. In July this year, after campaigning, the Belgian parliament announced the establishment of a commission to examine the country's colonial past. The detrimental role of the World Bank is important here. In the 1950s, King Leopold II of Belgium ran up debt that financed projects in Belgian Congo, some of which was spent in Belgium. In 1960, this debt was unfairly transferred to the Congolese people at independence.
>
> According to the Committee for the Abolition of Illegitimate Debt, this was clearly illegal under international law and unthinkable for Patrice Lumumba, prime minister of the new state's first government, to pay back. Congo's current unsustainable debt load, which exists in part due to the unwillingness of the World Bank and IMF to write off odious debts, continues to this day. (p 3)

Only recently is the premise of hide-and-seek of the ex-colonial nations changing, albeit slowly. Slaves wearing metal collars branded 'Moor' slaves, and kept by seventeenth century Dutch households, have recently appeared in museum exhibits.[46] Such displays are being made feasible in the aftermath of the 2020 Black Lives Matter movement though they have a long way to go. Also coming into view is the fact that some portraits, much admired by appreciators of high art, by masters such as Rembrandt, are of slave drivers.[47] Unfortunately, little evidence exists of slaves because they could own, and leave behind, nothing. Court testimony of some slaves who were caught after failed attempts to run away and executed, provides scattered evidence.[48]

Spain, Portugal and colonialism

These countries took the institution one step further by annihilating live populations of the Americas, doing away with their well-developed religions based on the Earth's relation with humans, replacing them with a stern brand of Catholicism that had little to do with the natural development of the continents, literally stealing all their treasures and transporting them back to their home countries. The much-celebrated Columbus who reigned from Hispaniola (today's Dominican Republic) from 1492, imprisoned a cache of slaves in the tunnels under his own governor's quarters, actually revealing extreme ruthlessness towards a race that had expressed nothing but total trust in welcoming their European raiders. The cruelty of the Spanish conquistador Hernán Cortés (1485–1547) towards the Aztecs of Mexico materialized in a trail of bloodshed that subsequent conquistadors would emulate. They included Francisco Pizarro against the Incas in Peru, Pedro de Alvarado against the Mayas in Central America and other conquerors of the Americas. Cortés' success in bringing down the mighty Aztec empire quickly became legendary in Spain. Most of his soldiers had been peasants or younger sons of minor nobility with little to look forward to in terms of wealth or prestige. After the conquest, his men who were given land, then enslaved native people, and confiscated gold. That, in turn, led thousands more to the New World, each following Cortés' bloody and gory actions including countless deaths of men, rapes of women and extraction of gold whose value remains immeasurable in current terms.

Spain's colonial rapacity continued into its Caribbean colonies in particular in Cuba where sugar plantations were introduced, and slave labour used.

[46] Rijksmuseum, Amsterdam, June 2021.

[47] For example, the wealth of Marten Soolman and Oopjen Coppit, celebrated subjects of Rembrandt portraiture, came from the slave dependent sugar trade.

[48] Such evidence exists, for example, from the interrogation of Wally, a slave in Surinam, subsequently executed with four others in 1707. This was painted by Dirk Valkenburg who had termed Wally a trouble maker, in a comprehensive, merry-making scene, such were the attitudes of the times.

Recently, Ferrer (2021) elaborated the role of the US in continually intervening to usurp the colony for commercial gain through encouraging rebel, mainly Black, subversion, and fighting a brutal war with Spain. Quintin Bandera, a Black general, led three wars against Spain. Indeed, many rebels were Black. Plantation owners such as Thomas Jefferson viewed Cuba as the 'southernmost limit' of the US. It was not just the southern states, but northern shipowners carried on the slave trade between Africa and Cuba even after the practice was abolished. After Spain was ousted and the US accepted Cuba's independence, the US introduced the Platt amendment that would allow the US army to enter Cuba at any point; and it limited the new government from signing treaties. Cuba went from one form of repression to another, and poverty remained unabated.

So much has been forgotten about it and, yet, so grave, wide and deep have been its reach that no further mention need be made on inequality and poverty other than as outcomes imposed and generated by extractors. Each of the regions of the world colonized by Europeans found itself in a debt and poverty trap. It may now be redeemed only through mass reparations from the North to the South until inequality among nations is removed and poverty eliminated. The proposal for reparations is neither new nor unique. Naoroji proposed it more than a century back in his 1906 presidential address to the Congress party, calling for reparations from Britain for India's sufferings. A revived proposal may appear untenable in the prevailing self-centric thinking of global leaders today. Yet the UN is already enabling the examination and discussion of the issue in its forums. The South cannot shy away from putting it up for serious global consideration as the only practical solution for the removal of global poverty with financing from reparations to compensate, at least substantially, for past extraction using unjustified suffering.

It would be erroneous for it to appear that only European countries have used slavery and indentured servitude for gains in their own material interests. The role of Japan, for example, in the enslavement of Koreans, or even within its own boundaries, cannot be bypassed. In Hokkaido, its northern most island, Japan systematically enslaved and isolated the Ainu, its original indigenous population for centuries, passing laws against them since 1899, taking 120 years to pass the first law against discrimination on the basis of ethnicity. Nevertheless, it has declined to apologize in any form for past treatment. The ramifications on the Ainu have included lower education, lower earnings, fewer jobs, presumption of laziness and less intelligence and other stereotypes. The annals of slavery across the world are indeed long and have had a wide reach.

It would be incorrect to single out one country alone by sanctimonious Western politicians and researchers alike who choose to exclude a veritable line-up of countries that indulged in similar inhuman isolation and extraction policies even where it led to annihilation. Accordingly, this chapter has covered the atrocities of many European nations, with a short citation of Japan, that caused long-term poverty and inequality in the colonies they ruled to achieve disproportionate material gains based, usually, on a conviction of their racial superiority. There is no escaping that fact.

The point of widely assignable blame across countries has been brought out by Overy (2021) in the context of the Second World War. While US President Franklin Roosevelt insisted on a liberal internationalism in the Atlantic Charter of 1941 committing to the idea of self-determination as a right for all peoples, Winston Churchill signed it reluctantly. Nevertheless, actual occurrences in the US did not reflect that commitment. Around 1942, just as Britain was jailing thousands of Indian independence seekers and even shooting them down, the US continued with its racial segregation policies that affected its daily life as well as its armed forces harshly. Further, neither government showed much interest in saving Jews from the Third Reich. Thus, Overy concluded that the allied powers could not be said to have fought for decent values, instead revealing a callousness towards it. Thus, he hypothesized a comparability between the allied and axis powers in that their ordinary denizens perpetrated terrible conditions, including annihilation, on selected portions – colonized and citizens alike – of their populations.

New poverty-generating global activities

Today, amusingly, such ex-colonial countries overwhelm their television channels with euphoric, exaggerated, if not false, accounts of their contributions in civilizing their colonies. There is little recognition by them of what actually occurred, that their actions in their colonies were atrocities that should call for pecuniary compensation at the international court of justice based in The Hague which, so far, has not convicted a single Western individual for past atrocities against humanity. Perhaps it is the fear of the extent of reparations that may be stipulated to transfer to ex-colonies that inhibits them from facing up to their past.

To conclude, there is continued opacity in large segments of today's advanced economies in perceiving Black poverty and inequality as the outcome of slavery, or global poverty as outcomes of indentured servitude or apartheid. Rather, the escalation of the manufacture and supply of arms by rich nations provides an underlying exacerbation of it. Instead of mounting global resources towards appropriate inter-governmental compensation, the perpetrating countries comprise huge military spenders even while cutting back their international aid budgets as the UK did in 2020. Often arms are sold by rich nations at high prices to fight unjustifiable or fabricated wars. It occurs at the opportunity cost of scarce resources that could be spent on containing extreme poverty and inequality across the globe. Recent examples are arms in the hands of Somalia and its quasi-autonomous region of Somaliland, both extremely poor, yet acquiring arms with the blessing of, or directly from, the West. Another example in their vicinity of another locational civil war is the ruthless suppression by the Ethiopian government of its compatriot rebels in its Tigray region with Western armaments. Another is the arming of Chad with the blessing of the West which has failed to officially and multilaterally query the reason for the rise of the Boko Haram extremists who have ravaged Sub-Saharan Africa. In every instance such as these, the involvement of the West in providing arms while behaving as if such arms transfer would be made only to the deserving party is fully visible without, however, making ostensible attempts to delve deep into the causes of the problems. In most such cases, the problems have arisen, in any event, with the West drawing unthinking borders through tribal regions while grossing up some areas without consideration of whether such areas comprised complementary tribal clans before they hurried out in the 1950s, 1960s and 1970s from colonial rule. There has been no apology, leave alone any voluntary action, towards monetary retribution for their past actions.

In Chapter 6, we explore if a crucial driver behind India's intractable problem of poverty and inequality is its millennia-old caste-based society.

References

Ali, Tariq. (2021) 'Winged words', *London Review of Books*, 43 (12): 17 June.

Almond, Douglas and Janet Curries. (2011) 'Human capital development before age five', in Orley Ashenfelter and David Card (eds) *Handbook of Labor Economics*, 4(B): 1315–1486. Amsterdam: North Holland.

Ashcroft, Bill, Gareth Griffiths and Helen Tiffin. (2007) *Post-Colonial Studies – The Key Concepts*. Abingdon-Oxon: Routledge.

BBC News. (2020a) 'Democrats introduce sweeping legislation to reform police', 9 June. www.bbc.com/news/world-us-canada-52969375, accessed 6 May 2021.

BBC News. (2020b) 'Edward Colston statue: Cases sent to Crown Prosecution Service', 17 September. www.bbc.com/news/uk-england-bristol-54191039, accessed 15 May 2021.

Bhambra, Gurminder K. (2021) 'Narrating inequality, eliding empire', *The British Journal of Sociology*, 72 (1): 69–78. Available at https://doi.org/10.1111/1468-4446.12804, accessed 1 May 2021.

Bhambra, Gurminder K. and John Holmwood. (2021) *Colonialism and Modern Social Theory*. Oxford: Polity Press.

Brown, Christopher. (2021) 'Later, not now', *London Review of Books*, 43(14): 25–28.

Boushey, Heather. (2019) *UnBound: How Inequality Constricts Our Economy and What We Can Do About It*. Cambridge: Harvard University Press.

Cameron, Hazel. (2013) *Britain's Hidden Role in the Rwandan Genocide: The Cat's Paw*. New York: Routledge.

Caplan, Gerald. (2008) 'Book Review: Silent Accomplice: the untold story of France's role in the Rwandan genocide', *Genocide Studies and Prevention: An international Journal*, 3(1): Article 10. Available at https://scholarcommons.usf.edu/cgi/viewcontent.cgi?article=1187&context=gsp, accessed 9 June 2021.

Carr, Shannon. (2015) 'Britain's hidden role in the Rwandan genocide: The Cat's Paw by Hazel Cameron', *Human Rights Review*, 16: 319–20. Available at https://doi.org/10.1007/s12142-015-0369-z.

Chen, Edwin. (1990) 'Mandela Speech Draws Cheers from Congress: South Africa', *Los Angeles Times*. Available at www.latimes.com/archives/la-xpm-1990-06-27-mn-631-story.html, accessed 13 August 2021.

Chetty, Raj, David Grusky, Maximilian Hell, Nathaniel Hendren, Robert Manduca and Jimmy Narang. (2017) 'The fading American dream: trends in absolute income mobility since 1940'. *Science*, 356(6336): 398–406. Available at doi: 10.1126/science.aal4617, accessed 1 May 2021.

Cooper, Kerris and Kitty Stewart. (2013) 'Does Money Affect Children's Outcomes?', CASE Reports casereport80, Centre for Analysis of Social Exclusion, LSE. Available at https://sticerd.lse.ac.uk/dps/case/cr/casereport80.pdf, accessed 20 August 2021.

Crosby, Alfred W. (2004) *Ecological Imperialism – The Biological Expansion of Europe, 900–1900*. New York: Cambridge University Press.

Currie, Janet and Rosemary Hyson. (1999) 'Is the impact of health shocks cushioned by socioeconomic status? The case of low birthweight', *American Economic Review*, 89(2): 245–250. Available at doi: 10.1257/aer.89.2.245, accessed 1 May 2021.

Currie, Janet and Duncan Thomas. (1999) 'Early Test Scores, Socioeconomic Status and Future Outcomes'. Available at SSRN: https://ssrn.com/abstract=149693, accessed 1 January 2023.

Dahl, Gordon B. and Lance Lochner. (2012) 'The impact of family income on child achievement: evidence from the earned income tax credit', *American Economic Review*, 102(5): 1927–56. Available at doi: 10.1257/aer.102.5.1927, accessed 1 May 2021.

Dalrymple, William. (2019) *The Anarchy – The Relentless Rise of the East India Company*. London: Bloomsbury Publishing.

Du Bois, W. E. B. (1935) *Black Reconstruction in America*. New York: Harcourt, Brace and Company.

Edlund, Lena and Wojciech Kopczuk. (2009) 'Women, wealth, and mobility', *American Economic Review*, 99(1): 146–78. Available at doi: 10.1257/aer.99.1.146, accessed 1 May 2021.

Ellsworth, Scott. (1992) *Death in a Promised Land: The Tulsa Race Riot of 1921*. Baton Rouge: LSU Press.

Ellsworth, Scott. (2021) *The Ground Breaking: The Tulsa Race Massacre and an American City's Search for Justice*. London: Icon Books Limited.

Ferrer, Ada. (2021) *Cuba: An American History*. New York: Scribner/ Simon and Schuster.

Fleming, David and Richard Benjamin. (2011) *Transatlantic Slavery: An Introduction*. Liverpool: Liverpool University Press.

Hicks, Dan. (2020) *The Brutish Museums: The Benin Bronzes, Colonial Violence and Cultural Restitution*. London: Pluto Press.

Gardner, Leigh and Tirthankar Roy. (2020) *The Economic History of Colonialism*. Bristol: Bristol University Press.

Gilroy, Paul. (2019) 'Never Again: Refusing Race and Salvaging the Human', The 2019 Holberg Lecture. Available at https://holbergprisen.no/en/news/holberg-prize/2019-holberg-lecture-laureate-paul-gilroy, accessed 1 October 2021.

Goldin, Claudia and Lawrence F. Katz. (2010) *The Race between Education and Technology*. Cambridge: Belknap Press of Harvard University Press.

Jefferson, Thomas. (1781) *Slavery and Racism*. Encyclopedia Britannica. Available at https://www.britannica.com, accessed 31 December 2022.

Kosicki, Piotr H. 2007. 'Sites of aggressor – victim memory: The Rwandan genocide, theory and practice', *International Journal of Sociology*, 37(1): 10–29. Available at www.jstor.org/stable/20628282, accessed 9 June 2021.

Liebow, Elliot. (1967) *Tally's Corner*. Boston and Toronto: Little, Brown and Company.

Lincoln, Abraham. (1862) 'Letter to Horace Greely,' August 22, in *Abraham Lincoln Papers: Series 2. General Correspondence. 1858–64*, quoted in *The Economist*, December 2020, p 118.

Moosvi, Shireen. (2008) *People, Taxation and Trade in Mughal India*. New Delhi: Oxford University Press.

Lukka, Priya. (2020) 'Repairing Harm Caused: What Could a Reparations Approach Mean for The IMF And World Bank?', *Bretton Woods Project*, 6 October. Available at www.brettonwoodsproject.org/2020/10/repairing-harm-caused-what-could-a-reparations-approach-mean-for-the-imf-and-world-bank/, accessed 8 October 2021.

Messer, Chris M. (2021) *The 1921 Tulsa Race Massacre*. Cham: Palgrave Macmillan. Available at https://doi.org/10.1007/978-3-030-74679-7, accessed 23 June 2021.

Moreno-Leguizamon, Carlos. (1995) 'A Critical Interpretation of Divergent Discourses About Drugs in an Urban Setting', Masters' Thesis, Washington DC: Howard University, unpublished.

MPR News. (2021) 'With Biden's backing, Democrats revive George Floyd police reform bill', 3 March. Available at https://www.mprnews.org/story/2021/03/03/with-bidens-backing-dems-revive-george-floyd-police-reform-bill, accessed 6 May 2021.

Mukerjee, Madhusree. (2010) *Churchill's Secret War – The British Empire and The Ravaging of India During World War II*. New Delhi: Tranquebar Press, Westland Ltd.

Naoroji, Dadabhai. (1901–02) *Poverty And Un-British Rule in India*. New Delhi: Nation Press.

Overy, Richard. (2021) *The Great Imperial War, 1931–1945*. London: Allen Lane.

Patel, Dinyar. (2021) *Naoroji: Pioneer of Indian Nationalism*. Cambridge: Harvard University Press.

Patnaik, Utsa and Shubhra Chakrabarti. (eds) (2017) *Agrarian and Other Histories: Essays for Binay Bhushan Chaudhuri*. New Delhi: Tulika Books.

Phillips, Barnaby. (2021) *Loot: Britain and the Benin Bronzes*. London: Oneworld.

Piketty, Thomas. (2020) *Capital and Ideology*. Translated by Arthur Goldhammer. Cambridge: Harvard University Press.

Piketty, Thomas. (2021) 'Capital and ideology: a global perspective on inequality regimes', *The British Journal of Sociology*, 72(1): 139–150. Available at https://doi.org/10.1111/1468-4446.12836, accessed 30 April 2021.

Prideaux, John. (2021) 'America is becoming less racist and yet more divided by racism', Race in America – Special Report, *The Economist*, 22 May, pp 3–12.

Ramey, Garey and Valerie A. Ramey. (2010) 'The rug rat race', Brookings Papers on Economic Activity, Economic Studies Program, The Brookings Institution, 41(1): 129–199. Available at www.brookings.edu/wp-content/uploads/2010/03/2010a_bpea_ramey.pdf, accessed 1 May 2021.

Rawley, James A. and Stephen D. Behrendt. (2009) *The Transatlantic Slave Trade: A History Revised edition*. Lincoln: University of Nebraska Press.

Reddy, Sanjay G. (2021) 'Beyond property or beyond Piketty?', *The British Journal of Sociology*, 72(1): 8–25. Available at https://doi.org/10.1111/1468-4446.12822, accessed 1 May 2021.

Rhodes, Jewell Parker. (2021) 'Writing history, uncovering truths', *World Literature Today*, 95(2): 44–47. Available at doi:10.7588/worllitetoda.95.2.0044, accessed 23 June 2021.

Roy, Thirthankar. (2020) *The Economic History of India, 1857–2010*. Fourth Edition, New Delhi: Oxford University Press.

Rogers, Nicholas. (2020) *Murder on the Middle Passage: The Trial of Captain Kimber*. Woodbridge: Boydell & Brewer.

Sen, Amartya. (1981) *Poverty and Famines: An Essay on Entitlement and Deprivation*. Oxford: Oxford University Press.

Sen, Nabendu. (1992) *India in the International Economy 1853–1913*. Calcutta: Orient Longman Ltd.

Shipman, Pat. (1994) *The Evolution of Racism*. New York: Simon and Schuster.

Shome, Parthasarathi. (2021) *Taxation History, Theory, Law and Administration*. Cham: Springer. Available at https://doi.org/10.1007/978-3-030-68214-9, accessed 1 May 2021.

Smith, John David and J. Vincent Lowery (eds) (2013) *The Dunning School: Historians, Race, and the Meaning of Reconstruction*. Lexington: University Press of Kentucky.

Spivak, Gayatri. (1987) *In Other Worlds: Essays in Cultural Politics*. New York: Methuen.

Stringer, Christopher, and Clive Gamble. (1993) *In Search of Neanderthals*. London: Thames and Hudson.

Taylor, Michael. (2020) *The Interest: How the British Establishment Resisted the Abolition of Slavery*. London: Bodley Head.

Thomas, Hugh. (2006) *The Slave Trade: The Story of the Atlantic Slave Trade: 1440–1870*. New York: Simon & Schuster.

Tobias, Phillip V. (1972) *Meaning of Race*. Johannesburg: South African Institute of Race Relations.

Tuhiwai Smith, Linda. (2021) *Decolonizing Methodologies: Research and Indigenous Peoples*. Zed Books: London.

Wallis, Andrew. (2006) *Silent Accomplice: The Untold Story of France's Role in the Rwandan Genocide*. London: I. B. Tauris.

Wilkerson, Isabel. (2020) *Caste-The Lies that Divide Us*. London: Allen Lane, Penguin Random House.

Wintz, Mark. (2010) *Transatlantic Diplomacy and the Use of Military Force in the Post-Cold War Era*, chs 4 and 5. New York: Palgrave Macmillan. Available at https://doi.org/10.1057/9780230113589, accessed 1 January 2023.

6

India's Caste Structure

Introduction

The caste structure has existed in India as long as its history has been recorded. Most Indians are familiar, even though not all may be comfortable with the concept and repercussions of caste on society. That unfortunately translates to a passive form of racism that does not openly resemble the racism of the West but is a variant of it. In an anthropological twist, this author recalls Indian visitors from suburbia visiting his home in the urban centre of Washington DC when he was residing there. They visited only during the day usually for lunch if the purpose of the visit was to have a meal. Typically, fear prevailed regarding entering Washington DC from the states of Maryland or Virginia, states to the north and south of Washington respectively where most Indians resided. The widely prevalent view was that, after sundown, Black violence could descend willy-nilly on neighbourhoods with a Washington DC address. They openly expressed their concern, however unfounded, within the confined safety of their own communities where they felt free to express their fears. Any protestation would be met with amusement at the complainant's contrary point of view or manner of living. Attitudes towards Africans resident in India are all too apparent *pari passu* with India's own worsening caste separation.[1] Inter-caste marriage can still lead to death in the vastness of non-urban areas.[2] The slide of society into silence and little opprobrium over caste-based lynching in recent years reflect the newly emerging realities of caste-based inequality in India.

Earlier, India did make significant attempts to recognize the gravity of exclusion, isolation and domination leading to poverty and inequality, and

1 See Rao (2009).

2 Even in the US, interracial relationships continue to meet obstacles. See, among many, Pundit (2016), in which interracial living is cogently presented in the context of a novel.

attempted various forms of compensation to attenuate their deleterious consequences. However, actual achievement has fallen short and caste discrimination, together with occasional atrocities, continues in large parts of India, in particular in the so-called Hindu belt comprising the Hindi speaking northern states or those with contiguous languages using the *Devanagari* script. Untouchability, despite being rendered unconstitutional in India's 1950 constitution, together with the caste system, continues to exist in many overt and covert forms, representing the primary obstacles, the fountainhead perhaps, of India's knee-breaking inequality and poverty. It is not always understood that by his surname, a person's caste is etched on his life at birth until death and that, sometimes, it continues even after that since cremations could be separated by location and rituals separated by caste in many locations.

Caste remains the testimonial for the dominant castes to discriminate against the lower-by-birth castes regarding choice of work, location of housing, access to shopping and movement across villages and entrance to religious edifices, marriage, and education, all adding up to economic distortions and limiting the capacity and capability, productivity and output of affected castes. Thus, as long as the caste phenomenon is not eradicated from Indian society, for example by abolishing surnames with penalty for their use in any form or disguise, poverty and inequality are likely to linger. However astute the design of economists' redistribution programmes may be, and as long as caste-based 'entitlement' is enjoyed as a matter of right in Indian rural society, there will lurk in the minds and hearts of the non-excluded, non-isolated, dominating segments of rural populations, routes to subvert those programmes or how to divert public sector awarded benefits in their own favour. For example, it is well-known that subsidized loans for the lower castes have been regularly diverted to the more powerful upper castes by using the legitimate beneficiaries as fronts. It is pertinent to cite Sen (1981) here who enunciated a concept of entitlement.

> the causation of poverty raises questions that are not easily answered … there are various intermediate levels of useful answers that are worth exploring. (p vii)

> Ownership relations are one kind of entitlement relations. It is necessary to understand the entitlement systems within which the problem of starvation is to be analysed. This applies more generally to poverty as such. (p 1)

Entitlement relations accepted in a private ownership market economy typically include the following, among others:

1. *trade-based entitlement:* one is entitled to own what one obtains by trading something one owns with a willing party (or, multilaterally, with a willing set of parties);
2. *production-based entitlement:* one is entitled to own what one gets by arranging production using one's owned resources, or resources hired from willing parties meeting the agreed conditions of trade;
3. *own-labour entitlement:* one is entitled to one's own labour power, and thus to the trade-based and production-based entitlements related to one's labour power;
4. *inheritance and transfer entitlement:* one is entitled to own what is willingly given to one by another who legitimately owns it, possibly to take effect after the latter's death (if so, specified by him).

Sen (1981) goes on to explain that market entitlements may be supplemented by rationing or coupon systems, even in private ownership market economies, such as in Britain during the Second World War[3] (p 2). Britain used sequencing of COVID-19 vaccines during the 2020–21 pandemic by sequestering the private sector medical system in place for its sole use by the state thus, in one stroke, altering the entitlement system.

In Sen's four basic classifications of entitlement or their variations, caste-based entitlement determined by the happenstance of birth does not appear. Caste may be viewed as akin to a 'sudden death' phenomenon after birth or as a boxing-in of an individual into certain occupational entitlements and location of living bound by inextricable and unchangeable rules of work and living as well as for the conduct of personal and social life. This is in direct opposition to Sen's (1981) concept of 'development as freedom'. The premise of this book is based on entitlement by compulsion or force, in favour of a minority and to the detriment of the larger population who have little role in determining the entitlements or their distribution. One outcome is the generation and continuance of inequality and poverty caused by the pecuniary and non-pecuniary returns laid out for different entitlement groups. This is what has occurred for millennia, and continues to occur in a significant portion of India, leading to production outcomes well within what economists call the production possibility frontier. Those authors who have attributed useful characteristics to the functioning of the caste system such as maintaining social order or the protection of all groups through the recognition of their respective rights, may have to reconsider their position since the system's deleterious ramifications must far outweigh its benefits.

[3] This may or may not be combined with price 'control', and that in its turn may or may not be combined with a flourishing 'black market'.

Antecedents of caste

The word *jati* in most Indian languages means 'species' or 'kind', denoting social categories, though it has come to refer primarily to caste.[4] All Hindus belong to a caste and those at the bottom of the heap and considered non-Hindus, are also given a caste name. Remarkably, this categorization occurs at birth reflecting the caste of the family to which a baby is born. Caste has percolated into other religious groups in India including Muslims, Christians, Sikhs and others, though not to tribal peoples who existed on Indian soil prior to the entry of northern Asian or European immigrants. What is noteworthy is that those tribals do not include the Dravidians who, according to the prevailing view, entered during a first immigration event. They were already inhabitants of India during a second immigration event, usually termed an Aryan invasion. Thus, the broadly recognized hypothesis, for example by Ambedkar (1947) is that the Dravidians had also immigrated into India and had a well-developed and articulated culture prior to the entry of the Aryans. There is considerable discussion regarding who conjured up the caste system and when.

In the caste system, marriage occurs within the same caste which the children also inherit. In most communities, a woman could marry a man of a higher caste but not vice versa. This is a practice that has continued from the early Hindu kingdoms of previous millennia. Further, subsequent religious conversions into Christianity or Islam could not eradicate caste. Thus, caste continues to exist in the Indian sub-continent, extending into Pakistan and Bangladesh that are primarily Muslim, Sri Lanka that is primarily Buddhist and Nepal which is primarily Hindu. This chapter narrows down to caste primarily prevalent in India.

An interpretation of the caste system is that it defines a division of labour. In practice many occupations are caste-specific, especially in the services and artisan sectors, such as for washermen and carpenters, transporters of live and dead animals, and several others whose jobs other caste members are unlikely to usurp.[5] Some of these occupations paid so little as wages or earnings that their members were likely to be born and die in penury or live off the charity of higher castes. Such conditions led necessarily to more loose eating habits, for example, beef by the removers of dead cattle. That, in turn, led to their untouchability. Thus, untouchability as an institution is of

---

4 Fuller (2003).

5 In urban India, however, occupations got widely distributed, for example, modern laundry and dry-cleaning services, leather products, dentistry and eating places were heavily geared towards a Chinese immigrant population that, however, receded somewhat after the 1962 Indo-Chinese War that left more than a dent in the bilateral relations of the two countries and led to considerable Chinese emigration.

a later vintage than the institution of caste. The caste condition was lifelong and there was no way of escaping it other than to leave the community and emigrate to urban areas, thereby becoming somewhat invisible (Das, 2015, pp 63–65). That too does not necessarily ensure anonymity as caste groupings continue to appear and prevail in towns and cities if not for anything else but for the safety and security of the lower-caste groupings in unfamiliar environments.

The foundational ethos of the caste system is the immobility across occupations from birth that it has been based on and the wall it creates against social mobility. Its immediate impact is to create social inequality. The most voluminous explanation of the caste system – its genesis, rules, implementation, power and evolution over time – has been developed and delineated in graphic detail by Ambedkar (1936). A synthesis of his research, findings and conclusions appears in Chapter 7. Castes are ranked hierarchically, Brahmins, or the priestly caste on the top, then proceeding downwards with other occupations. As indicated, occupations that are menial were at the bottom and also led to their being untouchable. They were later termed *Harijans* or the 'children of God' by Mohandas Karamchand Gandhi, or, later, Dalit,[6] or Scheduled Castes (SCs) (their official designation in India's constitution). Perhaps the lowest castes in Bihar and Bengal are the Dom and Chamar. The Dom cremate dead bodies of all castes, and the Chamar slaughters and produces animal hide. That there is no dignity of labour attached to these professions is symbolized by the fact that the terms Chamar and Dom comprise two of the most abusive terms of castigation of menials. How ironic then that, though rituals to be performed at death differ by caste, gender, status of marriage, regular death or suicide and so on, the final rites for all, categorized as of the lowest form of human activity, are carried out by the lowest Untouchable! Strangely, even though blind caste-based rules have been disappearing from urban social practices, at death, Indians tend to follow caste-based rituals such as differentiated number of days of mourning for husband, wife, children by age, adults by regular death or suicide and so on. This could, of course, reflect the deep sense of sorrow commonly felt at the moment of loss of a close family member at which time ignoring rules would take monumental courage to reject the prescriptions of the Brahminic almanac pushed forward by priests. Only the most advanced urban inhabitants have exited those Hindu rituals, replacing them with a

---

6 'Dalit' is a word for a community and an identity that are in the making. To call oneself Dalit, meaning 'ground down', 'broken to pieces', 'crushed', … 'the terms of exclusion on which discrimination is premised are at once refused and reproduced in the demands for inclusion.' See Rao (2009, p 1). Note that Dalit is not used in italics reflecting common usage.

compassionate wake after cremation in electricity-driven kilns (rather than on wood pyres), sometimes accompanied by songs invoking the Universe.

In between the Brahmins and Harijans are a large variety of other castes, who may not be present in every state of India. In many but not all villages, one populous caste or a combination thereof may exercise control over society and local politics. Such castes tend to be landholding, such as Rajputs and Jats in the north, and Mudaliars and Chettiars who are likely to be holders of land and financial wealth in Tamil Nadu, and sometimes even the Nadars, who are slightly lower in the caste hierarchy. Brahmins dominate through landholding only in a handful of cases including the Kavery delta in Tamil Nadu and Karnataka.

A question that arises is whether caste in India is linked to Indo-Aryan Persia of the Achaemenid era, its celebrated monarchs comprising Cyrus, his son-in-law Darius I, and Darius's son Xerxes who extended the empire, apart from others.[7] Persian history negates the possibility of caste, however. The Persians worshipped a trinity of divinities – Ahuramazda,[8] Anahita and Mithra – and held the fire to be divine. They comprised truth and justice, separable from the Lie – the *daiwa* or false gods. Their priests were called the Magi. Names were derived from the lines of the trinity. The trinity were not worshipped together, for example, Darius[9] and Xerxes worshipped Ahuramazda. Nevertheless, Darius's entourage was replete with Mithra names, thus revealing a mix of lineages in practice and eschewing any form of caste separation. The role of the Magi was more contained than that of the Brahmin. A Magus chanted theogony or hymns, implying that a layman did not suffice to complete an ablution; but the Magus was not a theologian. Cook (1983) pointed out that,

> By the end of the Persian empire ... the whole Aryan-Iranian race could be spoken of as being at one with the Magi in their doctrine of

---

7 Cyrus reigned between 559–530 BC and united prevailing Persian tribes and established an empire, extending it west to Palestine. Cambyses, Cyrus's son reigned between 530–522 BC followed by Cyrus's son-in-law Darius who reigned between 522–486 BC. Xerxes, the son of Darius, reigned between 486–465 BC. They and other successors of Cyrus extended the empire west to Egypt and Bulgaria, north to central Asia, and east to the Indus valley (Pakistan), converting the empire to the most powerful empire that existed. The length and wealth of the empire enabled the development of nuanced details in religious practices with an established heritage.

8 Ahura translates to Lord, and Mazda to Wise.

9 Darius possibly brought Zoroaster's (Zarathushtra) god from north-eastern Iran though he called his god Ahuramazda. He recognized one creator and omnipotent deity as Zoroaster did, coming close to becoming a monotheist. He did not speak of Justice or its enemy, the Lie (*daiwa*) though Xerxes, his son, introduced both in his *daiwa* inscriptions. See Cook (1983), p 156.

> cosmic dualism, which implies that they all had them as their priests. We thus find that the development of the catholic Zoroastrianism of the *Avesta*[10] seems … to have been working itself out in North-eastern Iran but that the religion that evolved was that of the Magi.
>
> The Magi were subject to their temporal masters … and not to the high priests (or) forming … its own hierarchy, doctrinal instruction, or endowments … some Magi were put in positions of trust; but there is no reason to suppose that they were able to assert themselves as a corporate body … In the Achaemenid era there does not seem to be evidence of a caste system like that which gave priests and judges a place next to the nobles in the social hierarchy. They may have been a tribe like the Levites,[11] but not a caste like the Brahmins. (pp 154–155)

It may thus be concluded that the Indo-Aryans of Persia cannot be linked with the severity, cruelty, perversity and absurdity of the caste system as it formed and took shape in India.

Genesis of caste

Early religious texts provide the first intimation of the prevalence of caste in India.

Hindu religious texts

Caste among settlers appears to have been established and sharpened on the Indo-Gangetic plains prior to the Vedic and later-Vedic periods. Sharma (1983) studied the genesis of the complex pre-iron society in the mid-Ganga plains that paved the way for the historically documented period. The use of iron appeared later and its quintessential role in the clearance of forests, enablement of settlements and a rise in economic productivity became increasingly apparent. Using ethnological analogies, Sharma (2017) pointed out that, as social formations in the mid-Ganga plains spread out in the later Vedic period, emerging unequal distribution of resources and agricultural surpluses could have given rise to the *varna* / caste system.

The original word for the major caste divisions was *varna* that encompassed Brahmins, who were priests based on the exclusive pursuit of religious scriptures; Kshatriyas, who were soldiers and from whom

---

10 The *Avesta* refers to the collection of primary religious texts of Zoroastrianism.

11 The Levites were priests of the Jews, but no exclusivity can be assigned to them for 'The history of the Levites is further obscured by the possibility that their ranks may have included representatives of all the tribes.' *Encyclopedia Britannica*, accessed on 1 January 2023.

rose leaders, kings and soldiers; Vaisyas who were traders and herders; and Sudras, who comprised more lowly occupations and served the other three groups (Sharma, 2016).[12] The origin of the caste system is claimed by scholars to be the last *mandala* or portion of the *purusha sukta*, a hymnal poem from the *Rig Veda* (1200 BCE) considered the oldest among all ancient texts, where the idea was first mooted. But how the institution came to be established and anchored remains uncertain. Historians continue to attempt to reconstruct the process, but the paucity of reliable data implies, at best, slow progress. The *mandala* describes how the world was created in a cosmic sacrifice of *purusha*, the primeval Man. *Purusha*'s mouth became the Brahmin, his arms the Kshatriya, his thighs the Vaisya, and his feet the Sudra. Accordingly, the hierarchy proceeds from head to feet of *purusha*. A benign interpretation of scholars – domestic and international – has been one of Hindu society as a unity of ranked classes, each performing different functions to sustain the system. Jaiswal's (2000) interpretation was that, though the caste system's evolution, present form and substance reflected many changes that the institution underwent over centuries, its origins were embedded in the ecology of Vedic settlements. Influences and practices of patriarchy and state formation played a crucial role in its evolution but the basic principles of separation of caste roles remained steadfast.

The entire caste hierarchy has been referred to as *jati* in the ancient religio-legal texts that together comprise the *dharmashastra*. As already explained, lowly groups such as the *Chandalas* and the *Dom*, who performed the lowliest functions of removing dead cattle and night soil, and carrying out cremations, fell below and outside the *varna* structure. Ambedkar (1936) illuminated the reader with minute details from ancient texts pertaining to the matter. Jha (2017) traced the first mention of *Chandalas* in the later Vedic literature (1000 to 600 BC) in the context of the *Purushamedha* (symbolic human sacrifice) dedicated to the deity, Vayu. He also elaborated on the *Nishadas* – fishermen and hunters – who were categorized around the same time as Sudras and, ultimately, as untouchables.

Modern scholars, both domestic and international, have tended to describe caste as a structure with different functions for sustaining, as a whole, an occupational classification distributed among the various castes. According to *Manusmriti*, or the Laws of Manu, which attained its final form about two millennia back, untouchables were created from illicit hypogamous unions between Sudra men and women of higher castes. No document

[12] Also see Jha (2017). The author describes the position of the shudras circa AD 600 in relation to their material conditions and their economic and social relations with members of higher castes / varnas. The untouchables are also discussed.

provides any firm evidence about the categorization evolving from such occurrences, however. Ambedkar (1936) developed a conceivable hypothesis that is elaborated in Chapter 7 of this book. Max Muller, a German scholar well-versed in ancient Hindu texts, maintained that Aryans invaded the Gangetic plains en masse and subordinated the indigenous population in the second millennium BC.[13] Their language was Indo-Aryan or Indo-European in which subsequent Hindu texts were scribed and Hindu systems of living – including racial segregation – came to be based. The two evolved languages were Sanskrit and Dravidian-Tamil. Amplifying Max Mueller, Thapar (2003) indicated,

> That Aryan should have been interpreted in racial terms is curious, since the texts use it to refer to persons of status who speak Sanskrit and observe caste regulations. The equation had still wider ramifications. It appealed to some of those working on Dravidian languages, who proposed that there was a Dravidian race speaking Dravidian, prior to, and distinct from, the Aryan. They quoted in support the fact that Indo-Aryan is an inflected language, and therefore quite distinct from the Dravidian languages which are agglutinative. Gradually, Proto-Dravidian was projected as the original language and came to be equated with Tamil, which is not a historically or linguistically valid equation. Proto-Dravidian, like Indo-European, is a hypothetical language reconstructed from known Dravidian languages of which Tamil was one. (p 13)

Thapar (2003) reported that Jyotiba Phule, an authority on the Dalits, took a position in the late nineteenth century that Sanskrit-speaking brahmins had descended from the Aryans who were alien to India, and that the indigenous peoples who were the castaways into lower castes were the rightful inheritors of the land. This appears to match Max Muller's position that racial difference was the genesis of caste.[14] Thapar also indicated that most modern scholars later took the view that there was little evidence that the caste system emanated from fair-skinned *arya* or Aryan invaders defeating the *dasa* or dark-skinned Dravidians who were prior inhabitants of the subcontinent.[15] This was the early view of Ambedkar as well who claimed that both the so-called Aryans and the Dravidians entered India from the North though the former came centuries after the entry of the latter. Thus,

---

13 See Thapar (2003), p 13.

14 See Thapar (2003) who quoted Max Muller being of the opinion that Aryan invaders originated in central Asia and invaded from Persia.

15 See Risley ([1915] 1969), who provided anthropometric information to establish his claim.

Thapar's conclusion was that 'Indo-Aryan speaking peoples' better describe the group than 'Aryans' (pp 14–15).

Yet, if caste was the instrument that dictated the division of occupations in reflection of categories such as the invaders and the conquered, or the *aryas* and the *dasas*, or the northern language group versus the southern language group, then it is difficult to oppose the hypothesis that caste-based rules must have been drawn up reflecting group differences, racial or not that, in turn, led also to exclusion, isolation and domination. And the very fact that lower castes earned a fraction of the hourly returns of upper castes, inequality and poverty could be viewed to have been automatically sanctioned as a way of life generated by the system itself, rather than through any inability of lower castes to work in equal measure to higher castes. Yet Thapar disagreed with the view that Indian culture had been static or that it had been essentially frozen on the basis of caste. To make her point, she cited changes that had occurred between politics and economic systems, or the vigorous mercantile activities of Indians over centuries that negated a position of static socio-economic pattern.[16]

The crucial question that remains, however, is not whether India had been able to manoeuvre within a given system but, rather, whether that system made any sense at all in light of the economic and social distortions that it brought about with its deleterious ramifications on productivity over the centuries by curtailing freedoms of movement, expression and occupation that got determined at birth and continued unto death. Obviously, the status quo of the structure made sense to a narrow coterie of the top castes to the detriment of the majority of the population.

Brahmanic dominance

The inexorable yet curious emergence of Brahmanic dominance was manifested in a growing need for priests – primarily through Brahmanic manipulation – in rituals and a growing elaboration of required sacrifices for every ritual that culminated in 16 priest categories who were tasked to perform them. The *Rajasuya yagya* for the coronation ceremony of the Pandavas of the *Mahabharata* (see next) took two years to perform. Even the *Ashwamedha yagya* based on the sacrifice of the horse, an animal said to have been introduced by the Aryans,[17] was a long, drawn-out process

---

16 She made a point that the chanting of the *gayatri* mantra, a hymn from the Rig Veda that is commonly chanted evoking the solar deity, has taken on varying renditions over subsequent millennia, a point that is not entirely clear in this context. The crux of the matter is that the chanting continues by upper-caste Indians and hardly ever by Indians as a whole. See Thapar (2003), pp xxiv– xxv.

17 This statement has been questioned recently by selected historians based on archaeological observations and remains a matter of unresolved controversy.

performed by priests. The length of a *yagya* to no small extent reflected the complexity they increasingly assumed for the consecration of a king – who were not necessarily born into the warrior caste – and could acquire legitimacy only through lengthy priestly anointment procedures. Indeed, of the priest categories, the Brahmins were a single category that eventually consolidated its power and displaced other priest categories. In the end, Brahmins could be said to hold ritual power with Kshatriyas holding ruling or administrative power. The power sharing produced an equilibrium between them, the determination of which had little to do with the majority of the population that comprised the lower castes. Interestingly, in their references to Brahmins, the ancient texts did not necessarily view them as godlike but, rather, as possessing an entitlement to material benefits. Indeed, there were also occasional reference to their greed.

References to caste and the supremacy of Brahmins are found in the 5th century BCE *Ramayana*, or the story of Rama, and the 4th century BCE *Mahabharata*, or the story of the great Bharat, that is, India.[18] Note must be taken of the plentiful references to Brahmins; yet these references are not often discussed in their own terms in prevailing or emerging analyses. The earliest known references to the conduct of governance in the context of dynastic accounts are found in the *Ramayana* and the *Mahabharata*, while, much later, Kautilya's *Arthashastra* written during the Maurya period (321 to 185 BCE), comprises direct instructions for how to govern. Further to the East, Lord Shang of China and, to the West, Plato of Ancient Greece, provided comparable treatises, albeit founded on different tenets of governance, reflecting the mores of society in which they lived and observed.[19]

The *Ramayana*, as recounted in *Ramrajya*, or the Rule of Rama, was one in which lies were not spoken or heard since people did not know dishonesty, and where the virtuous, godlike king[20] represented his people through every aspect of kingship. Muniapan and Satpathy (2010) asserted that the seven books in Valmiki's *Ramayana* contain multiple dimensions of life and governance including 'philosophy, spirituality, politics, economics, sociology, culture, literature, language, poetry, (and) technology' (p 645).

[18] A reading of Dutt (1898) illustrates the point.

[19] Subsequent to Hinduism and Buddhism, religions founded in rural societies stipulated rules and guidelines declared by prophets, for example, in the Bible of Christianity, Guru Granth Sahib of Sikhism, and the Quran of Islam. In combination, they comprise a formidable set of insights on guidance regarding the manner of living, interacting, administering and dying, in each of those societies where they emerged.

[20] Rama is described as Vishnu, the god, in bravery, godlike in benevolence and justice and attractive like the full moon. He equals the earth in perseverance but is like the fire of conflagration in his wrath.

When Rama leaves for the forest and assigns Bharata, his brother, to govern in his absence, he instructs Bharata to take the responsibilities of the art and craft of governance. Rama implores,

> I hope that superior servants are assigned superior works only, mediocre servants in mediocre works and inferior servants in inferior works. I hope your income is abundant and your expenditure, minimum. I hope your treasure does not reach undeserving people. O, Bharata! I hope that your expenditure goes for the cause of divinity, 'manes',[21] *brahmanas*, unexpected visitors, soldiers and hosts of friends.
>
> I hope you are regularly giving your army the daily provisions and the suitable salary to them without any delay … I hope that you seek to conciliate by the following three means – gifts, a loving mind and polite words – the aged, children and foremost, physicians … I hope you are not honouring the materialistic *brahmanas*, my dear brother! These men are skilled in perverting the mind, ignorant as they are and thinking themselves to be learned and reaching to their logical acumen, these men of perverted intellect preach meaninglessly, in the presence of eminent books on righteousness.
>
> Are you cherishing all those who live by agriculture and cattle rearing, O, dear brother? … providing them what they need and abstaining from what they fear. All the citizens are indeed to be protected by the king through his righteousness.[22] (pp 651–59)

Thus, as early as the 5th century BCE *Ramayana*, Indians accepted the supremacy of Brahmins listing them next to divinity while, at the same time, distinguishing the good from the materialistic Brahmins.

The popular understanding of the *Mahabharata*[23] is as an epic of sacrifice and war, of which the *Bhagwat Gita*, or the Song of God, is the most universally familiar. Here, He (Krishna) relates to man (Arjuna), the craft of war and the justification to conduct it under certain circumstances. However, as the longest known written document produced by humankind to date, it constitutes eighteen *parvas* or books spanning every major facet of societal governance. For example, the *rajdharma* or kingship and statehood focus of *shantiparvam* that relates to peace, is spread over 130 chapters. It comprises the counsel of Bhishma, sage and uncle to the Pandavas who were the victors over the Kauravas, their cousins, at the Kurukshetra War. This part could be viewed as a treatise for

---

[21] Manes may be derived from 'an archaic adjective manus – good (Wikipedia). This could have allegiance to *manushya* or human being in modern Sanskrit derived languages.

[22] Muniapan and Satpathy (2010).

[23] Or Great India.

post-conflict government formation and its functioning, with details of the roles and responsibilities and state activity of a dutiful king (Sharma, 2003).

The *Mahabharata*'s preponderance in modern India's psyche despite its focus on caste categories is noteworthy. The following selected couplets from the *Mahabharata* are cited, in this instance from the *Astra Darsana*, or the archery tournament, in which a competition takes place between the Kurus (Kauravas) and the Pandavs (Pandavas). What is surprising is the number of times Brahmins are mentioned and extolled. To quote,[24]

The Gathering

Skill in arms attained these princes from a *Brahman* warrior bold,
Drona, priest and proud preceptor, peerless chief of days of old!
Answered then the ancient monarch, joyful was his royal heart,
'Best of *Brahmans* and of warriors, nobly hast thou done thy part!' (p 2)

And the people of the city, *Brahmans*, *Vaisyas*, *Kshatras* bold,
Men from stall and loom and anvil gathered there, the young and old, (p 3)

Offerings to the gods immortal then the priestly warrior made,
Brahmans with their chanted *mantra* worship and obeisance paid, (p 4)

The Anointment of Karna

Brahmans chanted sacred *mantra* which holy books ordain,
And anointed Karna monarch, king of Anga's fair domain! (p 11)

Journey to Panchala

For when travelling with their mother, so it chanced by will of fate,
They were met by pious *Brahmans* bound for South Panchala's State,

And the pure and holy *Brahmans* hailed the youths of noble fame,
Asked them whither they would journey, from what distant land they came.

---

[24] The page numbers relate to Dutt's (1898) translation. The spellings of words reflect Dutt's own use.

"Heard ye not," the *Brahmans* questioned, "in Panchala's fair domain,
Drupad, good and gracious monarch, doth a mighty feast ordain?" (p 15)

Noble gifts we take as *Brahmans*, bless the rite with gladsome heart,
Share the feast so rich and bounteous, then with joyful minds depart.
Thus, the righteous sons of Pandu with the *Brahmans* took their way,
Where in South Panchala's kingdom mighty Drupad held his sway. (p 16)

And disguised as pious *Brahmans*, sons of Pandu begged their food,
People knew not Kuru's princes in that dwelling poor and rude.

The Wedding Ceremony

Brahmans came from distant regions with their sacred learning blest,
Drupad with a royal welcome greeted every honoured guest. (p 17)

Pandu's sons in guise of *Brahmans* mix with *Brahmans* versed in lore,
Mark proud Drupad's wealth and splendour, gazing, wondering evermore! (p 19)

The Bride

Then a *Brahman* versed in *mantra,* ancient priest of lunar race,
Lights the Fire, with pious offerings seeks its blessings and its grace, (p 19)

The Suitors

And he knew the warlike brothers in their holy *Brahman* guise,
Pointed them to Valadeva, gazing with a glad surprise! (p 21)

Trial of Skill

Stood like SURYA in his splendour and like AGNI in his flame, –
Pandu's sons in terror whispered, Karna sure must hit the aim!
But in proud and queenly accents Drupad's queenly daughter said:

"Monarch's daughter, born a *Kshatra*, *Suta*'s son I will not wed!"
Karna heard with crimsoned forehead, left the emprise almost done,
Left the bow already circled, silent gazed upon the Sun! (p 22)

The Disguised Arjun

Hushed the merry sound of laughter, hushed each suitor in his shame,
Arjun, godlike son of Pritha, from the ranks of *Brahmans* came!
Guised as *Brahman* young and holy and like INDRA's rainbow bright,
All the *Brahmans* shook their deerskins, cheered him in their hearts' delight!
Can a *Brahman* weak by nature, and in warlike arms untrained,
Wield the bow which crowned monarchs, long-armed chieftains have not strained?
Sure the *Brahman* boy in folly dares a foolish thoughtless deed,
Shame amidst this throng of monarchs, shall it be the *Brahman*'s meed?
Youth in youthful pride or madness will a foolish emprise dare, –
Sager men should stop his rashness and the *Brahman*'s honour spare!
"Shame he will not bring unto us," other *Brahmans* made reply,
Rather in this throng of monarchs, rich renown and honour high, (p 23)

Like a tusker strong and stately, like Himalay's towering crest,
Stands unmoved the youthful *Brahman*, ample-shouldered, deep in chest,
He will do the feat of valour, will not bring disgrace and stain,
Nor is task in all this wide earth which a *Brahman* tries in vain!
Ask not if 'tis right or foolish when a *Brahman* tries his fate,
If it leads to woe or glory, if "tis mean or wonderous great!
Let this young and daring *Brahman* undertake the warlike deed,
Let him try and by his prowess win the victor's noble meed!"
While the *Brahmans* deep revolving hopes and timid fears expressed,
By the bow the youthful Arjun stood unmoved like mountain crest! (p 24)

And the *Brahmans* shook their deerskins, but each irritated chief
In a lowly muttered whisper spake his rising rage and grief!

Drupad in the *Brahman*'s mantle knew the hero proud and brave,
'Gainst the rage of baffled suitors sought the gallant prince to save, (p 25)

The Tumult

Spake the suitors, anger-shaken, like a forest tempest-torn,
As Panchala's courteous monarch came to greet a *Brahman*-born:
Shall he like the grass of jungle trample us in haughty pride,
To a prating priest and *Brahman* wed the proud and peerless bride? (p 25)

And this rite of *swayamvara*, so our sacred laws ordain,
Is for warlike *Kshatras* only, priests that custom shall not stain!
If this maiden on a *Brahman* cast her eye, devoid of shame,
Let her expiate her folly in a pyre of blazing flame!
Leave the priestling in his folly sinning through a *Brahman*'s greed,
For we wage no war with *Brahmans* and forgive a foolish deed!
Much we owe to holy *Brahmans* for our realm and wealth and life,
Blood of priest or wise preceptor shall not stain our noble strife!
On they came, the angry monarchs, armed for cruel vengeful strife,
Drupad midst the holy *Brahmans* trembling fled for fear of life! (p 26)

Krishna to the rescue

Krishna knew the sons of Pandu though in robes of *Brahmans* dressed,
To his elder, Valadeva, thus his inner thoughts expressed:
Krishna rose amidst the monarchs, strove the tumult to appease,
And unto the angry suitors spake in words of righteous peace,
Monarchs bowed to Krishna's mandate, left Panchala's festive land,
Arjun took the beauteous princess, gently led her by the hand. (p 27)

What may be deduced from the 35 references to Brahmins in contrast to a handful of references to Kshatras (Kshatriyas), Vaisyas and Sutas (Sudhras)?[25]

[25] See Dutt (1898), pp 2–27.

First, Brahmins are the most revered of the four castes. Second, their supremacy and piety are unquestioned. Third, their rights are enormous; yet they cannot easily usurp a Kshatra bride, that is, inter-caste marriage is not easily accepted even though, in the ultimate analysis, there is deference to a Brahmin even in this matter.[26] Fourth, there appears to be some contradiction regarding their physical prowess for, though they are 'Brahman warrior bold', subsequently they are criticized for wanting to marry a Kshatra. Nevertheless, this is accepted since much is owed to Brahmins for the 'realm, wealth and life' of others. Indeed, it is the Kshatra woman who is found shameful for selecting a Brahmin to marry, an act that deserves expiation in 'a pyre of blazing flame'. Interestingly, however, the population of the city – 'Brahmans, Vaishyas, Kshatras' – are all allowed at the gathering though Sudhras are not mentioned, a practice that continues in many an Indian village where Sudhras are banished to live outside the circumference of the village proper. The genesis of this practice is described in Chapter 7.

It is this practical recognition of the sway of the caste system even while being fully aware of the exploitation already being carried out by Brahmins, that is noteworthy. Surely this should reflect a deep superstition regarding afterlife and what might befall anyone, in particular perhaps the king, if his Brahmins were not satiated with land, tax exemptions and the expropriation of cash through revenue sharing.

But its manifestations grew more monstrous with time. The virulence of caste emerged in a variety of experiences lived in different parts of India. One of the worst instances prevailed in rural Bengal until the mid-eighteenth century whereby Kulin Brahmins, a sub-caste of the Brahmins, took up as their occupation, marrying every pre-pubescent girl with no other suitable bridegroom in a village to save her and her family from perfidy and, thus, banishment from the village. This reflected a rule that a girl's marriage could not be held after puberty, possibly a *diktat* from the Brahmins themselves. The Kulin Brahmin, often old, travelled from village to village marrying such girls and spending a night with them and moving on. The *diktat* covered even the ruling *zamindar* – land owning, revenue collector – families. When the old, perennial bridegroom died, the news was sent from village to village and all his brides would be made a '*sati*', that is, burnt alive on a funeral pyre. *Sati* flourished in other forms as well. The death by a disease such as cholera, small pox or typhoid of a young man, occurrences that were not uncommon, would result in his young widow's being burnt alive on the funeral pyre of the husband. One excuse for the inhumane practice was to protect her from being physically assaulted in widowhood. *Sati* – woman sacrificed to fire – was abolished on 4 December 1829, at the urging of

[26] See Shome (2021), ch. 2, for reference to the fact that in some subsequent Hindu kingdoms, Brahmins were allowed to marry lower castes but not vice versa.

Raja Rammohan Roy who, as a young man, had seen his sister-in-law being burnt alive at the funeral pyre of his elder brother. Roy worked in cooperation with William Bentinck, a reform-minded Governor General of India. According to Fisch (2000), 'Wherever the prohibition had taken place, widow-burning soon ceased almost completely, although it never vanished completely. Occasional cases were reported even after 1947. The last highly publicized Sati was the death of the 18-year-old Roop Kanwar in Deorala, Rajasthan, on 4 September, 1987' (pp 109–10).

It is also known that the Hindu kings of India who took their religion and the caste system to south-east Asia as far back as the first millennium CE, established structures with crucial powerful roles accorded to Brahmins. While Buddhism emerged and prevailed widely for a period in India, it faded with the consolidation of Hinduism by the Adi Shankaracharya (788 CE–820 CE) and its re-adoption by powerful kings; and the preeminent position of Brahmins was restored. However, Buddhism established itself in South-East Asia. In Cambodia, Buddhism asserted itself from the reign of Jayavarman VII (reigned 1181–1220 CE) and continued thereafter. Buddhism spread south to Sri Lanka and east to Myanmar and South-East Asia, and further east to China, Korea and Japan, carried back mainly by travelling monks. In the process, Buddhism, by and large, eradicated caste. In India, Hinduism did not lose its primary position again and caste took hold as a strong force. The essential difference between the two regions today is the absence or presence of caste.[27] In one, inclusion of all activities by anyone and, in the other, exclusion and isolation, with selective allocation of activities to different pre-determined groups by birth, became the rule.[28]

Indeed, Bagade (2021), in a review of Phule's (1827–90) work, pointed out how early authors consistently brought caste and its ramifications to the forefront of intellectual awareness. He described Phule's work as bringing the caste question to the universal conceptual category of slavery. It was a harbinger to Wilkerson's (2020) analogy of caste and slavery discussed earlier in Chapter 5. Phule elaborated the material, social and psychological bondage of the caste system, initiating a struggle for freedom from the caste bondage. Bagade (2021) described how Phule had elaborated on the impact of prevalent caste structures. To quote, 'He not only identified structures and processes of the exploitation and oppression operating under caste but also unravelled the social condition of slavery structured under the Brahmanical hegemony'

[27] This does not imply that ethnic groupings with considerable income differences have not risen in Buddhist majority countries such as in Sri Lanka against Tamil Hindus, or in Myanmar against Rohingya Muslims. But the minorities cannot be said to be separated into specific occupations.

[28] The grasp of caste with its deleterious effects remains strong in Islamic Pakistan as well. See Lieven (2011), p 34, and pp 38–39.

(p 197). Bagade also described Phule's pursuing of *Sarvjanik Satyadharma*, an alternative approach to the process of Sanskritization which he linked to Brahmanical ideology (Bagade, 2021, p 198). The role of Brahmanism in shaping a society that designs social and economic exclusion and isolation stares in the face of Indian society, and its heavy burden continues to this day. Essentially it has disabled capabilities in basic education, primary health and lifetime earning capacity, in turn affecting freedom and happiness by stratifying society. It should not be unsafe to say, therefore, that unless the role of the extraordinary institution of caste is singed successfully, the reality of India's truncated socio-economic development is likely to remain intact and, relatedly, poverty and inequality to remain an indelible feature of Indian society. By contrast, China essentially got rid of the burden of the feudal features of religions such as Taoism and Confucianism in the form of all beliefs connected to superstition, spirits or links to ancestors or even family through Mao Zedong's ruthless eradication of historical baggage through a cultural revolution in the 1960s.[29] Nevertheless, there appears to be a resurgence of religions in contemporary China with their concomitant challenges of societal stratification and growing income inequality.

Use of caste by the colonists

Between mid-eighteenth and nineteenth centuries – the first century of British rule in India – the caste system appears to have become less rigid or hierarchical. But this changed in the second century of British rule when the British introduced land revenue policies whose returns were better assured through local caste hierarchy. Thus 'the 'traditional' Indian village with its 'traditional' caste system was, in large part, a product of the British Raj' (Fuller, 2003, p 480). The British legal system in India also leaned on the *Dharmashastra* with its Brahmanical legal code. Elaborate classification and enumeration of caste were introduced together with tenurial categories and religious distinctions. Social subdivisions were defined by caste (other than for tribal people) which became the institutional keystone of Indian society.

The decennial census also sharpened categories by caste, beginning 1871. The 1910 Census introduced three categories: (i) Hindus; (ii) Tribals; and (iii) Untouchables. The last two categories were called essentially 'not Hindus at all.' The census provided a list of excluded Hindus. While the ancient *Smriti* had listed 12 communities, by 1935, 429 untouchable communities had been listed by state, segregated in non-intersecting communities, a system that had 'no parallel in the history of the world' (Ambedkar [1947],

[29] Most historians agree the cultural revolution began in 1966 when party chiefs in Beijing issued the 'May 16 Notification' and officially came to an end when Mao died on 9 September 1976 at the age of 82. See Phillips (2016).

p 265). Between the lists, only one community was common, exposing the impracticality, if not anomaly, of such categorization.

The caste of every citizen was recorded until 1931, with a rank order and the total number under each category which was taken as the framework for society, with pan-Indian uniformity. Thus, though the British did not create, they imbued caste with a 'centrality and inflexibility which it had not had before. In Bayly's phrase (1988: ch. 5), colonialism 'consolidated' 'traditional' caste society in India (cf. Cohn 1987: chs 8, 10, 22 and passim)' (Fuller, p 481). Whether the emphasis, elongation and use of caste was carried out due to malice against the resident population by stirring the pot, or whether it was their meticulousness for meaningless detail[30] is debatable. Perhaps it was a mix of the two.

The census reports, together with volumes entitled, *Castes and Tribes*, provided an 'official' ethnography of thousands of different castes but were unable to detail if and how the caste system worked in different locations. Only after independence, 'village studies' between the 1950s to 1970s provided analytical descriptions of village society including castes and social change. Analysed post-independence, a body of Western researchers concluded that 'traditional' villages and 'traditional' caste systems got anchored in the colonial period.

Counter-positioned was Dumont ([1966] 1970) who, in his *Homo Hierarchicus* converted caste from a village-based concept to that of Indian society as a whole whose unity, in his view, reflected the pan-Indian existence and religious ideology of the caste system. It suggested that the caste system was based on complementarity. A Brahmin's purity reciprocally depended on the impurity of an untouchable who served him and the completion of whose responsibilities enabled the functioning of the Brahmin and all castes in between, all of them having interlocking functional relationships with one another. In this view, traditional Indian society was hierarchical but holistic while western society was individualistic and based on economic interests and relations. In Chatterjee's (1993) description of Dumont,

> Brahmans cannot do without the menial castes if their economic services are to be provided. The unity of identity and difference – vide Dumont, the unity of purity and pollution – gives us the *ground* of caste as a totality or system … . ([T]he) ground for defining the totality of caste relations as a system. (p 176)

Chatterjee (1993) observed two prevailing views on caste,

30 See Dickens (1837) ch. 1, for a fictional account of meticulous nonsense practised by the Pickwickians, a club of 'smallwigs' in Victorian England.

> All arguments about the rule of colonial difference, and hence about the inherent incapacity of Indian society to acquire the virtues of modernity and nationhood, tended to converge upon this supposedly Indian institution. (p 173)

> The first is to deny the suggestion that caste is essential to the characterisation of Indian society. This position has been especially favoured by the nationalist Left … . The second is to … retain caste as an essential element of Indian society … a caste system makes Indian society different from the Western. What is denied, however, is … that caste is necessarily contradictory to, and incompatible with, a modern and just society. (p 174)

What may be derived is that the caste system exemplified a society that was in contraposition to western society. Since Dumont's work, comparative analyses of social inequality have not overlooked the role of caste. It is the contention of this book that caste determines income inequality and poverty, that, by rational inference from an imposed classification at birth that assigns income earning capability, caste automatically imposes – perpetrates – economic capacity by hierarchy. Inequality terminates in poverty.

Subsequent studies emphasized alternative ideologies possessed by all non-Brahmin castes including Kshatriyas, Vaisyas and Sudhras extending right to Harijans at the bottom (Madan, 1982). Such differences are expressed through various means including food restrictions – vegetarianism and non-vegetarianism in general but also through more detailed specifications – and conjugal mores and customs expressed through Hindu marriage laws, and in various other ways. Thus, according to such studies, ritual purity representing Brahmanical values are not unique determinants of status. Rather, Kshatriya-like castes and kingly dominance rather than religious pre-eminence, may be viewed to comprise the cornerstone of the pertinent social structure.

Some scholars have claimed that low castes reject the pretensions of the Brahmins and other high castes, or even that they deny the ideological premises of the caste system altogether (Gough [1981] 1989). Harijans are more likely to pay lip-service to caste values and only defer to the higher castes because they are too weak to resist them openly, economically, and politically (Das, 2015). In private, they assert their own sense of self-worth and display an awareness of how claims to high status depend on control of material resources (Mencher 1974; Kapadia 1995). However, hierarchy within untouchable castes who may be worried about their rank in relation to one another also exists. Biardeau ([1981] 1989) observed that the emerging emphasis on 'agency' and 'resistance' had led some authors to 'overlook the complexity of Brahmanical religious ideology. Dumont's original hypothesis of a monolithic caste system effectively comes under scrutiny in that he ignored variations in the practice of the caste system. Nevertheless, little proof exists of major variations from the central monolith of the *varna*-based caste practices prevalent in deep-rooted village structures in the depths of India.

Thapar (2003) pointed to caste as a variegated entity, forming different clusters in different parts of India. Close identities between religious sects and castes have been found to be frequent in Indian religion so much so that independent sects have been cast as Hindu religions (in the plural) by scholars (p xxviii–ix). In some regions, landowning groups and in others, trading groups, can be dominant allowing different freedoms to, and restrictions on, castes. This probably has allowed wealth – rather than caste – ranking as the determinant of power in a few such regions. There, caste would have a less rigid or frozen control on society (p xxvii). While this reality could be representative of urban or semi-urban society and pockets of semi-rural and rural society, the grip of caste remains strong and powerful in much of rural society and in small mufassil towns in the periphery.

In the same vein, Fuller (2003) pointed out that Dumont's ([1966] 1970) 'substantialization' conveyed a transformation of caste whereby 'interdependent, complementary relationships among hierarchically ranked castes (gave) way to competitive opposition among separate groups perceived as substantively different from each other' (p 487). What has been explained earlier is that complementarity cited by analysts is more a one-sided relationship in favour of the more powerful in the caste hierarchy and, by definition, cannot be for both sides. This is because the less powerful can have no choice in selecting or rejecting the relationship. At least behind the scene, caste-based domination and decision making have to prevail. In this entire literature, therefore, there is certainly an ardent, if not apologetic, search for a duality, of an equilibrium structure, of complementary within caste hierarchy. That is a fallacy since that view is oblivious of the lack of choice by the lower castes as well as to the truncated capability and productivity that caste must have caused to society over millennia.

Caste in contemporary India

In a post-independence case study, Ramkheri, a village in Madhya Pradesh, was followed over several decades (1954–56, 1983 and 1992) by Mayer (1960, 1996). He concluded that caste rank had become less sharply 'defined', but untouchability had stood its ground as did caste endogamy. It appeared that cultural difference and separation had replaced the more ostensible Brahminic ritual purity. This was interpreted as substantialization as each caste became defined by its own culture and way of life though, paradoxically, this also led to more inequality within each caste. Mayer asserted that statements by villagers such as 'there is no caste left' was 'never meant to be a statement of fact' but that caste inequality could no longer be legitimately defended in public while cultural difference could. Villagers replaced caste or *jati* by community or *samaj*. The new terms could be 'a coded means to assert the status of one's own caste and to justify inequality among castes. … substantialization is an ideological shift which sharpens the divide between public and private behaviour and expression.' Beteille's (1996) work claimed that urban areas differed regarding caste in that it had become increasingly irrelevant in many areas of life; for example, caste may help in finding a job though meritocracy may reign.

However, caste liaisons matter in the acceptance of a marriage though it has to be admitted that instances of arranged inter-caste marriage do occur in large cities such as Mumbai and Kolkata. Beteille's position that caste does not enter the mind or action of most of the urban intelligentsia does, however, raise the question of what percent of the urban population comprises that intelligentsia, that is, what is the relevance of their view in the context of the entire urban population? Caste does still obstruct choice in marriage and lead to unhappiness over and above excluding a person from stepping on to the career ladder. Thus, multiple livelihood activities of an urban dweller continue to be determined by an accident of birth.

Banerjee et al. (2009) found that, 'First, there is no reason to expect that economic growth by itself will undermine caste-based preferences in marriage. Second, caste-based preferences in marriage are unlikely to be a major constraint on growth' (p 34). Banerjee et al. (2013) used matrimonial advertisements in Bengal to analyse the role of caste in a selection of middle-class marriage partners. They found that, 'caste is highly valued in terms of preferences … (However,) in equilibrium, caste (does) little to alter the matching patterns on non-caste attributes' (p 33). Further,

> 30 percent of people in the sample do not marry within their caste. In part, this is due to heterogeneity in caste preferences, with some people having caste-neutral preferences … (and) about 40 percent of the sons and daughters of respondents eventually marry through a channel other than the ads (e.g., through friends and family networks), and 20 percent enter into a 'love marriage.' This suggests that while economic forces have not been able to undermine the role of caste-based preferences on marriage market outcomes, these preferences themselves might be undergoing changes. (p 70)

More recently, Chakraborty (2021) pointed out that, even in a literate state like Kerala, the labour force participation of women remained low with marriage as the most significant determinant of women's economic future and caste, denoting that marital status continued to remain a persistent feature. Indeed, the parents of prospective brides were not unlikely to avoid their children marrying outside their caste even at the cost of sacrificing education – no education versus a master's degree – of the bridegroom. The author concluded that caste continued to be an important element in the preference pattern for marriage partners.

Caste among non-Hindus

Muslims, Christians, Sikhs and other non-Hindus are also found to be hierarchically ranked in India, usually integrated into their local caste hierarchies prior to conversion (Ahmad, 1973). In some localities, a Muslim community may be the dominant *jati* such as the Meos of north Rajasthan and south Haryana (Jamous, 1996) or the Syrian Christians in southern Kerala (Fuller, 1976). Meos consider themselves Rajputs; Syrian Christians, claiming descent from Saint Thomas the Apostle's Brahmin converts, enjoy a status similar to the landholding Nayars. Elite Muslims may adhere to a pan-Islamic community beyond India, their status categorized by reference to their Arabian origins, or descent from the Prophet, or ancestral traditions of Islamic learning. Lower-status Muslims may be perceived as descendants of low-caste converts. Indian Muslims, therefore, could resemble Hindu castes.

Ironically, the partition of India did not demolish or disable caste differentiation in the predominantly Muslim Pakistan as Lieven (2011) has discussed. He quoted Ibbetson (1883),

> An old agnostic is said to have summed up his philosophy in the following words: 'The only thing I know is that I know nothing and I am not quite sure that I know that.' His words express very exactly my own feelings regarding caste in the Punjab. My experience is that it is almost impossible to make any statement whatever regarding any one of the castes we have to deal with; absolutely true though it may be for one part of the province, (not so) … as regards the same people in some other district. (p 38)

Lieven's subsequent analysis revealed that an effective caste system continued in post-independent Muslim Pakistan. The word *Zat* is related to the Sanskritised (Indian) word *jati*. Pakistan also uses *Qaum* to mean tribe or ethnicity over and above nation. The latter, used in Balochistan province, is reminiscent of the old, tightly-knit clans of Scotland controlled by autocratic chieftains. Pathans divide their tribes into rival sub-tribes, with new leaders in every generation. In Punjab, that is, in its Pakistan portion in the west, the same caste differences exist in the form of Rajputs, Jats, Gujjars and others.[31] Indeed their origin is Kshatriya whether in India or Pakistan though, unlike

[31] Gujjars gave its name to the state of Gujarat in India and the city in Pakistan by the same name.

in India, they do not possess a collective political identity in Pakistan. Lieven found, however, that they shared 'a strong sense of superiority to everyone else, a strong preference for marrying each other' as well as a definitive clan cooperation (p 39). Loyalty and mobilization get stronger with local sub-clans such as the Chauhan Rajput, Alpial Rajput and others. Lieven (2011) claimed that 'The Sayyids and Qureishis are groups peculiar to Islam, being (ostensibly) descendants of the Prophet and his clan, and therefore of Arabic origin. Yet their role and status in South Asian Muslim society has certain limited affinities to that of the Brahmins in South Asian Hindu society' (p 39).

Lower castes of the Hindu system also prevail in Pakistan including the *kammi* artisan and service groups in towns and villages and, below them, rather unbelievably perhaps, the untouchables and tribals. They are so far down the system that no one even bothers much if they are Muslim, Hindu or – what most really are – pre-Hindu animist. As in India, this last grouping is the most vulnerable in Pakistani society, liable to be preyed on economically and sexually by local dominant lineages and by the police.

Other groupings that Lieven brought to notice were *khandan* – or 'joint family', in which descendants of one male ancestor lived under one roof using one kitchen[32] and *biradiri* (from the Indo-European 'brothers') as a single family. Thus, religion may have separated Pakistan from India in 1947 but, ironically, Pakistan carried casteism with it from India and practices it within its own boundaries.

Nevertheless, with the appearance of Hindu nationalistic politics, Muslim antipathy to internal caste-like groupings has sharpened. Sikhs too have moved away from caste divisions since the 1980s as caste is increasingly perceived as a stamp of Hindu society. However, caste feelings have not disappeared totally from the top layers of either group.

Caste and current politics

Back in colonial India, the Commissioner for the 1911 Census of Bengal reported that Bengalis generally believed that the census was designed 'to fix the relative position of different castes and to deal with questions of social superiority', and 'hundreds of petitions were received from different castes … requesting that they might be known by a new name, be placed higher up in the order of precedence, be recognized as Kshatriya and Vaishya, etc.' (Srinivas, 1966, pp 95–96).

With the British toying with limited Indian self-government from 1919, caste-based associations began to exercise political pressure at the regional level to give it shape. Kumar (2021) described a memorandum to

[32] *Ekannavarti* or 'rice prepared in one pot' in Hindu nomenclature.

the Simon Commission in 1928 in which members of the All-India Adi Hindu Mahasabha, Cawnpore (an association of former 'untouchable' castes) brought to the Commission's attention that school textbooks castigated 'untouchables' as low, mean, illegitimate and willed (p 239). Clearly caste groups had begun to find avenues to pursue means to bring their overall dire condition to the attention of the governing authorities. Since independence, such associations intensified their political agendas and roles, for example, through intensified demands for quotas for public sector education and jobs based on 'reservations' for caste categories (see next discussion) with demonstrated success on an internationally comparative basis.

India's 1950 constitution guaranteed equal fundamental rights for all citizens together with freedom from discrimination on grounds of race, caste, sex or place of birth, and equality of opportunity in public appointments; it also abolished untouchability. The constitution provided for the 'reservation' of seats in parliament and state legislatures, and of posts in government services, for the SCs and Scheduled Tribes (STs), the newly termed erstwhile Harijans or untouchables. The formulation along those lines may be attributed to Bhimrao Ramji Ambedkar (1891–1956), political thinker and activist, an untouchable himself, known as the father of the constitution. It was his interpretation that equated political universalization to caste equality (see Chapter 7). The constitution also recognized other 'backward classes' (OBCs), but did not define them or specify provisions in their favour. Subsequently, however, several state governments adopted measures for OBCs, for example in the reservation of posts akin to those for SCs and STs guaranteed by the central government. These attempts clearly revealed an intention, a determination perhaps, to rid India of its ancient inequalities, an endeavour not witnessed in any advanced country to a comparable extent.

Piketty (2020) revisited inequality between India's earlier discriminated lower castes – Dalits and Adivasis – and the rest of society. Piketty (2021) argued that reservations actually provided an excuse for advantaged groups from paying taxes for adequate and comprehensive provision of socio-economic services including education, health and basic infrastructure. To buttress his point, he cited Shah et al. (2021) who argued that economic growth had not erased, but entrenched, caste and race in India. Another instrument to reduce inequality, land redistribution by communist state level governments in Kerala and West Bengal, was not supported by the central government. Even Ambedkar, the Dalit leader, did not exhibit a stance in favour of land redistribution. The *Bhoodan* – gift of land – movement initiated in 1951 by Vinoba Bhave, a Gandhian, was successful while he lived though it receded later.[33]

[33] Bhave (1895–1982) walked from village to village with his followers with the objective of convincing landowners to transfer their excess land to the landless. The Bhoodan

In sum, the struggles for and by SC, ST and OBC 'communities' continued and culminated in various manifestations including mass conversions to Buddhism and Christianity and in separately identifiable political representations. They emerged as 'a specific political subject, a non-Hindu, a political minority, and finally, a suffering subject that required state protection' (Rao, 2009). Efforts to redress complex cultural forms of discrimination thus produced a unique set of religion related outcomes and political attempts at resolving the problem of Dalit suffering. This explains why caste has grown rather than diminished in significance as democracy has taken root in India, producing a form of politics that forefronts collective rights and group emancipation rather than individual autonomy. This book proposes an approach to the caste issue that challenges received accounts of democratization in the form of a radical human prescription for any future path to be followed in the concluding Chapter 11.

Rao (2009) argued that Dalits continued to comprise caste subalterns, and could enhance their rights including equality and citizenship not just due to the formal delegitimization of caste but also by forming sub-caste clusters and exercising voting power that converted 'historic suffering and humiliation' – the experience of being 'ground down', being 'broken'. This was 'central to the identity of the Dalit as both a non-Hindu minority and an inaugural political-ethical subject' (p xii). However, Rao admitted that Dalits continued to suffer stigmatization and comprised,

> a historical and contemporary object of suffering. Rising Dalit militancy has been offset by new formations of anti-Dalit violence: brutality against inter-caste liaison, land grabs, and other forms of economic violence, especially against more prosperous Dalits, sexual humiliation of Dalit women, ritual murders, and the desecration of Dalit commemorative sites. (p xiii)

Though electoral politics in independent India cannot be said to have been solely determined by caste categories in particular in metropolitan urban areas, there has been a strong underlying current of caste influence, if not

---

Movement was initiated by Mahatma Gandhi's disciple Vinoba Bhave in April 1951 and witnessed landowners gifting land to the landless. Within six years, about 1.9 million hectares were collected into a land bank. The subsequent Bhoodan Act entrusted government to distribute the land. The movement later transformed into the *Gramdan* (gifted village) movement, which sought donations of entire villages to achieve equal distribution among all village residents. Sometimes three-quarters of a village would donate land. Tribal areas, currently under vigorous land acquisition, were major participants in the *Graamdaan* movement. Both the movements eventually receded though the land bank survived. See Mahapatra (2020).

diktat, as one moves from urban towards rural locales. This process has occasionally resulted in Dalits consolidating forces, or a large lower caste such as the Yadavs narrowing down to successful political consolidation and rule at the level of a state. Such concentration has no doubt produced the chief minister of Uttar Pradesh state, where Dalits and Yadavs held governments alternatively during the years 1989–2017.[34] That was followed by a rightwing Hindu nationalist government that proved the weakness and ephemeral nature of Dalit power. A similar role could be identified in the Jat community of Haryana after the erstwhile larger state of Punjab was divided into two in 1966, one exclusively for majority Sikhs and another for majority Jats. The political power of the Jats, a consolidated peasant caste, has reflected their control over land and their emergence as farmers functioning successfully within the market economy.

Reaction against reservation

In 1990, the role of reservation in Indian politics gathered steam. V. P. Singh, then Prime Minister, initiated the implementation of recommendations of an enquiry commission (the Mandal Commission) that had been issued ten years earlier. It included reserving 27 per cent of public sector jobs for OBCs. This was in addition to 22.5 per cent already reserved for the SC-ST categories, the total thus adding up to almost 50 per cent. The decision was defended using the achievement of social equality as an argument, but it was also to draw electoral support from the large OBC communities in northern India. It led to severe violence from the higher castes causing deaths, and was challenged in the courts. Nevertheless, the subsequent government implemented it in 1991 while facing mild protests, and it was approved by the Supreme Court in 1992. Caste anchored in more strongly in the political landscape of the 1990s (Radhakrishnan 1996). Subsequently, the southern states of Karnataka and Tamil Nadu increased reservations further to 69 per cent.

The consolidation of Dalit political power translated into their supporting the Hindu nationalists of the Bharatiya Janata Party (BJP) that is currently in power at the centre as well as in an increasingly large number of states. It may be asked why. Perhaps because the BJP's platform has been, sporadically, one of uniting all Hindus, paradoxically including Dalits into the fray. So

[34] 1989–91 (Samajwadi Party [SP] led by Mulayam Singh Yadav belonging to the Yadavs, considered a lower caste of herdsmen), 1993–95 (SP of Mulayam Singh Yadav with Bahujan Samaj Party [BSP] led by Mayawati, a Dalit, 2003–07 (SP of Mulayam Singh Yadav), 2007–12 (BSP-Mayawati), and 2012–17 (SP-Akhilesh Yadav) after which the Bharatiya Janata Party (BJP) took over the government, headed by Yogi Adityanath, a Hindu priest, under the auspices of Narendra Modi, the prime minister at the centre.

far, the BJP has won seats in a first-past-the-line system which reveals that everywhere it has won by narrow margins. It is, therefore, likely that the lowest castes, especially Harijans who do not consider themselves to be Hindus and are exploited by upper castes in rural communities, would not be so pliable as to join in with a Hindu supremacist grouping. Indeed, instead of being eradicated, caste differences appear to have been sharpened in Indian politics and rural society. Reservation may have temporarily provided solace and a kind of social protection for nearly 70 percent of India's lower castes reflecting India's unique policy attempts at equalization of public access and rights. But they would be better off if caste differences were actually neutralized and society achieved social equality in its full meaning lest it should lose the tentative political, and associated economic, foothold it has achieved in some states.

A form of equalization is a transfer through public redistribution of tangible assets such as land apart from private endeavours such as the *Bhoodan* movement of Vinoba Bhave. Though land reform was relatively successful in some Indian states where land was transferred from absentee landlords to peasants, it did not occur in most states successfully or occurred only on paper with subalterns appearing as the face, rather than the real, recipients of such transfer. Sarkar (2012) examined the challenges faced by reform-oriented political projects in governing antagonistic elements of class, caste, gender and religion. He studied the experience of the Left Front Government (a coalition of several[35] Left and Leftist political parties) which governed the state of West Bengal for 34 years between 1977–2011. He found that the lack of land ownership or freedom from oppression and bodily toil remained a fundamental political problem that determined the course and dynamics of governance, pointing to the limits of agrarian modernity. While the government redistributed land, secured tenancy contracts, improved agricultural productivity and had an impact on caste relations in rural areas, the restructuring created a new dominant class under which the earlier role of the Panchayat – rural government – receded. A policy framework to assist marginalized groups was lacking, and they had to help themselves for survival, employing covert strategies. Antagonisms developed and an atmosphere of consent and cooperation failed to develop. Reflecting the Left rule's dithering normative policy basis, their tenure finally collapsed, and a populist setup replaced it in May 2011.

[35] The six founding parties of the Left Front comprised the Communist Party of India (Marxist) or the CPI(M), the All India Forward Bloc (AIFB), the Revolutionary Socialist Party (RSP), the Marxist Forward Bloc (MFB), the Revolutionary Communist Party of India (RCPI) and the Biplabi Bangla Congress (BBC), and articulated a common programme. In 1981, the Communist Party of India, the Democratic Socialist Party and the West Bengal Socialist Party joined the Left Front.

Sarkar (2011) further pointed to challenges of land acquisition by government from affected families, sometimes leading to their oppression. If the state upholds the law, it should accept the democratic values of disagreement and dissent and plurality of modes of existence. This does not always happen. Therefore, where socio-economic reform including land reform, has not occurred or has failed, Dalit power, in particular of Adivasis, has tended to demonstrate itself outside the political spectrum. Whatever changes have occurred to benefit low castes in urban areas have not been matched in rural or extreme interior areas where the vast majority of the Indian population lives. New scholarly work that is emerging provides evidence of it. Reflecting anthropological fieldwork, Kunnath (2021), for example, focused on the agency of the very poor – Dalits and Adivasis – in rural India who participate in rebel governance. During 50 years of armed struggle, they have successfully established *Janathana Sarkar* – people's government – with the objective of complete social overhaul in a radical form of democracy of the poor. Not being a part of the established political system, they have met with violent government repression but have, nevertheless, grown over the fifty years of their existence. Summing up his 20-month research in and around Krantipur, the centre of Maoist governance, Kunnath (2020) observed,

> The effect of the State's ruthless crackdown on the Maoist movement was being felt in the forest villages. The security forces were gradually closing in on Krantipur from all sides. More police camps were being built, and thousands of troops moved into the forest areas. Fear was growing all over the place. The villagers were being stopped, searched, arrested and tortured.

However, he also found a certain degree of dominance by the Maoist superiors over the Dalits and Adivasis which was resented by them. He found that there was room to enhance agency – self-governance – of the poor in those areas despite violence exercised on them by the state. It is also a strong reflection of the continuance of poverty among the lowest caste groupings in India's remote areas.

Division of incomes by caste

Under one rubric, Bhaduri (2005), in a long essay, mentioned several related aspects including acute caste, religion and gender prejudices as causing gross inequality in Indian society. He asserted his view as a three-step sequence. First, reflecting India's low per-capita income, a growth-oriented strategy is essential. Second, growth and distribution must be interwoven, reinforcing each other in the formulation of economic policies. Third, the combined approach has to be buttressed by policies to root out structural inequalities in caste, gender and religious discrimination. This three-pronged approach continues to be needed today since only the first pillar has been achieved, the second has worsened, and the third has not achieved its potential. They now need further strengthening as fissures in the form of caste and religious discrimination and atrocities against women have escalated during the last decade.

Appeasing caste consequences by an array of subsidies to selected groups who historically suffered exclusion has been India's policy response. Thus, selection to exclude, then isolate, followed by selection to appease is what explains the sweep of India's poverty and inequality experience and its attempts at alleviating them. Nevertheless, statistical evidence on caste divisions across income deciles has been reported by Bharti (2018), revealing income inequality according to caste groupings. His raw data are used here to draw conclusions. Caste codes reflect a particular classification, including Muslims and Others, as in the following list:

- Dalits, Adivasis and OBC's are coded as they are, regardless of their religion;
- Brahmins are coded as Brahmins;
- all Hindus[36] who are not categorized previously are coded as Forward Caste (FC);
- all Muslims, who are not coded previously, are coded as Muslims;
- the rest of the population is grouped as Others.[37]

Bharti's figures reveal what is termed 'representational inequality' (RI) in wealth across castes. To illustrate by taking the OBC population for example, if it comprises 45 per cent of the overall population, perfect representational equality will imply a representation of 45 per cent OBC population in all deciles. A deviation from this would imply representational inequality. A higher representation (than the population share) for any caste group in the top decile, will also increase RI. That caste group would be a beneficiary of the inequality. On the other hand, a higher representation (than the population share) of a caste group in the lower deciles also increase RI, but that caste group would be a victim of the inequality.

---

[36] There are five major religions in India – Hinduism, Islam, Christianity, Buddhism and Sikhism.

[37] FC comprises those who do not fall under SC, ST or OBC. It consists of castes and sub-castes such as Brahmins, Rajputs, Banias and others who are not covered by reservation for employment or education in public institutions.

Using raw statistics presented by Bharti, the population share of any group, for example, Scheduled Tribes, ST in any decile can be calculated. For example, for the top decile of the rural population in 2002, it was:

Population Share (ST, 2002, Top 10%) = [RI (ST, 2002, Top 10%) + 1] * Population Share (ST, 2002)

This turns out to be 2.84 as highlighted in Table 6.1. Similar calculations are made for all caste groupings in different wealth deciles to arrive at the

Table 6.1: India: population shares of caste groups in given wealth deciles (%)

	2002			2012		
	Bottom 50%	**Middle 40%**	**Top 10%**	**Bottom 50%**	**Middle 40%**	**Top 10%**
India						
ST	10.89	5.45	2.24	13.01	5.95	2.32
SC	27.00	13.60	3.74	24.79	13.90	3.94
OBC	39.07	42.70	31.82	41.39	47.06	36.16
FC	14.89	28.65	43.09	14.34	24.78	40.55
Muslim	9.00	6.50	3.70	7.01	5.82	3.38
Others	0.70	1.98	10.55	0.68	1.64	8.75
Rural						
ST	13.11	6.55	**2.84**	16.09	8.17	2.88
SC	28.71	14.04	3.40	26.38	15.25	5.15
OBC	39.45	45.33	38.19	40.09	49.88	42.76
FC	11.72	25.91	35.74	11.54	19.29	30.67
Muslim	7.81	5.49	3.64	6.33	5.36	2.45
Others	0.42	1.53	11.50	0.53	1.18	11.23
Urban						
ST	3.77	2.02	1.55	4.69	2.49	1.93
SC	20.73	11.35	3.78	20.24	11.46	2.83
OBC	37.82	35.00	24.04	43.99	41.09	30.30
FC	25.27	38.24	52.20	21.91	35.60	50.82
Muslim	12.59	9.08	4.02	9.24	6.26	3.80
Others	1.58	3.50	9.80	1.21	2.40	7.10

Source: Calculations based on Tables 10 and 18 in Bharti (2018). All India Debt and Investment Survey (AIDIS), 2012, is the last survey year

proportion of population in a particular decile in 2002, for all of India, and divided into rural and urban. The exercise is repeated for 2012.

The results are converted to easy-to-read Figures 6.1 (rural) and 6.2 (urban). In the case of the rural population, what is observed is that only for the forward class (FC) and the category Others did the top decile have a higher representation than the remaining 90 per cent of the population. By contrast, in the SC, ST as well as the Muslim populations, the share in the top decile declined significantly. As was to be expected, their shares were much higher than those of the FC and Others in the lower half of the population. Thus, despite government attempts at redressing inequality through various non-pecuniary transfers, the state of inequality remained strongly reflective of the descending order of castes.

Essentially the same conclusion may be drawn for the urban population in which the FC and Others occupied much higher shares in the top decile and lower shares in the lower deciles, while the OBC and SC occupied high positions in the bottom half of the urban population. However, it is noteworthy that the FC also occupied a high percentage of 21.91 per cent in the lower half of the urban population, as opposed to only 11.54 per cent in the lower half of the rural population. This could reflect the challenges of urban life also for the FC. Thus, a variety of revealing conclusions may be drawn. It is hoped that new insights may be obtained from the next survey

Figure 6.1: Proportion of different caste groups: rural (2012)[1]

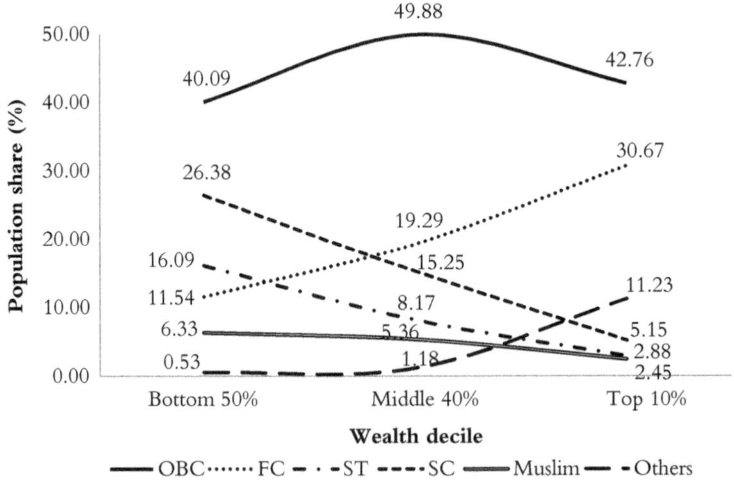

[1] Note that, ideally, each column (under 50%, 40% and 10%) should add up to 100. Based on the numbers, the addition yields numbers close to 100. Any difference can be attributed to statistical errors.

Source: Drawn using Table 6.1

Figure 6.2: Proportion of different caste groups: urban (2012)

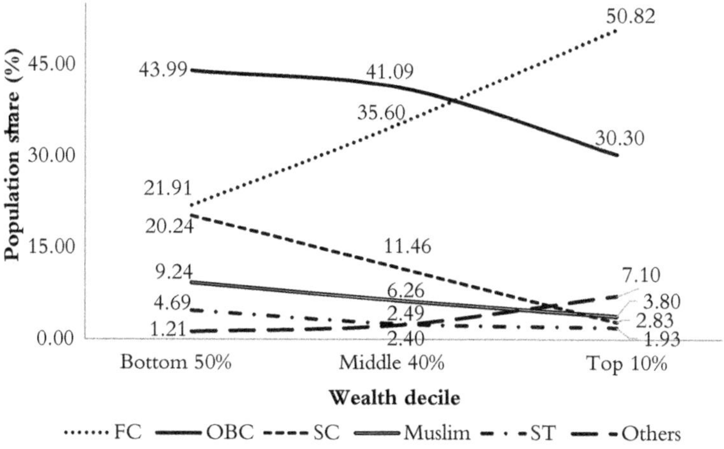

Source: Drawn using Table 6.1

Table 6.2: Caste reservation and budget allocation

Year	**2014**	**2019**					
Seats reserved in Lok Shabha (Lower House) (%)							
Scheduled Castes (SCs)	15.5	15.5					
Scheduled Tribes (STs)	8.7	8.7					
Financial year	**2015–16**	**2016–17**	**2017–18**	**2018–19**	**2019–20**	**2020–21**	**2021–22**
% of central government budget allocated to SC-ST welfare	2.9	2.8	3.8	3.9	4.2	3.9	6.0

Source: Sustainable Development Goals, National Indicator Framework, Progress Report 2021, National Statistical Office (NSO), Ministry of Statistics and Programme Implementation, Government of India

regarding emerging trends if any, regarding caste divisions within different wealth deciles in India.

One aspect on the political front is to be recognized, however. Currently, almost a quarter of the seats in the lower house of parliament are reserved for the SC-ST categories (Table 6.2), a phenomenon that is unknown in advanced country democracies. India's achievement is worth noting in light of global experience and practices that have failed to correct for such historical injustices. In the case of the United States, there has been a failure to correct for prior injustices towards non-white races through reforming legislative representation. On the contrary, county boundaries have been continually redrawn to diminish their representation.

Table 6.2 also reveals that the central government in India has steadily increased the budget allocation for SC-ST welfare in a short period of time, from less than 3 per cent in 2015–16 to 6 per cent in 2021–22, again a hallmark absent in other international instances. It is, nevertheless, correct to point out that, despite such salient measures, there is a long distance to be traversed for all manifestations of caste differences to be erased.

References

Ahmad, Imtiaz. (ed) (1973) *Caste and Social Stratification among the Muslims*. New Delhi: Manohar Publications.

Ambedkar, Bhimrao Rami (1936) *Annihilation of Caste: Speech*. India: B. R. Kadrekar.

Ambedkar, Bhimrao Rami (1947) *Who Were the Shudras? How They Came to be the Fourth Varna in the Indo-Aryan Society*. India: Thacker and Co.'s.

Bagade, Umesh. (2021) 'Seeking freedom from slavery and ignorance: Phule's theorisation of knowledge and education', in Vikas Gupta, Rama Kant Agnihotri, Minati Panda (eds) *Education and Inequality: Historical and Contemporary Trajectories*. Hyderabad: Orient BlackSwan, ch. 5, pp 160–208.

Banerjee, Abhijit, Esther Duflo, Maitreesh Ghatak, and Jeanne Lafortune. (2009) 'Marry for What: Caste and Mate Selection in Modern India'. National Bureau of Economic Research, Working Paper 14958, May. Available at http://www.nber.org/papers/w14958, accessed 6 October 2021.

Banerjee, Abhijit, Esther Duflo, Maitreesh Ghatak, and Jeanne Lafortune. (2013) 'Marry for what? Caste and mate selection in modern India', *American Economic Journal: Microeconomics*, 5(2): 33–72, May. Available at https://www.aeaweb.org/articles?id=10.1257/mic.5.2.33, accessed 6 October 2021.

Bayly, Christopher A. (1988) *Indian Society and the Making of the British Empire*. Cambridge: Cambridge University Press, pp 162–23.

Beteille, Andre. (1996) 'Caste in contemporary India', in C. J. Fuller (ed) *Caste Today*. Delhi: Oxford University Press, pp 162–23.

Bhaduri, Amit. (2005) *Development with Dignity: A Case for Full Employment*. New Delhi: National Book Trust. Available at https://catalogue.nia.gov.au, accessed 20 August 2021.

Bharti, Nitin Kumar. (2018) 'Wealth Inequality, Class and Caste in India, 1961–2012'. WID.world Working Paper 2018/14, World Inequality Lab, 20 November. Available at https://wid.world/document/n-k-bharti-wealth-inequality-class-and-caste-in-india-1961-2012/, accessed 14 June 2021.

Biardeau, Madeleine. [1981] (1989) *Hinduism: The Anthropology of a Civilization*. Reprint. Delhi: Oxford University Press.

Campion, Sonali. (2016) 'Educate, agitate, organise – a short biography of Dr B. R. Ambedkar', 26 April. Available at https://blogs.lse.ac.uk/lsehistory/2016/04/26/educate-agitate-organise-a-short-biography-of-dr-b-r-ambedkar/, accessed 2 January 2023.

Chakraborty, Lekha. (2021) 'Why Indian states need to incorporate gender budgeting in their fiscal planning', *The Wire*, 16 August. Available at https://thewire.in/society/gender-budgeting-human-development-index, accessed 17 August 2021.

Chatterjee, Partha. (1993) *The Nation and Its Fragments*. Princeton: Princeton University Press, pp 173–75.

Cohn, Bernanard S. (1987) *An Anthropologist among the Historians and Other Essays*. Delhi: Oxford University Press.

Cook, John M. (1983) *The Persian Empire*. Bungay, Suffolk: J. M. Dent / The Chaucer Press.

Das, Veena. (2015) *Affliction – Health, Disease, Poverty*. New York: Fordham University Press.

Dickens, Charles. (1837) *The Posthumous Papers of the Pickwick Club*. London: Chapman and Hall.

Dumont, Louis. [1966] (1970) *Homo Hierarchicus: The Caste System and Its Implications*. London: Weidenfeld and Nicolson, pp 225–28.

Dutt, Romesh CIE.[38] (1898) *Mahabharata – The Epic of Ancient India*. London: J. M. Dent and Co.

Encyclopedia Britannica. 'Levite: An ancient Israelite history', The Editors of Encyclopedia, www.britannica.com/topic/Levite, accessed 1 January 2023.

Fisch, Jörg. (2000) 'Humanitarian achievement or administrative necessity? Lord William Bentinck and the abolition of sati in 1829', *Journal of Asian History* 34(2): 109–34. Available at www.jstor.org/stable/41933234, accessed 15 June 2021.

Fuller, Christopher J. (ed) (1976) 'Kerala Christians and the caste system', *Man, (n. s.)*, 11: 53–70. Available at https://ehrafworldcultures.yale.edu, accessed 2 January 2023.

[38] Companion of the Indian Empire (CIE) within the 'Most Eminent Order of the Indian Empire' instituted by Victoria in 1878 upon assuming the title of Empress of India..

Fuller, Christopher J. (2003) 'Caste', in Veena Das (ed) *The Oxford India Companion to Sociology and Social Anthropology*, Vol. 1. New Delhi: Oxford University Press, pp 477–501.

Gough, Kathleen. [1981] (1989) *Rural Society in Southeast India*. Cambridge: Cambridge University Press.

Ibbetson, Denzil. (1883) *Punjab Castes*. Lahore: Civil and Military Gazette Press. (Reprinted, Lahore: Sang-e-Meel [2001] p 1.)

Jaiswal, Suvira. (2000) *Caste: Origin, Function and Dimensions of Change*. New Delhi: Manohar Publishers.

Jamous, Raymond. (1996) 'The Meo as a Rajput caste and a Muslim community', in C. J. Fuller (ed) *Caste Today*. Delhi: Oxford University Press.

Jha, Vivekanand. (2017) *Candala: Untouchability and Caste in Early India*. New Delhi: Primus Books.

Kapadia, Karin. (1995) *Siva and Her Sisters: Gender, Caste, and Class in Rural South India*. Boulder: Westview Press.

Kumar, Arun. (2021) 'Rethinking inequality and education: crime, labour, and the school curriculum in Indian reformatory schools (1880s–1920s)', in Gupta, Vikas, Rama Kant Agnihotri, Minati Panda (eds) *Education and Inequality: Historical and Contemporary Trajectories*. Hyderabad: Orient/ BlackSwan, ch. 7, pp 225–52.

Kunnath, George. (2020) 'Doni the anthropologist's dog: a scent of ethnographic fieldwork', *Anthropology Now*, 12(3): 106–21. Available at doi: 10.1080/19428200.2020.1884482, accessed 28 June 2021.

Kunnath, George. (2021) 'Janathana Sarkar (People's Government): Rebel governance and agency of the poor in India's Maoist guerrilla zones', *Global Studies in Culture and Power*, 45-62. Available at https://doi.org/10.1080/ 1070289X.2021.1928981, accessed 10 June 2021.

Lieven, Anatol. (2011) *Pakistan: A Hard Country*. London: Penguin Books.

Madan, T. N. (1982) 'The ideology of the householder among the Kashmiri Pandits', in T. N. Madan (ed) *Way of Life*. New Delhi: Vikas Publications, pp 302–58.

Mahapatra, Richard. (2020) Where is Bhoodan Land? *DownToEarth*, 30 November. Available at https://www.downtoearth.org.in/blog/wheres-bhoodan-land-34263, accessed 26 May 2021.

Mayer, Adrian C. (1960) *Caste and Kinship in Central India: A Village and Its region*. London: Routledge and Kegan Paul.

Mayer, Adrian C. (1996) 'Caste in an Indian village: change and continuity 1954–1992', in C. J. Fuller (ed) *Caste Today*. Delhi: Oxford University Press.

Mencher, Joan P. (1974) 'The caste system upside-down, or the not-so-mysterious East', *Current Anthropology*, 15: 469–93.

Muniapan, Balakrishnan, and Biswajit Satpathy. (2010) 'The relevance of *Valmiki Ramayan* in developing managerial effectiveness', *International Journal of Indian Culture and Business Management*, 3(6): 645–68. Available at doi:10.1504/IJICBM.2010.035670, accessed 1 May 2021.

National Indicator Framework. (2021) *Sustainable Development Goals Progress Report*, National Statistical Office (NSO), Ministry of Statistics and Programme Implementation, New Delhi: Government of India.

Phillips, Tom. (2016) 'China breaks official silence on Cultural Revolution's "decade of calamity"', *The Guardian*, London, 17 May.

Piketty, Thomas. (2020) *Capital and Ideology*. Translated by Arthur Goldhammer, Massachusetts: Harvard University Press.

Piketty, Thomas. (2021) 'Capital and ideology: A global perspective on inequality regimes', *The British Journal of Sociology*, 72(1): 139–50. Available at doi.org/10.1111/1468-4446.12836, accessed 30 April 2021.

Pundit, Adwit. (2016) *Potomac Turning*. India: Partridge.

Radhakrishnan, P. (1996) 'Mandal Commission Report: a sociological critique', in M. N. Srinivas. (ed) *Caste: Its Twentieth Century Avatar*. New Delhi: Viking, pp 203–20.

Rao, Anupama. (2009) *The Caste Question – Dalits and the Politics of Modern India*. Ranikhet/New Delhi: Permanent Black/Orient Blackswan.

Risley, Herbert. [1915] (1969) *The People of India*. Delhi: Oriental Books.

Sarkar, Swagato. (2011) 'The impossibility of just land acquisition', *Economic and Political Weekly*, 8 October, xlvi(41): 35–38. Available at www.researchgate.net/publication/275644573_The_Impossibility_of_Just_Land_Acquisition, accessed 29 June 2021.

Sarkar, Swagato. (2012) 'Between egalitarianism and domination: governing differences in a transitional society', *Third World Quarterly*, 33(4): 669–84. Available at www.researchgate.net/publication/254353070_Between_Egalitarianism_and_Domination_governing_differences_in_a_transitional_society, accessed 29 June 2021.

Sen, Amartya. (1981) *Poverty and Famines: An Essay on Entitlement and Deprivation*. Oxford: Oxford University Press.

Shah, Alpa et al. (2021) *Ground Down by Growth – Tribe, Caste, Class and Inequality in 21st Century India*. London: Pluto Books.

Sharma, Ram Saran. (1983) *Material Culture and Social Formations in Ancient India*. India: Macmillan.

Sharma, Ram Saran. (2016) *Sudras in Ancient India: A Social History of the Lower Order Down to Circa A.D. 600* (3rd edn). New Delhi: Motilal Banarsidass Publishing House.

Sharma, Ram Saran. (2017) *The State and Varna Formation in the Mid-Ganga Plains: An Ethnoarchaeological View*. New Delhi: Manohar Publishers.

Sharma, Sanjeev Kumar. (2003) 'Good governance in ancient India: Remembering kingship in *Shantiparvam* in *Mahabharat', Journal of Political Science and Public Administration*, 6(1): 109–23, India.

Shome, Parthasarathi. (2021) 'Taxation in ancient India', in *Taxation History, Theory, Law and Administration*. Springer Texts in Business and Economics. Cham: Springer, ch. 2. Available at https://doi.org/10.1007/978-3-030-68214-9_2, accessed 5 May 2022.

Srinivas, M. N. (1966) *Social Change in Modern India*. Berkeley: University of California Press.

Thapar, Romila. (2003) *The Penguin History of Early India: From the origins to AD 1300*. New Delhi: Penguin Books.

Wikipedia. (2023) 'On Manes', Available at https://en.wikipedia.org>wiki>Manes, accessed 1 January 2023.

Wilkerson, Isabel. (2020) *Caste: The Lies that Divide Us*, United Kingdom: Penguin Random House.

7

Untouchability: Ambedkar and Early Reformers

Introduction

This chapter presents in a nutshell the development of untouchability as progressively enunciated in Brahmanic law. It could explain to some extent the pre-conditions of non-Brahminic low-caste birth into a drudgery of life, a condition that, in many instances, ends only with death. It draws from the work of Ambedkar (1936) and supplements it from the works of other scholars. Ambedkar (1891–1956), the father of India's constitution, himself belonged to the Scheduled Caste (SC). What is not so well-known is his unsurpassed treatise on caste and untouchability, sorting through ancient texts to identify what they had to say on caste matters, the confusion they caused, their irrationality and their dogma, yet the power they held, and continue to hold on Hindu society.

The chapter also explores the role and efforts made by early Indian reformers to subdue the virulence of untouchability and caste if not to eradicate them and, essentially, their failure to do so despite their own exemplary lives with regard to the abrogation of caste practices. Several examples are given and instances are provided from the literature of Tagore, the Nobel laureate from Bengal, and the writings of Kalki, the Tamil literary figure, despite which they encountered lack of success in their endeavours.

Ambedkar's analysis of Hindu *shastra*

The untouchable caste Ambedkar was born into is known as Mahar, a group which was viewed by the British as 'inferior village servants'. Nevertheless, Ambedkar's father became an Indian Army officer; hence Ambedkar could attend school though teachers were often reluctant to mark the exams of such lower-caste boys. Ambedkar was the first in his community to graduate from high school who, subsequently, graduated in economics and politics from Bombay University. There he met Sayaji Rao III, the Maharajah of the princely state of Baroda, who was in favour of the removal of untouchability. He sponsored Ambedkar's further education at Columbia University, New York, where he completed a Masters degree and a PhD. He also attended the London School of Economics (LSE). During this period, Ambedkar wrote on various issues including a history of caste in India.

In 1917, Ambedkar's studies were terminated as a result of the First World War. Back in India, when he was appointed as a Professor at the Sydenham College of Commerce and Economics in Bombay, other faculty members would object to him using the communal water jug. He began campaigning for Dalit rights and, in 1919, gave evidence to the British in favour of separate electorates and reserved seats for untouchables and religious minorities. In 1920 he started a weekly paper in the Marathi language, which criticized the caste hierarchy and called for a Dalit awakening and mobilization against inequality.

Ambedkar clashed with the Congress party over the issue of untouchability. In 1932, when the British attempted to provide for separate electorates for minorities, including untouchables, Mohandas Karamchand Gandhi began a fast until death, hence Ambedkar felt obliged to withdraw his position. In 1936, Jat-Pat Todak Mandal, a Hindu reformist group working to eradicate the caste system, invited Ambedkar to deliver their annual lecture in Lahore. Upon learning its contents, the group considered it offensive to Hinduism and revoked the invitation. Subsequently, Ambedkar self-published it as a book, *Annihilation of Caste.* In this book, he discussed the atrocities faced by the lower castes and the need to destruct the caste system and untouchability, suggesting ways in which caste-based discrimination could be stopped. Of course, there were many others who also discussed caste and untouchability in their various aspects but, at the end of it, even Ambedkar had a limited impact on the caste system as a whole though India made untouchability unconstitutional in indelible ink and introduced pacifiers to protect and advance the affairs of the lower castes.

Continuing with their differences through the 1930s, Ambedkar penned two texts in the 1940s criticizing the Congress and Gandhi, considered the Father of the Nation. At India's independence in August 1947, Jawaharlal Nehru, the first prime minister, nevertheless invited Ambedkar to be Minister of Law and Justice. Shortly thereafter, the Constituent Assembly appointed him Chair of the Drafting Committee for India's new constitution. He died a few years after the ratification of the constitution.

Ambedkar elaborated on caste and its ramifications in his work, elaborating that caste is determined at birth. This is explained in the *Purusha Sukta,* verses 11 and 12, which is a part of the *Rig Veda,* elaborated further next. *Manusmriti* describes the divinity and infallibility of the *chaturvarna,* essentially a four-tier *varna* or caste system. The *Purusha Sukta* raises the structure from de facto to de jure or elevates the actual to the ideal, giving it the sanction of law in the form of a permanent warrant. The Egyptians, Greeks or Romans did not articulate any such irreversible classification, even though there is a tendency to compare Roman and Brahmanic law. The former accommodated some flexibility in moving across groups under defined circumstances while the latter forbade it, except for the possible worsening of one's *varna* for misdemeanours of various kinds (though not so for Brahmins committing misdemeanours).

Ambedkar viewed any comparison of Roman with Brahmanic law as laughable. He recounted several accounts of the birth of the *varna* system. Scholars had a field day in classifying the *Vishnu Purana*'s solar and lunar races. The solar race was learned and comprised sage-like kings. They composed hymns among which was the immortal *Gayatri Mantra* of the *Rig Veda* composed by King Vishwamitra. Given their nature – in contrast with the servile lunar race – they had conflicts with the Brahmins. They also flouted meaningless Brahmin rules, though this culminated in the annihilation of the Kshatriyas at large (elaborated next). Ripley (1899, p 97) identified four races listed in Chapter 6 of this book. Of these, Ambedkar went into meticulous detail on the Shudras.[1] The *Mahabharata*'s Chapter XXXIII of the *Sabha Parva* speaks of the Republic of Shudras. Elsewhere, Indo-Aryans are called Indo-Iranians and derogatorily referred to as *Dasyu*. Ambedkar (1947) speculated whether the *Dasas* of the *Rig Veda* were the same as the *Dahaka* of the *Zenda Avestha* of Persia, in which case India's *Dasa* community could not have been native to India (p 104). In fact, the *Rig Veda* informs that they were not only not savages – primitive or aboriginal – but had been more powerful than the Aryans, and were actually of Aryan stock (elaborated later). In a war between the two, the Aryans won only because the gods *Indra* who reigned over the heavens and *Agni*, the fire god, helped them. Later Vedic literature refrained from mentioning the *Dasyus* or *Dasas*.

If it is accepted that the Dasas were also not native like the Aryans, then the question arises in what ways the two could have been different. It is evident that the later *Dharma Sutras* opposed the Shudras, disallowing them from studying the Vedas and banning them from having the *upanayana*, an essential ceremony for an individual to be included as a high caste person. Yet, alternative sources such as the *Samskara Ganapati* reveal that Shudras could indeed have *upanayana*. Ambedkar (1947) elaborated that,

> the *Chhandogya Upanishad* (iv: 1–2) relates the story of one Janasruti to whom the *Veda Vidya* was taught by the preceptor Raikva. Janasruti

[1] Recall that he himself was a Shudra and suffered from this categorization throughout his life.

> was a Shudra. What is more is that Kavasha Ailusha was a Shudra. He was a Rishi and the author of several hymns of the Tenth Book of the *Rig Veda*. (p 108)

In the ultimate analysis, even *Manusmriti* indicates that, after six generations of an impure mix of caste has taken place, the Shudra difference vanishes (p 110). To emphasize, Kautilya in *Arthashastra* states, 'A Shudra who is not a born slave but Arya in birth,' implying that a Shudra could have been Aryan. They are also described as participating in the king's investiture and could even occupy ministerial posts (pp 111–14).

Accordingly, Ambedkar concluded: (1) Shudras were Aryans; (2) Shudras were Kshatriyas; and (3) some Shudras were kings among ancient Aryan communities. Illustrating his last point, he cited from the *Shantiparva* of the *Mahabharata* that Paijavana, famous for his elaborate sacrifices, was a Shudra king. He speculated that he was the same as Sudas of the *Rig Veda* which describes him as Kshatriya. That Sudas too was a 'mighty' king is established through his coronation by the sage Vasistha (alias Brahmarishi) listed in the *Aitareya Brahmana*.[2] And the *Rig Veda* describes him as a philanthropist whom the Brahmins called Atithgva (the doyen of philanthropists).

But was Sudas also Aryan? Excerpts from the *Bhagavata Purana* indicate that the dynasty from Manu to Sudas included Bharata who was an Aryan; hence Sudas too must have been Aryan. But then, what is a Shudra after all? The explanation may be as follows. Primitive societies were divided into clans, phratries, moieties and tribes. All four *varna* categories had a 'tie of kinship' – a *jati, sajata* – while clans by themselves were from a single ancestor. Weber (1858), an early German Indologist concluded that Shudras were 'an Aryan tribe which immigrated into India before the other *varnas*. This may be asserted from the observation that Brahmins, Kshatriyas and Shudras, all performed the same sacrifices for success and well-being' (pp 130–31).

The *Satapatha Brahmana* and the *Taittriya Brahmana* do not mention Shudras though they mention the creation of three *varnas*. The *Purusha Sukta* mentions four *varnas* but is itself not mentioned in the *Samheeta* of the *Vedas*. While containing some hymns, it appears as a miscellany of the *Rig Veda* and a supplement to the *Atharva Veda*. Thus, the *Purusha Sukta* with its four *varnas* appears to have been an add-on at a later point of time.[3] It is not unlikely that this was done to clinch the superiority of Brahmins through

---

2 See Haug (1922), Vol II, pp 523–24.

3 Further it was in narrative form and not in verse as the *Vedas* were, except for verses 11 and 12 in which the four *varnas* are mentioned. Also, these appear in question-answer form quite different from the *Vedas* themselves, as if to ensure that, through pondering, there will be acceptance of the four *varnas*.

different insertions of subordinate law including that of widow burning.[4] In the same way, Shudras could have been added in as a fourth *varna* to give *chaturvarna* – the four *varna* structure – the sanction of the *Vedas*.

The next question is, what events might have led the Kshatriyas to give effect to the Shudra offshoot, and how come the latter took on the role of near slaves? Ambedkar described the rise of the priestly class comprising 17 types at its high point. He asked what the cause of malice against the Shudras could have been. He provided an answer through a violent conflict between King Sudas and Vasistha, a Brahmin renunciate.[5] The genesis of the quarrel was the replacement by Sudas of Vasistha with Vishwamitra, another Brahmin sage as his court *purohit*, or priest. After all, Vishwamitra was the author of the *Gayatri Mantra*, the hymn of universal consciousness that became quintessential in the successful completion of the sacred thread ceremony for investitures of all types.[6] The clincher was that Shakti, Vasistha's son and *sadgurushishya* or disciple, was burnt alive by Sudas for having defeated him in public debate. The outcome was that Sudas was vanquished by Vasistha in war.

The *Puranas,* early religious texts, go through additional conflicts between Brahmins and kings – Vena, Pururavas, Nahusha, Nimi, Sumukha, all descendants of Ishvaku – in which the kings lost due to their lack of humility in a slide during which even Brahmin forest hermits gained kingdoms. This process resulted in the insertion of a fourth – the lowest – *varna*, with the erstwhile kings grouped into it, their lineages cast aside forever. The final blow was the refusal by Brahmin priests to perform *upanayana* of these Shudras, that is, the teaching of the Vedas by a Vedic Brahmin who performed the ceremony to the enunciate and, with that, to pass on a gotra – heritage, lineage linked to the Vedic Brahmin – from father to son.[7]

The machinations by Brahmins in forming cast-iron rules left the defeated kings without a respectable *varna* and perpetrated a class that could have, since, suffered exclusion and, over time, isolation and exploitation. Convinced that the *Purusha Sukta* was its genesis, Ambedkar called it 'perverse, criminal in intent and anti-social in its results,' (p 32) due to its assertion that the 'classes were created by God' though they knew well that they were later insertions into the *Rig Veda*. Max Mueller too called the system 'imagination run riot, absurd priest-craft, superstition created by idiots and madmen' (p 41).

---

4 By replacing the word '*Agre*' with '*Agne*' (fire). This Ambedkar termed 'Brahmin forgeries' (p 137).

5 A sage who played a veritably deterministic – not infrequently destructive – role in setting up and applying the class structure.

6 Hindu children have recited the *Gayatri* into present times.

7 These events are, by and large, corroborated by analysts of India's ancient texts including Max Mueller (1912); Muir (1868) and others.

However, Ambedkar demonstrated that Shudras and women were given *upanayana* by the Indo-Aryans in the form of the *Upa* ceremony though that right was withdrawn later. For the women, the withdrawal happened as the age of marriage approached eight, the same as the age of *upanayana*, thus merging the two events. The Shudras lost the right as a result simply of the refusal to conduct *upanayana* by Brahmin priests for them. Further, property ownership began to be considered irrelevant since it was linked to the necessity to conduct sacrifice; hence that right came to be withdrawn too. Also, without the ceremony, the initiation of education vanished. And, as recounted by Ambedkar, without the right to property and right to knowledge, both social status and personal rights of Shudras evaporated. Such was the Brahmin's implementation of his weapon of vengeance.

Reflecting the continuation of the system into India's modern history, it may not be surprising that, whether a person was not a Shudra and, therefore, had the right to upanayana, has been considered in the justice system. For example, does the Kayastha, a sub-caste, have the right to upanayana? If yes, he is a Kshatriya, otherwise a Shudra. The establishment of non-Shudra status was quintessential for upanayana, only the performance of which guaranteed the recognition of Kshatriya status including for a royal coronation. To take an example, Chhatrapati Shivaji (1630–80) of Maharashtra, known for his valour and successes against the Mughals and the primal symbolic hero of Maharashtrians today,[8] could not conduct his own *rajyabhishekh* – coronation – since he was considered a Shudra until Balaji Avaji, his personal secretary, collected evidence that Shivaji was a descendant of Sisodiya Kshatriyas who were Rajputs from Mewad. The only priest who agreed to conduct the ceremony was found in Benaras but baulked at the last minute until propitiated with further dole-outs of cash. Shivaji's coronation occurred in 1674. His grandson Shahu (who reigned between 1708–49) appointed Balaji Vishvanath Bhat, a Chitpavan Brahmin, as Peshwa[9] in 1714. Balaji's son Baji Rao I, also called Baji Rao Ballal Balaji Bhat, secured hereditary succession to the peshwa-ship of the Maratha confederacy (administering between 1720–40). Subsequently, when the Brahmin Peshwas assumed complete control at the termination of Shahu's reign, they excluded Shivaji's great grandson from being recognized as a Brahmin. However, a Brahmin conference in Satara eventually reinstated his status.

---

8 Shivaji expanded his military, captured and built forts, formed a navy, established the foundation of a Maratha empire, promoted Marathi and Sanskrit languages, replaced Persian as the court language, introduced progressive civil rule and administrative structure, yet had to carry the burden of his early categorization as a non-Kshatriya with its long reach of opprobrium.

9 Peshwa, chief minister or *mukhya pradhan*, were hereditary Brahmins and originally headed the advisory council of Shivaji.

The determination of an exact caste and associated ceremonies that had to accompany, or were allowed, in the caste categories became increasingly unclear with time. Court cases appeared from 1837[10] in which the Privy Council considered whether there were any Kshatriyas left in India. However, the Privy Council could not define any test by which a Kshatriya could be distinguished from a Shudra. Rather, the question would have to be resolved separately for every disputed case (p 162). In one case, a question was raised whether the Kayasthas of Bihar were Kshatriyas or Shudras.[11] The Bihar Kayasthas claimed that they were different from the Kayasthas of Bengal, the Upper Provinces or Benares who were Shudras. Nevertheless, the court would not make any distinction and held that the Kayasthas of Bihar were Shudras. The validity of this judgement was, however, not accepted by the Allahabad High Court[12] (p 162–63).

Another case considered whether the Kayasthas of Bengal were Kshatriyas or Shudras in which the High Court of Calcutta decided that they were Shudras.[13] From the High Court, the case was taken to the Privy Council but the matter was left open. Between 1916–26, the High Court gave two decisions that held that intermarriages between Kayasthas of Bengal and Tantis[14] and Doms,[15] who were two of the lowest sub-castes, were legal since they were sub-castes of Shudras (hence the Kayasthas were also Shudras).[16] This was contrasted for the Kayasthas of Bihar by Mr Justice Jwala Prasad in Patna, the capital of Bihar,[17] in a judgement of 47 pages that cited instances from *Purana* and *Smriti* in which Kayasthas had been referred to, thus concluding that the Kayasthas of Bihar were indeed Kshatriyas

---

10 Chuohirya Run Murdan Syn *Versus* Sahub Purhulad Syn, 7, M.I.A.18.

11 Raj Coomar Lall *versus* Bissessur Dyal, in I.L.R.10 Cal. 688.

12 Tulsi Ram versus Behari Lai. In I.L.R.12 All. 328.

13 Asita Mohan Ghosh versus Nirod Mohan Ghosh Maulik, reported in (1916) 20 Cal. W.N.901.

14 (1921) 48 Cal. 626. Bishwanath Ghosh versus Srimati Balai Desai.

15 (1924) 51 Cal. 788. Bholanalh Mitter versus King Emperor.

16 It is to be wondered whether any categorisation of Bengal Kayasthas into Kshatriya or Shudra would have mattered at all for already dissension in their midst was rife. A common limerick cited among specific Bengali Kayastha sub-groups especially among zamindari families even in the 1960s when arranged marriages were commonplace, ran like this: 'The Ghosh dynasty is at the top, the Bose is known for his charity, the Mitra is devious, the Dutta is a turncoat.' That virtually excluded the latter two marrying into the former two who allowed in surnames such as Deb, Guha and Shome among marriageable clans. When queried why, for example, the Dutta had such a poor reputation, a prevalent explanation was that he was not really a Kayastha, oblivious of the reality that the courts had long determined that all of these surnames were Shudras.

17 (1926) Ishwari Prasad versus Rai Hari Prasad Lai. Reported in I.L.R. 6 Patna 506.

(pp 163–164). It is not hard to conclude that the categorization of caste and sub-caste was, and remains, a conundrum of confusion.

Ambedkar next tackled the emergence of untouchability. He posed the question whether Shudras were always untouchable. He counted that, in 1948, of a total Indian population of 358 million, there was an 85 million strong lower rung comprising Aboriginal Tribes (15 million), Criminal Tribes (20 million) and Untouchables (50 million). In other words, almost 60 per cent of the lower rung comprised Untouchables which he called 'an abomination'. He calculated that untouchability was a later addition to the Shudra class and was linked to beef eating that became a necessity as the Shudras, dictated by the upper castes, were obliged to handle beef, removing carcasses, curing leather, and performing menial tasks such as removing night soil that paid miniscule wages, slowly but surely leading to the eating of dead animals.[18]

Accordingly, Ambedkar hypothesized that untouchables, who were 'broken men' defeated in war by the Brahmins, suffered the atrocities of isolation and extraction that followed. That, in turn, led several of them to adopt Buddhism, at one point 60 per cent of the population having converted to Buddhism which allowed the consumption of beef.[19] Those who did not reconvert to Hinduism became Shudras, the period of this development being attributed to around 400 AD. It coincided with the re-entry of Brahmins into the royal courts beginning with the Gupta period (following the Mauryas who had converted to Buddhism earlier).[20]

Manu's *Prayashchit Mayukha* revealed the abhorrence of Buddhists by dictating that if a Hindu touched a Buddhist, the former would have to have a bath. Buddhists were carnivorous for Buddha had allowed three – and later five – types of 'pure flesh' to be consumed comprising 'unseen, unheard, unsuspected' meat, and later added any animal having suffered 'natural death or killed by a bird of prey' (Watters, 1904).[21] That became the magic wand of opprobrium of the Brahmins for their castigation of Buddhists. Thus, even though Vedic evidence had existed of beef eating among Hindus including Brahmins, it was a convenient Brahminic ploy to link beef eating to primitivity, impurity, defilement and pollution (p 242).

---

[18] See Mistry (1995) where examples of this phenomenon and its occurrence are described through real-life situations in his masterpiece, *A Fine Balance*.

[19] Buddha opposed the caste system, propagating that a person's actions were the measure of who a person was, as well as the authority of Brahmin priests, their scripture and rituals.

[20] See Shome (2021), ch. 2. Emperor Ashoka (3rd century BCE) converted to Buddhism after winning a war in Kalinga (today's Odisha) and perceiving its devastation. Thereafter he focused on public works and formed a series of edicts.

[21] Watters (1904), p 55, where he derives these observations from Yuan Chwang, a Chinese traveller.

This became converted to hereditary untouchability (p 265). Ambedkar clarified that Buddhists and non-Buddhists who consumed beef became untouchable as mentioned in the *Veda Vyas Smriti*.[22]

Reflecting the negative attitude towards beef eating even today, an elaboration should be useful. The *Rig Veda* (X.91.14, X.72.6) says, 'for *Agni,* were sacrificed horses, bulls, oxen, barren cows and rams, with a sword or axe. The *Taittiriya Brahmana* from the *Kamayshti* further describes which cows should be sacrificed: 'dwarf ox to Vishnu, drooping horned bull with a blaze on the head to Indra, a black cow to Pushan,' and so on. For another sacrifice, the *Panchasaradiya Seva* specifies, 'immolate 17 five-year-old humpless dwarf bulls and as many dwarf heifers under three years old'.

The *Apastambha Dharma Sutra* at 14, 15 and 29 says that the cow and bull are sacred and therefore should be eaten.[23] The *Atreya Brahmana* describes how a *yajna* – ceremonial religious sacrifice – should be performed. The types of wood to make the *yupa* – sacrificial post to which the sacrificial animal was tied – are described with meticulous detail of the performance itself including exactly how the animal was to be positioned, killed and skinned. After the sacrifice, seventeen Brahmins shared the carcass so that few other people could share it as well.

Indeed, cow sacrifice and consumption at *Madhuparka,* a gathering of guests, became so central that they were let off before guests arrived so that goat, ram or deer could be served instead. For absolution, the Brahmin who did the slaughtering, uttered, 'Far may it be from us,' three times. Page after page is taken to describe in excruciating detail which parts are to be offered to the gods, and which are to be discarded. They are a 'guide to heaven' who do the division of the 36 pieces, and are described in detail for the 17 Brahmins present. In effect, the Brahmins slaughtered and consumed the animal amongst themselves without sharing with others present or those financing the sacrifice. The rationale was that, through the sacrifice to *Agni-Soma,*[24] who represented a conglomeration of all deities, the person carrying out the act released himself from being sacrificed; hence no one else should touch the sacrificed meat.

Despite such a high incidence of beef consumption, once Brahmins imposed a ban on it, untouchability in Hindu society emerged for all who consumed it; further, untouchability was imposed from birth to death without the possibility of reversal. The Hindu Gupta dynasty made cow slaughter *mahapataka,* a capital punishment (Bhandarkar, 1940, pp 78–79).

---

[22] They comprised the *Antyajas*. See Kane (1941), p 71.

[23] Yet, the same *Sutra* at 1, 5, 17 and 29 lays down a prohibition on the eating of cow's flesh (pp 324–25).

[24] *Agni* (fire, or light and heat), *Soma* (water) and *Vayu* (air or energy) empower all life.

It permitted consuming a dead cow but that rendered the consumer an untouchable. The non-reversal of his condition had to be imposed to ensure the departure of Buddhism from Hindu society and the assurance of reinstatement of Brahmanism in its place. And, for their own protection, the adoption of vegetarianism was quintessential for a new-found purity that was explained through the *Advaita* philosophy which recognized a single supreme entity in which all life – human and animal – was sacred. Ambedkar observed that shifting to vegetarianism from a predominantly carnivorous culture symbolized a strategic move to establish supremacy over Buddhism and any challenge from *Bhikshus* or Buddhist monks. Recall that, after all, the appearance of Manu was 400 years later by when matters had already fallen into place.

It would follow that untouchables were obliged to live outside the boundaries of settlements to ensure the purity of others.[25] To clinch their own re-establishment, Brahmins abandoned the *yajna* as a form of worship through cow sacrifice and replaced it with working on royal courts to finance the building of temples in homage to Hindu gods including Shiva, Vishnu, Krishna and others in an emulation of the stupas that were already in existence or were being built by Buddhists. The fact that the settled agrarian population had revealed signs of opposition to cow sacrificial rituals as their cattle stock – an asset – got depleted, helped in the process of change.

When untouchables began to be mentioned in Hindu *shastras,* they were termed *Antya* or *Anta* (born last). It is noteworthy that Shudras are *savarna* (inside the *varna* system) while the untouchables are *avarna* (outside the *varna* system). Ambedkar claimed that this possibly did not imply the end of creation, but the end of the village settlement. Be that as it may, untouchable categories in western societies that had existed such as the Fuidhirs – those who broke the bond of union – of Ireland, and the Alltudes – of different blood – of Wales, eventually disappeared, but they did not disappear from India where society was simply transformed into (i) non-beef eating Hindus, and (ii) beef eating untouchables. Ambedkar insisted that 'beef eating is the root of untouchability'.

Examining occupations mentioned in Vedic literature, untouchability could not have existed in Vedic times. Manu mentions there is no fifth *Varna* while *Narada Smriti* mentions a fifth class as slaves, not as untouchables. *Asparshya* – untouchable – goes back to Gautama in the *Dharma Sutra* prescribing a ritual bath after touching one such as a *chandala. Antya* and *Antyaja* are mentioned in the later *Smriti*'s, but they are not described as untouchable. Touching is allayed by a bath as prescribed by Gautama, Vashistha and Bandhyaan in

[25] They often had to live in locations from where (polluted) wind or breeze would not blow towards the settlements.

Dharma Sutra and by Manu. Ambedkar concluded that there is no evidence that untouchability or impurity was practiced with full veracity by any other caste than the Brahmins.

In 185 BC, Brihadratha, a Buddhist Mauryan king, was assassinated by Pushyamitra, his Brahmin commander-in-chief, that led to the overthrow of the Buddhist Mauryas by the Brahmins. *Manusmriti* argued in favour of this regicide. However, Buddhism survived to the second century AD which could be taken as the time of the emergence of untouchability. By 400 AD, Fah-Hian, a Chinese traveller, observed that only chandalas hunted and sold flesh while others did not. Yet, there was never complete clarity, for example, even circa 600 AD, Bāṇabhaṭṭa, the author of *Harsha Charita*, wrote that chandalas were not untouchable[26] (Ridding, 1896). Yet in 629 AD, Yuan Chwang, another Chinese traveler who stayed in India for 16 years and left detailed accounts, wrote that butchers, scavengers, fishermen and other such communities were forced to live outside the village and that they had to 'sneak along on the left side when they were in the hamlets'[27] (p 387). Thus, it may perhaps be concluded that untouchability indeed prevailed after 600 AD.

Essential failure of early social reformers

Caste, Shudras and untouchability, and the poverty and inequality that are built into them, continue in India's societal framework today, in particular in rural societies. Given that India made the practice of untouchability unconstitutional and hence illegal, its incidence felt to the present day as a matter of everyday life must imply that its weight is imparted well beyond illegality. In this section, a point is made through a spattering of personalities that, through India's pre-independence 18–20th century renaissance, the caste feeling might have disappeared among much of the reformist upper castes who were visibly leading the independence movement across subcontinental India. However, they were essentially unable to eradicate the practice from the vast swathes of the land. A quotation from a reading by Ramnarayan (2021) from a recent biography of Kalki Krishnamurthy (1899–1954), a Tamil Brahmin reformer-poet-litterateur illustrates,[28]

> The lectures of Swami Vivekananda had first developed in the lad a hatred for the practice of caste distinctions and untouchability. This

[26] Banabhatta lived during the era of King Harshavardhana (606–47 AD) of Thanesar who reigned over northern India.

[27] Watters (1904), p 147.

[28] The biography of Kalki is by Sunda (2022). The reading was prior to its publication.

loathing increased as he noted the hypocrisy in the observance of rituals, and the fraudulent, selfish actions in the so-called *vaidika* community, who were regarded as the true followers of the scriptures. The songs of Subramaniya Bharati (1882–1921), a Brahmin and a mystical Tamil poet, filled with nationalistic fervour and resonating with anti-caste feelings in his compositions, also fuelled the boy's abhorrence of caste. To illustrate with a rhyme addressed to a little child,

> There is no such thing as caste –
> It is a sin to divide people as higher and lower
> Those who are just, educated and cultured,
> Those who have much love –
> They are superior.

Bharathi's devotional song, 'Nandalala,' the infant Krishna, invoking the colour of a crow, further revealed his depth of understanding of the colourlessness of divine existence, yet much of the depiction of Krishna in the present day on annual calendars appears to be blue in a rejection or, perhaps fear, of black.

> Until then, the youngster had not seen any Tamil-born who had actually abjured caste distinctions and untouchability. It was no surprise, therefore, that the boy saw Rajaji[29] as a valiant hero.
>
> For the youth of today, it would be difficult to understand the struggles undergone by the social reformers of those years. Sea voyages overseas, sitting down to meals with untouchables, a non-brahmin's presence when a Brahmin took his meal, even accepting drinking water from someone who belonged to a lower caste – all these and more were punished with social ostracism. In short, it was easier to go to prison, than to work for social reform. (Ananda Vikatan 5 May 1935, reprint in *Vellimani*, 12 December 1947)

As a writer, Kalki's views on untouchability and caste are cogently expressed in his 1925 short story, 'Poison Cure', in which, through a parable-like tale, he takes the view that there should be no discrimination against anyone on any grounds. He was touched by the writings of Rabindranath Tagore who also wrote on untouchability, as described next. He indicated that Tagore's poem, *Gitanjali* and *The Gardner*, inspired him as did short stories such as

---

[29] Shri Chakravarti Rajagopalachari (1878–1972), was a statesman, writer, lawyer and independence activist. He was also the first Indian-born governor-general as well as the last as India became a republic in 1950.

The Hungry Stones. They filled his heart and intoxicated him as he had felt when he had touched Tagore's robe some years before.

Novelists and poets of the day commonly included caste and untouchability as essential components of their major works. To take one example, the 1917–33 novel, *Srikanto*, by Sarat Chandra Chattopadhyay (1876–1938) is not only an account of the protagonist's life adventures but an eye-opening description of the minute sub-caste groupings and distancing and separation among them that existed in the Bengal of his times.[30] Rabindranath Tagore's 1938 opera, *Chandalika*, composed around Prakriti, a Chandala girl, poignantly narrates the story of an untouchable girl. The scene opens with a vendor of yogurt entering the village and villagers cautioning in unison against touching Prakriti. Thus,

> Don't touch her, Don't touch her!
> For then the yogurt will be useless
> Don't you know that?

The entrance of Ananda, a Buddhist Bhikshu, changes everything. As he pleads,

> Give me water, please give me water,
> The sun is oppressive, the path ahead is long, Please give me water.
> I am distressed by the heat and am parched. Please give me water,
> I am so tired. Please give me water.

Prakriti responds,

> Forgive me my lord, please forgive me – I am the daughter of a Chandala.
> The water of my well is unholy,
> I am not worthy of the blessed deed of giving you water,
> (As) I am the daughter of a Chandala.

Ananda nevertheless accepts water from Prakriti and departs, leaving her in a stunned state.

If leaders such as Jatindra Nath Das (1904–29), Mohandas Karamchand Gandhi (1869–1948), Kalki Krishnamurthy (1899–1954), Ramakrishna Paramahansa (1836–86), or Chakravarti Rajagopalachari (1878–1972), Rabindranath Tagore (1861–1941), Swami Vivekananda (1863–1902) and a myriad other pre-independence national political and religious leaders

---

[30] Written between 1917–33 in different magazines and subsequently consolidated.

and social reformers of the Indian Renaissance transcended caste with its characteristics of exclusion and isolation, then why did Indian society continue with caste, and even untouchability, unperturbed well after their times?

Even several contemporary novelists such as Rohinton Mistry (1995) in *A Fine Balance* (mentioned earlier), Arundhati Roy (1997) in *A God of Small Things* and others have depended on class, caste and untouchability as quintessential elements in their writings – some of which have been acclaimed as masterpieces – as if they cannot but return to caste and separation issues that are still very much there, not as disappearing shadows, but as a lingering presence in India's prevailing culture. It is as if Indians, irrespective of their socio-economic backgrounds, continue to hold on to the straw that defines and individualizes India and Indians among nations, tied to caste and untouchability in an intrinsic, internecine way.

The answer to the mystery of failure to convey by the top social revolutionaries against caste to the vast sea of India's population possibly lies in their inability to transmit their beliefs not only to society as a whole but, often, even within their own families. Their views generally remained elevated at their own ethereal level, unable to extricate them from the depths of family customs and beliefs, leave alone being able to dive into the grassroots of society on a large scale. The allocation of names in the South and surnames in the North at birth stamps a person's caste in the Indian subcontinent.

The caste system remains the Achilles' Heel of the Indian peoples, continuing to reduce them as human beings shackled by societal barriers and obstacles that eat into their capabilities. They are the type of impediments that comparable societies have long forsaken and moved forward ahead of India, sometimes coming from much farther behind. Thus, the caste system grew from a system driven mainly by the exclusive economic advantage to be reaped by selected, small groups to an institution more complex and more vicious. It is embodied by an aversion to touch or social mixing, and even the sharing of knowledge for no explicable reason other than the accident of birth. Even India's 1950 Constitution which made untouchability unconstitutional failed to eradicate it. On the contrary, ironically, nothing could be more helpful to the beneficiaries if the continuance of caste and the existence of untouchability could be used for political advantage in the formation of governments in a country divided by politics and buttressed by caste hatred and untouchability.

References

Ambedkar, B. R. (1936) *Annihilation of Caste: Speech*. India: B. R. Kadrekar.

Ambedkar, B. R. (1947) *Who Were the Shudras? How They Came to be the Fourth Varna in the Indo-Aryan Society*. India: Thacker and Co.'s.

Bhandarkar, Devadatta Ramakrishna (1940). *Some Aspects of Ancient Indian Culture*. India: University of Madras.

Chattopadhyay, Sarat. (1917–33) *Srikanto*. Republished in India Penguin Modern Classics series, (2009) Aditya Publishers, (2018) and others.

Haug, Martin. (1922) *The Aitareya Brahmanam of the Rigveda*, Vol. 2. Allahabad: Sudhindra Nath Vasu, M. B., at the Panini office. Available at https://archive.org/details/in.ernet.dli.2015.104262, accessed 3 January 2023.

Kane, Pandurang Vaman. (1941) *History of Dharmashastra*, Vol. II, Part 1. Poona: Bhandarkar Oriental Research.

Krishnamurthy, Kalki. (1925) '"Poison Cure", a short story', translated by Gowri Ramnarayan, 1999.

Max Müller, Friedrich. (1912) *A History of Ancient Sanskrit Literature So Far as it Illustrates the Primitive Religion of the Brahmans*. India: Panini Office, Bhuvaneshwari Ashrama.

Mistry, Rohinton. (1995) *A Fine Balance*. New York: Vintage Random House.

Muir, John (1868) *Original Sanskrit Texts on the Origin and History of the People of India*, Vol. I. London: Trubner & Co.

Ramnarayan, Gowri. (2021) *Kalki Krishnamurthy: His Life and Times*, a translation of 'Ponniyin Pudalvar', the Tamil biography by 'Sunda' MRM Sundaram. Available at www.kalkibiography.com.

Ridding, C. M. (Translated). (1896) *The Kadambari of Bana*. Oriental Translation Fund, New Series, Vol. II. London: Royal Asiatic Society. Available at www.gutenberg.org/files/41128/41128-h/41128-h.htm, accessed 3 January 2023.

Ripley, William Z. (1899) *The Races of Europe: A Sociological Study* (Lowell Institute Lectures). New York: D. Appleton & Co.

Roy, Arundhati. (1997) *The God of Small Things*, IndiaInk, New Delhi.

Shipman, Pat. (1994) *The Evolution of Racism*, New York: Simon and Schuster.

Shome, Parthasarathi. (2021) Taxation in Ancient India, in *Taxation History, Theory, Law and Administration*. Springer Texts in Business and Economics. Cham: Springer. Available at https://doi.org/10.1007/978-3-030-68214-9_2.

Stringer, Christopher, and Clive Gamble. (1993) *In Search of Neanderthals*. London: Thames and Hudson.

Subramaniya, Bharathi. (1882–1921) *Poems*. Available at www.poemhunter.com/subramanya-bharathi/poems, accessed 3 January 2023.

Sunda, M. R. M. Sundaram. (2022) *Kalki Krishnamurthy – His Life and Times*, Sudarshan Graphics Private Limited, Chennai.

Tagore, Rabindranath. (1938) *Chandalika*, reproduced by Champak Library, Kindle and several others.

Tobias, P. V. (1972) *Meaning of Race*. Johannesburg: South African Institute of Race Relations.

Watters, Thomas. (1904) *On Yuan-Chwang's Travels in India (629–645 A.D.)*, Vol. I., (eds) T. W. Rhys Davids and S. W. Bushell. London: Royal Asiatic Society. Available at www.rarebooksocietyofindia.org/book_archive/196174216674_10153425489631675.pdf, accessed 16 June 2021.

Weber, Albrecht. (1858) *Indische Studien: Beiträge für die Kunde des indischen Alterthums*. Berlin: F. Dümmler.

PART III

Sectoral Effects

Put a Woman in Charge
Way back when, in the beginning of time,
Way back when man made the fire then the wheel,
Went from a horse to an automobile,
He said "The world is mine;" he took oceans and sky,
He set borders, built walls – he won't stop till he owns it all,
And here we are standing on the brink of disaster.
Enough is enough is enough is enough.
I know the answer – Put a woman in charge.
The time has come – We've got to turn this world around.
Call the mothers, call the daughters,
We need the sisters of mercy now – she'll be a hero, not a fool.
She's got the power to change the rules.
She's got something that men don't have –
She is kind and she understands.
So let the ladies do what they were born to do.
Raise the vibration and make a better place for me and you.
Put a woman in charge.
We're gonna feel the magic when the girls take over;
It's gonna be fantastic – we need more women in charge.
Put a woman in charge.

Keb Mo[1]

---

[1] Song released by Kevin Roosevelt Moore (b. 3 October 1951), a post-modern blues songwriter and singer, on 28 September 2018. He has been described as 'a living link to the Delta blues that travelled up the Mississippi River and across the expanse of America'.

8

The Rural-Urban Divide

Introduction

The 2022 World Development Indicators, World Bank, indicate that 65 per cent of the total population comprises the rural population. Of this, 55 per cent engage in agricultural activities according to the Department of Agriculture and Farmers' Welfare, Government of India (GOI). Nevertheless, agriculture's share in gross domestic product (GDP) has declined steadily since India's independence. Current shares have diminished significantly when seen against the relative size of the rural population.[1] The continuation of differences between rural and urban sectors informs the higher incidence of poverty and the extent of inequality between the sectors. Comparing various sectors, Table 8.1 reveals that the share in GDP of agriculture and forestry and fishing has declined while those of mining, manufacturing and services – and their components – have increased. In particular, those of trade and the financial services have increased indicating that sectors that have habitually participated in and are accessed by the relatively rich and wealthy in the organized sectors have gained at the cost of others – the poorer. It points to a lop-sided development pattern for a primarily rural society with labour-intensive agriculture.

Ideally, the rate of return to capital use and the rate of return to the supply of labour should approach each other over time. A rate of return from capital

---

1 The share in GDP diminished from 57 per cent in 1950–51 to 52 per cent in 1960–61, 46 per cent in 1970-71, 40 per cent in 1980-81, 33 per cent in 1990-91, 29 per cent in 1997–98, 17 per cent in 2006–07, and 14 per cent in 2011–12 at 2004–05 prices, in contrast to occupying 43 per cent of the geographical area. See Thakur (2012) whose data are reported to be sourced from the 1999–2000 *Economic Survey*, GOI. Thakur's figures after 2006–07 differ somewhat from those from the World Development Indicators shown in Chapter 2, Appendix 2.2, Table 2.9.

According to the Ministry of Statistics and Programme Development, GOI (2021), the share in GDP was 16 per cent in 2020–21.

Table 8.1: India: sectoral composition of GDP

Economic activity				**Share (%)**				
Year	**1971**	**1981**	**1991**	**2001**	**2011**	**2018**	**2019**	**2020**
Agriculture, forestry and fishing[1]	38.1	31.7	27.3	21.6	17.2	16.0	16.7	18.3
Industry (including construction)[2], of which	22.4	26.1	26.4	26.5	30.2	26.4	24.2	23.2
manufacturing	15.0	16.8	15.7	15.3	16.1	14.9	13.3	13.0
Services[3] (data from the World Bank)	35.8	33.9	37.8	43.8	45.4	48.5	49.9	49.3
Financial year	**1971–72[4]**	**1981–82**	**1991–92**	**2001–02**	**2011–12[5]**	**2018–19**	**2019–20**	**2020–21[6]**
Services (data from the NSO)[7], of which	38.4	40.4	45.0	52.0	49.0	53.4	55.0	53.9
Trade, hotels & restaurants	8.7	12.1	12.6	14.9	17.4	18.6	18.9	16.4
Transport, storage & communication	4.2	4.7	6.3	7.7				
Financing, insurance, real estate & business services	13.0	11.1	12.9	14.8	18.9	20.6	21.2	22.1
Community, social & personal services	12.5	12.4	13.3	14.6	12.7	14.1	14.9	15.4

Note: [1] Agriculture includes forestry, hunting, and fishing, as well as cultivation of crops and livestock production. [2] Industry includes manufacturing. It comprises value added in mining, manufacturing (also reported as a separate subgroup), construction, electricity, water and gas. [3] Services as defined in World Bank data include wholesale and retail trade (including hotels and restaurants), transport, and government, financial, professional and personal services such as education, health care and real estate services. Also included are imputed bank service charges, import duties, and any statistical discrepancies noted by national compilers as well as discrepancies arising from rescaling. However, the breakup is not provided. [4] GDP at current prices (base year, 2004–05) for years 1971–72 to 2001–02. NSO data give greater breakdown of the services sector. [5] GDP at current prices base year, 2011–12) for years 2011–12 to 2020–21. [6] Provisional estimates. [7] From base year 2011–12, Trade and so on, includes hotels, transport, communication and services related to broadcasting; financing and so on, includes financial, real estate and professional services; community services and so on, includes public administration, defence and other services.

Source: World Development Indicators, World Bank (last updated on 30 July 2021) and National Statistical Office (NSO), Ministry of Statistics and Programme Implementation (MSoPI).

markets that persistently exceeds the rate of return from offering work, disrupts that balance. This disequilibrium has been unfolding for decades in the world's democracies and glaringly so in India – and it has exacerbated the rural-urban divide. This chapter analyses the existing and growing rural-urban divide causing income inequality, in particular in India. Some proposals of redressal are presented in Chapter 11.

Drivers of rural-urban migration

A few observations contrasting India and China may help to assess how the two economies moved over time with respect to their agricultural sectors. Agriculture – rural activities – continues to provide the livelihood of over half of India's population though accompanying structural and economic reforms have not kept up (Gulati et al., 2021a). While the grain sector still dominates India's cropped area, China, after meeting its domestic demand for food, has transformed its agriculture over the past four decades. From the late 1970s, it diversified agriculture, with a focus on high-value commodities and commercialization. Its off-farm rural employment has also increased, an observation that has also been noted for India by Binswanger-Mkhize (2013). What emerges on the whole is that India has a distance to go in terms of modernization and commercialization in agriculture when compared to China.

Such differences could explain, to a good extent, the phenomenon of rural-urban migration in India though widespread agreement regarding the drivers of rural-to-urban migration appears to be lacking, with recent scholars emerging with an array of perspectives on the matter. Using census data and district level data, Mitra and Murayama (2009) enquired what lay behind inter-state and intra-state migration and found that the relatively poor and backward states revealed large population mobility primarily in search of a livelihood and that women were likely to move as accompanists of males. This was corroborated by Imbert and Papp (2020). Using survey data on seasonal migration, they concluded that probably rural–urban migrants were generally willing to accept up to a 35 per cent lower wage at rural public works to avoid migration. Binswanger-Mkhize (2013) observed that the rural non-farm sector had grown rapidly, generating a large number of jobs. Such diversification through self-employment had been a means to increase incomes, with farming sometimes becoming a part-time activity. This finding was, of course, not altogether surprising since, in the absence of rapid agricultural growth or market access to its products, it would be expectable that alternative means would have to be found for an adequate living. Yet Kalamkar (2009) appeared to have taken a different position from this in that the lack of development in agriculture had led to its inability to absorb surplus urban labour. In a way, this could have contributed to poverty.

In slight variations to the previously mentioned positions, Bhagat and Keshri (2020), using 2011 census data, suggested that developed and urbanized states registered net gains in migration while less developed states recorded net losses. Thus, it was the search for livelihood that was driving migration. Using panel data for 1991–2011, Tripathi (2021) suggested that higher per-capita state income attracted rural to urban migration. Ali (2018) recommended a slew of needed policy actions to buttress the incomes of the rural sector, including to,

> follow an integrated and intensive farming system to have higher and sustainable agricultural and livestock production and productivity; process the produces in the production catchment to minimize post-harvest losses and get better quality fresh and processed products for consumers; have an economic utilization of agricultural residues, wastes and processing by-products for feed and/or compost to enhance animal health and soil fertility for better productivity; do the marketing of fresh and value-added products through designated cooperative bulk and/or retail markets with minimum possible number of middlemen-intermediaries; have more employment for rural men and women and thereby more income to farmers-producers of raw materials. All these when planned and implemented successfully, the rural-urban gap in prosperity and living comforts would be minimized and people may start reverse migration from urban to rural areas in search of better food, environment, health, happiness and longevity. (p 11)

While such observations may be philosophically comforting, the reality is elsewhere when considered on a mass scale as the rural-urban divide indeed continues unabated in the absence of clear government direction.

Selected poverty indicators of the rural-urban divide are shown in Table 8.2. The indicators – poverty rate and poverty gap ratio – are explained in some detail in the two footnotes respectively to the table. It presents the information at the level of state governments[2] thus revealing the presence of regional variation in poverty. Unfortunately, the information is dated but comprises the latest issued by the government despite their earlier quinquennial routine, a matter that has been raised at domestic and international research levels.[3]

---

2 A Union Territory is not a state. It is a sub-national level region that is governed by the central government.

3 Mehrotra and Parida (2021) pointed out, 'India has not released its Consumption Expenditure Survey (CES) data since 2011–12. Normally a CES is conducted by the National Sample Survey Office (NSO) every five years. But the CES of 2017–18 (already conducted a year late) was not made public by the GOI. Now, we hear that a new CES

Despite the date of the information, regional disparities are likely to have continued to a great extent and the table is intended as a window into that perspective. The first column (Total) orders sub-national governments at an increasing level of poverty which shows significant regional dispersion in poverty. It also emerges that, in every state administration, rural poverty is much higher than urban poverty, with the exception of West Bengal where the difference is small. This could reflect 34 years of communist rule (1977–2011) during which land reform transferred land to landless agriculturists from absentee landlords but urban areas were neglected as a result of which public services deteriorated to very low levels. Note also that Union Territories (UTs) that are mainly urban obviously reported no rural poverty.

Mehrotra and Parida (2021) attempted to extrapolate the 2011–12 figures to 2019–20 using the five-yearly labour surveys (Employment-Unemployment Rounds) and gauging the population share of those below the poverty line. As Table 8.2 reveals, both rural and urban poverty headcount ratios worsened in the last decade and, therefore, of India as a whole. As may be observed, poverty rose faster in rural areas. The authors emphasized, 'What is stunning is that for the first time in India's history of estimating poverty, there is a rise in the incidence of poverty since 2011–12'. Also, to be noted is that this conclusion was arrived at prior to the 2019–21 COVID-19 pandemic that would have made conditions worse.

Mehrotra and Parida's (2021) numbers showed how that trend changed. Thus, between 1973 and 1993, the absolute number of poor had remained constant (at about 320 million poor), despite a significant increase in India's total population. Between 1993 and 2004, the absolute number of poor fell by a marginal number (18 million) from 320 million to 302 million, during a period when the GDP growth rate had picked up after the economic reforms. It is for the first time in India's history since the Consumption Expenditure Survey (CES) began that we have seen an increase in the absolute numbers of the poor, between 2012–13 and 2019–20 . . . . Between 2004–05 and 2011–12, the number of the poor fell by 133 million, or by over 19 million per year. By contrast, not only has the incidence of poverty increased since then, but the absolute increase in poverty is totally unprecedented.

Using data between 1957–2012, Datt, Ravallion and Murgai (2016) found that there was a downward trend in poverty measures since 1970 with an

is likely to be conducted in 2021–22, the data from which will probably not be available before end–2022.' *The Hindu*, 4 August.

Table 8.2: India: rural-urban poverty

State/Union Territory (UT)	Poverty headcount ratio[1]			Poverty gap ratio[2]	
	2011–12				
	Total	Rural	Urban	Rural	Urban
Dadra and Nagar Haveli	1.0	1.6	0.0	-	-
Puducherry	2.8	0.0	3.4	3.7	0.8
Gujarat	5.1	6.8	4.1	3.3	1.6
Madhya Pradesh	7.1	9.1	5.0	8.3	3.9
Jammu and Kashmir	8.1	8.5	4.3	1.9	1.0
Tamil Nadu	8.2	9.9	3.7	2.5	1.1
Rajasthan	8.3	7.7	9.2	3.2	1.6
Andhra Pradesh	9.2	11.0	5.8	1.6	0.9
Chandigarh	9.7	17.1	6.3	-	-
Goa	9.9	12.9	9.8	0.7	0.7
Lakshadweep	9.9	0.0	12.6	-	-
Jharkhand	10.3	11.5	7.2	6.9	4.9
Himachal Pradesh	11.2	11.6	10.3	1.0	0.8
Tripura	11.3	15.8	6.5	2.2	1.7
West Bengal	11.3	11.6	10.5	3.7	2.7
Mizoram	11.9	12.5	9.3	7.5	0.6
Uttar Pradesh	14.0	16.5	7.4	5.7	5.3
Sikkim	14.7	16.1	10.7	1.0	0.5
Haryana	16.6	21.5	10.1	2.1	1.8
Manipur	17.4	24.2	9.1	6.6	6.1
Orissa	18.9	19.9	16.5	7.0	3.2
A and N Islands	20.0	22.5	14.7	-	-
Nagaland	20.4	35.4	6.4	3.8	1.8
Kerala	20.9	24.5	15.3	1.6	0.8
Daman and Diu	21.8	1.6	22.3	-	-
Uttarakhand	29.4	30.4	26.1	1.3	1.6
Maharashtra	31.6	35.7	21.0	4.7	1.6
Assam	32.0	33.9	20.5	5.8	3.8
Punjab	32.6	35.7	17.3	1.2	1.6
Bihar	33.7	34.1	31.2	6.2	6.8
Arunachal Pradesh	34.7	38.9	20.3	9.8	4.9
Meghalaya	36.9	38.8	32.6	1.6	1.5

Table 8.2: India: rural-urban poverty (continued)

State/Union Territory (UT)	Poverty headcount ratio[1]			Poverty gap ratio[2]	
	2011–12				
	Total	Rural	Urban	Rural	Urban
Karnataka	37.0	40.8	24.8	3.3	3.1
Delhi	39.3	62.6	15.4	1.8	1.6
Chhattisgarh	39.9	44.6	24.8	9.0	5.2
India (2011–12) (NSO)	21.9	25.7	13.7	5.1	2.7
India (2019–20) (M&P)	25.9	30.5	15.5	-	-

Note: [1] The national poverty line appearing in this table indicating state-wise division, uses the recommendation in the 2009 report[1] (Government of India, 2009).[2] The poverty gap ratio (PGR) is defined as the gap by which the mean consumption of the poor below poverty line falls short of the poverty line. It indicates the depth of poverty; the higher is the PGR, the worse is the condition of the poor.

[1] In 2011, the planning commission decided that the national poverty line will be raised in accordance with the recommendations of an expert group chaired by the Suresh Tendulkar. This poverty line was comparable at the time to the international poverty line of World Bank, at $1.09 (now raised to $1.90 to account for inflation) person per day. See Gaur and Rao (2020), and Mehrotra and Parida (2021).

Source: Sustainable Development Goals, National Indicator Framework, Progress Report 2021, NSO, Ministry of Statistics and Programme Implementation (MoSPI) and Mehrotra and Parida (M&P). A dash (-) indicates that data are not available.

acceleration post-1991 despite rising inequality. Faster poverty decline came with higher growth and a more pro-poor pattern of growth (p 1).

Impact of government policy

Government's policies on land and agriculture have been repeatedly fallacious. For example, a 2015 Land Acquisition Bill lacked economic fundamentals in its structure if not intent. Appendix 8.1 illustrates diagrammatically in what way it could have affected the relative positions of landowners or agriculturists versus industrialists, worsening the position of the former. Several authors subsequently critiqued the proposed Act as it had been drawn up. Kale (2015) pointed out,

> there should be a balance between the need for developmental activities and the need to protect the affected people. i.e landowners, tenants, labourers whose livelihood is dependent on land. Resettlement and rehabilitation should be properly done because … in the past, 100 percent resettlement and rehabilitation have not been done by government. The concept of 'public purpose' should be perfectly

> defined and elaborated by law … . This bill should not be accepted as it is formulated. It should be revised because it is useful up to some extent and harmful to (a greater) extent. (p 140)

The 2020–21 extended nation-wide *annesan* (fast) by farmers also illustrated how erroneously government tried to implement procurement policies to the detriment of farmers' wellbeing. Such policies followed several government declarations for improving the farmer's condition. Take one example, that of the 2016–17 annual government budget. After two seasons of drought when median farmer income was less than Rs 30,000 (approximately $447.29[4]) per annum, the then finance minister made a declaration that farmers' incomes would be doubled in five years. It is not known what background calculations had buttressed the statement, for it would have necessitated an annual economic growth rate of 16–17 per cent as against the 6–7 per cent that was being experienced. The question necessarily arose as to how this 10 percentage points per annum difference would be closed but no answer was provided in any follow-up document (Government of India, 2018).

Recently, Gulati et al. (2021b) have underscored the erroneous government policy that aims to merely increase agricultural GDP. Such policy did not necessarily improve the welfare or wellbeing of farmers. Thus, farm incomes failed to grow in states such as Gujarat and Maharashtra despite agricultural growth. On the other hand, in states such as Odisha, Bihar and, to some extent, Uttar Pradesh, average agricultural growth rates were relatively low, yet farmers' incomes grew rapidly. How the fruits of GDP growth are divided among the various types of owners of factors of production can be extremely important. This finding is along the lines of Majumdar's (2021) finding that the current government's aim of doubling the 2015–16 level of farmer incomes by 2022–23 was unlikely to be realized. Calculations have been made by several observers to point this out (Chandrasekhar and Mehrotra, 2016; Ramadas et al., 2018, and others).

To sum up, despite promises of building up rural infrastructure and irrigation, the fact is that Indian agriculture remains so deeply rain-fed and that irrigation has been so neglected or funds so pilfered that it is obvious that no government could achieve the needed output outcomes within a five-year frame.

Taking another example, a minimum support price (MSP) of 50 per cent above cost was also promised to farmers. In fact, for wheat, cost had increased slightly less than MSP in the previous three years and, for varieties of lentils, cost had risen faster than MSP, leave alone MSP being 50 per cent higher than cost. There was little wonder at the spate of farmer suicides

[4] At the average exchange rate of $1 = Rs 67.07 for 2016–17.

as they faced unrepayable debt as a result of policies. All this happened even as the intelligentsia appeared to be in favour of greater funding for recapitalization of banks than the budget allocated, the main beneficiaries of which would be the already rich and wealthy who had depleted bank coffers through non-repayment of bank loans and mounting non-performing assets (NPA). They were 'the elephants that hide amidst the mice' as a Latin American finance minister once confided to this author regarding his own country. The previously mentioned study by Majumdar (2021) undertook a detailed econometric analysis to establish that the MSP outcome could not have redressed farmer distress since it failed to recognize the class-related structural constructs that ruled rural production and circulation processes. She concluded that agrarian distress pitted against the growing wealth of private traders could be altered only through changing the underlying agrarian class structure.

A nostalgic recollection is in a song by poet Dwijendralal Ray (1863–1913) taught to children in their early years,

> *Dhan Dhanya Pushp Bhara Hamara Yeh Vasundhara*
> Our earth, with its abundance of crops and the richness of flowers
> Holds within its midst a land that is the most beautiful of all lands
> This land is built of dreams and bound by memories
> This, the land of my birth, the queen of all lands, is ne'er to be found anywhere else … I pray that I breathe my last in this land where I was born.

That era has gone. Squalor surrounds urban and rural environments. After every shower, roads reduce to dirt patches. Farmers commit suicide on their parched, unirrigated land under debt burdens that break their backs. Indian society has become inured to farmer suicides even by the hundreds in Vidarbha and elsewhere. Cowed down with fear, few question what has been happening. Yet, crops rot or are meals for mice for lack of storage or transport facilities The role of corruption raises its head time and again and has to be confronted.[5] That a state government's interest in an enquiry to trace the use of hundreds of billions of rupees spent to achieve one per cent of budgeted irrigation objectives was quashed by the same political party at the centre – reflecting the intransigent position taken by a coalition partner in the UPA-II government – is just one case in point.

Water pollution has affected parts of India in a particularly harmful way. Punjab, once the granary bowl of India and home of the Green Revolution,

5 International indices put India's corruption at such high levels that it would be foolhardy to convey that it will be an easy task.

today stands vitiated by chemicals in its soil, its farmers impoverished and, from all accounts, many obliged to seek sustenance from unlawful and socially unacceptable activities. A state that was also the pride of India for its *jawans* – soldiers – and farmers has now been reduced to street protests that is being quashed ultimately for the benefit of a handful of industrial houses that are likely to corner the absorption of farm produce at oligopolistic prices. In the same way, the same houses have captured sectors such as telecom and oil by driving out competition and at the behest of a government dominated from the same regional base and community.

Often media finds it more comfortable to interpret rural–urban migration as a sign of progress. Much of the truth lies, however, in the inability of farmers to obtain adequate and clean water to cultivate land as reported by emigres from Bihar, Jharkhand, Odisha, Rajasthan, West Bengal and elsewhere to urban hubs such as Bangalore, Delhi, Mumbai and Pune. It is often driven more by desperation than by choice. The prevailing shyness of raising questions needs to be punctured and bold actions recommended and taken.

To move forward, Saini and Gulati (2021) have emphasized that dispassionate analysis of what went wrong and a concurrent evaluation of all major programmes are needed so that they can be meaningfully modified with improved delivery objectives. In the final analysis, farmers' economic situation and the alleviation of their poverty and malnutrition have to be achieved as early as possible. Only then their demand for market products could increase, a well-rounded rural-urban-rural nexus meaningfully develop, and a multiplier effect be activated. Such an eventuality would be far more preferable to farmers carrying on with their perennial trek to urban boundaries to eke out a living under challenging conditions, an option that is not their first one as found in the analysis of Imbert and Papp (2020).

References

Ali, Nawab. (2018) 'Checking rural migration through enhancing farmers income and improving their living conditions', *Indian Farming*, 68(1): 07–11. Available at https://icar.org.in/sites/default/files/Checking%20Rural%20Migration.pdf, accessed 11 August 2021.

Bhagat, Ram B. and Kunal Keshri. (2020) Internal migration in India, in Martin Bell, Aude Bernard, Charles-Edward and Yu Zhu (eds) *Internal Migration in the Countries of Asia: A Cross-national Comparison.* Cham: Springer. Available at https://doi.org/10.1007/978-3-030-44010-7_11, accessed 7 February 2023.

Binswanger-Mkhize, Hans P. (2013) 'The stunted structural transformation of the Indian economy: agriculture, manufacturing and the rural non-farm sector', *Economic and Political Weekly*, 48(26/27): 5–13. Available at www.jstor.org/stable/23527235, accessed 10 August 2021.

Chandrasekhar, S. and Nirupam Mehrotra N. (2016) 'Doubling farmers' incomes by 2022', *Economic & Political Weekly*, 51(18): 10–13. Available at www.epw.in/journal/2016/18/commentary/doubling-farmers-incomes-2022.html, accessed 12 August 2021.

Datt, Gaurav, Martin Ravallion and Rinku Murgai. (2016) 'Growth, Urbanization, and Poverty Reduction in India'. World Bank Policy Research Working Paper No. 7568. Available at SSRN: https://ssrn.com/abstract=2733906, accessed 8 August 2021.

Gaur, Seema and N Srinivasa Rao. (2020) 'Poverty Measurement in India: A Status Update'. Working paper No. 1/2020, Ministry of Rural Development, Government of India. Available at https://rural.nic.in/sites/default/files/WorkingPaper_Poverty_DoRD_Sept_2020.pdf, accessed 4 August 2021.

Government of India. (2009) 'Report of the Expert Group to Review the Methodology for Estimation of Poverty', Chaired by S. D. Tendulkar, Planning Commission, New Delhi.

Government of India. (2015) 'The Right to Fair Compensation and Transparency in Land Acquisition, Rehabilitation and Resettlement (Amendment) (LARR) Bill', New Delhi.

Government of India. (2018) 'Report of the Committee for Doubling Farmers' Income', Volume VIII, Ministry of Agriculture & Farmers' Welfare, New Delhi, February.

Government of India. (2020a) 'Farmers' Produce Trade and Commerce (Promotion and Facilitation) Act', New Delhi.

Government of India. (2020b) 'Farmers' (Empowerment and Protection) Agreement of Price Assurance and Farm Services Act', New Delhi.

Government of India. (2020c) 'Essential Commodities (Amendment) Act', New Delhi.

Government of India. (2021) *Sector-wise GDP of India*, Ministry of Statistics and Programme Implementation, New Delhi, 17 June.

Gulati, Ashok, Ritika Juneja and Jikun Huang. (2021a) 'Overview of India, China and Israel', in *From Food Scarcity to Surplus*. Singapore: Springer. Available at https://doi.org/10.1007/978-981-15-9484-7_2, accessed 11 August 2021.

Gulati, Ashok, Shweta Saini and Ranjana Roy. (2021b) 'Going beyond agricultural GDP to farmers' incomes', in Gulati A., Roy R. and Saini S. (eds) *Revitalizing Indian Agriculture and Boosting Farmer Incomes*. India Studies in Business and Economics, pp 281–318. Singapore: Springer. Available at https://doi.org/10.1007/978-981-15-9335-2_10, accessed 11 August 2021.

Imbert, Clément and John Papp. (2020) 'Costs and benefits of rural-urban migration: evidence from India', *Journal of Development Economics*, 146: 102473. Available at https://doi.org/10.1016/j.jdeveco.2020.102473, accessed 11 August 2021.

Kalamkar, S. S. (2009) 'Urbanisation and agricultural growth in India', *Indian Journal of Agricultural Economics*, 64(3): 442–61. Available at www.shram.org/uploadFiles/20170822025552.pdf, accessed 11 August 2021.

Kale, Vinayak B. (2015) 'Land Acquisition Bill 2015: Problems and Perspectives (2015)', *International Refereed Multidisciplinary Journal of Contemporary Research*, Special Issue III: 138–40. Available at www.researchgate.net/profile/Rahul-Pardeshi-5/publication/349092454_RAINFALL_CHANGE_OF_COLLAPSE_AGRICULTURAL_LAND_USE_IN_SOLAPUR_DISTRICT/links/601f411d92851c4ed55471ae/RAINFALL-CHANGE-OF-COLLAPSE-AGRICULTURAL-LAND-USE-IN-SOLAPUR-DISTRICT.pdf#page=142, accessed 9 August 2021.

Majumdar, Sayonee. (2021) 'A class-focused theory of minimum support price and agricultural distress in India', *A Journal of Economics, Culture & Society*, 33(1): 71–97. Available at doi: 10.1080/08935696.2020.1847017, accessed 11 August 2021.

Mehrotra, Santosh and Jajati Keshari Parida. (2021) 'Poverty in India is on the rise again', *The Hindu*, 4 August. Available at https://www.thehindu.com/opinion/lead/poverty-in-india-is-on-the-rise-again/article35709263.ece, accessed 4 August 2021.

Mitra, Arup and Mayumi Murayama. (2009) 'Rural to urban migration: a district-level analysis for India', *International Journal of Migration, Health and Social Care*, 5 (2): 35–52. Available at https://doi.org/10.1108/17479894200900011, accessed 4 August 2021.

Ramadas, Sendhil, S. J. Balaji, P. Ramasundaram, Anuj Kumar, Satyavir Singh, Ravish Chatrath and G. P. Singh. (2018) 'Doubling Farmers Income by 2022: Trends, Challenges, Pathway and Strategies'. Research Bulletin No. 40, ICAR-Indian Institute of Wheat and Barley Research, Karnal, pp 1–54. Available at 10.13140/RG.2.2.24608.28169, accessed 12 August 2021.

Saini, Shweta and Ashok Gulati. (2021) 'Indian agriculture under PM Modi 1.0 2014–2018', in Gulati A., Roy R. and Saini S. (eds) *Revitalizing Indian Agriculture and Boosting Farmer Incomes*. India Studies in Business and Economics, pp 321–51. Singapore: Springer. Available at https://doi.org/10.1007/978-981-15-9335-2_11, accessed 11 August 2021.

Thakur, Babita. (2012) 'Declining share of agriculture in GDP: a serious concern', *International Journal of Engineering Research and Technology*, 1(8) October: 1–8. Available at www.ijert.org, accessed 9 August 2021.

Tripathi, Sabyasachi. (2021) 'Why is the rural to urban migration rate in India so low? An empirical analysis', *The Review of Regional Studies*, 51(1): 1–16. Available at https://pdfs.semanticscholar.org/863d/c1a2e6da02f0d965cb890a4ebd3856d86d23.pdf, accessed 9 August 2021.

9

Women, Children and Demographic Dividend

Introduction

In this chapter, we address inequality encountered and suffered by women and children. Realizing what the prevailing conditions of children are, we ask whether the promised demographic dividend from a large youth population is likely to occur or if it is likely to remain an unrealizable promise. The growth of India's population has been explosive. Total population was 0.4 billion in 1950, 0.5 billion in 1960, 0.6 billion in 1970, 0.7 billion in 1980, 0.9 billion in 1990, 1.1 billion in 2000, 1.2 billion in 2010, and had been projected at 1.4 billion in 2020–21 (United Nations, 2019). While the rate of increase has declined in the 2000s, the sheer volume increase continues to put heavy pressure on economic resources, and this becomes doubly burdensome in light of starkly worsening inequality and the provision of socio-economic infrastructure. In this chapter, we begin with the state of gender inequality and continue with the ramifications for children's education. We leave the condition of rural and mufassil healthcare, coupled with government's recent policy announcement regarding universal healthcare, to Chapter 10.

Gender inequality

Gender is another area in which inequality is high globally and in India. Chancel et al. (2021) provided estimates of gender inequality in global earnings,

> Gender inequalities remain considerable at the global level, and progress within countries is too slow … Overall, women's share of total incomes from work (labor income) neared 30% in 1990 and stands at less than 35% today (in 2015–2020). Current gender earnings inequality remains very high: in a gender equal world, women would earn 50% of all labor

> income. In 30 years, progress has been very slow at the global level, and dynamics have been different across countries, with some recording progress but others seeing reductions in women's share of earnings. (p 16)

The authors looked also at India and found,

> Gender inequalities in India are very high. The female labor income share is equal to 18%. This is significantly lower than the average in Asia (21%, excluding China). This value is one of the lowest in the world, slightly higher than the average share in Middle East (15%). The significant increase observed since 1990 (+8 p.p.) has been insufficient to lift women's labor income share to the regional average. (p 198)

The condition of women in India was poignantly described by Mehta (2014) in an instance of how women converted work into self-expression (which was perhaps not feasible in real life) while reporting on Ansari households in Barabanki, Uttar Pradesh,

> Through the process of making [a] quilt, the producer tells a story about herself … and by incorporating the quilt in her personhood, the quiltmaker embeds in herself the capacity to transform external materials, making them re-emerge as a product of her nature. (p 234)

> in deciding the types of designs for the quilt, workers hark back to a past to argue for or against a design – the past must inform the present in affirmation or negation … . Women remember how an embroidered design fared in the ensuring of a good marriage, or turned out to be not particularly propitious … a well-remembered past links a motif or a rag to a particular marriage or a particular person. … Patchwork constitutes an eternal present. (p 253)

Thus, the women found a sure way to leave an indelible mark of their lives that would perhaps not be feasible verbally, in everyday life.

As in the case of the rural-urban divide, the female-male divide is another gaping breach of equality in India. The position of women lags behind that of men in most socio-economic indicators. Table 9.1 categorizes the relative position of women versus men in rural vis a vis urban areas between 1951–2021. It reveals several points:

1. The female-male ratio in total population (the sex ratio) has hardly changed between 1951–2021, remaining 48.6/51.4 and 48.7/51.3 in the rural and urban areas respectively. Thus, the female component has remained 5 per cent lower than the male component over 70 years of

Table 9.1: Population shares and growth of population

Share of total population (%)											
Year	**Total**		**Rural**			**Urban**			**AAEGR**[1]		
	Female	**Male**	**Total**	**Female**	**Male**	**Total**	**Female**	**Male**	**Total**	**Female**	**Male**
1951	48.6	51.4	82.7	83.5	81.9	17.3	16.4	18.1	1.3	1.3	1.2
1961	48.5	51.5	82.0	83.0	81.1	18.0	17.0	18.9	2.0	1.9	2.0
1971	48.2	51.8	80.1	80.9	79.3	19.9	19.1	20.7	2.2	2.2	2.3
1981	48.3	51.7	76.7	77.4	76.0	23.3	22.6	24.0	2.2	2.2	2.2
1991	48.1	51.9	74.3	74.8	73.8	25.7	25.2	26.2	2.1	2.1	2.2
2001	48.3	51.7	72.2	72.7	71.7	27.8	27.3	28.3	2.0	2.0	1.9
2011	48.5	51.5	68.8	69.1	68.6	31.2	30.9	31.4	1.6	1.7	1.6
2021[2]	48.7	51.3	65.5	65.8	65.1	34.5	34.2	34.9	1.1	1.1	1.1

Note: [1] Average annual exponential growth rate (AAEGR) = (1/n) * log (current year's population / population as reported in years back), where n is the number of years in between. [2] Report of the Technical Group on Population Projections, November 2019, National Commission on Population, Ministry of Health and Family Welfare (MoHFW).

Source: Women & Men in India 2020, Social Statistics Division, National Statistical Office, Ministry of Statistics and Programme Implementation, Government of India

independence. It surely implies prevailing adverse societal conditions and concomitant family preferences and interventions in various forms, none of which can be salutary.

2. The rural population in proportion of total population has declined from 82.7 per cent to 65.5 per cent while that of the urban population has doubled from 17.3 per cent to 34.5 per cent. Therefore, the current population is divided broadly into 2/3 rural and 1/3 urban.
3. The female component of the rural population has been higher than the male though the margin of difference has narrowed. On the other hand, the female component of the urban population has been lower than the male though, here again, the margin has narrowed.
4. The average annual exponential population growth rate (AAEGR) jumped between 1951–61 during the first decade after independence from 1.3 per cent to 2.0 per cent, then remained stable at 2.2–2.0 per cent until 2001 for 40 years, after which it steadily declined over the next 20 years to 1.1 per cent in 2021.
5. In parallel, the AAEGR for the female population remained slightly lower than that of the male, though the female rate exceeded the male rate in 2001–11. It does remain somewhat of a mystery that, in terms of population growth rates, women have not fared too poorly compared to males in the new millennium (Table 9.1). This may comprise a fledgling sign towards gender evenness in their growth rates during the current millennium.

The latest National Family Health Survey (NFHS-5) (2019–21) based on 636,699 households in state/union territories (UT) and districts reported a reversal of the female-male sex ratio. Oddly, it covered 724,115 women and 101,839 men, and reported a female-male sex ratio at 1020/1000, changing from 991/1000 in 2015–16. Further, though the female-male sex ratio at birth continued to be lower than 1:1, it improved from 919/1,000 to 929/1,000. A wide variation existed among the states.

In a recent study, Deshpande (2021) assessed advances made by women in female labour force participation (FLFP), concluding that women's involvement in paid work remained low and questioned what measures might enable its advancement. She pointed out that an increase in FLFP led to lowering the son-preference phenomenon as has occurred in Bangladesh and South Korea. She conceded that the son-daughter stereotype was diminishing as more parents recognized the higher contribution of daughters in their lives than sons. As was pointed out in Table 9.1, the sex ratio at birth had improved though the male proportion remained higher. Despite such progress, Deshpande made the point that paid work opportunities for women continued to be laggard and their responsibility was perceived as primarily home-making.

Several studies have identified gender markers of poverty and inequality in the field of international development, revealing that gender-based inequality is not confined to India but is universal. Women do two-thirds of the work, but earn one-third of total income and own less than one-tenth of the resources. Women are discriminated against more than men reflecting their relative lack of economic power. Several studies exist that have identified gender markers of poverty and inequality in the field of international development. Bradshaw et al. (2017) cautioned on statistical data that limited the strength of conclusions regarding what should be paramount in understanding the multiple processes accounting for gender bias in determining poverty burdens. Such limitations revealed the lack of a set of tools that could successfully measure or monitor poverty by gender.

Macro-econometric studies have found greater gender equality to be associated with a positive impact on economic growth, though higher economic growth may not improve gender equality (Kabeer, 2016). The causal pathways cannot explain such asymmetry. Kabeer (2019) examined selected impact assessment studies that used randomized control trials (RCTs) to test the impact of transferring assets to women in extreme poverty in West Bengal and Sindh. She concluded that RCTs failed to meet their own criteria for establishing causality. Also, their explanations for the patterns of outcomes observed were limited. Hence, she recommended mixed approaches that did not depend exclusively on RCTs.

Authors have also studied gender inequality in regions of India. Jha and Nagar (2015) looked at regions and social classes and speculated on aspects that prevented economic growth from trickling down to improve the lives of the Indian poor including women. They found arriving at a comprehensive view on gender inequality in India to be complex since inequality existed in every field including education, employment opportunities, income, health, cultural and overall socio-economic environment. They emphasized the need for a multi-dimensional approach to conclude on gender inequalities in India. In her study, Kohli (2017) narrowed down on the depth of penetration of gender inequality reflecting the nature of patriarchy in Indian society, manifested in foeticide, infanticide, and the continuing perception of girls as a liability.

Another state level study by Arora (2012) found certain links between state level gender inequality and the per-capita income of a state. Overall, higher per-capita income was associated with lower gender inequality, and lower per-capita income in states with high inequality. Further, lower trade openness was also associated with higher gender inequality.[1]

---

1 Unexpectedly, however, Arora indicated that the 'study also found that even in high per-capita income states such as Punjab and Haryana, gender inequality is high. Both child mortality and under-5 mortality rates are much higher for girls than boys in these two states' (p 157).

Arora correctly pointed to the need for improved access to education and better health facilities as necessary conditions to facilitate women's contribution to economic growth, but she also highlighted women's increased participation in the labour force to reduce gender inequality. In fact, despite economic growth, women's conditions may languish without being fully evident.

The state of Kerala may be a case in point. On the one hand, the Human Development Index (HDI) there (0.763) was the highest in India in 2019. Kerala also had the highest literacy rate of 94 per cent, being 96 per cent for men and 92 per cent for women, as against 82 per cent and 65 per cent respectively for all India. Life expectancy at birth of women was 77.8 years as against 70.4 years for all India, and maternal mortality rate was 430 per 1 million live births as against 1,130 for all India. While such indicators are usually cited in favour of Kerala, there are certain alarming characteristics emerging as well. The female-to-male sex ratio at birth (the number of females born per 100 males) in Kerala has been worsening in recent years. It has been singled out as 'gender discrimination even before birth' (Chakraborty, 2021). A sharp decline has occurred from 1,047 in 2015–16 to 951 in 2019–20 (983 in urban and 922 in rural Kerala). This indicator of prenatal gender selection is a clear sign of societal regression possibly driven by the re-emergence of dowry with an increasing emphasis on gold even as world gold prices have escalated.

Das et al. (2015) queried the low participation rate of women in India. Using household survey data, they found, conditional on demographic characteristics and education, as well as state-level labour market flexibility, that the labour force participation of women had languished behind that of men. They concluded that appropriate social spending on education and enhanced labour market flexibility would improve workforce participation of women and encourage women to move into formal sector jobs from the informal sector.

To take specific examples, Priya (2020) studied women in the construction sector which is the largest employer in India – after agriculture – absorbing more than 31 million workers. Priya's conclusions were based on an anthropological examination of 100 migrant workers in various construction sites in Coimbatore in Tamil Nadu state. More than 35 per cent of them were women who worked without opportunities to improve their position to masonry or supervision and, of course, their wages were much lower than men. Rizvi and Vinaik (2020) examined the state of women in the corporate sector. They found that, though women's participation in the corporate sector had increased in recent years, the mindset towards women remained frozen. Using secondary data, they concluded that much scope remained in the corporate sector as well as in government to ensure fair and equitable treatment of working women in India.

Despite some advances, ubiquitous gender-specific violence continues in Indian society. Going back, extreme violence was perpetrated on women at its 1947 Partition graphic descriptions of which have been provided by authors such as Menon and Bhasin (1998); Menon (2013); Butalia (2017) and others. Karlekar (2004) explained that a social attitude favouring the suppression of the phenomenon of violence against women was no small cause for its continuance. Once married, girls found themselves exposed to a new set of unfamiliar relationships, the equilibrium of which may be determined by pecuniary factors, mainly the dowry that she brought in. If considered low, abuse – emotional, verbal, physical – could follow, a matter that has been examined by an array of sociologists, for example, Uberoi (1995) and Verghese (1997). Wife abuse – beating and battering – that is not uncommon in many – including Western – societies, assumes an additional bite when the perception of an insufficient dowry is added in as an instigating factor.

Chakraborty (2021) studied the incidence of crimes against women which continues to be a significant threat in India. The highest component – one third – of all crimes against women was 'within own home' under cruelty by the husband or his relatives. Three dowry-related deaths in Kerala in June 2021 of women in their early twenties created an uproar, bringing to the forefront dowry's deep-rooted position in society even in Kerala, often cited as India's showcase for women's advancement. Education of a girl was found to be a relatively insignificant determinant in tackling these social evils as educated girls were also compelled to marry within their caste with parents paying huge sums of money as dowry (see Chapter 6).

India has not outlawed rape within marriage unless the wife is below 18 years of age. Thus, India remains one among only 36 countries where marital rape is not a crime.[2] As Table 9.2 reveals, crimes against women have escalated, rising by more than 23 per cent in the five years since 2015. The various categories of crimes within the total and their sharp rise are, indeed, also an eye-opener. For example, dowry-related and cruelty against the wife now represent higher proportions, buttressing the discussion of the condition of the married woman made previously. Inequality of women versus men that continues in many forms and manifestations obviously needs strong laws to counter it if only as a beginning point.

---

[2] As per an exception clause in Section 375 of the Indian Penal Code, 1860, sexual intercourse by a man with his own wife, with the wife not being under 15 years of age, was not considered rape. The Supreme Court increased the age to 18 years though, it is to be noted that it militates against the Right to Equality included in Article 14 of the Indian constitution. The high court of Kerala has recently opined that marital rape was a form of cruelty and comprised grounds for divorce.

Table 9.2: Major crimes committed against women

Share (%)					
Type of crime	**2015**	**2016**	**2017**	**2018**	**2019**
Rape (Sec. 375 to 376 IPC)	10.5	11.5	9.0	8.8	7.9
Kidnapping and abduction (Sec. 363 to 373 IPC)	18.0	19.0	18.4	19.2	17.9
Cruelty by husband and relatives (Sec. 498-A IPC)	34.4	32.6	29.1	27.3	30.9
Assault on women with intent to outrage her modesty (Sec. 354 IPC)	25.0	25.0	23.9	23.6	21.8
Insult to the modesty of women (Sec. 509 IPC)	2.6	2.2	2.1	1.8	1.7
Dowry Prohibition Act, 1961	3.0	2.9	2.8	3.4	3.3
Others	6.3	6.9	14.7	15.9	16.5
Total number of crimes against women	329243	338954	359849	378236	405861

Source: Women & Men in India 2020, Social Statistics Division, National Statistical Office, Ministry of Statistics and Programme Implementation, Government of India

Not to mention the condition of the widow which is likely to be worse than that of a married woman, would be a serious oversight. Widowhood is a double-edged sword when the abuse comes from one's own children. But sexual assault of widows has not been unknown including that of migrant widows to Kashi – Benaras – when it was common practice for them to emigrate there once widowed in particular from Bengal. The rape en masse of Sikh widows in Delhi after Indira Gandhi's assassination in 1984 is another example among several other instances that stare in the face of Indian society.

A push for the inclusion of women remains a perennial struggle in Indian society. An example is the recent exhortation by the supreme court to government to allow women to sit for the entrance examination scheduled from September 2021 for the National Defence Academy, the thrust point for top jobs in the armed forces. Accordingly, it instructed the Union Public Services Commission (UPSC) which oversees the government entrance examination system to issue appropriate notifications to publicize the matter. This reflects the armed forces' reticence thus far in opening it up to women in clear sight of robbing them of the highest posts in the defence system. In fact, women were not allowed 'permanent commission' in the armed forces and had to do with finite contracts until, in 2020, the supreme court pushed it in.

Table 9.3 reveals that the proportions of women versus men represented in the upper and lower houses of parliament and in the council of central government ministers are woefully behind their proportion in total

Table 9.3: India: female political representation (%)

	2004	2009	2014	2016	2018	2019	2020
Seats held by women							
Lok Sabha	8.3	10.9	11.4	-	-	14.4	-
Rajya Sabha	-	-	12.8	11.1	11.5	-	10.3
Panchayati Raj Institutions	-	-	46.1	-	-	44.4	-
Women in Central Council of Ministers	10.3	9.0	15.6	12.0	12.2	10.5	9.3

Source: Sustainable Development Goals, National Indicator Framework, Progress Report 2021, National Statistical Office, Ministry of Statistics and Programme Implementation, Government of India

population, though their representation at local government level is closer though not equal to their population share.

Children's condition

Reflecting the crucial link between the condition of children and the demographic dividend, India's child performance will be compared with a selection of countries, from birth through school years, to understand if the demographic dividend that was anticipated was likely to be achieved or whether it might turn into a nightmare. Will the new National Education Policy (NEP), for example, help alleviate the formidable challenges over and above redesigning school curricula? These aspects comprise the subject matter of this section.

What is the condition of India's children? To begin, a huge proportion of them have to leave high school primarily for the pressure of having to feed themselves (Save the Children, 2017).[3] In fact, many of them get into the work of adults. Dreze (2003) cited a poll of Delhi residents in which nearly 90 per cent agreed that 'our country's biggest failure has been in the field of education' (p 978). The constitution's goal of universal education has not been met. A survey in backward states found almost 90 per cent parents indicated their interest in educating girls while 100 per cent expressed a similar wish for boys. This interest did not translate into practice, reasons comprising the monetary effort needed to purchase books, slates, fees, clothes and other expenses, apart from releasing the children from other chores, coupled with the fear that leaving school would be an irreversible

[3] It is a not-for-profit, non-governmental organization (NGO) that works for children's rights. Its Global Childhood Report comprises a useful source of information.

backward turn for the child. Thus, under such trying circumstances, parents would have to be strongly convinced that the effort of sending children to school would be worthwhile. Dreze cited the manifestations of educational deprivation as including dependence on child labour for a family's survival, quoting a spokesperson for the Coalition Against Child Labour as saying, 'How can we make our country fully literate when (millions) of our children are engaged in full-time jobs as child labourers?' (p 979). Indeed, Nieuwenhuys (2003) cited ten studies that showed that 'poor children who are not employed perform crucial work, often in the domestic arena, in subsistence agriculture, and in the urban informal sector' (p 945). Thus, whether children are in employment or not, they appear to be performing unpaid – likely to be high quality – work in any event.

Work conditions of children can be Dickensian as in Victorian England. Karlekar (2004), citing various studies, pointed to beatings and lashings of defenceless children leading to substantial injury and extreme corporal punishments by parents 'when the child shirked work' (p 315). Further, the female child, considered inferior, physically and mentally weak, and sexually vulnerable, faced inequality in the household versus the male child. This encouraged early marriage thus continuing a woman's status of physical confinement through life as well as of diminished intra-household entitlements (Sen, 1983) of health care, nutrition, education and material assets. Various studies have offered evidence of lower access to material resources by girls than boys. Discrimination in food has been found to occur in upper- and middle-class households as well, thus indicating that it was more in the nature of gender discrimination than being determined by household incomes.[4]

Save the Children sources data from the World Bank, United Nations Educational, Scientific and Cultural Organization (UNESCO), other United Nations offices for global population, United Nations Children's Fund (UNICEF), World Health Organization (WHO) and others. It enables a discussion of children's condition in a cross-country context. The criteria to assess early end-of-childhood comprise eight indicators. They are: under-five mortality (per 1,000 live births), malnutrition causing stunting (percentage for 0–59 months), exclusion from primary and secondary school (percentage of age 5–17), child labour in adult roles (percentage of age 5–17), percentage of teenage girls married or in union, and births per 1,000 teenage girls (both for girls aged 15–19) and percentage of displacement through conflict or victims of homicide (deaths per 100,000 among age 0–19).

---

4 Evidence is also provided of boys receiving more milk and eggs than girls and taboos against giving girls meat or fish.

Table 9.4: Selected countries: childhood condition – rank and score

Country	Score (1–1000)			Rank[1]	
	2000[2]	2017	2021	2017	2021
China	861	928	942	41	45
Bangladesh	575	680	722	134	140
Brazil	785	821	815	89	108
India	632	754	789	116	118
Indonesia	721	793	816	101	107
Nepal	543	680	740	134	137
Pakistan	540	621	690	148	147
Sri Lanka	867	903	915	61	63

Note: [1] Increase in the rank number of a country shows that it is in a worse condition than countries with lower rank numbers. [2] The values of for 2000 are extrapolated backwards and reported in the 2019 Report. The number of countries considered in each reported year are, accordingly, 172 in 2017, 176 in 2000 and 2019, and 186 in 2021.

Source: Global Childhood Reports, 2017, 2019 and 2021, Save the Children

Eight countries are compared to assess India's performance on the basis of its prevailing score and rank among those countries. Table 9.4 reveals that, though India's score and rank in the 2000–21 period were better than those of Bangladesh, Nepal and Pakistan, they remained considerably below those of China, Brazil, Indonesia and Sri Lanka. Also to be noted is that only China and Sri Lanka reached a score of above 900 during 2017–21.[5] Surprisingly, Brazil experienced a decline in the score of six points between 2017–21, the only such instance among the sample countries. The difference in India's rank compared to China and Sri Lanka was striking. Thus, India has a long way to go in order to achieve an internationally acceptable degree of childhood wellbeing. Merely having remained ahead of Bangladesh, Pakistan or Nepal cannot be considered a hallmark of success.

The derivation of the score needs elaboration. Since each of the eight indicators is measured differently, it has to be 'normalized' or brought down to a common denominator. Thus X_N, a normalized indicator value, equals $(X - L) / (H - L)$, where X is a country's actual value for that indicator, L (Worst) is the highest observed value for the indicator[6] among all countries, and H (Best) is the lowest possible value for the indicator which is zero

[5] Among advanced European economies and the US, the scores ranged between 984 for Norway and 948 for the US.

[6] As elaborated before, the indicators are set in terms of deficiencies. Therefore, higher observed indicator values show worse performance.

Table 9.5: Selected countries: children's indicators[1]

Country	Child mortality (per 1000)		Severely malnourished[2] (%)		Out of school[3] (%)	
	2015[4]	2019[4]	2011–16	2015–20	2011–16	2015–19
China	10.7	7.9	9.4	8.1	11.6	7.6
Bangladesh	37.6	30.8	36.1	28.0	28.0	28.1
Brazil	16.4	13.9	7.1	7.0	7.3	6.9
India	47.7	34.3	38.7	34.7	18.6	20.3
Indonesia	27.2	23.9	36.4	30.8	14.3	12.6
Nepal	35.8	30.8	37.4	31.5	13.4	9.0
Pakistan	81.1	67.2	45.0	37.6	42.9	38.3
Sri Lanka	9.8	7.1	14.7	17.3	10.1	5.0
World	42.5	37.7	23.2	21.3	17.8	16.9

Note: For definitions see the discussion on Save the Children above. [2] Data reflect the most recent year available for particular country during the reference period. [3] The same fact applies here as in 2. [4] For these categories, 2015 data are found in the 2017 Report, and 2019 data are found in the 2021 Report.

Source: Global Childhood Reports, 2017 and 2021, Save the Children

for all eight indicators. The overall score for a country is calculated by summing X_N for all eight indicators and dividing the sum by eight, then multiplying by 1,000 to get numbers between 0–1,000 (with 1,000 being the best possible score).

Country scores, when taken together, allow an ordering of countries. For 2021 for example, India was ranked 118 out of 186 countries. India's score reflected an improvement of 35 points – from 754 to 789 – during 2017–21. This improvement fell short of improvements made by Bangladesh (42), Nepal (60) and Pakistan (69) though that did not enable them to reach India's score. China and Sri Lanka, already with high scores, did not of course improve much further, though Brazil, as already mentioned, experienced a small decline in score. Indonesia (23) showed only lacklustre improvement.

Table 9.5 deconstructs the overall picture into selected indicator components using data as available. Thus, India reduced its child mortality during 2015–19 as did every sample country. Over a longer period 2011–20, India made an improvement of 4 per cent in reducing severe malnourishment (stunting),[7]

[7] At present, a quarter of Indian babies are wasted, and half suffer from malnutrition or stuntedness.

Table 9.6: Selected countries: child–adult indicators[1]

Country	Begins work life[2] (%)		Marries[3] (%)		Child-mother (per 1000 girls)		Victim of extreme violence (deaths per 100,000)
	2011–16	2015–20	2011–16	2014–19	2016	2018	2016
China	…	…	3.1	2.1	6.5	7.6	0.5
Bangladesh	4.3	6.8	44.2	32.4	84.4	82.3	1.5
Brazil	8.1	5.4	3.9	15.1	62.7	57.9	17.9
India	11.8	11.8	21.1	16.2	24.5	12.1	1.3
Indonesia	6.9	6.9	12.8	9.4	48.0	46.9	2.8
Nepal	37.4	21.7	24.2	27.1	62.1	64.4	1.6
Pakistan	…	12.8	13.1	13.5	37.7	38.6	6.0
Sri Lanka	2.5	1.0	9.0	6.0	14.8	20.7	0.8
World	12.6	12.6	14.4	16.0	50.4	44.0	3.3

Note: [1] For definitions see the discussion on Save the Children above. [2] Data refer to the most recent year available for particular country during the reference period. Thus, the data reflect the manner in which they are presented. [3] The same fact applies here as in 2.

Source: Global Childhood Reports, 2017, 2020, and 2021, Save the Children

while Sri Lanka deteriorated. In particular, Sri Lanka's worsening is surprising though its testy political environment may provide a clue. Tellingly, India and Bangladesh's indicator for out-of-school children worsened during 2011–19. This is lamentable in light of an improvement in every other sample country and in the global average.

Table 9.6 focuses on what may be termed 'child-adult' indicators. There was no improvement in India in reducing child labour. Bangladesh's condition worsened in reducing child labour and Indonesia made nil progress in reducing child labour, while Brazil and Sri Lanka did improve. Perhaps Nieuwenhuys's (2004) observation on child labour that it needed to be examined under an alternative lens, is worth quoting,

> The dissociation of childhood from the performance of valued work is considered a yardstick of modernity … . The problem of defining children's roles in this way is that it denies their agency in the creation and negotiation of value … the moral condemnation of child labour assumes that children's place in modern society must perforce be one of dependency and passivity. This denial of their capacity to legitimately

> act upon their environment by undertaking valuable work makes children altogether dependent. (p 331)

Nieuwenhuys wondered as to what extent commitment to the basis of the childhood ideal such as free education, cheap housing, free health care, sports and recreation facilities and family welfare and support services could be financed from available social surpluses in developing countries. On the other hand, he said, 'working for pay offers opportunities for self-respect (though) it also entails sacrificing childhood' (p 339). Mainly, this anthropologist's expressed view was that the condition of work for child labour should be ensured by delinking it from the strict principles of modernity and through proper pay and work conditions, thus improving the self-esteem of the child. In other words, in order to pursue the education objective, the prevalent conditions of the working child should not be abandoned; rather, improvement in his or her work condition should be ensured.

An area in which India made good progress was reducing the incidence of child marriage during 2011–19, though the picture of other countries was mixed. Bangladesh, Indonesia and Sri Lanka improved. China – already with a high score – made progress, while Nepal, Pakistan and Brazil worsened. Indeed, Brazil's worsening appears surprising. India's 2018 score for child-mother was considerably better than all sample countries other than, expectedly, China. This Indian achievement is noteworthy (see Table 9.6).

Last is the indicator that perhaps cries out for attention the most, that of the violent cutting short of a child's life. Here again India ranks just after China and Sri Lanka from the top, a commendable score despite its poverty, while Brazil is by far the worst. Recently, a report succinctly presented much information on the prevailing challenges relating to Brazil's abject race relations in the city of Rio de Janeiro and the children who are often caught in between, even losing their lives.[8]

In sum, India is making progress in improving its children's condition though certain component indicators have stagnated. Overall, India has to run much faster to improve its global rank. Another conclusion is that Brazil's reputation for violence appears corroborated with respect to its children. To emphasize again, pure macroeconomic indicators are meaningless in a vacuum that excludes socio-economic indicators. This could be nowhere more relevant than in India.

Demographic dividend

India and the international community have pointed to the possibility of a demographic dividend from its relatively young population that India

---

[8] *The Economist* (2021).

Figure 9.1: Selected countries: share of age-group 15–64 in total population

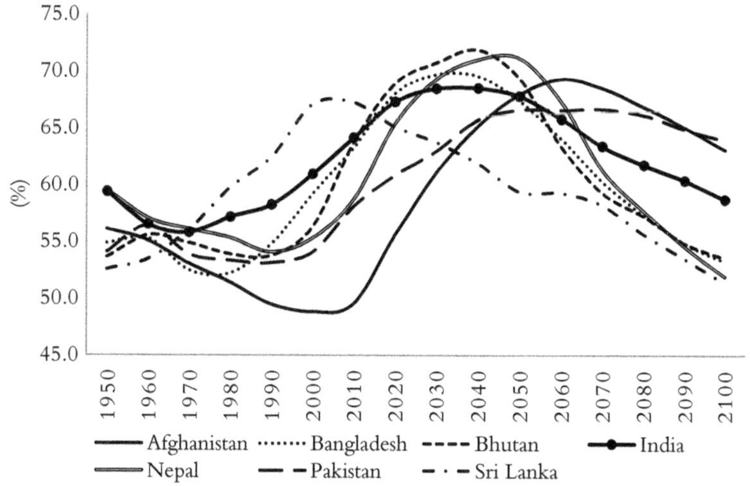

Note: Figures show estimates for the period 1950–2020 while, for the period 2020–2100, projections are based on the probabilistic projections.

Source: World Population Prospects 2019, Online Edition. Rev. 1. United Nations, Department of Economic and Social Affairs, Population Division

could reap until mid-century. United Nations data reveal the share of the working age group of 15–64 years in total population in South Asia as well as their trends. They indicate growth in the share, until 2040 in Bhutan and India, until 2045–50 in Nepal and Pakistan, and until 2060 in Afghanistan (Figure 9.1). The challenge is to convert this growing population into productive citizens through the enhanced provision of nutrition, health and education.[9] Rural-urban migration will be steep in all of South Asia, with urban India likely to reach 50 per cent of the population by 2050,[10] adding a further onerous dimension of absorptive capacity and the implied need for socio-economic infrastructure in health, nutrition and education.

The Indian middle class[11] is marginal in terms of the size of the population comprising less than 9 per cent (Chapter 4, Table 4.1). It should find

[9] It is conceptually comparable to the challenge of converting savings into productive investment rather than into non-performing assets as has emerged increasingly in Indian banking experience thus vitiating positive economic outcomes of a high savings rate. In the same way a rapidly growing population could become a country's liability rather than being an asset.

[10] Ghani (2011) projected the urban population of India at 47.8 per cent for 2040 (p 240).

[11] The middle-class population was 32 million in 1980, 70 million in 2013, 73 million in 2015 and 79 million in 2019 reflecting the last available population data. (World Inequality Database).

financing the necessary socio-economic infrastructure an uphill task unless every paisa is spent perspicuously in this endeavor to improve children's condition. To recall, in 2015–16, 41 per cent of rural babies under five years were stunted, more than 38 per cent underweight, and more than 21 per cent wasted.[12] Looking at the urban component, the figures were 31 per cent stunted, more than 29 per cent underweight, and 20 per cent wasted. Thus, for urban babies, the numbers were 20–25 per cent less bad for stunting and underweight than for rural babies[13] (NHFS-4). Whatever the case may be, adequately financing nutrition, health and education remains a formidable task.

Mother's education had a strikingly salient effect on outcomes. As per the NFHS-4, 51 per cent of children born to mothers with no schooling were stunted, compared with 24 per cent of children born to mothers with 12 or more years of schooling. The corresponding proportions of underweight children were 47 and 22 per cent, respectively. Also, 18 per cent of infants had a birth weight of less than 2.5 kg. Low birth weight decreased with an increase in the mother's schooling and household wealth status. Only 15 per cent of births to mothers having 12 or more years of schooling had a low birth weight, compared with 20 per cent of births to mothers having no schooling (NFHS-4 Report).

Education numbers appear less alarming. There is 100 per cent rural and urban primary (I–V) school enrollment for six- to ten-year-olds. For secondary (VI–VIII) level, it is 80 per cent for rural and 90 per cent for urban; for IX–X, over 60 per cent for rural and over 80 per cent for urban; and, for XI–XII, 40 per cent for rural and 60 per cent for urban. Female attendance ratios decrease with levels of education, and are 5 to 15 per cent less than those for male. It may be gleaned from Table 9.7 that, in 2005–06, the female to male enrolment ratio fell rapidly as the level of education increased from primary level – 87 per cent – to higher education – 62 per cent. By 2015–16, the gap had narrowed to 93 per cent–86 per cent, showing a more rapid improvement for female students in higher education.

These achievements reflected to no small extent the Right to Education Act (RTE) introduced by the UPA-I government in 2009 which attempted to address the assurance made in India's constitution, 'The State shall endeavor to provide, within a period of ten years from the commencement of this Constitution, for free and compulsory education for all children until

[12] India National Family Health Survey (NHFS-4), 2015–16.

[13] The prevalence of stunting and underweight has decreased since 2005–06, especially for stunting, which declined from 48 per cent in 2005–06 to 38 per cent in 2015–16 and underweight declined from 43 per cent to 36 per cent (NFHS-4, 2015–16, p 293). Over this same time period, the prevalence of wasting has remained about the same (20 per cent in 2005–06 and 21 per cent 2015–16).

Table 9.7: Female-male enrolment ratios in stages of education

Females per 100 males enrolled					
	Primary	**Upper primary**	**Secondary**	**Senior secondary**	**Higher education**
Year	**(I-V)**	**(VI-VIII)**	**(IX-X)**	**(XI-XII)**	
2005–06	87	81	73	72	62
2010–11	92	89	82	79	78
2015–16	93	95	91	90	86
2018–19	92	94	92	93	NA

Source: Women & Men in India 2020, National Statistical Office, Ministry of Statistics and Programme Implementation, Government of India

they complete the age of fourteen years' (Article 45). The RTE required education to adhere to a set of principles and standards including a maximum teacher-student ratio of 1:30, minimum teacher qualifications, and free and compulsory education. Enrolment increased rapidly in every level of school education, and there was a clear movement towards closing the gap between female and male enrolment in every level of school education with the proportion of female to male enrollee reaching 90 per cent in 2018–19 from around 70 per cent in 2005–06 (Table 9.7). However, discontinuation of schooling ranges broadly between 10 per cent in primary, to 20 per cent for secondary and with varying percentages for higher levels.

The incidence of discontinuation of education, shown in Table 9.8, vitiates somewhat the enrolment figures. A few broad observations may be made. (1) Discontinuation increases with age until the secondary level, then declines. (2) This is the case with both rural and urban components. (3) Discontinuation is higher in the rural component than in the urban component. (4) In both rural and urban components, discontinuation among girls remains higher than for boys in the primary/middle level but, after that – in secondary and higher secondary levels, girls are likely to discontinue somewhat less than boys including for post-graduate studies. It is possible to speculate perhaps that girls are weeded out from earlier stages of education faster than boys but, if they can survive the higher attrition in the early stages, they would have proven their mettle; hence a lower proportion of them are forced out from secondary, higher secondary and post-graduate levels.

The reasons for discontinuation reported in the 2020 National Statistical Office (NSO) survey are shown in Figure 9.2. They are similar to those discussed in Dreze (2003) and Save the Children (2017) as indicated already. In other words, the reasons that push children out of school have not changed much. The need to join domestic activities and to get married for girls and

Table 9.8: Discontinuation from different education levels[1]

Level of last enrolment	Percentage of students								
	Rural			Urban			Total		
	Male	**Female**	**Person**	**Male**	**Female**	**Person**	**Male**	**Female**	**Person**
Pre-primary	5.1	9.6	7.2	3.3	4.4	3.8	4.5	7.9	6.0
Primary	9.1	12.3	10.6	6.9	9.0	7.8	8.5	11.6	10.0
Upper primary/middle	17.5	19.1	18.2	14.9	15.5	15.2	16.9	18.3	17.5
Secondary	21.4	20.2	20.8	17.6	16.6	17.1	20.4	19.2	19.8
Higher secondary	10.7	9.7	10.3	8.8	7.7	8.3	10.1	9.0	9.6
Diploma/certificate (below graduate)	10.7	20.2	13.3	9.7	16.4	11.7	10.3	18.6	12.7
Graduation	5.6	6.7	6.0	4.4	3.8	4.2	5.0	5.2	5.1
Post-graduation and above	3.9	2.8	3.4	1.6	1.5	1.5	2.5	1.9	2.2
Diploma/certificate (graduate and above)	10.1	4.0	7.8	4.2	1.9	3.4	6.7	2.8	5.3
All	13.2	14.7	13.8	9.5	9.7	9.6	12.1	13.2	12.6

Note: [1] Percentage of persons dropped out among ever enrolled persons of age 3 to 35 years for different levels of last enrolment.

Source: Women & Men in India 2020, National Statistical Office, Ministry of Statistics and Programme Implementation, Government of India

economic activities for boys comprise the main drivers.[14] Financial constraints comprise the second driver in the case of both girls and boys, perhaps obliging both to become economically or domestically active. Disinterest in continuing studies, including that of parents, also features as an element. But the lack of quality – medium of instruction and comprehensibility expressed in an inability to cope – also comprise explanations. Distance from school, perhaps indicating an association with constrained finances, is also a factor in discontinuation.

To sum up, while Indian children are enrolling in school, many leave before completion mainly reflecting financial constraints of the family; and the vicious circle of under-age, under-nourished mothers bearing under-nourished babies keeps repeating. Some government programmes such as mid-day meals have helped retain children in school despite the many challenges and shortcomings of these programmes though, overall, the objective of universal education is far from having been achieved. It may be safe to conclude that a demographic dividend cannot be realized at the current accomplishment rates for education, health and nutrition.

Moving from the quantity of education, its quality remains suspect for the majority of even privileged children. There is little standardization in curricula, lesson plans or requirements, with testing varying widely. Even within a state, the method varies in different schools. One pervading expectation is that students should be able to memorize rather than be allowed to think freely or innovate. Whether India is successfully changing systemic rote learning to thinking independently remains a question. Are children taught the appreciation of art? Do they have time to read a classical novel in its entirety and judge its merit by the time they are out of school? Are they allowed to express themselves, even if chaotically, if they wish to, without being reprimanded? Can they critique the teaching of their teachers in class? An incongruity appears to be the emphatic commendation of high achievers and a focus on the poorly faring students whose performance needs to be improved in the interest of the school's reputation. The middling majority is, more often than not, left to fend for itself, as it neither brings any glory nor poses any serious threat of disrepute.

In another setback, the quality and outcomes of education appear to have collapsed as a result of the 2020–21 COVID-19 pandemic as reflected in an 'emergency report' based on a survey of 1,400 school children in under-privileged households across India (Bakhla et al., 2021). Much of the severe deterioration reflects the unavailability of laptops and online

[14] This nomenclature of 'domestic' and 'economic' is awkward as if domestic duties are not economic, but it is the official nomenclature of the NSO (see Figure 9.2).

Figure 9.2: Reasons for discontinuing education[1] (2018)

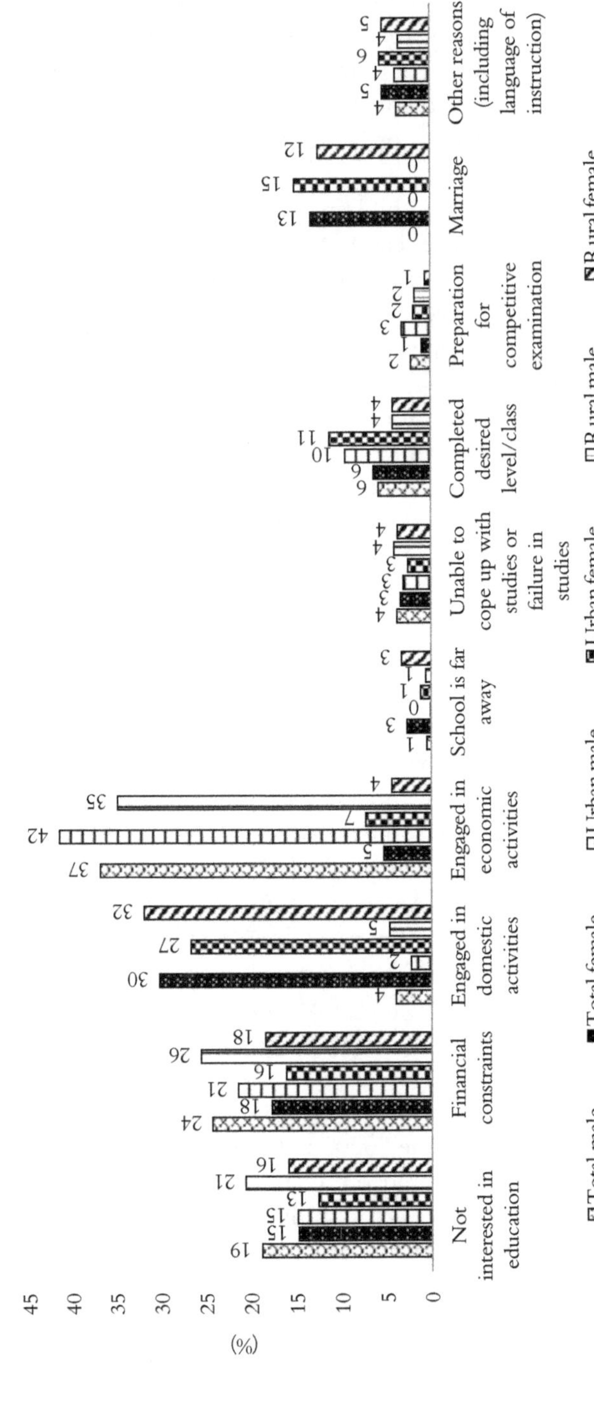

Note: [1] Percentage of ever enrolled persons of age 3 to 35 years currently not attending education and their distribution by major reason for not attending.

Source: Women & Men in India 2020, National Statistical Office, Ministry of Statistics and Programme Implementation, Government of India

education for the vast majority of children. An entire generation could be bypassed in terms of basic literacy even as students country-wide are promoted, essentially without testing. Overall, India has to run much faster to improve its global rank in children's education. To reiterate, at its current rate of progress, a demographic dividend is unlikely to be achieved in India if the entire population of children – from rich, middle and poor households – is considered.

Education policy and caste

In the statistics presented previously, an aspect that is missing is information on the precarious education for lower castes during the British era due to which a reservation policy became essential in the post-independence era. Phule (1980) observed regarding the status of education of the *shudras*, that denial of access to education inflicted ignorance and slavery upon the *shudratishudra* (lowest of the low) castes. This denial reduced them to docility, unable even to recognize the injustice and the robbing of human rights in their prevailing condition. Subsequently, Gupta (2021) commented on the matter. Describing Nambissan's (1996) work, he pointed to their persistent struggle for access to schooling and in facing considerable antagonism from caste Hindus. To quote,

> Nambissan emphasized the dual character of British education policy in India, which at one hand pronounced that 'no boy be refused admission to a government college or school merely on the ground of caste', and on the other hand simultaneously emphasized that this principle be applied with due caution. Moreover, institutionally, a number of options were made available by the administration … the untouchables were also persuaded to set up their own special schools under the government grants-in-aid system … official reports in the late nineteenth and early twentieth century are replete with accounts of the many trials and tribulations and humiliating experiences of Dalits and 'untouchables' who persevered to receive an education whether in 'common' or in 'special' schools. Official and missionary sources also reveal the aspirations of untouchable castes with regard to education. However, separate schools provided for the untouchables were inefficient and for the most part 'one-teacher' schools. Night schools were popular, however, only bare minimum of reading and writing skills were given to lower and labouring castes in such schools. Recruiting suitable teachers for special schools was an acute problem; individuals from lower castes and the Muslim community formed the bulk of teachers in schools that catered to untouchables. (pp 22–23)

Nancharaiah (2002) argued that the British opted for a deliberate policy to focus higher education on brahmins and other upper classes … social disabilities such as untouchability became obstacles to the education of Dalits. They were obliged to stay away from the main village and thus from schools (p 24).

Zelliot (2014) explained that founders of night schools and hostels were often not educated themselves, stressing the non-brahmin status of such educational reformers. Bhattacharya (2002); Nambissan (2009); Majumdar and Mooij (2011) and others pointed to inequality arising from the choice of curriculum both pre- and post-independence that further consolidated the power of the dominant castes, spreading cultural imperialism and colonial values.

Another challenge was posed by the many full-fledged languages of India with independent scripts, the use of English as *lingua franca* from colonial times, and the prevalence of Sanskrit, the ancient language used in Hindu epics, and Urdu spoken by the Muslim population. Post-independence, Jawaharlal Nehru, the first prime minister of India, was particular not to endorse a regional language policy in schools reflecting his concern for national integration (King, 1997). The Ministry of Education with Maulana Abdul Kalam Azad as minister, implemented a three-language formula for school education as recommended by the Secondary Education Commission set up by the Government of India (1952–53) (p 38). Nevertheless, which language(s) would be used in school education became a volatile issue that has not been resolved to date, degenerating into a political instrument of consecutive governments. The victims of the confusion have been India's children, in particular the poor and from the lower castes, who cannot opt for the more marketable English medium schools. Not rarely, they have to learn and regurgitate what they have been taught in languages far from the language they are most familiar with. If they could express themselves in their own language, certainly their performance levels would have been superior.

To redress the inequality in education brought about by caste separation, Section 12 of the RTE stipulated that a quarter of the seats in private schools and special category schools such as *Kendriya Vidyalaya, Navodaya Vidyalaya* and Sainik School be reserved for disadvantaged communities. It sought to suppress any exclusivity of status, income or caste in particular in private schools as did the midday meals that had to be shared by all children alike with a preference to hire cooks from the lower castes (SC/ST). However, there was a wide variation in the application of Section 12, with some states including Odisha, Uttar Pradesh, Punjab and Kerala allocating between 0–7 per cent of seats to SC/STs, while others such as Bihar, Karnataka, Uttarakhand, Tamil Nadu and New Delhi reaching 31–45 per cent (Chiriyankandath et al. 2020). Therefore, caste has been a knot that has been tough to untangle in several states.

Subsequently, the Twelfth Five Year Plan encouraged the promotion of non-governmental profit-making organizations in education in 2013.[15] An outcome-based, rather than an input-based approach was proposed. Nevertheless, delays in enacting enabling laws perhaps reveal a lack of urgency in how education has been perceived by governments, with India's literacy rates languishing at rates below that achieved by China as far back as in 1982 (Chiriyankandath et al., 2020).

A New Education Policy (NEP) was drafted anew in 2019. It eschewed the commercialization of education, yet promoted the privatization of education through unregulated philanthropic and not-for-profit entities. It promised a 6 per cent of gross domestic product (GDP) expenditure allocation for education that has remained unfulfilled. While the NEP made provisions for volunteers in education which as a policy should be welcome, analysts have expressed fears of education's politicization through such means (Batra, 2021).

In light of emerging policy, whether the role of government schools should be de-emphasized needs to be seriously weighed if it is to be assumed that, by and large, the lower castes would be better protected in a system of government schools. After all, instances continue to appear in which teachers arrange seating in classrooms along caste lines (Kumar, 2021, p 225). Khare (2019) conducted an ethnographic study of government schools, focusing on teachers who involved students, parents and the community. They used activity-based learning and used digital modes. The teachers, students and parents worked together in the village community to bring about change (p 65). Reflecting that those schools were a part of the government school system, the question must be asked whether such a system would not be preferable for assurance of lower caste education in an as-yet caste-ridden society. It is a comprehensive monitoring and evaluation (M&E) of government schools that is lacking and that is what is needed to be stepped up before replacing it with an altogether new system perhaps.

The NEP, at first glance, is a document on education policy whose objective is the improvement of skills for the 21st century, with proposals that aspire to fulfil that aim. It brings children of 3–5 years within the formal education system and proposes a mission of foundational literacy and numeracy, free breakfasts in addition to the currently provided free lunches in government schools, and vocational education along with internships from the sixth grade. The proposed new curricula appear to say relatively little in terms of the enhancement of quality education through those means. Many education policies have dotted the past, and only actual

15 See Vol. 3, ch. 21.

implementation could indicate its success or failure. Despite the 2009 RTE, the real challenge remains the poor standard of foundational learning as the Annual Status of Education Reports (ASER) point out each year.[16] The test of NEP, therefore, lies in how far it can alter quality deficiency. India currently spends 3 per cent of GDP on education, which needs to be increased to 6 per cent of GDP if the NEP objectives are to be achieved, according to the government itself.

That magnitude of resource allocation for education has not occurred in the past and resource constraints may not allow for it to occur soon. Gupta (2021) has raised a fundamental issue with the NEP in that

> it pushes vigorously for the centralisation of many crucial aspects of education from pre-primary to higher levels, such as the preparation of curricular frameworks (including a set of values and skills), admission procedure, evaluation of students, award of scholarships, and coordination of research etc. … In pressing further centralisation, it seems to ignore the fact that Education falls within the Concurrent List of the Constitution where usually it is subject to be legislated upon by the state governments. (p 65)

To conclude, the evidence of extreme poverty afflicting children appears from time to time which cannot be ignored, for such evidence stares in the face of academic research. To take one example, in October 2018, the BBC in a series on modern day slavery, had a one-hour coverage on India. It bared scores of little boys and girls being transported across the country and disappearing from their parents' grasps who said they had no financial ability to search for their children at any future date. Even where children stayed with parents, it was alarming. A three-year-old being put to collect mica in a mine was explained by the mother in simple terms: the children had to chip in to try to return the debt into which they were born. In other words, the parents were incalculably burdened with debt mainly reflecting their caste status, miniscule wages and a tight grip on their labour by upper caste managers of their indentured servitude. The world too watched this bioscope. Despite the statistical evidence and analysis of the progress in children's education, India cannot look away from the severely abysmal condition of many of its children in the present era. To cite Bhattacharya's

[16] ASER 2019 'Early Years,' was conducted in 26 districts across 24 states in India, covering a total of 1,514 villages, 30,425 households, and 36,930 children in the age group four to eight. Sampled children's enrollment status in pre-school or school was collected. Children did a variety of cognitive, early language, and early numeracy tasks; and activities to assess children's social and emotional development were also conducted. All tasks were done one-on-one with children in their homes.

(2018) succinctly conveyed statement on this depressing matter, ' how many more decades will it take? That is a more important (question) than when India will become the third largest economy in the world in terms of PPP or whether India is the fastest growing economy in the world'. And no wonder many a social science activist view India's poverty eradication as a failure and that the achievement of the UN's sustainable development goal (SDG) of 'leaving no one behind' by 2030 as extremely unlikely, if not impossible.

References

Arora, Rashmi Umesh. (2012) 'Gender inequality, economic development, and globalization: a state level analysis of India', *The Journal of Developing Areas*, 46(1): 147–164. Available at doi:10.1353/jda.2012.0019, accessed 12 August 2021.

ASER Centre. (2019) 'Early years', Annual Status of Education Reports, New Delhi. Available at www.asercentre.org, accessed 5 January 2023.

Bakhla, Nirali, Jean Dreze, Vipul Paikra and Reetika Khera. (2021) *Locked Out: Emergency Report on School Education. Children's Online and Offline Learning (SCHOOL) Survey*. The School Team. Available at https://counterviewfiles.files.wordpress.com/2021/09/locked-out-emergency-report-on-school-education-6-sept-2021.pdf, accessed 13 September 2021.

Batra, Poonam. (2021) 'India's education problematique and state betrayal: NEP 2020 and beyond', in Vikas Gupta, Rama Kant Agnihotri and Minati Panda (eds) *Education and Inequality: Historical and Contemporary Trajectories*. Hyderabad: Orient BlackSwan, ch. 23, pp 608–41.

Bhattacharya, Sabyasachi (ed) (2002) *Education and the Deprivileged: Nineteenth and Twentieth Century India*. New Delhi: Orient Longman.

Bhattacharya, Bipul. (2018) 'Letter to the Editor', *Business Standard*, 22 October.

Bradshaw, Sarah, Sylvia Chant and Brian Linneker. (2017) 'Gender and poverty: what we know, don't know, and need to know for Agenda 2030', *Gender, Place & Culture*, 24(12): 1667–1688. Available at doi:10.1080/0966369X.2017.1395821, accessed 16 August 2021.

Butalia, Urvashi. (2017) *The Other Side of Silence: Voices from the Partition of India*. New Delhi: Penguin Books.

Chakraborty, Lekha. (2021) 'Why Indian states need to incorporate gender budgeting', *The Economic Review of Kerala*, January. Available at https://thewire.in, accessed 5 January 2023.

Chancel, Lucas Thomas Piketty, Emmanuel Saez and Gabriel Zucman. (2021) 'World Inequality Report 2022', World Inequality Lab. Available at https://wir2022.wid.world/www-site/uploads/2021/12/WorldInequalityReport2022_Full_Report.pdf, accessed 15 December 2021.

Chiriyankandath, James, Diego Maiorano, James Manor and Louise Tillin. (2020) *The Politics of Poverty Reduction in India – The UPA Government 2004 to 2014*. Hyderabad: Orient BlackSwan.

Das, Sonali, Sonali Jain-Chandra, Kalpana Kochhar and Naresh Kumar. (2015) 'Women Workers in India: Why So Few Among So Many?', IMF Working paper WP/15/55, Asia and Pacific Department, International Monetary Fund. Available at www.imf.org/external/pubs/ft/wp/2015/wp1555.pdf, accessed 12 August 2021.

Deshpande, Ashwini. (2021) *Intersecting Identities, Livelihoods and Affirmative Action – How Social Identity Affects Economic Opportunity for Women in India*. Andhra Pradesh: Krea University and Initiative for What Works to Advance Women and Girls in the Economy (IWWAGE). Available at https://iwwage.org/wp-content/uploads/2021/04/Intersecting-Identities-Livelihoods-and-Affirmative-Action.pdf, accessed 13 September 2021.

Dreze, Jean. (2003) 'Patterns of literacy and their social context', in Veena Das (ed) *The Oxford India Companion to Sociology and Social Anthropology*, Volume 2. United Kingdom: Oxford University Press, pp 974–97.

Ghani, Rebecca. (2011) '40 million children have no access to the most basic healthcare services', *BMJ*, Available at https://doi.org/10.1136/bmj.d4667, 22 July, accessed 5 January 2023.[17]

Government of India. (1952–53) *Report of the Secondary Education Commission*, New Delhi. Available at http://indianculture.gov.in, accessed 5 January 2023.

Government of India. (2020) 'Women and Men in India', Social Statistics Division, National Statistical Office, Ministry of Statistics and Programme Implementation, New Delhi.

Gupta, Vikas. (2021) 'Some perspective on education in modern India', in Vikas Gupta, Rama Kant Agnihotri and Minati Panda (eds) *Education and Inequality: Historical and Contemporary Trajectories*. Hyderabad: Orient BlackSwan, ch. 1, pp 3–86.

India National Family Health Survey (NFHS-4). (2015–16) (FR339). International Institute for Population Sciences (IIPS), Mumbai. Accessible at www.tbdiah.org, accessed 5 January 2023.

International Institute for Population Sciences (IIPS) and ICF. (2017) *National Family Health Survey (NFHS-4), 2015–16: India*. Mumbai: IIPS. Available at https://dhsprogram.com/pubs/pdf/FR339/FR339.pdf, accessed 20 August 2021.

[17] *BMJ* is a weekly peer-reviewed medical trade journal published by the trade union associated with the British Medical Association (BMA).

International Institute for Population Sciences (IIPS) and ICF. (2020) *National Family Health Survey (NFHS-5)*. 'India and State Factsheet Compendium'. Mumbai: IIPS. Available at http://rchiips.org/nfhs/NFHS-5_FCTS/COMPENDIUM/NFHS-5%20India%20and%20State%20Factsheet%20Compendium_Phase-II.pdf, accessed 29 November 2021.

Jha, Priti and Niti Nagar. (2015) 'A study of gender inequality in India', *International Journal of Indian Psychology*, 2(3): 46–53. Available at doi:10.25215/0203.045, DIP: 18.01.045/20150203, accessed 12 August 2021.

Kabeer, Naila. (2016) 'Gender equality, economic growth, and women's agency: the "endless variety" and "monotonous similarity" of patriarchal constraints', *Feminist Economics*, 22(1): 295–321. Available at doi:10.1080/13545701.2015.1090009, accessed 16 August 2021.

Kabeer, Naila. (2019) 'Randomized control trials and qualitative evaluations of a multifaceted programme for women in extreme poverty: empirical findings and methodological reflections', *Journal of Human Development and Capabilities*, 20(2): 197–217. Available at: doi:10.1080/19452829.2018.1536696, accessed 16 August 2021.

Karlekar, Malavika. (2004) 'Domestic violence', in Veena Das (ed) *Handbook of Indian Sociology*. New Delhi/New York: Oxford University Press, pp 308–30.

Khare, Shirish. (2019) *Ummid Ki Pathshala* (1st edn). Varanasi: Agora Publication.

King, Robert D. (1997) *Nehru and the Language Politics of India*. Delhi: Oxford University Press.

Kohli, Sugandha. (2017) 'Gender inequality in India', *International Journal of Humanities & Social Science Studies (IJHSSS)*, III(IV): 178–85. Available at www.ijhsss.com/old/files/15_ph6h6r3a.-Sugandha-Kohli.pdf, accessed 12 August 2021.

Kumar, Arun. (2021) 'Rethinking inequality and education: crime, labour, and the school curriculum in Indian reformatory schools (1880s–1920s)', in Vikas Gupta, Rama Kant Agnihotri and Minati Panda (eds) *Education and Inequality: Historical and Contemporary Trajectories*. Hyderabad: Orient BlackSwan, ch. 7, pp 225–52.

Majumdar, Manabi and Jos Mooij. (2011) *Education and Inequality in India: A Classroom View*. London: Routledge.

Mehta, Deepak. (2014) Women's work: quilt making and gift giving, in Veena Das and Ranendra K. Das (eds) *Sociology and Anthropology of Economic Life I: The Moral Embedding of Economic Action*, Vol. 1. New Delhi: Oxford University Press, pp 234–53.

Menon, Ritu and Kamla Bhasin. (1998) *Borders and Boundaries: Women in India's Partition*. New Delhi: Kali for Women.

Menon, Jisha. (2013) *The Performance of Nationalism: India, Pakistan, and the Memory of Partition*. New York: Cambridge University Press.

Nancharaiah, G. (2002) 'Dalit education and economic inequality', in S. Bhattacharya (ed) *Education and the Deprivileged: Nineteenth and twentieth Century India*. New Delhi: Orien Longman, pp 163–80.

Nambissan, Geetha B. (1996) 'Equity in education? Schooling of Dalit children in India', *Economic and Political Weekly*, 31(16/17): 1011–24.

Nambissan, Geetha B. (2009) 'Exclusive and Discrimination in Schools: Experiences of Dalit Children'. Working Paper Series, Vol. 1, no. 1. Indian Institute of Dalit Studies and UNICEF.

Nieuwenhuys, Olga. (2003) 'The paradox of child labour and anthropology', in Veena Das (ed) *The Oxford India Companion to Sociology and Social Anthropology*, Vol. 2. Oxford: Oxford University Press, pp 939–55.

Nieuwenhuys, Olga. (2004) 'The paradox of child labour and anthropology', in Veena Das (ed) *Handbook of Indian Sociology*. New Delhi/New York: Oxford University Press, pp 331–44.

Phule, Jyotirao. (1980) 'Keer-Malashe', in *Mahatma Phule Samgra Wangmay*. Mumbai: Maharashtra Rajya Sahitya Sanskriti Mandal.

Priya. (2020) 'Perception of gender equality: a comparative study of young men and women', in N. M. P. Verma and Alpana Srivastava (eds) *The Routledge Handbook of Exclusion, Inequality and Stigma in India* (1st edn) India: Routledge. Available at https://doi.org/10.4324/9780429295706, accessed 12 August 2021.

Rizvi, Halima Sadia and Mansi Vinaik. (2020) 'Inequality, gender and policy initiatives: inequality, gender and policy initiatives' in N. M. P. Verma and Alpana Srivastava (eds) *The Routledge Handbook of Exclusion, Inequality and Stigma in India* (1st edn). India: Routledge. Available at https://doi.org/10.4324/9780429295706, accessed 12 August 2021.

Save the Children. (2017, 2019, 2020, 2021) 'Global Childhood Reports'. Available at https://www.savethechildren.org/us/about-us/resource-library, accessed 12 August 2021.

Sen, Amartya. (1983) *Poverty and Famines: An Essay on Entitlement and Deprivation*. Oxford: Oxford University Press.

The Economist. (2021) 'One city, two worlds – race in Brazil', 14 August, London, pp 35–37.

Uberoi, Patricia. (1995) 'Introduction', in Patricia Uberoi (ed) *Family, Marriage and Kinship in India*. Delhi: Oxford University Press, pp 1–44.

United Nations. (2019) 'Population Division Statistics', World Population Prospects, Geneva: United Nations Publications.

Verghese, Jamila. (1997) *Her Gold and Her Body*, 2nd edn. Ghaziabad: Vikas Publishing House.

Zelliot, Eleanor (2014) 'Dalit initiatives in education, 1880–1992', in Parimala V. Rao (ed) *New Perspective in the History of Indian Education*. New Delhi: Orient BlackSwan, pp 45–67.

10

Nutrition, Health, Sanitation, Water and Climate Change

Introduction

In this chapter, we selectively examine the significance of nutrition and health as well as the role of clean water, for example, what is likely to happen to the poor if natural resources such as water are insufficiently available to them; what is the extent of food security and its effects on nutrition and health including on the urban poor? How do urban pollution and the lack of sanitary facilities affect the poor? And how forest inhabitants' flailing rights impinge directly on the poor. Some of India's new laws created legal entitlements over discretionary disbursements and demarcated new identification markers for beneficiaries (Chiriyankandath et al., 2020). Were they sufficient? These are some of the questions that will be addressed.

Nutrition and health

Under a Common Minimum Programme (CMP), India's United Progressive Alliance (UPA-I) government (2004–09) introduced a number of social insurance measures reflecting a Right to Food Campaign (RFC) that included the universalization of an existing midday meal programme, the Mahatma Gandhi National Rural Employment Guarantee Act (MGNREGA) and the Forest Rights Act. In its second term, the United Progressive Alliance government (UPA-II, 2009–14) introduced additional programmes including the National Food Security Act (NFSA) and a reform of child development. By then, important architects of the earlier programmes had left, and the new efforts came under critical expert examination. Desai and Vanneman (2015) have assessed that they were not successful in expanding India's Public Distribution System (PDS) targeted to poor households or in strengthening the Integrated Child Development Scheme (ICDS) for child nutrition. Access to subsidized grains via the PDS was not linked to improved child nutrition, and the ICDS had a limited reach despite its universal application. The authors proposed that such programmes should begin with the identification of undernourished children and districts where they were located. This should be followed up with targeting severe and moderate malnutrition, rather than merely focusing on cereal distribution as was the case with the NFSA. Chiriyankandath et al. (2020) argued that a good part of the explanation of their relative lack of success was political, the UPA-II coalition being less assertive than UPA-I. Consequently, the CMP was weakened in terms of its objective, from monitoring its implementation to one of 'attention to the priorities … which was an exercise high in rhetoric and low in substance' apart from being 'tainted by a long list of scandals' (p xxi).

A National Rural Health Mission (NRHM) was introduced during UPA-I as a top policy priority. It pledged 2–3 per cent of gross domestic product (GDP) on health, a national health insurance scheme for the poor (the *Rashtriya Swasthya Bima Yojana* (RSBY)) and an urgency in controlling communicable diseases, the objective being a diminution of out-of-pocket expenses on health that is known to cause regression back into poverty among households.

Some studies, for example, by Vellakkal et al. (2017) claimed that NRHM reduced inequality in the access to healthcare and neonatal mortality, and increased the incidence of breastfeeding and immunizations. There were attempts at governance reform, an increase in the number of institutional deliveries, promotion of non-governmental organizations (NGOs) for delivery, and decentralization to the village level, all of which led to improved co-ordination with other schemes in health, sanitation and drinking water. However, the sustainability in the supply of healthcare and accessibility for the poor reflecting a small budget were called into question, NRHM expenditure in the first five years being 0.2 per cent of GDP (Dreze and Sen, 2013).

Supply of healthcare in India is among the lowest in the world on a per-capita basis. This is especially so as we go down the income scale, at the bottom of which there is little availability of hospitals or even health centres, doctors, nurses or surgical and laboratory equipment. The availability of beds in government hospitals across Indian states serves as a useful indicator. The World Health Organization (WHO) guidelines recommend 3.5 hospital beds per 1,000 population. While the global average for 2017 was 2.9 beds per 1,000 population, India had around 0.5 beds per 1,000 population. India remains low among comparable nations such as Sri Lanka and Bangladesh in terms of design, application, regulation and assessment of availability of hospitals or, more generally, government policy in healthcare; indeed, it is more comparable to countries in Sub-Saharan Africa.

Singh et al. (2020) reported the availability of government hospital beds for major states in India from the 2019 National Health Profile. They observed a total of 7,13,986 beds in government hospitals, amounting to 0.55 beds per 1000 population. States that lay below the national average per 1000 population were, beginning from the bottom, Bihar, Jharkhand, Gujarat, Uttar Pradesh, Andhra Pradesh, Chhattisgarh, Madhya Pradesh, Haryana, Maharashtra, Odisha, Assam and Manipur, accounting for some 70 per cent of the population. Bihar had only 0.11 beds while West Bengal had 2.25 beds and Sikkim had 2.34 beds. States with a generally good reputation for the provision of healthcare had surprisingly low numbers, with Delhi having 1.05 beds, Kerala 1.05 beds and Tamil Nadu 1.1 beds. The seniors (aged 60 and above) fared better, with allocated government beds being 5.18 beds for 1,000 population. State-wise, Kerala had 7.4 beds, Tamil Nadu 7.8 beds, West Bengal 7.7 beds, and Karnataka 8.6 beds, while the northern and central states had relatively lower availability.

The bottom line is that healthcare provision has to speed up in India given the reality of low government supply of hospital beds. For matters to improve, government should recognize the special features that characterize the healthcare industry and enable the private sector to step in on a significant scale. However, the industry typically has high setup costs, followed by high operational costs, reflecting the need for high-skilled manpower, expensive equipment often embedding imported medical technology that usually has around seven-year investment cycles, medicines and consumables. Such characteristics, in turn, render it prohibitive for most Indians to avail of high-quality healthcare.

Erroneous policy is reflected in the tax and financial structure as well. A gap in domestic manufacturing obliges hospitals to import major medical equipment, such as magnetic resonance imaging (MRI), computed tomography (CT) scan, linear accelerators and other equipment. Hospitals pay a countervailing duty (CD) of 12 per cent on imports that is equivalent to the central government's domestic excise tax. Similarly, a special additional duty (SAD) of four per cent is imposed to achieve comparability with the state-level value-added tax (VAT). Thus, it is understandable that these two taxes have to be paid. However, customs duty on imported equipment is additionally imposed at 7.5 per cent to 10 per cent. This is typically couched in the argument of protecting 'infant' industry, though, in reality, it is merely an easy means of collecting revenue, a practice that should be eschewed rather than being resurrected after decades of efforts to move away from high customs barriers. Tax incentives in government budgets demarcated by a minimum number of hospital beds for a hospital, or the distance of location from urban centres, have also not worked because they do not reflect market or field realities. The incentive criteria keep changing through various budgets without such changes being backed by survey-based micro-information. And there is little practice of meaningful Social Impact Assessments (SIA) of changing government expenditure policies in order to redirect policies towards more rational alternatives.

In addition, a consequence of continuing exchange rate depreciation of the rupee has been that the cost of imported equipment has risen. Further, with exchange rate depreciation, all three previously mentioned duties yield higher revenue in terms of rupees. This poses additional net cost to the healthcare sector, and it is likely that the increased burden has to be borne by both healthcare providers and patients. By contrast, equipment for setting up planetariums, solar energy equipment and research equipment are exempt from customs duty. It is not as if these should not be exempt, but it is difficult to perceive why healthcare, reflecting its urgency, should not feature among exempted items if any exemptions are to be given. To give another example, the Reserve Bank of India (RBI) encourages banks to extend long-term loans to the infrastructure sector with flexible structuring to absorb potential contingencies. Public infrastructure projects can raise loans at lower interest rates than that of commercial projects and have repayment periods of 10–25 years as against five-seven years for commercial projects. Hospitals, by contrast, do not command infrastructure status. Utility rates for hospitals also remain higher than for industries in most states. falling in the highest of the graded brackets.

On the whole, therefore, healthcare cannot be said to have been a preferred sector in government policy or resource allocation. Yet hospitals are required to provide treatment under the Employee State Insurance (ESI) and central and various state government health insurance schemes at regulated rates prescribed by the central and the state governments. The rates are revised at infrequent and unpredictable intervals without detailed analysis.[1] Prinja et al. (2019) reported considerably higher costs than government prescribed ones.[2]

Policy anomalies abound. To take the example of one state, while Karnataka launched a health insurance scheme for above-poverty-line (APL) households, the scheme covered 449 medical procedures at the same base package rates as another insurance scheme for the below-poverty-line (BPL) population. With little effective cost sharing for reducing input costs while creating a price cap by stipulating provision of health insurance to APL households at BPL rates, not only is a financial burden created for hospitals and their operations but the quality-of-service provision as a result may also be questioned. In addition, irregular and delayed payments by government

---

1 For example, detailed price specifications are made by the Central Government Health Scheme (CGHS) for prices of an array of cardiovascular and cardiac surgery & investigations, ranging between Rs 0.16 million to Rs 0.19 million, without prices being necessarily ordered in terms of surgical complexity (2014 Bengaluru rates updated as on 17 May 2021) that can quite easily bear heavily on a middle-class household budget, leave alone a lower income one.

2 They reported prices ranging between Rs 0.12 million and Rs 0.32 million for comparable medical procedures.

strain the cash flow of hospitals, pending payments reaching above Rs 10 million in metropolitan cities.

To conclude, without a strong and serious resuscitation from government, catching up with WHO guidelines is unlikely to occur in India's healthcare. A good beginning would be for government at every level, while improving public sector healthcare, to effectively eradicate bottlenecks and constraints placed along the way of growth of the private healthcare sector that is increasingly attending to the needs of the poor as an integral part of their overall mission.

Sanitation

One of the 2015 Sustainable Development Goals (SDGs) of the United Nations (UN) relates to the enhancement of the availability of water and sanitation over the next 15 years, to 'ensure availability and sustainable management of water and sanitation for all' (Goal 6). It does not stand alone but has synergies with the other SDGs, in particular poverty eradication (SDG 1), ending hunger by improved nutrition (SDG 2), ensuring healthy lives and promoting well-being (SDG 3), education (SDG 4), gender equality (SDG 5), inclusive cities (SDG 11), life below water (SDG 14) and terrestrial ecosystem (SDG 15). Leaving behind the *nirmal bharat abhiyan* scheme of the previous government initiated in April 2012[3] that attempted to improve sanitation, the *swachh bharat mission* (SBM) was subsequently launched by the National Democratic Alliance (NDA) government on 2 October 2014. In its first year, Rs 42.6 billion were committed over a period of five years, then it decreased to Rs 28.5 billion in the revised estimates. It decreased further to 26.3 billion in the second year, increasing to 65.3 billion in the revised estimates. Despite the swings in allocation, SBM appears to have made strides in the right direction though media has reported various hiccups related to the scheme.

Table 10.1 uses data reported in 2021 by the World Health Organization-United Nations Children's Fund (WHO-UNICEF) complex. It reveals advances made by India in the 2000–20 period, with the proportion of the population with improved basic facilities rising from 15 per cent to 71 per cent, unimproved facilities declining from 6 per cent to 2 per cent, and open defecation declining from 74 per cent to 15 per cent. The rural-urban

[3] *Nirmal* remained unattained. There was little evidence of any centrally sponsored *nirmal* scheme that went to local – as opposed to state – governments. Social impact analyses (SIAs) were essentially absent under *nirmal*. Indeed, many states failed to set up state finance commissions to ensure constitutionally guaranteed financing of municipal or *panchayat* expenditure programmes. The lack of quick success of *nirmal*, therefore, was not surprising.

Table 10.1: India: proportion of population using different levels of sanitation services

		Proportion (%)			Change (%)		Average annual (%) change	
	Year	2000	2011	2020	2004–14	2015–20	2004–14	2015–20
Population (million)		**1057**	**1250**	**1380**	**15**	**5**	**1.40**	**1.06**
	At least basic[1], of which	**15**	**45**	**71**	**109**	**26**	**8.05**	**4.79**
Improved	Safely managed[2]	7	27	46	151	29	10.72	5.33
Total	Limited[3] (shared)	5	10	12	49	7	4.41	1.49
Unimproved	Unimproved[4]	6	4	2	-40	-39	-4.86	-8.90
	Open defecation[5]	74	41	15	-48	-49	-6.19	-11.96
	At least basic, of which	**2**	**36**	**67**	**225**	**35**	**13.92**	**6.34**
Improved	Safely managed	<1	26	51	293	37	17.83	6.75
Rural	Limited (shared)	<1	6	8	138	11	10.45	2.36
Unimproved	Unimproved	5	4	2	-29	-21	-3.33	-4.60
	Open defecation	92	54	22	-45	-44	-5.60	-10.40
	At least basic, of which	**48**	**65**	**79**	**29**	**12**	**2.57**	**2.23**
Improved	Safely managed	21	30	37	31	12	2.82	2.30
Urban	Limited (shared)	17	19	19	6	0	0.59	0.06
Unimproved	Unimproved	8	4	<1	-58	n. a.	-8.08	-18.37
	Open defecation	27	13	<1	-60	n. a.	-8.37	-23.15

Table 10.1: India: proportion of population using different levels of sanitation services (continued)

Note: improved facilities include flush/pour flush toilets connected to piped sewer systems, septic tanks or pit latrines; pit latrines with slabs (including ventilated pit latrines); and composting toilets. [1] Use of improved facilities that are not shared with other households. [2] Safely managed includes disposed in situ, emptied and treated, wastewater treated, latrines and other, septic tanks, and sewer connections. Use of improved facilities that are not shared with other households and where excreta are safely disposed of in situ or removed and treated off-site. [3] Use of improved facilities that are shared with other households. [4] Use of pit latrines without a slab or platform, hanging latrines or bucket latrines. [5] Disposal of human faeces in fields, forests, bushes, open bodies of water, beaches or other open places, or with solid waste.

Source: WHO/UNICEF Joint Monitoring Programme for Water Supply, Sanitation and Hygiene (JMP) Database and Progress on Household Drinking Water, Sanitation and Hygiene 2000–2020: Five years into the SDGs. Geneva: WHO and UNICEF, 2021

variation in improved facilities was 67–79 per cent in 2020. Table 10.1 provides further details in the provision of unimproved facilities and their rural and urban components. While such improvements have to be lauded, SBM's objective of the replacement of open defecation with basic toilets in five years remains to be fulfilled, however.

Another observation worth making is that the annual percentage improvements in the improved – safely managed, and limited – facilities were consistently better during the United Progressive Alliance (UPA) governments (2004–14) while the cutbacks in unimproved facilities and in open defecation were more rapid during the Bharatiya Janata Party (BJP) led governments (2014–20). The latter clearly has to do with their promise to eradicate open defecation in five years, though it remains to be fully accomplished. This issue is dealt with in greater detail next.

One aspect of sanitation that has a particular connotation for urban areas is the growing presence of urban slums and their immediate effects on sanitation and longer-term ramifications such as the inadequacy of housing (UN, 2020).[4] There is a variety of deprivations suffered by the urban poor that may not be fully reflected in prevailing slum related statistics that actually obfuscate important components and fail to lead to substantive policy action. Patel et al. (2020) used a large dataset from the 2011 Census comprising 1 per cent of India's urban population to track the extent and nature of housing deprivation and showed that India's official slum statistics underestimated its extent. They developed a Slum Severity Index to indicate that different levels of deprivation could be used to identify the most deprived populations and, thus, to target the neediest among slum populations. They also described the types of interventions that would be most beneficial, explaining that only such a targeted approach could help in meaningfully achieving the SDG goal for basic services and housing for the urban poor.

The authors admitted, however, that details such as the levels of access to water such as distance to the source of water, or sanitation such as whether sewage was safely managed, remained unaddressed in their investigation due to the lack of information from the Census. They, therefore, emphasized the need for censuses for slum enumeration and for information on details that would allow appropriate analysis to move forward in the future. Only then the role of exclusionary practices and policies affecting housing outcomes for marginalized groups could be assessed. What becomes clear from research studies such as theirs is that government produced data are not an end but an initial point from which further analysis needs to be carried out to decipher the reality of urban poverty and its various manifestations.

---

4 With 1 billion people living in slums worldwide, the definition of slums varies across countries.

Table 10.2: Cross-country: open defecation

	(% of population)								
	Total			Rural			Urban		
Country	**2000**	**2010**	**2020**	**2000**	**2010**	**2020**	**2000**	**2010**	**2020**
Bangladesh	17	7	<1	20	9	<1	5	2	<1
Cambodia	87	53	19	98	62	25	37	17	<1
Ethiopia	77	47	17	87	54	21	22	13	3
Haiti	37	26	18	52	41	31	10	9	8
India	74	44	15	92	57	22	27	14	<1
Nepal	69	39	10	77	44	11	20	12	4
Pakistan	38	22	7	55	33	12	5	3	<1
Peru	19	11	4	50	32	13	7	4	2
Sri Lanka	5	2	<1	6	3	<1	3	1	<1
Vietnam	18	8	3	22	11	4	5	3	1

Note: <1: Values less than 1 reported as in JMP database.

Source: WHO/UNICEF Joint Monitoring Programme for Water Supply, Sanitation and Hygiene (JMP) Database (updated July, 2021)

Table 10.2 examines the incidence of open defecation in India compared to a cross-section of comparable countries. Despite India's improvements, it lags behind Nepal, Pakistan and Bangladesh, the last having eradicated it altogether. India is in a better position than Cambodia, Ethiopia and Haiti, but is significantly behind Peru, Vietnam and, in particular, Sri Lanka. The percentage improvements made by sample countries are also impressive, ranging around two-thirds during 2010–20 (with Bangladesh at 100 per cent), having speeded up from around 40 per cent during 2000–10. The statistics indicate that open defecation in urban areas has been eradicated altogether in Bangladesh, Cambodia, India, Pakistan and Sri Lanka. Clearly this outcome reflects the efforts being made by the signatories of the UN SDGs in the area of sanitation.

Table 10.3 attempts to analyse the effect of including India with its cohorts in South Asia. While numbers are presented over the 2000–20 period, just a comparison of 2020 figures proves revealing. For example, open defecation for South Asia excluding India was 5 per cent of the population while including India in the group increases the proportion to 12 per cent. On the other hand, India has performed better in the basic service and safely managed components so that its inclusion improves the performance of the group as a whole. Clearly, India has to push its effort more intensively in eradicating open defecation in its rural areas.

Table 10.3: South Asia: latrines

		(% of population)														
		Total					**Rural**					**Urban**				
		Improved					**Improved**					**Improved**				
Region	**Year**															
		Basic service	**Limited (shared)**	**Safely managed**	**Unimproved**	**Open defecation**	**Basic service**	**Limited (shared)**	**Safely managed**	**Unimproved**	**Open defecation**	**Basic service**	**Limited (shared)**	**Safely managed**	**Unimproved**	**Open defecation**
South Asia including India	2000	9	6	9	13	63	2	2	4	13	79	28	16	22	12	22
	2010	17	10	26	9	37	10	7	25	10	49	33	18	29	8	11
	2020	25	13	45	6	12	16	10	49	7	19	40	19	37	3	1
South Asia without India	2000	12	8	17	34	30	5	6	16	36	38	29	14	24	27	6
	2010	17	12	29	26	17	11	10	29	28	23	31	16	30	20	3
	2020	22	15	42	17	5	16	13	44	19	7	34	18	36	12	2

Source: WHO/UNICEF Joint Monitoring Programme for Water Supply, Sanitation and Hygiene (JMP) Database (updated July, 2021)

It is now time for India to undertake a wide-ranging exercise in SIA and Monitoring and Evaluation (M&E) of the sustainability as well as the correct interpretation of SBM. This should include, for example, not only the number of latrines but also the availability of water needed for their adequate functioning. India's new statistics are being examined with caution by researchers, numbers that are likely to have been prepared by government for multilateral submission. Gautam (2019) emphasized the need for measurement and verification, as well as the need for community-led approaches for the construction of toilets rather than a super-imposed number orientation. Bharat et al. (2020) undertook an examination of the status of sanitation in rural and urban India for achieving and sustaining open-defecation free (ODF) status. They pointed to how a re-emergence of poor sanitation could affect negatively the positive achievements of SDG-6; therefore, any regression from the achieved position had to be carefully monitored and arrested.

The aversion to use toilets could reflect a lingering fetish against touching, ingrained in Hindu practice, that forbids a person to sit on a reusable toilet to defecate, together with other irrational such beliefs and mores. While the urban middle classes have, by and large, discarded such views, a portion of the far larger rural population remains to be convinced. Therefore, the introduction of squatting, rather than sitting, latrines may be more practical for rural India. The incidence of latrine use or sustained change in behaviour remains unmeasured (Lahiri et al., 2017). Gautam (2019) and others brought to focus that the number of persons using open defecation was higher than 500 million in 2017 (while the previous Table 10.1 implies a number of around 110 million in 2020), and cautioned against its deleterious impact on diseases such as diarrhoea and also its longer-term effects including stunting and malnutrition.

There have been other reported challenges. Built toilets were used as storage, one reason being the unavailability of sufficient water (Lakshmi, 2015). The impact of water on India's sanitation levels is linked to water availability. While dams get built despite their effect on environmental degradation, they generate a scarcity of water that, on occasion, has led to sensitive conflict situations among states (Karnataka versus Tamil Nadu) and regions (West Bengal versus Bangladesh, as well as India versus Pakistan). Despite the obvious links among the various SDGs, there appears to be relatively little long-term planning or little rehabilitation of displaced communities or replenishment of flattened forest cover. It is one thing to sign international agreements on these matters; it is another to adhere to them or achieve assigned targets. In the final analysis, it would be erroneous not to conclude that the SBM comprises correct policy revival; nevertheless, it is likely to fail unless buttressed by a robust, palpable implementation and monitoring structure. Without comprehensive impact assessment of programmes, meaningful and convincing conclusions cannot yet be drawn.

Table 10.4 shows the last available information on the incidence of night soil removal by hand in selected Indian states reported in the 2011 Census. Uttar Pradesh had by far the highest incidence in both rural and urban areas. But West Bengal had a high number for its rural and Tamil Nadu for its urban components. Assuming that this occupation is assigned to the lowest castes will not lead to a serious error. Can the higher castes of India, or the rest of the global community, imagine the life-long ignominy of the lowest castes of India related to caste-imposed night soil removal? It should be highlighted that those who hand carry excreta through urban and village streets, are sometimes the subject of mockery for being of such low caste groups, and are relegated to live that life due to their accident of birth into the *atishudra* – lowest of the low – caste group. With the drastic cutback in open defecation, however, it may only be hoped that night soil removal by human hands would also have declined though this is not yet reported in available statistics.[5] An additional challenge would be for them to find alternate lines of work for it is likely that the willingness to absorb them would be low at least in the initial stages.

[5] Also note that night soil removal pertains to unflushable toilets and not just to open defecation.

Table 10.4: India: top 10 states' night soil removal by humans (%)[1]

States	Total	Rural	Urban
Andhra Pradesh	1.30	0.55	3.41
Assam	2.79	2.72	2.97
Bihar	1.71	1.67	1.83
Jammu and Kashmir	22.46	27.43	8.48
Maharashtra	1.21	0.73	2.56
Manipur	1.27	1.04	1.90
Odisha	3.34	3.23	3.62
Tamil Nadu	3.48	1.75	8.36
Uttar Pradesh	41.05	37.44	51.21
West Bengal	16.42	19.78	6.91
Total	95.02	96.34	91.25

Note: [1] India = 100%

Source: Census 2011

Water

The deterioration of groundwater quality has caused segments of society to slide back into poverty. Bhallamudi et al. (2019) have tested this deterioration in two southern Indian towns (Namakkal and Erumaipatti) and its impact on sanitation. Thirty-two open and deep bore wells were monitored for two years. The presence of fecal matter to a specified extent showed that bacteriological contamination occurred through fractures and fissures as urbanization occurred. Paradoxically, open defecation areas were less polluted than densely toileted areas. Therefore, they concluded that it was not just the provision of toilets but on-site waste management systems that were essential to achieve appropriate effluent quality.

Ground water levels have been depleting and degrading as India's population pressure raises the demand for water rapidly. Weak institutional architecture to harvest rain water or manage water resources, and negligence in allocating much needed financial resources to the water sector have worsened the situation. Scholars have called India's sustainable water resource management dysfunctional (Tiwari, 2019). Water pollution has affected parts of rural India permanently. The northern state of Punjab, once the granary bowl of India and the home of the Green Revolution, stands vitiated by chemicals in its soil, its farmers impoverished. One ramification of recession and unemployment has been a growth in the drug supply chain across the border. A state that was also the pride of India for its *jawans* – youth soldiers – is now dotted with youth lamenting the long wait for immigration visas to Canada, New Zealand, the

UK or the US. An example of the southern state of Karnataka may also be cited. There, the farmers (other than in Gulbarga district) are better off than those in Vidarbha district of Maharashtra. Nevertheless, scenes were witnessed in which Kannadiga farmers revolted against water sharing, seriously fearing bankruptcy if they shared water with Tamil Nadu. The genesis was more economic than ethnic in particular reflecting that Kannada-, Malayalam-, Tamil- and Telugu-speaking peoples have lived by and large harmoniously in the vast lands of Karnataka for centuries. Thus, the deteriorating quality and scarcity of water both have worsened the poverty condition or raised the fear of poverty in different parts of India.

Amelioration of the severe challenge made an appearance through the 2016 National Water Framework Bill. It is not as though water security opportunities for the efficient use of water do not exist in the agriculture sector. But it is an inefficient, while being the largest, user of water. As future industrial and domestic demand adds pressure on water resources, problems are expected to multiply. The effects of climate change add another dimension to the challenge. Local participation in water resource management would comprise a more bottom-up approach that would benefit wastewater recycling, rainwater harvesting and their management.

Water governance is acknowledged as an important factor for sustainable development. Focusing on eight states – Andhra Pradesh, Arunachal Pradesh, Karnataka, Maharashtra, Tamil Nadu, Telangana, Uttar Pradesh and Uttarakhand – and using survey data, Ahmed and Araral (2019) analysed whether water governance had improved in accordance with the UN SDGs. They scored 17 indicators covering water law, policy and administration and concluded that average scores had improved over two surveys conducted in 2014–15 and 2017–18. They attributed the improvement to better provision of clean drinking water. Nevertheless, there appears to be a range of conflicting views on the matter.

A strong critique of the National Water Policy (NWP) at the central and state levels was made by Pandit and Biswas (2019) who found that NWP did not make any perceptible difference in improving water management in India. They criticized it as an exercise on paper with 'lofty drafting and policy prescriptions that are divorced from reality' (p 1) without specialist input or emphasis on implementation. Rani (2021) found regional – spatial and temporal – disparities in the availability of safe drinking water. Nevertheless, using 1981–2011 Census data, India was found to have advanced in the access to safe drinking water from 38 per cent in 1981 to 85.5 per cent in 2011. A rural-urban disparity of 49 percentage points was reduced considerably to 9 per cent. Access to drinking water within household premises also improved. Tamil Nadu scored the highest with Punjab and Himachal Pradesh, while Manipur and Odisha trailed behind.

Using 1976–2008 time series data, Ridzuan (2021) made the point that inequality had actually increased water pollution, and that inequality and corruption in implementation were equal determinants of water pollution in India. This would imply that reduction in inequality and reduction in corruption would benefit water quality. At the same time, increases in water pollution widened inequality in India. The author checked the robustness of the results against various sensitivity tests. One reason among many as to why inequality increased water pollution could be that higher inequality led to greater mistrust regarding a social contract among the poor. That resulted in lower cooperation to protect public resources. Also, higher inequality forced more people to worry mainly about earning a daily living rather than about the environment or the state of wellbeing.

Climate change

Climate change is a global phenomenon that is at every continent's door. Intensification of the 2017 hurricane Harvey in the US occurred after travelling over unusually warmer ocean temperatures (2 degrees C) in the Gulf of Mexico, before landfall. It cost the US 60 lives and caused enormous economic damage.[6] The 2021 hurricane Ida that struck with enormous force from Louisiana in the south to New Jersey in the north took 43 lives in the states of Connecticut, New Jersey, New York, and Pennsylvania, of which 23 were in New Jersey alone. The sea surface warming in the Gulf has occurred over a century and is continuing. The Arctic Report Card also describes how sea surface temperature (SST) is increasing in the Arctic Ocean and adjacent seas. Seas of Alaska and Greenland have the largest warming trends – 1/2 degree C per decade since 1982. Instances can be drawn from other seas and continents including Antarctica where a chunk as large as the US has broken off and is floating. And, reflecting changes in climatic patterns, large areas of Australia, California, Europe and Siberia are suffering fires with unabated intensity.

India's exposure to the effects of climate change is no less daunting. Recent weather events in the Indian sub-continent deluging the western state of Kerala, the northern state of Bihar and the nation state of Nepal as

6 Shunondo Basu of Bloomberg New Energy Finance, New York, reported that supply in energy markets declined severely during the days of the storm and immediately thereafter. Refinery shutdowns and disruptions to pipeline infrastructure caused a sudden supply constraint. Gasoline prices rose nationwide. Given that natural gas was the primary fuel source for power generation, its demand was down significantly. Crude oil tankers drifted on the Gulf, unable to deliver at ports. The relatively rapid recovery in the shale oil sector enabled resumption of normal operations buttressed by government financial support. By contrast, as a post-climate event period unfolds, it typically takes long for infrastructure to be reinstated methodically in India's environment. To no small extent it appears to reflect leakage of relief funds, a matter India has found challenging to grapple with.

well as the eastern states of Odisha and West Bengal have brought under the lens the matter of ocean warming and climate change. Cities such as Mumbai and Kolkata habitually get inundated while Delhi is experiencing uncharacteristic strength of rain storms. Such events affect the poor the most since they tend to live in low-lying areas in poorly constructed homes that can more easily fall victim to the wrath of the weather. What is revealing is that the pattern of climate change disasters is also changing in India. Thus, for example, meteorological reports have revealed that flood-prone districts in Bihar were no longer the only ones to be affected. Also, the intensity of rains increased even where total rainfall remained the same. Thus, unexpected flash floods – rather than just embankment breaches – increased. Reflecting the increasing uncertainty in patterns, preparations tend to become less than adequately targeted.

As per the UNICEF, the 2017 deluge in the Indian subcontinent cost 1,288 lives, with 40 million people (16 million children) being affected. Germanwatch (2021) revealed that poor countries were the worst sufferers. India was extremely vulnerable, ranking seventh in climate risk among 180 nations. Table 10.5 shows that, in 2019, only Mozambique, Zimbabwe, Bahamas, Japan, Malawi and the Islamic Republic of Afghanistan were affected more than India. Even South Sudan, Niger and Bolivia in the top ten were less affected. Germanwatch documented that, in 2019, India's damage was upwards of $69 billion in purchasing power parity, with 2,267 dead.

In 2019, the monsoon, which typically lasts from June to early September, continued for a month longer than usual, with the surplus of rain causing major hardship. From June to the end of September, precipitation was 110 per cent of the normal per annum figure. The highest rainfall since 1994 was recorded. Floods caused by the heavy rains were responsible for 1,800 deaths across 14 states and led to the displacement of 1.8 million people. Overall, 11.8 million people were affected by the intense monsoon season with economic damage estimated to be US $10 billion. Furthermore, with a total of eight tropical cyclones, 2019 was one of the most active cyclone seasons on record for the northern section of the Indian Ocean. Six of the eight cyclones intensified to become 'very severe'. The worst was Cyclone Fani in May 2019, which affected a total of 28 million people, killing 90 people in India and Bangladesh and causing economic losses of US $8.1 billion.[7] India's precarious condition in climate risk danger (Table 10.5) has reflected a high incidence of associated fatalities, together with financial and per-capita GDP losses. Also of interest are the positions of Japan and South Korea which are high on the list reflecting their exposure to various climate challenges whose incidence has increased in recent years.

7 See Germanwatch (2021) for a cross-country report.

Table 10.5: Climate Risk Index (CRI): top 10 most affected countries

Ranking 2019[1] (2018)	Country	CRI score	Fatalities	Fatalities per 1,00,000 inhabitants	Absolute losses (in million US$ PPP)	Losses per unit GDP in %
1 (54)	Mozambique	2.67	700	2.25	4930.08	12.16
2 (132)	Zimbabwe	6.17	347	2.33	1836.82	4.26
3 (135)	Bahamas	6.50	56	14.70	4758.21	31.59
4 (1)	Japan	14.50	290	0.23	28899.79	0.53
5 (93)	Malawi	15.17	95	0.47	452.14	2.22
6 (24)	Afghanistan	16.00	191	0.51	548.73	0.67
7 (5)	India	16.67	2267	0.17	68812.35	0.72
8 (133)	South Sudan	17.33	185	1.38	85.86	0.74
9 (27)	Niger	18.17	117	0.50	219.58	0.74
10 (59)	Bolivia	19.67	33	0.29	798.91	0.76

Note: [1] Out of 180 countries.

Source: Global Climate Risk Index 2021, Germanwatch

Thus, climate change is affecting advanced economies and developing countries alike. Nevertheless, there is an ensuing concern regarding global climate inequality. Chancel et al. (2021) noted that,

> Addressing large inequalities in carbon emissions is essential for tackling climate change … Global income and wealth inequalities are tightly connected to ecological inequalities and to inequalities in contributions to climate change. On average, humans emit 6.6 tonnes of carbon dioxide equivalent (tCO2e) per capita, per year. ... the top 10% of emitters are responsible for close to 50% of all emissions, while the bottom 50% produce 12% of the total. (p 16)
>
> [T]hese inequalities are not just a rich vs. poor country issue. There are high emitters in low- and middle-income countries and low emitters in rich countries. In Europe, the bottom 50% of the population emits around five tonnes per year per person; the bottom 50% in East Asia emits around three tonnes and the bottom 50% in North America around 10 tonnes. This contrasts sharply with the emissions of the top 10% in these regions (29 tonnes in Europe, 39 in East Asia, and 73 in North America) … the poorest half of the population in rich countries is already at (or near) the 2030 climate targets set by rich countries, when these targets are expressed on a per capita basis. This

> is not the case for the top half of the population. Large inequalities in emissions suggest that climate policies should target wealthy polluters more. So far, climate policies such as carbon taxes have often disproportionately impacted low and middle-income groups, while leaving the consumption habits of wealthiest groups unchanged. (p 17)

The authors pointed out that

> India is a low carbon emitter: the average per capita consumption of greenhouse gas is equal to just over 2 tonnes of carbon dioxide equivalent (tCO2e). These levels are typically comparable with carbon footprints in sub-Saharan African countries. The bottom 50%, middle 40% and top 10% respectively consume 1, 2, and 9 tCO2e/capita. A person in the bottom 50% of the population in India is responsible for, on average, five times fewer emissions than the average person in the bottom 50% in the European Union and 10 times fewer than the average person in the bottom 50% in the US. (p 198)

Given the harsh reality, perhaps it is every country's responsibility to minimize the causes and effects of its own worsening natural disasters brought on by climate risk. Though the UN-established Inter-governmental Panel on Climate Change (IPCC) indicated that they had not found a definitive link, nevertheless a large portion of the scientific community postulated the existence of a link between climate change and a greater number of major hurricanes as a percentage of total tropical cyclones in a season. Planet Earth cannot get away from the self-harm it is inflicting. The previous US President Donald Trump's 2017 abrogation of the 2015 Paris Agreement on climate change – a global commitment to limit global temperature increase to 1.5 degrees C and to allocate adequate financial resources to achieve it – was a massive setback for the international community. The current US President Joe Biden's re-entrance has been a fillip. Nevertheless, even as the UK hosted the most recent global climate summit in October 2021, it was entering new contracts for the exploration of its seas near the Shetlands for natural gas as was the US sanctioning contracts on its home soil. The outcome of the summit revealed a continued lack of commitment despite its rosy declarations.

The seriousness of the most advanced economies to tackle climate change can, therefore, be called into question. In this light, extracting promises from large middle-income and poor countries such as Brazil, China and India to cut back on the depletion of forest cover or to use less coal for industrial production is also likely to fall on deaf ears as was the case in the October 2021 summit. It is no wonder that many global experts on climate change have pronounced that humanity has already lost the battle on climate change, if there ever was a battle as such.

India's lack of mitigation, and absent or slow rehabilitation, are tough to measure reliably. Clearly, the brunt of the ramifications is on the silent rural majority. The relocation of *adivasis* is a precondition to the construction of irrigation or electricity projects, as is their rehabilitation after setting aside their rights to preserve the green cover. Nevertheless, they all suffer due to bureaucratic hurdles and conflicts of interest with a direct adverse impact on poverty. There is a need for full frontal confrontation on corruption in disbursements after climate emergencies or ensuring property rights of the indigenous SC/ST populations. Otherwise, India will remain unable to pick up and move forward in eliminating the impact of natural disasters precipitated by the increasingly complex ramifications of climate change that have begun to hit India's vast geographical expanse year after year.

To recall government's inaction to do the right thing in matters of relocation and reimbursements, a case involving Union Carbide, a private multinational company, may be recalled. On 2 December 1984, the chemical methyl isocyanate (MIC) was leaked from a pesticide factory of the Union Carbide India Ltd. Union Carbide's agreement with the Indian government assigned the relocation and rehabilitation of the victims to the responsibility of government in exchange for compensation paid only to government – rather than directly to the victims – in what was considered to be a paltry sum by international standards.[8] The relocation and rehabilitation remain glaringly incomplete, with medical impacts unattended and unfinanced.[9] They are unlikely to be ever completed.[10] If government has ignored extensive domestic and international media coverage, academic investigations and documentaries on this globally publicized case, it may be easily surmised how many *adivasis* have been relocated or reimbursed as a result of the

[8] The motivation behind the nature and amount of compensation remains a matter of debate.

[9] Eckerman (2005) in her book, *The Bhopal Saga*, recalled what a victim told him, 'Death would have been a great relief. It's worse to be a survivor'. Thirty years later, there is no closure in the case. Thousands of survivors of the Bhopal gas tragedy continue to face a lack of healthcare facilities. After the factory was closed, whatever remained inside was sealed and kept there. Gas victims' welfare organizations have been demanding its removal for years. Many petitions have been languishing in the high court and the Supreme Court for removal of the plant's poisonous remains. See 'Bhopal gas tragedy', *Business Standard*. Available at tragedy#:~:text=On%20the%20night%20of%20December,India's%20first%20 major%20industrial%20disaster, accessed 23 April 2021.

[10] The wait for justice for the survivors of Bhopal in one of the world's worst industrial catastrophes, continues after 38 years of the disaster with consecutive governments having given up on the cause, as indicated by organizations fighting for their rights. See Ellis-Petersen (2019) for a comprehensive coverage of the ramifications of the tragedy.

dislocation or slide into poverty brought about by its infrastructure projects, the beneficiaries of which are often the powerful. Such policies, unless meaningfully planned with the best intentions, are likely to, in effect, transfer real incomes away from those at the bottom of the income ladder to those who are at least in the middle if not higher up.

References

Ahmed, Masood and Eduardo Araral. (2019) 'Water governance in India: evidence on water law, policy, and administration from eight Indian states', *Water*, 11(10): 2071. Available at https://doi.org/10.3390/w11102071, accessed 15 July 2021.

Bhallamudi, S. Murty, R. Kaviyarasan, A. Abilarasu and Ligy Philip. (2019) 'Nexus between sanitation and groundwater quality: case study from a hard rock region in India', *Journal of Water, Sanitation and Hygiene for Development*, 9(4): 703–713. Available at https://doi.org/10.2166/washdev.2019.002, accessed 31 August 2021.

Bharat, Girija K., Nathaniel B. Dkhar and Mary Abraham. (2020) 'Aligning India's Sanitation Policies with the Sustainable Development Goals (SDGs)', TERI Discussion Paper. Available at https://www.teriin.org/policy-brief/discussion-paper-aligning-indias-sanitation-policies-sdgs, accessed 31 August 2021.

Chancel, Lucas Thomas Piketty, Emmanuel Saez and Gabriel Zucman. (2021) 'World Inequality Report 2022'. World Inequality Lab. Available at https://wir2022.wid.world/www-site/uploads/2021/12/WorldInequalityReport2022_Full_Report.pdf, accessed 15 December 2021.

Chiriyankandath, James, Diego Maiorano, James Manor and Louise Tillin. (2020) *The Politics of Poverty Reduction in India – The UPA Government 2004 to 2014*. Hyderabad: Orient BlackSwan.

Desai, Sonalde and Reeve Vanneman. (2015) 'Enhancing nutrition security via India's national food security act: using an axe instead of a scalpel?' *India Policy Forum*, 11: 67–113. Available at https://www.ncbi.nlm.nih.gov/pmc/articles/PMC4811376/, accessed 15 July 2021.

Dreze, Jean and Amartya Sen. (2013) *An Uncertain Glory: India and Its Contradictions*. London: Allan Lane.

Eckerman, Ingrid. (2005) 'The Bhopal Saga – Causes and consequences of the world's largest industrial disaster', *Prehospital and Disaster Medicine*, the official journal of the National Association of EMS Physicians, 20 (S1). Available at www.researchgate.net > publication > 2590407811, accessed 6 January 2023.

Ellis-Petersen, Hannah (2019) 'Bhopal's tragedy has not stopped: the urban disaster still claiming lives 35 years on'. *The Guardian*, London, 8 December. Available at www.theguardian.com > cities > dec > bhopals-tragedy-, accessed 6 January 2023.

Gautam, Ankur. (2019) 'Understanding behavior change for ending open defecation in rural India: a review of India's sanitation policy efforts', in Naoyuki Yoshino, Eduardo Araral and K. E. Seetha Ram (eds) *Water Insecurity and Sanitation in Asia.* Tokyo: Asian Development Bank Institute. Available at www.adb.org/publications/water-insecurity-and-sanitation-asia, accessed 31 August 2021.

Germanwatch. (2021) 'Who suffers most from extreme weather events? weather-related loss events in 2019, and 2000–2019', Global Climate Risk Index, Bonn. Available at www.germanwatch.org/en/19777, accessed 20 September 2021.

Government of India. (2005) 'The Mahatma Gandhi National Rural Employment Guarantee Act', New Delhi: Ministry of Rural Development.

Government of India. (2011) *Census of India 2011.* Available at https://censusindia.gov.in > census.website > data-, accessed 7 January 2023.

Lahiri, Shaon, Rosaine N. Yegbemey, Neeta Goel, Leja Mathew and Jyotsna Puri (2017) *Promoting Latrine Use in Rural India. 3ie Scoping Paper 8.* New Delhi: International Initiative for Impact Evaluation.

Lakshmi, R. (2015) 'India is building millions of toilets, but that's the easy part', *Washington Post*, 4 June. Available at www.washingtonpost.com/world/asia_pacific/india-is-building-millions-of-toilets-buttoilet-training-could-be-a-bigger-task/2015/06/03/09d1aa9e095a-11e5-a7ad-b430fc1d3f5c_story.html.

Pandit, Chetan and Asit K. Biswas. (2019) 'India's national water policy: "feel good" document, nothing more', *International Journal of Water Resources Development*, 35: 1015–28. Available at https://doi.org/10.1080/07900627.2019.1576509, accessed 15 July 2021.

Patel, Amit, Phoram Shah and Brian E. Beauregard. (2020) 'Measuring multiple housing deprivations in urban India using Slum Severity Index', *Habitat International*, 101: 102190. Available at https://doi.org/10.1016/j.habitatint.2020.102190, accessed 15 July 2021.

Prinja, Sankar, Yashpal Sharma, Jyoti Dixit, et al. (2019) 'Cost of treatment of valvular heart disease at a tertiary hospital in north India: policy implications', *PharmacoEconomics*, 3: 391–402. Available at https://doi.org/10.1007/s41669-019-0123-6, accessed 20 September 2021.

Rani, Seema. (2021) 'Evaluating the regional disparities in safe drinking water availability and accessibility in India', *Environment Development and Sustainability*, 24(5): 1–24. Available at https://doi.org/10.1007/s10668-021-01631-6, accessed 15 July 2021.

Ridzuan, Sulhi. (2021) 'Inequality and water pollution in India', *Water Policy*, 23(4): 985–99. Available at https://doi.org/10.2166/wp.2021.057, accessed 31 August 2021.

Singh, Prachi, Shamika Ravi and Sikim Chakraborty. (2020) 'COVID-19: Is India's health infrastructure equipped to handle an epidemic?', *Brookings*, 24 March . Available at www.brookings.edu/blog/up-front/2020/03/24/is-indias-health-infrastructure-equipped-to-handle-an-epidemic/, accessed 20 September 2021.

Tiwari, Piyush. (2019) 'The water conundrum in India: an institutional perspective', in Naoyuki Yoshino, Eduardo Araral and K. E. Seetha Ram (eds) *Water Insecurity and Sanitation in Asia*. Tokyo: Asian Development Bank Institute. Available at www.adb.org/publications/water-insecurity-and-sanitation-asia, accessed 31 August 2021.

United Nations. (2005) 'Global housing crisis results in mass human rights violations'. Geneva: Press Release, 5 March 2020. Accessed 6 January 2023.

Vellakkal, Sukumar, Adyya Gupta, Zaky Khan, David Stuckler, Aaron Reeves, Shah Ebrahim, Ann Bowling and Pat Doyle (2017) 'Has India's national rural health mission reduced inequities in maternal health services? A pre-post repeated cross-sectional study', *Health Policy and Planning*, 32(1): 79–90. February. Available at https://pubmed.ncbi.nlm.nih.gov/27515405/, accessed 16 September 2021.

WHO-UNICEF. (2017) *Progress on Drinking Water, Sanitation and Hygiene: 2017 Update and SDG Baselines*. Geneva: World Health Organization.

WHO-UNICEF. (2021) *Joint Monitoring Programme for Water Supply, Sanitation (JMP) Database and Progress on Household Drinking Water, Sanitation and Hygiene 2000–2020: Five Years into the SDGs*. Geneva: World Health Organization.

PART IV

Radical Humanism

> As soon as you say the topic is civil disobedience, you are saying our problem is civil disobedience. That is not our problem... . Our problem is civil obedience. Our problem is the numbers of people all over the world who have obeyed the dictates of the leaders of their government and have gone to war, and millions have been killed because of this obedience.
>
> Howard Zinn[1]

1 In November 1970, after his arrest due to his engagement in a Boston protest at an army base to block soldiers from being sent to Vietnam. He took part in a debate with the philosopher Charles Frankel on civil disobedience. 'The Problem is Civil Disobedience', speech at John Hopkins University, Baltimore, November 1970.

11

Blueprint for Addressing Poverty and Inequality

Always take sides. Neutrality helps the oppressor, never the victim. Silence encourages the tormentor, never the tormented.

Elie Wiesel[1]

Introduction

The concluding chapter proposes a range of policies based on a spirit of 'radical humanism' that could successfully address the challenges of extreme poverty and deepening inequality in India. Why this term is being used may be explained by the radical nature of the proposals while being based on a humanism whose objective is to vanquish poverty and inequality. Earlier chapters had, at various points, explained the need to combine economic, socio-economic and anthropogenic aspects, not shying away from subjectivity to justify a set of arguments and proposals that are found acceptable to traditionalists (Levinas, 2006). The term 'radical humanism' was brought up by Amery (2009), in illustrating his experience in a Nazi concentration camp of enduring torture and its supply chain. To quote Gilroy (2019),

> In *At the Mind's Limits*, Amery ... interprets his own experience of being tortured and explores it forensically ... in grasping the philosophical and political meanings of what he had endured in the concentrationary universe and its supply chains ... respond(ing) to those trials by becoming a combative proponent of what he called a 'radical humanism'... the outspread wings of 'the bird of prey' he called the Gestapo. In those talons, he had acquired a stake in the politics of

1 Author, political activist and Holocaust survivor, from his acceptance speech of the Nobel Peace Prize, 1986.

> dignity which could answer the governmental actions that had brought racial hierarchy so disastrously, yet legally, to life … shatter(ing) the flimsy, social conventions of his civilized, inter-cultural childhood, and then hung him from a ceiling hook by his dislocated arms in the dimly lit 'business room' of the Breendonk fortress in Belgium: 'everyone went about his business and theirs was murder'. (p 4)

Amery's recounting of his past is reminiscent of that of the helpless, castaway *atishudra*, at least metaphorically, both conditions reflecting the accident of birth. Perhaps this imagination is inept reflecting that it is not possible to imagine life experience in either condition unless one has actually lived it. Ironically, technology has contributed useful, eye-opening illustrations of this condition in recent times.[2] Should children in modern schools not be shown such reality documentaries, rather than spending time primarily on video games? That contemplation, recognition and follow-up action are what radical humanism is about and the policymaking authorities in any country and no less in India, should reflect on such measures in formulating education policy rather than merely regurgitating old curricula and reorganizing them at the margins to put a mark of any ruling government.

It is crucial for any government to be particularly cautious of surreptitious breezes of intolerance initially fanned by private interested parties and culminating in unfathomable concentration of wealth, with government losing sight of pathways to a solution, or precipitated with tacit approval. This has occurred or is occurring in several present-day democracies including the US, Brazil and India and was legislated in September 2022 by the UK in justification of propelling higher economic growth. Several European countries are at the cusp of voting in governments that are likely to adopt comparable policies. Plutocracy and kleptocracy are the order of the day in dictatorships such as China, Russia, Belarus and a plethora of others. To recall Levi (1974),

> Every age has its own fascism, and we see the warning signs wherever the concentration of power denies citizens the possibility and the means of expressing and acting on their own free will. There are many ways of reaching this point, and not just through the terror of police intimidation, but by denying and distorting information, by undermining systems of justice, by paralyzing the education system,

---

2 Netflix, in the final episode of a series entitled, *Crime Stories: India Detectives*, based on investigations by Bengaluru police, take up a case entitled, 'The Stolen Baby'. In a heart-rending illustration of abject poverty, a baby of street dwellers that is probably sold, and associated petty crime are brought to the attention of the audience. Another case of a British Broadcasting Corporation (BBC) documentary on children born into parental debt and being sold off into disappearance has already been cited.

> and by spreading in a myriad subtle ways nostalgia for a world where order reigned, and where the security of a privileged few depends on the forced labour and the forced silence of the many. (Gilroy, p 3)

Strongly founded democracies, even if in hibernation, have been able to reverse any course to fascism. An eventual return to democracy has occurred time and again, however long – decades, even a century – that may take under different circumstances. It is not just the loss of the freedom of expression but the growing concentration of wealth and worsening poverty that come to grip society that have imploded and have given birth to new and better courses. Nevertheless, this has occurred at great interim cost to society in the form of wars that are relatively short events that bring concentrated human suffering, or may be protracted, drawn-out events lasting longer than a lifetime. Thus, large proportions of the population may be born and die without any change in their economic or social condition.

To quote Gilroy (2019), '(The) collective work of salvage … is likely to involve more than pulling imperiled fellow beings from the sea, for it is our own humanity that needs to be rescued from the mounting wreckage. There is still time for that operation, but not much' (p 14). To successfully address resultant poverty and inequality, policies of equal strength and ferocity – of radical humanism – have to be employed. Policy prescriptions are often made in a dry, formulaic, and predictable pattern. It is important at this time to think out of the box. Over and above tax policies and direct transfer policies that are albeit important and have had a good run with positive outcomes, this chapter proposes policies that have remained underdiscussed or underutilized.

What innovations are feasible under the current set of possibilities for India? Among domestic measures that should be introduced are, for example: (1) setting up a youth task force to register, tabulate and publish the names and associated details of all farmers who have committed suicide; (2) taking explicit measures to restore the rural-urban, agricultural-non-agricultural balance including raising agricultural engineering institutes to the same level of competence as Indian institutes of technology (IITs) and refraining and withdrawing from deifying the latter; (3) developing and publishing accurate accounts of bank and non-bank credit by economic sector (agricultural, non-agricultural and others) and by income and wealth deciles of recipients; and (4) following up policy announcements such as the intention to provide health insurance to the poor (and many such announcements) with the actual provision and filling of posts of doctors, nurses and assistants in public sector health centres. This has to be complemented with adequate economic infrastructure to run rural health centres many of which languish in dire straits.

Other steps would be to: (5) provide a step-up for women, legally assuring them public sector posts in direct proportion to their population share; and

(6) ensure entrance to government schools, colleges and professional degree institutions according to caste definitions in the interim, while (7) abolishing the use of caste names through the constitution whose effects are likely to take time to fructify in Indian society.

There is an important international measure that has to be picked up by previously colonized countries and pushed ahead. This comprises (8) reparations from previous colonizers. The pervasive and persistent transfers by the colonizers from their colonies to home countries may be considered the primary explanation of the conversion of previously economically better-off and socially better organized societies into economic penury and reductive societies. That position cannot be reversed, or poverty and inequality eradicated without international reparations. If such reparations are honestly calculated and undertaken, cross-country inequality should significantly diminish. Some of these aspects will be considered later in the chapter.

Tax policy

Tax policy changes must be made innovatively so as not to disrupt productive activity. Nevertheless, the crux of tax policy has to be based on higher tax incidence on the rich and wealthy enabling transfers in kind and cash to the poor. Changes in policy should aim to increase individual income and wealth taxes, which are low by global standards while rationalizing the corporate income tax without affecting its basic rate structure (Shome (2021a)).

The sharp edges of the Goods and Services Tax (GST) need to be smoothened quickly to facilitate compliance and reduce evasion, the absence of which adds to inequality. Crucial GST measures include the introduction of auto-population of tax return forms in order to check tax evasion. GST rates should not be increased since that would hurt the commoner's consumption basket in particular that of the poor. Short-term international taxes such as the Equalization Levy (EL) on the digital economy[3] have to continue to garner and protect revenue from this sector in the absence of progress in its taxation mechanisms in multilateral discussions. Note must, however, be taken of unilateral measures by the US against every country that has introduced an EL-like tax. Last but not the least, rapid reform of tax administration, with a customer (taxpayer) focus and away from retrospective application of taxes, is imperative to push up investment and gross domestic product (GDP) growth.

---

[3] In 2016, India introduced an EL at 6 per cent on the amount received from specified services provided by a non-resident taxpayer not having a permanent establishment (PE) in India. In 2020, the rate was reduced to 2 per cent while extending the base to include all e-commerce companies (Shome, 2021b; Rejoinder, ch. 7, p 192). The tax will continue until a tax is introduced multilaterally through the OECD.

A common observation made in discussions is that Indians pay tax only at top income levels. This is incorrect since the vast majority of Indians pay various taxes on production and consumption – indirect taxes – that do not differentiate between rich and poor. Reflecting that indirect taxes comprise about half or more of the total tax collected at the central government level, and account for almost the entirety of state and municipal taxes, India's poor and very poor pay their full share in taxation. If the revenue collected from the numerous cesses that governments collect from economic activities (rather than from income tax) are added, then the burden on the poor increases. Indeed, the share of tax burden from indirect taxes may be higher or much higher on the poor than on their richer counterparts since their budgets overwhelmingly reflect consumption rather than saving. Thus, the fallacious argument in which upper income groups find succour and solace, should be set aside.

By and large, continuing erroneous tax policies of consecutive governments have exacerbated inequality. Nevertheless, government may perhaps be perceived to have taken the right decision in recent years to reduce the headline corporate income tax rate along comparable international lines to promote the achievement of higher economic growth. This will, however, reduce tax revenue at least in the short to medium term. Therefore, it is crucially needed to be accompanied by complementary tax and expenditure measures; this has not occurred yet. Instead, to contain the fiscal deficit, in its January 2021 annual budget, government cut back expenditures on nutrition and education implying a setback for poverty and inequality amelioration.

Income and dividend taxes

A short recounting of India's experience with various income related taxes at the individual level may be revealing. Marginal individual income tax rates were slashed in the 1997–98 central government budget to encourage work effort. Currently, however, India's income tax structure is generally lower than international rates and there is urgency to raise the tax structure up. This is justified next.

First, to correct for India's low individual income tax rates, income tax policy should re-emphasize progressivity in the tax structure. The prevailing regressive tax structure needs reform through improving the individual income tax rate structure from 10, 20 and 30 per cent to, say, 10, 20, 30, 35, 40 and 45 per cent to make it comparable with other countries.[4]

[4] There is little justification to continue with a 30 per cent marginal rate for the highest incomes. Introduction of bands of Rs 10–20 million, Rs 20–30 million, Rs 30–40 million, and so on, is justified even when they are compared internationally on a rupee-to-dollar, rather than on a purchasing power parity (PPP) basis.

Second, capital gains taxation remains flawed. Until 31 March 2018, capital gains from the stock market were free of tax after just one year of holding since that was deemed 'long term'. Since 1 April 2018, long term capital gains over Rs 0.1 million on listed equity shares per financial year became taxable at the rate of 10 per cent without the benefit of indexation. Yet, an elderly couple selling a home after whatever number of years of possession has to pay capital gains tax.

Third, an elderly person acquiring a second flat at retirement even in his or her same cooperative, that is likely to have been made possible from accumulated incremental small savings, is taxed on the second property, while blanket exemption is given to ownership of a single house irrespective of value or height in blatant oversight of equity considerations and under the world's view. Clearly, this exemption should be limited to a consolidated value of Rs 50–100 million for all owned properties, thus rationalizing the tax on residential property by converting its base to value rather than the number of properties owned.

Fourth, the tax on dividends remains at 10 per cent. Instead, it should be the marginal tax rate applicable to the assessee. The argument that the company has already paid a tax on the distribution of dividends (DDT) can be countered in different ways. The latter's rate, at 20 per cent, is below the top income tax rate. hence there is room for higher taxation at the marginal income-tax rates. Therefore, the DDT should be fully merged with the income tax. Or, a tax deducted at source at 30–40 per cent could be applied and small owners could adjust it against their probable, smaller tax deducted at source (TDS) on interest.

Fifth, the argument that a lower tax on dividends is needed to attract foreign direct investment (FDI) has been irrelevant for some time. India's foreign exchange reserves rose to $605 billion for the week ended 4 June 2021.[5] The rupee appreciated 4 per cent against the dollar during financial year 2020–21, leading to pressure on exports.

Sixth, there are small elements in the structure that stare out for correction. One such is the exemption from the gift tax for expenditure on weddings. The mammoth sizes of Indian weddings are globally notorious. Even elephants have been transported to European wedding destinations such as Italy for wedding celebrations. Such practices comprise an avenue for spending black money that is accumulated over time for conspicuous consumption. The least that can be done is to identify such instances in the tax structure and remove them (Shome, 2021a, ch. 15).

[5] 'India's Forex Reserves: $600 Billion And Counting ...', *Bloomberg Quint*, 11 June 2021. Available at https://www.bloombergquint.com/business/indias-forex-reserves-600-billion-and-counting, accessed 18 June 2021.

Table 11.1: Global millionaires and billionaires, 2021

				Global wealth tax	
Wealth group ($)	**Number of adults**	**Total wealth ($ bn)**	**Average wealth ($ m)**	**Effective wealth tax rate (%)**	**Revenues (% global income)**
All above 1m	6,21,65,200	1,74,216	2.8	1.0	1.6
1m–10m	6,03,19,500	1,11,059	1.8	0.6	0.6
10m–100m	17,69,200	33,588	19	1.3	0.4
100m–1b	73,800	17,070	231	1.5	0.2
1b–10b	2,470	7,051	2,855	2.3	0.2
10b–100b	157	4,128	26,293	2.8	0.1
Over 100b	9	1,321	1,46,778	3.2	0.04

Note: Numbers of millionaires are rounded to the nearest ten.

Source: World Inequality Report, 2022, p 20

Economic policy cannot be cast in stone or etched by ideology alone. It is social science, and has to bend to reflect changing socioeconomic realities. Redressing the alarming worsening in income inequality should not be dependent only on tax policy, but that will be a beginning. It should be complemented with clearly targeted expenditure policies for the bottom 50 per cent of the population.

Wealth, gift and inheritance taxes

Wealth taxes have not been popular across the globe in recent years. Among the 37 Organization for Economic Co-operation and Development (OECD) countries, the number of countries with taxes on the net wealth of individuals grew from eight in 1965 to 12 in 1996, but fell to five by 2019. Among the five – Colombia, France, Norway, Spain and Switzerland – the share of the net wealth tax in total tax revenue varies widely, from 0.19% in France to 3.79% in Switzerland (Ghatak, 2021).

Such low taxation of wealth has been occurring *pari passu* with an increase in the income and wealth inequalities in all country groupings. Examining this aspect, Chancel et al. (2021) demonstrated the extent of global wealth concentration as shown in Table 11.1.

Such wealth concentration justifies the introduction of a global wealth tax. For that to occur, countries would have to be willing to look at such a possibility multilaterally. Revenue from such a tax could also comprise a continuing transfer of resources from the rich to the poorer countries that would mostly coincide with the objective of reparations from ex-colonial to ex-colonized countries. The transfers could be targeted to expenditures on education, health and ecological balance without which it would be unlikely for inequalities to be held down.

In an ordering of nations, India is among the very poor countries, and its income and wealth distribution and growing concentration continue to draw the surprise and shock of much of the world even if that may not be so to Indians in the uppermost income groups themselves. In India, where 0.001% of the top income cohorts are enjoying the most rapid increase in wealth concentration in the entire world, a tax on wealth is imperative for equity and growth. A tax on wealth would have little adverse effect on productivity provided that the design of its structure is simple and, commensurately, its administration is effective and honest. If well conceptualized and fairly implemented, it should also generate good revenue.

To recall, a 1 per cent tax on net wealth exceeding Rupees 3 million existed in India from the late 1950s but was removed in 2015 reflecting its low revenue productivity. That was due to tax evasion and poor tax administration. It was replaced by a 2 per cent surcharge on the 'super rich' at incomes exceeding Rs 10 million annually. A reintroduction of the wealth tax is justifiable for several reasons. (1) Global indicators reveal a significant increase in the wealth gap and wealth concentration across the world. (2) Wealth buildup in recent years has often been through destabilizing speculation such as the financialization of global commodity markets that has had little to do with market fundamentals that reflect underlying market demand and supply conditions. (3) Accumulated wealth is often economically unproductive. (4) Tax administration capability has improved in emerging economies to better track and cover wealth in the tax base. And (5) with international tax harmonization by means of double taxation avoidance arrangements (DTAAs), foreign tax credit for wealth tax is possible.

In India, three characteristics should comprise a wealth tax. (1) It should include both real and financial wealth in the tax base. (2) It should have a high threshold so that only the significantly wealthy get included in the tax net. And (3) it should not have prohibitive rates, say 0.25 per cent between Rs 0.5 billion and Rs 1 billion, and 0.5 per cent above Rs 1 billion that would provide some progressivity to the structure.

In addition to a wealth tax, India needs to reintroduce gift and inheritance taxes. The government position taken that such taxes yielded little revenue is not valid any longer with much improved automation and information through artificial intelligence (AI) and the prevalence of property tax at the local government level that has become the mainstay of many municipal corporations. The crucial need for these taxes becomes obvious from a cross-country comparison (Table 11.2). Not only advanced economies have rates ranging between 40–60 per cent, but even South Africa has a rate of 25 per cent for both taxes. Can there be any rationale for a country as poor as India

Table 11.2: Selected countries: headline inheritance and gift tax rates (%)

Country	Inheritance tax rate	Gift tax rate
Chile	25	25
France	60	60
Germany	50	50
India	0	0[1]
Japan	55	55
Republic of Korea	50	50
Netherlands	40	40
South Africa	25	25
United Kingdom	40[2]	40[3]
United States	40[4]	40

Note: [1] There is no gift tax liability on the donor. However, any sum of money aggregating to Rs 50,000 or more received during the relevant tax year without consideration or for an inadequate consideration by an individual from any person not being a relative is subject to income tax in the hands of the recipient. [2] It is only charged on the part of one's estate that is above the threshold. [3] If there is inheritance tax to pay, it is charged at 40 per cent on gifts given in the three years before death. Gifts made three to seven years before death are taxed on a sliding scale known as 'taper relief'. [4] There is no inheritance tax. However, there is an estate tax with a top rate of 40 per cent.

Source: PwC, Worldwide Tax Summaries, 2021

not to legislate these taxes? It can only be hoped that Indian policymakers will heed this urgent call as early as possible.

Corporate income tax

India's main corporate income tax (CIT) rate was reduced to an average of 27.69 per cent from financial year (FY) 2019–20 through a Taxation (Amendment) Ordinance on September 20, 2019. A special taxation regime was introduced:

- for existing manufacturing companies (under Section 115BAA) the CIT rate was reduced to 25.17% (22% + 10% SC + 4% HEC); and
- for new manufacturing companies (under Section 115BAB) the CIT rate was reduced to 17.16% (15% + 10% SC + 4% HEC).[6]

These rates are comparable with prevailing advanced economy rates, for example, 25.8 per cent in Netherlands, 25 per cent in China, 21 per cent in

[6] Surcharge (SC) and Health and Education Cess (HEC).

the US, 19 per cent in the UK and 12.5 per cent in Ireland. Therefore, there is little room for India to increase its corporate income tax rate at this time.

However, what can and should be done is not to extend additional tax incentives for five years and to make every effort to cut them back to increase neutrality across the corporate sector and protect tax revenue. The focus should, instead, be on improving the ease of paying taxes, a criterion in which India recently ranked lower (115) than China (105) in a cross-country comparison (World Bank, 2020 and Shome, 2021a).

Tax administration

Over the last two years, government has announced a number of taxpayer-friendly measures including that tax assessments will be carried out in a faceless manner, that is, no taxpayer will be called to the tax administration to physically face tax officers. While in theory this is a commendable break from the past, it may be asked why then taxpayers, by and large, have been making complaints about its functioning (Krishnan, 2022). The policymakers, rather than the tax administration alone, have to give particular attention to this issue through taxpayer surveys over and above receiving selective taxpayer representations that lack anonymity. Only then meaningful conclusions could be drawn and appropriate action taken. Otherwise the usefulness of a presumably helpful instrument such as faceless assessment is likely to recede rapidly.

In terms of penalty, it is difficult to anticipate success without cleansing the tax administration of corruption by legislating immediate suspension and removal of officers based on taxpayer complaints. This has been no easy task since the Vigilance Department has been generally unable to incarcerate officers despite evidence of corruption; in fact, it is more often than not that such functionaries have been reinstated with backpay and interest. The government's own Tax Administration Reform Commission (TARC, 2015) provided ample evidence of that. At the same time, India is among the countries with the least likelihood of a taxpayer being jailed for tax evasion unlike practices in advanced economies including in China where capital punishment is not unknown for such an infraction. India too must introduce strong legislation facilitating long jail terms for tax evaders. The challenge to this is that Indian governments have been observed to use their intelligence arms and tax departments to mete out vengeance against their detractors, as is known to occur in backward countries.

At what pace India's cash use has been increasing compared to Brazil and China is noteworthy (see Chapter 2, Table 2.2). Several measures could be taken to arrest this phenomenon instead of surprising the populace with unanticipated demonetization and other such moves that would affect the poor most adversely as it did the last time. Post demonetization, cash circulation dipped to 8.7 per cent of GDP in 2016 but, since then, it climbed back on a rising trajectory. Measures that should be taken include the following.

First, track for the next five years, the cash in circulation in terms of GDP, the objective being an observable decrease.

Second, track the number of non-cash transactions and whether their growth is approaching the gigantic leaps that China has achieved.

Third, among non-cash components, to what extent are more Indians using net banking and increasing the use of credit transfers and direct debits. Banks should implement helpful programmes to educate even zero-balance accountholders to use net banking. Without these changes, a salient ramification of any demonetization – to quickly move from cash to non-cash use – will remain unachieved.

Considerable obstacles remain in modernizing India's administrative capabilities that are impeded by high cash use; nevertheless, efforts to reform them cannot take a backseat for, otherwise, tax evasion and, correspondingly, corruption in the administration are unlikely to be stamped out.

Goods and Services Tax (GST)

The introduction of a GST was the outcome of a decade-long (2007–17) effort. It has now been in place for more than five years. Several points have emerged since its introduction revealing the need for improvement including the streamlining of tax compliance and control of tax evasion. Urgent administration reform required include the following.

First, reduce the number of rates and classifications. The voluminous list of tariffs in the GST structure indicates its departure from global norms and makes GST compliance challenging for taxpayers. In turn, a high incidence of litigation as in the previous domestic indirect tax regime, continues.

Second, step back from the newly introduced rule that a dealer or trader can be picked up for audit in any state. This implies that a taxpayer has to respond to a tax administration in any state where he is trading rather than in his home state where he is based. This makes post-tax compliance onerous for the majority of medium and small taxpayers. This practice was not prevalent under the previous state-level value-added tax (VAT).

Third, replace the joint administrative powers of the central and state tax administrations over the same taxpayer even at low turnover levels. Currently, this comprises a heavy compliance burden on taxpayers who have to face and deal with both levels of tax administration. Instead, information exchange among various tax administrations should be carried out more intensively to reduce the high incidence of tax evasion in specific sectors and in particular regions.

Fourth, introduce auto-population of GST return forms connecting output tax and input tax. Without it, there is no automatic cross-check, and the essence of GST is absent. The three GST Forms – 1M, 2A and 3B – were intended to be electronically linked, but they are not. Form 3B should have been automatically (electronically) populated as soon as the GST registration number of a taxpayer was entered in Form 1M or 2A. Ideally, there should be no requirement or possibility for a taxpayer to enter information into the three forms separately. This has led to GST evasion since carrying out manual cross-checks of all related return forms is impractical to expect from the tax administration.

There are also fundamental changes needed in the complex structural design of the GST. To note a few of them:

First, the crux of a GST is to have a broad base that, in turn, enables a low tax rate to yield a certain amount of tax revenue. Instead there are multiple rates including inverted rates. That implies output tax rates are lower than input tax rates, thus leading to input tax credit (ITC) accumulation in the hands of taxpayers that they can receive credit for only in future years.

Second, petroleum products contribute one-fourth to half of the different states' revenues. The states have been opposed to including it in the GST base to maintain their hold over this stream of revenue. This leads to economic distortions as explained next and should be corrected. The GST Council which is a combined central and state government policy making body comprising policymakers at the ministerial level retains an enabling provision to tax petroleum, and the centre prefers to include petroleum in the GST base. But states have been steadfast in their resistance to do so. This has to be reconsidered and there should be a via media for petroleum to be included in the GST base.

Third, keeping petroleum out leads to double cascading or 'tax on tax'. Petroleum users cannot take ITC, and the petroleum sector itself cannot take ITC for its own inputs. Therefore, the petroleum sector causes significant distortions in the allocation of resources across the supply chain in the economy as a whole.

Fourth, stamp duty which is a tax on immovable property has been excluded from the GST base so that ITC is not allowed for this tax. In turn, this leads to cascading generated in the construction sector.

If the required structural changes are made, the GST should be more revenue productive since resource misallocation would be reduced, thus generating higher GDP growth and, in turn, more revenue. In particular, revenue needs cannot be minimized in the post-pandemic environment and, if utilized judiciously, the GST could become a productive source of revenue for supporting socio-economic programmes.

Finally, a sustained increase in selective excises on conspicuous consumption comprising extreme luxury goods that has become the wont of the super-rich should be employed. This should be carried out rather than effectively increasing (through inflation) excises on domestic gas and petroleum consumption that hits the middle class badly and benefits a small class of suppliers.

Use of earmarked taxes/cesses

India uses several cesses that are collected for intended use in specific sectors such as education, though their actual destination does not match the intended purpose. This anomaly needs to be corrected. Government bears an obligation to ensure full and transparent utilization of earmarked monies just as payers of the cess have a right to seek information on whether the earmarked funds have been used for their specified objectives. Recent analysis by Kotha and Talekar (2021) revealed that Rs 940 billion in funds collected through the secondary and higher education cess since 2007 continue to remain in the Consolidated Fund of India. To quote,

> This is alarming because the funds have not been transferred or utilized despite a relevant sub-fund having been created in August 2017.[7] The cess continues to be levied as a newly-branded health and education cess. Access to education is a real challenge in India and contributors rightfully expect the money to be utilised for bridging the existing gaps. Unfortunately, this is not the case. In such a situation, it is argued that cess taxpayers have the right to seek utilisation of the earmarked monies. Acknowledging and adopting the rights-based discourse is the first step in realising the rights and identifying adequate remedies. (p 117)

When the GST was introduced in 2017, certain other cesses that had existed such as the Hygiene Cess, Farmer Welfare Cess and Infrastructure Cess were repealed with the intention that those expenditures would be allocated

---

[7] Comptroller and Auditor General of India, Report No 2 of 2019– Financial Audit, Accounts of the Union Government, https://cag.gov.in/webroot/uploads/download_audit_report/2019/Report_No_2_of_2019_Accounts_of_the _Union_Government_Financial_Audit.pdf.

from the general fiscal budget. Its actual outcome has not been reported, though the repeal of a statute does not diminish the rights or obligations accrued or incurred.[8] As Kotha and Talekar pointed out, the delivery of good governance is instrumental for building credibility of the tax system and increase voluntary compliance.

After having made a range of tax policy-oriented recommendations with the alleviation of inequality in mind, we now proceed to describe selected expenditure-oriented policies that require enhanced budgetary allocation in particular for socio-economic objectives. Recommendations are not added for the range of food and cash transfer policies embedded in the government budget on which there already exists a detailed literature to which we referred in earlier chapters.

Selected expenditure policies

Health and sanitation

Government needs to adopt meaningful policies reflecting the precarious condition of public hospitals and the state of nutrition; in particular that of the very poor children. To buttress its own budget provision, government could encourage private sector provision in a massive way in a public-private participation (PPP) scheme that should be designed in a way attractive for the private sector to opt into. In addition, the private sector should be encouraged to invest on its own with a proper Monitoring and Evaluation (M&E) mechanism that should transcend the possibility of corrupt practices of both parties. Efficacy of implementation remains the crux of the matter.

A few solution-oriented prevalent practices that have appeared in the private sector may be exemplified. A private group charges its hospital patients reflecting their ability-to-pay. It is based on a three-tier charging system giving access to the poor of the same quality healthcare as to the richer households. Another model comprises a small investment by an organization combined with a somewhat larger government contribution, while a reliance on private donations also features. This model has enabled almost half a million prosthetic limbs to be fitted across the globe by a single Indian organization. These are good examples of the existence and survival of private-sector led programmes with government participation.

The government should increasingly enable more of such worthy private sector models by cutting out bureaucratic hurdles that have tended to thwart widespread progress. Instead, the common experience has been for government to clamp down on non-governmental organization (NGO) activities that has sent out wrong signals across the world. Some NGOs

8 *General Clauses Act 1897* (India) Act No 10 of 1,897, s 6. 2017–18, 7.

may admittedly falter as a few members of a large fraternity might, but that does not mean that the entire sector should be viewed or treated in such a suspicious manner that the sector itself gets truncated or obliterated. This is especially as government has proven itself insufficient or incapable of fulfilling the needs of health and nutrition provision.

In the area of sanitation, it may be worth recalling when Mohandas Karamchand Gandhi uttered, *Karo pahale, kaho pichhe* – do it first, then speak – he actually cleaned out night soil of the Bihar Harijan, a lesson that should be revived in school teaching. In an earlier era after India's independence, by the time the experience of middle to high school came to an end, tasks following Gandhi's example were meted out to privileged students in many schools who were required to do social work in urban slums or rural locales. Rhetorically, how many children are going through a syllabus of this kind of activity in Indian schools today? Thus, youth involvement could complement PPP action in the delivery of sanitation and education in the wide expanses of India.

Studies could be conducted in some districts and lessons could be drawn based on government reporting of action taken. For example, the 2013–14 Budget of Berhampur Municipal Corporation in Ganjam district of the state of Odisha provided details of its budget allocation in garbage collection, solid waste management, drainage, public toilet, water supply, housing, roads and bridges, street lighting, parks, livelihood, infrastructure and project assistance. It asserted that it wanted mandatory public disclosure of documents, allocation to ensure citizen participation, increased allocation for the urban poor and for basic services including water, garbage, drainage and public toilets. It would also implement a development outcome budget to ensure effective government management and accountability.

Ganjam district has reported more recent implementation schemes[9] including 1,042 projects in urban infrastructure amounting to Rs 580.00 million, comprising roads, community centres, drains and guard walls. Further, 707 projects were being completed, with an estimated 76,000 urban residents being benefited through the scheme. Regarding water supply, during FY 2018–19, 16,364 applications were received from the public out of which 13,978 connections were completed. Comprehensive coverage of piped water supply to every household in urban local bodies (ULBs) of Ganjam District was to be achieved by December 2019 with new project proposals in the pipeline. Monitoring committees had been formed in ULBs that would collect grievances from the public and transmit them to the proper authorities to enable early disposal of problems.

---

[9] District Urban Development Agency. 2019 'District Reports', Ganjam District, Odisha state, https://ganjam.nic.in/duda/.

Open defecation is monitored under the *Swachh Bharat* Mission (SBM) umbrella. Thus, 18 ULBs have been declared open defecation free (ODF). The processing of non-biodegradable waste is being carried out in material recovery facilities in 18 ULBs; 17 are constructing micro composting centres where waste can be converted into soil conditioner and organic fertilizer. A fecal sludge seepage management plant has been constructed in Mahuda, Berhampur, where human waste can be treated and converted to soil conditioner. Four ULBs of Ganjam district have been tagged to this plant. The other 13 are ready to construct similar plants in their areas. The example of Berhampur may be extended to Odisha as a whole in its water access, sanitation, and hygiene (WASH) programme. Its 2021–22 budget has allocated Rs 120 billion in investment in piped drinking water to achieve the goals of the Buxi Jagabandhu Assured Water Supply to Habitation (BASUDHA) and *Jal Jeevan* missions and for the operation and maintenance of water supply systems.[10]

The budget provides other details on sanitation improvement, urban sewerage household latrines, providing Rs 2 billion for the rural component of SBM and, notably, Rs 300 million for the distribution of sanitary napkins.

This is a good moment to undertake an M&E exercise with the co-operation of the government. If the Berhampur efforts have been successful, it would comprise an example for other ULBs to follow. Whatever bottlenecks are identified could point towards pitfalls to avoid. The central government should pick up more such instances and give concrete shape to the SBM to arrive at convincing conclusions.

Recent instances of cleaned cities in other states that have come to light are Kolkata in West Bengal run by Trinamool Congress (an opposition party at the centre), and Vadodara in Gujarat ruled by the Bharatiya Janata Party (BJP) (the ruling party at the centre). The central government should rise above politics and convey these examples to other metropolitan cities with budget allocations enabling official visits and lesson learning. Funds should also be allocated for urban conversion projects. In Kolkata, the installation and management of public toilets, garbage compactors after collection, disinfecting drains, cleaning up lakes, rejuvenating parks and constructing attractive walkways, completing flyovers and clearing away leftover concrete and rubble under them were palpable steps viewed and experienced by its denizens. Similarly, Vadodara was cleaned up and a healthy environment emerged.

By contrast, and contrary to anticipation, Bengaluru in Karnataka has suffered rapid deterioration. The collapsed condition of its roads has been rendered proverbial by the media. Heaps of garbage at street corners, and

[10] Government of Odisha (2021), Berhampur Municipal Corporation Budget (2021–22).

its many parks and lakes have become a perennial sight. Varanasi too has been unable to achieve a full cleanup despite the initiation of the prime minister (PM)'s SBM campaign at the city's *Assi Ghat* (the 80th staired access to the Ganges in Varanasi). Delhi became India's most polluted city, indeed, globally so. The Delhi government introduced an odd-even license plate policy for vehicles to operate in city streets and the Supreme Court reassuringly endorsed it. What happened to that policy? It is useful to go into the past and assess available candidates for M&E to draw lessons rather than only looking forward to design and construct ever-new programmes. The lesson is that only the empowerment of, and honest co-operation among, the central, state, district and city governments, as well as the private sector, and NGOs, can achieve sustainably better sanitation, hygiene and safe water in a complex environment stricken with poverty such as India. Poverty has made the achievement of environmental objectives enormously challenging. Despite the strong hand that appears to be increasingly applied on them, NGOs have to continue their efforts towards poverty alleviation in India. It is up to the policymakers to consider the matter serious enough for that objective to be delivered with some success.

Some analysts have been providing frameworks with which to work on sanitation improvement. Gautam (2019) has suggested methods for integrative behaviour change in open defecation through cogent interventions. Success can be achieved only if a local population could be convinced of the health benefits of using toilets. That could come in the way how information, education and communication are framed, making toilets more appealing by targeting social and cultural norms and improving or adding functionalities accordingly. Most important is the assurance of a steady supply of water to the toilets that has been reported to vary by location and region. Verification of implementation has to be based on building capacities at the grassroots and local NGO levels to monitor and report slippages and provide their reasons. Further, local pharmacies and health centres should be obligated to log and report health outcomes.

Water

History has demonstrated time and again that competition over economic resources, if not reasonably, rationally and quickly contained, can result in ethnic wars with disastrous consequences. The Indian water wars need examination in this light since buried in them are unanticipated outcomes for the Indian nation (see Chapter 10). On the one hand, admittedly, economic progress cannot be stopped. For example, the Narmada Dam and other dams must be built in a country as large as India with intensive need for the availability of water. The solution is not to stop construction but to ensure environmentally friendly and technically robust construction and completion of rehabilitation – and that these are not thwarted by corruption. Admittedly, cross-country indices put India's corruption at such high levels that it would be foolhardy to convey that it will be an easy task, but that is the only route to success.

Shah (2019) described the prevailing water and sanitation conditions in India that are affected by adverse institutional, operational and financial management. That is likely to have a deleterious impact on food production already being affected by climate change and as the population crests over the next several decades. The central government has adopted an approach toward water supply and sanitation policies that favours decentralized solutions, rather than centralized treatment that could install piped sewerage more widely with an autonomous regulatory agency that oversees and manages water and sanitation at the state and national levels. Shah highlighted the benefits of a dedicated policy, renewed institutional support and a focus on financial sustainability and citizen involvement, taking a similar stance as researchers in the area of sanitation. Given the consensus found among such analysts, a policy of a grand coalition and co-operation appears to be the solution for India to achieve wide water availability, sanitation and eradication of open defecation.

A question that arises is sustainability through appropriate financing. Tiwari (2019) suggested water resource development should shift to small, decentralized augmentation projects involving harvesting and watershed development to achieve better maintenance and upgradation of existing water assets. In the case of a large project, its impact on the environment, people, and their livelihoods has to be carefully assessed, for example, where cost recovery is possible versus where cross-subsidy or grants would be required. Needed fiscal support has to be given in reflection of government's obligations under the Right to Water assurance. Behind this, a strong support infrastructure would be essential including,

> a detailed information system that would cover complete resource mapping (availability, use, quality, seasonality in availability, meteorological data at an appropriate hydrological unit, at state, city, and village levels); asset mapping (level and condition); socioeconomic information at various levels; and cropping and irrigation patterns. There is also a need for a national clearing house to collate and provide information on good water resource management practices (traditional and non-traditional) to help agencies. (p 352)

Such agencies include irrigation departments and pollution control boards whose capacity and capabilities would need to be brought up to the modern age as opposed to their reputation as hotbeds of corruption, for example, in issuing clearance certificates.

Thus, it is a mix of large, canal-based surface irrigation projects and small decentralized irrigation channels that needs to be financed and achieved under strict operational and outcome monitoring. Emerging technological options such as rainwater harvesting and drip irrigation have to be given supreme importance in areas of sparse water availability following available international models. Given that water is often an important factor of production in industry, a cross-subsidy from industry to agriculture could be introduced through an earmarked industrial cess.

For urban areas, the government has recently introduced service-level benchmarks for water utilities that should provide data to develop plans for performance and service improvements. It is crucial to have a strong M&E application in practice so that the pervasive neglect of performance orientation in decision making and lack of performance data can be identified and corrected.

Legal barriers exist between land tenure and service provision, thus preventing expansion of water services to slums and squatter settlements, and diverting supply to the non-poor. The Jawaharlal Nehru National Urban Renewal Mission (JNNURM) had conceptualized better service delivery, and PPP and other innovative mechanisms to serve the poor, though success has been elusive. This could reflect its traditional approach of supply augmentation rather than an overhaul of the distribution networks. Therefore, Indian cities have been unable, by and large, to engage with small-scale providers to the urban poor. A corporate approach should be seriously contemplated here. Any fear that it would raise costs to the poor consumer is likely to turn out to be fallacious since, often, they end up paying large sums for water delivery by lorries operated by small private operators in situations of emergency that are neither few nor far between.

Water pollution cannot be controlled because the Central Pollution Control Board and state boards, while empowered to prevent, control and abate water pollution, cannot enforce the same effluent discharge standards, the result being that water supply is often polluted. Tax incentives for pollution control equipment specify particular abatement technologies without providing incentives for innovation. It is not too late to introduce taxes on polluting industries, and tax concessions for the adoption of innovation in abatement technologies, and for recycling. Informal regulation instruments such as green ratings should also be promoted further, though examples already exist of selected buildings qualifying for it in large urban settings.

Revival of neglected instruments

Among needed action, it is possible to identify a few that have existed in international experience as well as in India, though their roles would need a strong thrust in contemporary times. One is social service by Indian youth that may call for compulsory action. Another is a major push for women's upliftment in particular in visible political roles, guaranteeing their representation in powerful and high-value responsibilities. These aspects are addressed next.

A youth taskforce

Concerted youth-based efforts have occurred in the world for socio-economic development, for example, the French Doctors without Borders, the Chinese Barefoot Doctors or the US Peace Corps. Citing the example of contemporary China, a stint at the grassroots level in impoverished villages and towns continues to serve as a career-enhancing honour for high-level public sector officers, usually Communist Party members. For example, Malipo, a remote county in Yunnan province on the border with Vietnam, has been served by foreign ministry officers for three decades. The officers serve while taking into account their earlier education, for example, as teachers in primary schools or as water quality inspectors for rivers, or to guide residents in how to use market forces to their advantage. Some of them may assist in enhancing foreign investment after serving abroad in diplomatic assignments. Such assignments may last for as long as a couple of years. The reliance on party members reflects a desire to encourage a culture of honesty at all levels of the county administration. This participation has helped remove such counties – some 88 in number – from extreme poverty while, at the same time, comprising a step-up in the reputation of local governments.

Even India has tried an approach of exhortation of youth at the central and state levels in its post-independence phase through a National Cadet Corps (NCC) and other schemes though with limited success. At this exigent moment, that approach needs to be reinvented in the form of a youth task force and introduced on a war footing for the implementation of national development projects in particular for poverty alleviation. School leaving and college-graduating youth from every economic group should be asked, without exception, to serve the vulnerable rural and urban communities with government financing and appropriate training, as a compulsory service to the nation. The objective would be to implement guided measures to restore the rural-urban, agricultural-non-agricultural balance. Agricultural engineering institutes should be established on the same footing and high standards as IITs. Advanced students should be tasked with tracking reported data on bank and non-bank credit by economic sector so that any bias against the agricultural sector or rural industries can be quickly identified and corrective action taken by the authorities.

The youth task force should also be deployed to take on the responsibility of teaching in rural and urban schools for poor children, being assigned in their own states so that they can remain in easy access to their families, unless they themselves prefer to travel to the far corners of India. The youth should participate in monitoring the midday meals for school children over and above participating as teachers in primary and secondary schools.

The youth task force should also be asked to serve in rural health centres and in urban government hospitals that cater in particular to the urban poor. They should also be deployed to ensure the implementation of government's *swachh bharat* mission (SBM) and Open Defecation Free (ODF) programmes by monitoring the construction of toilets, reporting on the lack of availability of water and recording the incidence of their actual use as latrines.

How they are distributed among rural-urban, education or health functions should depend, to the extent feasible, on the students' subject preferences but they should be prepared to essentially serve in any sector. Evasion to being recruited should be subjected to heavy penalties. The service should be for one year for school leaving students, and for an additional year for college or university leaving students, with no exception of reduced tenures, in particular, for the children of the powerful and rich. Such a policy could be expected to be put in place and made operational without much opposition in a country whose armed forces are voluntary and there is no military draft. That being replaced by a compulsory service in the youth task force oriented to socio-economic policy rather than for preparation for war comprises a benign demand of the state. The incorporation and action of youth in itself would comprise a non-pecuniary income redistribution that would bring benefits to the poor.

At the same time, the private sector needs to play an active role, possibly comparable to that of government, in the provision of health care as a part of the corporate social responsibility (CSR) assigned to it by law. Government may even consider granting subsidies directly related to such participation based on clear criteria. In its segment of operations, the private sector could deploy the youth task force for the latter's learning as well as to assist in M&E activities carried out by government. Youth oriented in the study of banking and accountancy should be used to manage credit programmes for the very small borrower; and assigned to study and analyse the profiles of bank credit to the urban and rural sectors, and by size of loans and assets.

Regarding the first task, it may be argued that if education and health could be viewed as intangible assets that are transferred to a segment of the population, then tangible assets that should be seriously considered for transfer would include small and large components such as cattle and land respectively. Such programmes, once introduced, could also be monitored by youth. Authors such as Balboni et al. (2020) and Bandiera et al. (2017) have analysed samples of population in Bangladesh where the transfer of milch cows shared among very poor families at relatively low cost, led to a secular rise in their economic status. Indian youth could be put to use to help make such programmes successful in India. Appendix 11.1 contains a concise survey of this literature that points to the importance of such transfers in poverty eradication which is central to the proposition here. In India, the youth task force could be additionally deployed in the implementation of legislated land reform. Thus far, though it was relatively successful in several Indian states where land was transferred from absentee landlords to peasants, it did not occur in many states successfully or occurred only on paper with subalterns appearing as the face, rather than the real, beneficiaries of such transfer. Even where it was successful such as in the state of West Bengal in India, Sarkar (2011, 2012) found that the policies did not attain the final goal of assimilation across diverse groups mainly reflecting governance defaults.

Regarding the second task, youth with appropriate training should be guided in practical terms to work out the size and quality of debt that could assist the writing of recurrent government white papers on the quality and size of bank debt, rather than depending primarily on the banks' own versions thereof that can be full of homilies casting the banks in good light until the situation deteriorates so much that re-capitalization by government has to take place across the banking sector. Such studies can also be used to calculate and impose penalties including confiscation of assets of errant borrowers including large industrial houses for failure to service or amortize debt. It is bound to emerge that bank policy needs to change urgently from pursuing medium industry borrowers who have sunk between the cracks of shifting government regulations to examining large industry borrowers against whom little action is taken either by banks or government unless they fall into the bad books of government for reasons that are likely to be non-economic.[11]

Youth with other specializations could be made responsible for overseeing environmental projects at least in the aspect of rehabilitation and reimbursement of displaced groups and report their findings to government. This would keep government on the alert since such action has a tendency to slide into low priority status in a competition for the limited availability of public resources. Therefore, all in all, the youth task force should be involved in the country's education and mid-day meal programmes, health centres affecting the poor, and help achieve *swatchh bharat*, as well as analyse bank credit profiles and performance and, last but not least, track the rehabilitation of the displaced as a fallout from public sector projects such as highways and dams through tribal forest land. Based on their reports, government should feel obliged to take action on a regular basis; and, through direct action in providing education and primary health for poor children, the country as a

[11] Information on debt by size of bank debt is not only available, but the question has been raised several times in parliament. However, every time, government response has been to gloss over or obfuscate the information.

whole would gain immensely. In the first instance, this may be thought of as impractical but that is not so. As pointed out right at the beginning, other countries have done so. It is for India to pick itself up, assign serious social roles to its youth, imbue them with responsibility, and see them blossom into a generation of new Indians – a different sort of Indian than the ones trained at very low cost, merely comprising back-office service providers of the global IT sector or slash-and-burn policy implementers emanating from management institutes that help them emigrate to occupy positions in multinational enterprises (MNEs). There is nothing beneficial in such policies for India. A complete re-orientation in education that fundamentally alters its emphasis and outcomes, that utilizes it directly in national development and helps pull up those who are suffering in their state of poverty, is what is needed and what is achievable.

A step up for women

A step-up in women's status and their empowerment has to be a steadfast goal. Lower per capita income is associated with higher gender inequality; therefore, poorer states must push for raising their growth rates as rapidly as possible, together with better education and health of women. Whether their participation in the paid workforce is undergoing sustained improvement has to be continuously monitored, manifested in higher household income and reduction in poverty of the family. Lower fertility rates, lower child mortality and better education of children would accordingly be buttressed (Arora, 2012). Some authors have gone further by proposing the incorporation of gender budgeting in the fiscal planning of states (Chakraborty, 2021).

The Dowry Prevention Act dates back to 1961 though its punishment is a fine of only Rs 5000 or, in the worst case, jail of half a year. It reflects the deep-rooted hold of patriarchy and an associated convolution of the institution of marriage. This practice needs to be stopped not just in law but in practice. When prejudice-fed social mores such as dowry cannot be changed merely through encouragement or by passing a law, a stronger approach by the state through meaningful monitoring and commensurate legal action and punishment is needed. Implementation of measures to enhance the right to life and wellbeing for India's girls *pari passu* with strong ensured punishment for those who thwart such improvements is called for. A commitment to actual disbursement over and above gender budgeting should be given prominence with penetration in urban areas and, in particular, into the vast stretches of rural India. Chakraborty's (2021) work showed that gender budgeting and violence against women were inversely related in Indian states in the sense that, higher was the support of the state machinery for women, the lower was crime against women. A policy framework that includes gender budgeting can be a tool for accountability and social justice, but it needs a nuanced exploration to understand its potential. The objective has to be to identify how state machinery can support women with appropriate implementation tools in order to address often sensitive and hidden matters such as intra-household violence against women. It has to go beyond the establishment of 'short stay homes' for abused women in every state, though building such safe havens in itself is a crucial factor in supporting women, especially married women, in distress. Clearly, not only massive public investment but also creative vehicles for implementation are needed for women's safety in domestic and external circumstances.

Reforms in the political system

There are crucial political actions that need to buttress the menu of actions that has already been delineated. Political actions are needed both on the international front as well as in the domestic context. These are elaborated upon next.

International aspects

If it is agreed that colonialism, slavery and caste were the genesis of inequality and poverty, then steps must be taken to counter each of them. First, reverse the effects of the past through reparations from the colonizers to the colonized. Second, caste was, and is, a domestic practice and reparations to counter its effects have to take pecuniary and non-pecuniary forms. India has attempted to undertake action through its constitution though complete success is far from having been achieved. Slavery in the United States was also a domestic institution; and its ramifications continue to ripple through society to this day in the form of racism. Clearly it is not just anti-racism laws that have to be passed but the formulation of reparations that will redress the inequalities that slavery brought about. It can be carried out through massive domestic transfers if only the US government were willing to undertake such a task. Such domestic action would go a long way to redress inequality and vanquish poverty.

Lest it should be forgotten, cross-country reparations brought about by colonialism do not comprise foreign aid. The latter is a voluntary and flexible contribution while the former is tied to colonial exploitation or crime in the past. Colonialism and its portents have different connotations reflecting its intra- and inter-continental reach. In this case reparations have to be undertaken across international boundaries. That would call for massive global action and an elaborate framework for several channels of transfer to operate. It is likely to assume gigantic proportions, perhaps in the scale of the United Nations itself. There is no doubt that it would be a formidable task but the fact that already there is a considerable amount of analysis and proposals regarding the matter reveals the prevailing concerns of researchers and policymakers alike.

Buxbaum (2005) recounted the reparations to the Allied Powers from the Axis – mainly the Third Reich – pertaining to the after-effects of the Second World War. It imparted a sense of urgency to extract the maximum possible from the defeated party. It could be said to have begun in 1950 after the formulation of the Paris Reparation Agreement in 1946 and continued for four decades until the reunification of Germany in 1990. Germany's pre-war debt with various countries was also calculated and built into the calculations. In addition, the millions of victims on whose person and property harm was inflicted could also seek compensation for those wrongs. In 1952, West Germany agreed to pay Israel the cost of resettling Holocaust survivors and it resulted in considerable investment in its economy. It is this latter aspect that has direct relevance to reparations related to colonialism together with how a legal perspective may be developed for it.

Suggestions have also been made regarding the just compensation for waging an unjust war by the US to Viet Nam (Lerner, 2017) or for its exploitative and unilateral behaviour in international trade relations (Singh, 2017). Selected analysts are also raising issue with the impact of World Bank and International Monetary Fund (IMF) policies as having harmed countries where they imposed them, a comprehensive analysis having emerged by Lukka (2020). The argument is based on the premise that those policies hit mainly ex-colonized countries and left the poorest segments of such communities behind.

Often policies of multilateral organizations insisted on the privatization of social delivery institutions. To give a handful of examples with respect to economic programmes, they included water delivery systems in Tanzania, or the conversion of farmland from food crops to cash crops such as cotton in Sudan that accelerated the desertification of large tracts of land. These affected the lowest income deciles adversely. Other examples are multilateral lending for mineral extraction including that of coal, such as in the Philippines, Botswana and South Africa while advanced economies protect their own environment from the vagaries of climate change. For the developing economies that borrow, the long-term ramifications have turned out to be verging on climate disaster.

A first step that needs to be taken is the repudiation of all debt of the Global South to the Global North in a Truth and Reconciliation approach to reconciliation for the past and decolonization for all future (Lukka, 2020). However, second, this has to be followed by a matrix of the type and quantification of reparations that would translate into a Contract of Radical Humanism of a flow of funds from the North to the South until the books of accounts are cleared. In this debate, it appears that sometimes the objective of transfer of resources gets lost in whether and how there will be acknowledgment of the crimes committed against the South by the North.

While such acknowledgement should be vigorously pursued, it would be fallacy for it to be converted into a conduit to the stalling of funds transfer on a sustained basis. Let not the South get embroiled in broad platforms but, rather, focus primarily on finance – the calculation of reparations based on models projecting back to the past – and placing it formally on the table. Gains from finance are well understood by the North and that is the route and instrument that has to be used.

Some countries have initiated unilateral action. Tunisia's Truth and Dignity Commission, founded in 2013, issued a memorandum to the World Bank, IMF, and France for reparations for Tunisian victims of human rights violations. Lukka (2020) reported that it found that,

> [T]he IMF and World Bank bore 'a share of responsibility' for social unrest linked to historic structural adjustment policies. It claimed that both institutions pushed the Tunisian government to freeze wages and recruitment in the civil service, and reduce subsidies on basic consumer goods, which led to social crises and conflicts. The commission called for three acts of reparation: apology, financial compensation to victims, and cancellation of Tunisia's multilateral debt to these institutions. The IMF and the World Bank failed to respond to the commission's calls, while Tunisia once again had to resort to borrowing from the IMF to respond to the COVID-19 pandemic in April. (pp 3–4)

It is not surprising that economics-oriented multilateral organizations would not respond. Such efforts would have more success if countries actually took a joint stand and pursued the matter together. A United Nations (UN) route would be a preferred interim solution though some analysts have pointed out that even the UN has struggled to establish whether there is any legal basis for reparations that would be binding on member states (Dunham, 2017). Thus far the UN has attempted to facilitate dialogue between member states and provide expertise in the fields of international law, human rights, and international peace and security and on constraints to development that are directly relevant to reparations. To be noted, however, is that the International Court of Justice (ICJ) which is a judiciary body under the UN system and takes up cases of international legal standards has, so far, not taken up reparations issues. Dunham (2017) stated that,

> In this forum, individual postcolonial states could bring a legal case against a former colonial power, as long as they are both members of the UN, for damages (that) occurred under colonial rule. After examining the international legal precedence and evidence for the case, the

> court would then issue a binding judgement that would permanently settle the dispute between the two countries. The drawback to such an approach is that, because the UN has no mechanism to enforce these decisions, it would be up to individual member states to enforce the decision or to impose penalties, such as economic embargos, on states that refuse to implement the court's decision. The CARICOM group of Caribbean states have expressed their intention to bring a lawsuit against former colonial powers in this forum; however, court proceedings have yet to begin. (p 8)

Reflecting the limitations of the UN system, therefore, while it can play an important role in the initial years, eventually only the establishment of, and pursuit through, an independent global commission that is empowered politically and financially by the South, can perform the task comprehensively and successfully.

The need for joint action from the South is quintessential to confronting former colonial powers that raise issue with the legality of postcolonial reparations since actions during the colonial era were not illegal at that time. Therefore, in Dunham's (2017) view,

> Direct state-to-state or group-to-state negotiations are seen as the most effective means of pressing the reparation agenda. For instance, a recent case that was heard in the British High Court has led to reparations for a group of 5,000 Kenyan elders who were tortured under British colonial rule. It is often easier to bring a case to the domestic court system of the former colonial power than trying to navigate the complexities of the international system which may not even lead to a binding ruling. (p 5)

On 31 December 2020, the UN General Assembly adopted Resolution 75/237 calling for concrete action for the elimination of racism, racial discrimination, xenophobia and related intolerance, and former colonial powers for reparations – consistent with paragraphs 157 and 158 of the Durban Declaration and Programme of Action (DDPA)[12] to redress the historical injustices of slavery and the slave trade, including the transatlantic slave trade. Further, on 12 July 2021, the UN High Commissioner for Human Rights issued Report A/HRC/47/53 that declared,

[12] UN General Assembly (2020). DDPA was adopted by consensus at the 2001 World Conference against Racism in Durban, South Africa. It symbolizes the need for recognition at the national, regional and international level, that racism is a global concern, its eradication should be a universal effort, and that no country can claim to be free of racism. The DDPA is not legally binding yet has a strong moral value and is a basis for worldwide advocacy, see https://www.un.org/en/durbanreview2009/ddpa.shtml.

> Structures and systems that were designed and shaped by enslavement, colonialism and successive racially discriminatory policies and systems must be transformed. Reparations should not only be equated with financial compensation. They also comprise measures aimed at restitution, rehabilitation, satisfaction and guarantees of non-repetition, including, for example, formal acknowledgment and apologies, memorialization and institutional and educational reforms. Reparations are essential for transforming relationships of discrimination and inequity and for mutually committing to and investing in a stronger, more resilient future of dignity, equality and non-discrimination for all. (p 20)

The Report was a silver lining but when a one-day high-level meeting of the General Assembly at the level of Heads of State and Government was called to commemorate the twentieth anniversary of the adoption of the DDPA, Australia, Austria, Bulgaria, Canada, Croatia, the Czech Republic, France, Germany, Hungary, Israel, Italy, the Netherlands, New Zealand, the United Kingdom and the United States announced their boycott of the meeting scheduled for 22 September 2021 under the guise that it represented anti-Semitism.

This is exactly why a persistent, multilateral effort from the South is so important to take the issue forward because, while individual researchers and social thinkers from the North may profess or seriously believe in an equal, non-racial global society, their governments are unlikely to take an affirmative position on it. Irrespective of whether they are temerarious or fearful of likely reparations they would be judged to make, they have revealed their steadfast adherence to the premise of colonial extraction. This appears to be their fundamental, underlying stance that has not changed even after two decades into the new millennium.

That opposition is bound to turn around at some point if a critical mass emerges in favour of reparations. Caution is needed that the North does not continue to burrow into the confidence of the South with covert and overt payments selectively to nations and individuals in the South. Ultimately, the South has to be able to stand together despite its challenges and heterogeneity if ultimate success is to be experienced on the matter of justice in the form of international reparations from the ex-colonial to the ex-colonized countries as per the previously mentioned report of the UN.

The domestic side

India had once aspired for the endorsement by the United Nations General Assembly for inclusion in the Security Council. There is little to show in terms of moving forward in the area of strategic advancement or achievement that could lead to such a possibility. Such an eventuality would have been a significant step for India's poverty condition since the world would look directly at what standards India was establishing in terms of the welfare of its people. In addition, India has waited in the wings for an IMF quota increase while China has been fully successful just as with Security Council membership. Today, China's elevated position in all multilateral organizations has enabled it to assume not only the very top positions but also a significant proportion of high-ranking jobs in them. India does not compare with China in its reach or command over international resources that it could have used to its own benefit for society and security. Fortunately, India's role in the Group of Twenty (G20) nations was enhanced through active participation and its contribution in the OECD's formulation of recommendations to minimize tax avoidance by MNEs has been noted. Such roles have to be forged also in other directions including at the Security Council and IMF.

India's receding international reputation cannot be studied without placing its domestic politics under a magnifying glass. Observers tend to mention the political system in passing as if it were a 'soft' or, increasingly, a dangerous area to confront. However, efforts against poverty and inequality, shorn of the context of India's political system and associated corruption would, in the final analysis, remain toothless. On 10 October 2012, the prime minister had said,

> The mindless atmosphere of negativity and pessimism that is sought to be created over ... corruption can do us no good. ... Experience has shown that big-ticket corruption is mostly related to operations by commercial entities. It is, therefore, also proposed to include corporate failure to prevent bribery as a new offence on the supply side.[13]

Expressions and efforts to curb corruption should not be thwarted. Yet recent reports are that changes in law have charted an alarming course and tax raids appear to be used for the wrong reasons. Taking up the context of COVID-19 during which thousands of migrant workers were obliged to return to their villages without notice or any government support, the *Economist* (2021) reported,

> Mr. Sood's foundation ... helped some 90,000 people find their way home and average 4 million meals to the hungry. So much cash has poured in that the charity now grants scholarships to COVID orphans, sponsors jobs, pays for medical care, runs a blood bank and is

[13] Prime Minister's speech, 19th Conference of the Central Bureau of Investigation and State Anti-Corruption Bureaux. *Central Bureau of Investigation*, 10 October 2012, New Delhi. Available at https://cbi.gov.in/DesktopModules/MainDashboard/NewsPDF/19_ACB_PM_2012-10-10.pdf, accessed 9 October 2021.

> building a hospital. … there is no doubt that Mr. Sood's effectiveness at delivering relief made blustering politicians look bad … India's leaders have routinely abused tools of state power. … tax sleuths were rifling through his bookshelves. … an anti-money-laundering agency raided addresses associated with Harsh Mander, an activist who is perhaps India's most worthy candidate for the Nobel peace prize. Among Mr Mander's initiatives is a volunteer group that seeks to heal sectarian scars by quietly consoling the victims of attacks motivated by hatred. (p 50)

The newspaper went on to describe how India's tax administration pursued small news organizations such as Tax Laundry, Newsclick in February 2021, and the Dainik Bhaskar Group in July for reporting accurately on COVID-19 deaths, widely estimated at 4,50,000 at the time. Workers were held in their offices, phones confiscated and data copied. Another avenue was the closure of some 19,000 NGOs including local chapters of Amnesty International and Human Rights Watch.

Yet, a new law made political parties not liable for illegal acceptance of foreign donations in the past, and introduced a 'reformed' system allowing unlimited, anonymous gifts to political parties. The accounts of the giant PM Cares Fund, set up for COVID relief to which millions of state employees had to contribute, are not apparent. As the *Economist* pointed out, 'With a click of the button on the fund's website, foreign well-wishers can pour money in' (p 50).

What is apparent is that fundamental reform of the financing of politics and elections as well as associated government practices are crucial. It is not certain if anything other than a mass movement would bring India to successfully confront the challenges it faces. Though many an obstacle were placed against the progress of a recent farmers' movement, it could not be nipped in the bud. Instead, government, which had failed to pre-consult farmers or reassure them of the benefits of change, had to announce the withdrawal of the draconian laws it had introduced without adequate parliamentary debate. It is happenstance that the announcement preceded expected national elections.

Reform measures are indeed needed to confront tax evasion by those who continue to steal from the nation's welfare especially as tax evasion continues to finance elections. But repeated tax raids, and the way they are conducted against imagined adversaries, comprise erroneous policy for any democracy to be taken seriously. Rather, what needs to be done comprises: (1) contribution limits to political parties and candidates should be removed; (2) names of contributors to political parties and candidates should be required to be revealed; (3) persons should be able to announce his or her candidature from any party *pari passu* with a 'primary' process that would select a final party candidate rather than giving out electoral tickets to compete in an election based on graft or other favours; (4) free voting by members of parliament should be allowed rather than restricting voting along party lines; (5) responsibility should be affixed on political parties regarding their success or failure in matching outcomes with expressed objectives in party manifestos; and (6) among other policies that should be explicitly listed, a population policy should be included to reduce the fertility rate. Though the rate has declined in recent years, the absolute number continues to grow very rapidly in cross-country comparisons (see Chapter 3, Figure 3.3). Party manifestos should spell out a mix of incentives and disincentives addressed towards population control for the 2024 parliamentary elections.

Some of these proposals are likely to appear to be unachievable under the banners of any of India's governments of recent times, but they have to be hammered in through societal persistence. Media has to revive the instrument of courage, if not honesty, and play its part despite the challenging conditions it confronts. Otherwise, as power concentrates and corruption finds a safe haven, as cruelty on the lowest castes intensifies, and wealth concentration rates gallop to the global top, while preoccupation for the care of the poor and vulnerable recedes, it is unlikely that inequality will ever be realistically reduced, or poverty eradicated.

Concluding remarks

The thrust of the hypothesis in this volume has been that, unless the entire gamut of required economic, social-economic, anthropogenic and political reform measures are considered holistically and sincerely, poverty eradication and inequality alleviation will not be achieved comprehensively and will remain shrouded in obfuscated statistics and feckless intellectual noise. Any government will continue to remain absolved on the basis of small poverty-related actions that it takes in its annual fiscal budgets while continuing to hide behind a political system made overtly beneficial to the wealthy. The daily life of civil society has become near impossible. Corrupt local regulatory bodies, and associated scarcity of water and electricity and faulty sewerage that has led to massive flooding even in upper-class neighbourhoods have, in turn, brought out their denizens hurling stones and bricks. Conditions in urban slums are worse. Slum dwellers often pass ten or more hours daily without electricity, and are likely to receive just an hour of water. With every rainy season, dengue makes its inevitable return, nesting in stagnant water that fails to be drained or garbage cleared despite being budgeted for. In spite of such adversity, India's poor do not loot.

Yet, it is true that the mandated upward movements in the political, and commensurate social and educational, status of the backward classes are unique to India. It gives Indians hope. Indians are an active, optimistic people. Economic activity reigns over slothfulness. It is they who keep society functioning in contrast to the political oligarchs or the complacent, protected bureaucrats that have comprised formidable bottlenecks to the conduct of the daily life of the masses. An oligarchy of the bureaucracy and policymakers emerged as India's post-independence history evolved and became consolidated to serve vested interests in successive governments. Even as malpractices continue, no institution, including the once vibrant, globally reputed media, stands up with its earlier vigour, leave alone combat the slide. And those who do are harassed, jailed or face worse outcomes. Society has to be handed back to the people to forge a new social contract that could reinstate democratic institutions and generate a socio-economy in which poverty is eradicated and inequality tamed.

A consideration of (1) family orientation, framework and attitudes; (2) the role of traditions: the bipolar male-female divide, and non-acceptance of gender options; (3) fear and superstition that pervade family and societal practices; (4) belief in *karma* or the inevitability of suffering and in subsequent births to assuage it; and, last but not least, (5) associated acceptance of a presumed natural limit on human rights. They all need to undergo fundamental change in order for India to undergo a meaningful transformation of society and for all to recognize the eradication of poverty and alleviation of inequality as the topmost goals of society rather than as an annual fiscal budget allocation exercise that satisfies and absolves policy makers.

References

Amery, Jean. (2009) *At the Mind's Limits: Contemplations by a Survivor on Auschwitz and Its Realities*. Translated by Sidney Rosenfeld and Stella P. Rosenfeld. Bloomington: Indiana University Press. (First published in 1966.)

Arora, Rashmi Umesh. (2012) 'Gender inequality, economic development, and globalization: a state level analysis of India', *The Journal of Developing Areas*, 46(1): 147–64. Available at doi:10.1353/jda.2012.0019, accessed 12 August 2021.

Balboni, Clare, Oriana Bandiera, Robin Burgess, Maitreesh Ghatak and Anton Heil. (2020) 'Why Do People Stay Poor?' Paper presented at the Inequalities Seminar Series, International Inequalities Institute (III), London School of Economics, 29 September. Available at https://www.lse.ac.uk/International-Inequalities/Assets/Documents/Slides/III-Inequalities-Seminar-Slides/Why-do-people-stay-poor-slides.pdf, accessed 4 October 2021.

Bandiera, Oriana, Robin Burgess, Narayan Das, Selim Gulesci, Imran Rasul and Munshi Sulaiman. (2017) 'Labor markets and poverty in village economies', *Quarterly Journal of Economics*, 132(2): 811–70. Available at https://doi.org/10.1093/qje/qjx003, accessed 4 October 2021.

Banerjee, Abhijit and Esther Duflo. (2008) 'Mandated empowerment: handing antipoverty policy back to the poor?', *Annals of the New York Academy Sciences*, 1136(1): 333–41. Available at https://doi.org/10.1196/annals.1425.019, accessed 22 June 2021.

Bari, Faisal, Kashif Malik, Muhammad Meki and Simon Quinn. (2021) 'Asset-Based Microfinance for Microenterprises: Evidence from Pakistan (February 1)', CEPR Discussion Paper No. DP15768. Available at SSRN: https://ssrn.com/abstract=3783994, accessed 30 June 2021.

Berhampur Municipal Corporation. (2021-22) 'Annual Budget', Berhampur. Odisha. Available at https://openbudgetsindia.org/organisation/berhampur-municipal-corporation, accessed 5 October 2021.

Buxbaum, Richard M. (2005) 'A legal history of international reparations.' *Berkeley Journal of International Law*, 23(2): 314–346. Available at www.researchgate.net/profile/Richard-Buxbaum/publication/241796497_A_Legal_History_of_International_Reparations/links/55ce3bf508ae6a8813848aa9/A-Legal-History-of-International-Reparations.pdf, accessed 8 October 2021.

Chakraborty, Lekha. (2021) 'Why Indian states need to incorporate gender budgeting in their fiscal planning', *The Wire*, 16 August. Available at https://thewire.in/society/gender-budgeting-human-development-index, accessed 17 August 2021.

Chancel, Lucas Thomas Piketty, Emmanuel Saez and Gabriel Zucman. (2021) 'World Inequality Report 2022', World Inequality Lab. Available at https://wir2022.wid.world/www-site/uploads/2021/12/WorldInequalityReport2022_Full_Report.pdf, accessed 15 December 2021.

Colonial Reparations. (2021) 'Reparations at the United Nations', *Newsletter*, September. Available at www.colonialismreparation.org/en/, accessed 8 October 2021.

District Urban Development Agency. (2019) 'District Survey Report', Ganjam District, Odisha state. Available at https://ganjam.nic.in/about-district/, accessed 5 October 2021.

Dunham, Anna. (2017) 'Should There be Reparations to Post-Colonial States?', ODUMUNC 2017 Issue Brief, Old Dominion University. Available at https://www.odu.edu/content/dam/odu/offices/mun/2017/ib-2017-fourth-reparations-final.pdf, accessed 8 October 2021.

Gautam, Ankur. (2019) 'Understanding behavior change for ending open defecation in rural India: A review of India's sanitation policy efforts', in Naoyuki Yoshino, Eduardo Araral and K. E. Seetha Ram (eds) *Water Insecurity and Sanitation in Asia.* Tokyo: Asian Development Bank Institute. Available at https://www.adb.org/publications/water-insecurity-and-sanitation-asia, accessed 31 August 2021.

Ghatak, Maitreesh. (2021 'India's inequality problem', *The India Forum*, 2 July. Available at www.theindiaforum.in/article/does-india-have-inequality-problem, accessed 2 July 2021.

Gilroy, Paul. (2019) 'Never Again: Refusing Race and Salvaging the Human', The 2019 Holberg Lecture. Available at https://holbergprisen.no/en/news/holberg-prize/2019-holberg-lecture-laureate-paul-gilroy, accessed 1 October 2021.

Government of Odisha. (2021) 'Highlights of Annual Budget, 2021–22', Finance Department. Available at https://finance.odisha.gov.in/sites/default/files/2021-02/Budget%20highlights%202021-22-Eng.pdf, accessed 5 October 2021.

Kotha, Ashrita Prasad and Pradnya Satish Talekar. (2021) 'Earmarked taxes: an Indian case study', *eJournal of Tax Research*, 19(1): 97–120. Available at SSRN: https://ssrn.com/abstract=3880472, accessed 28 September 2021.

Krishnan, S. (2022) 'Faceless Assessment in India, with a Rejoinder by PVSS Prasad,' in P. Shome (ed) *Prevailing and Emerging Dilemmas in International Taxation.* Gurugram: International Tax Research and Analysis Foundation and Oakbridge Publishers, pp 227–68.

Lerner, Adam B. (2017) 'Understanding India's case for colonial reparations', *PacificStandard*, 23 May. Available at https://psmag.com/economics/indias-case-for-reparations, accessed 8 October 2021.

Levi, Primo. (1974) 'A past that we believed should never return', *Corriere della sera*, 8 May.

Levinas, Emmanuel. (2006) *Humanism and the Other.* Urbana: University of Illinois Press. (First published in French in 1972.)

Lukka, Priya. (2020) 'Repairing Harm Caused: What Could a Reparations Approach Mean for The IMF And World Bank?' *Bretton Woods Project*, 6 October. https://www.brettonwoodsproject.org/2020/10/repairing-harm-caused-what-could-a-reparations-approach-mean-for-the-imf-and-world-bank/, accessed 8 October 2021.

PwC[14]. (2021) 'Worldwide Tax Summaries'. Available at www.pwc.com/gx/en/services/tax/worldwide-tax-summaries.html, accessed 7 January 2023.

[14] Earlier, Price Waterhouse Coopers.

Sarkar, Swagato. (2011) 'The impossibility of just land acquisition', *Economic and Political Weekly*, 8 October, xlvi(41): 35–38. Available at www.researchgate.net/publication/275644573_The_Impossibility_of_Just_Land_Acquisition, accessed 29 June 2021.

Sarkar, Swagato. (2012) 'Between egalitarianism and domination: governing differences in a transitional society', *Third World Quarterly*, 33(4): 669–684. Available at https://www.researchgate.net/publication/254353070_Between_Egalitarianism_and_Domination_governing_differences_in_a_transitional_society, accessed 29 June 2021.

Shah, Tamanna M. (2019) 'Water supply and sanitation: PPP "good practices" from India', in Naoyuki Yoshino, Eduardo Araral and K. E. Seetha Ram (eds) *Water Insecurity and Sanitation in Asia*, pp 128–54. Tokyo: Asian Development Bank Institute. Available at https://www.adb.org/publications/water-insecurity-and-sanitation-asia, accessed 31 August 2021.

Shome, Parthasarathi. (2021a) *Taxation – History, Theory, Law and Administration*. Cham, Switzerland: Springer Texts in Business and Economics.

Shome, Parthasarathi. (ed) (2021b) *Reimagining International Taxation*, Rejoinder to ch. 7, pp 189–96. Gurugram: ITRAF, Oakbridge Publishers.

Singh, J. P. (2017) *Sweet Talk: Paternalism and Collective Action in North-South Trade Relations*. Stanford: Stanford University Press.

Tax Administration Reform Commission (TARC). (2015) *Executive Summary*, Volume I, Government of India, Ministry of Finance TARC/Report/36/2014-15, New Delhi.

The Economist. (2021) 'A raid against dissent'. 2 October. London. Available at www.economist.com/asia/2021/10/02, accessed 7 January 2023.

Tiwari, Piyush. (2019) 'The water conundrum in India: an institutional perspective', in Naoyuki Yoshino, Eduardo Araral and K. E. Seetha Ram (eds) *Water Insecurity and Sanitation in Asia*. Tokyo: Asian Development Bank Institute. Available at https://www.adb.org/publications/water-insecurity-and-sanitation-asia, accessed 31 August 2021.

UN General Assembly. (2020) 'Durban Declaration and Programme of Action (DDPA)', World Conference against Racism. Durban, South Africa.

UN High Commissioner for Human Rights. (2021) 'OHCHR Report on Promotion and Protection of The Human Rights and Fundamental Freedoms of Africans and Of People of African Descent Against Excessive Use of Force and Other Human Rights Violations by Law Enforcement Officers'. United Nations General Assembly. Available at https://undocs.org/en/A/HRC/47/53, accessed 11 October 2021.

World Bank. (2020) *Ease of Doing Business 2020*. Washington, DC: World Bank. Available at doi:10.1596/978-1-4648-1440-2, accessed 1 May 2021.

World Inequality Lab. (2022) 'World Inequality Report'. Available at https://wir2022.wid.world/executive-summary/, accessed 8 January 2023.

Zinn, Howard. (1970) 'The problem is civil disobedience' (November). First printed in Hugh Davis Graham, (ed) *Violence: The Crisis of American Confidence*, Baltimore: Johns Hopkins Press, (1971) pp 154–62. (Reprinted in Howard Zinn, *The Zinn Reader: Writings on Disobedience and Democracy*, New York: Seven Stories Press [1997] pp 403–11.)

APPENDIX 2.1

Cash Use in India: A Cross-Country Comparison

The Bank of International Settlements Red Book of March 2021 reported 2018 figures which enable a comparison of cash use in Brazil, China and India. To begin, cash in circulation in terms of GDP has been higher in India (11.3 per cent) than in China (8.9 per cent) though in Brazil it has been much lower (3.8 per cent) reflecting a mammoth successful attempt in the 1990s towards non-cash use. Accordingly, India's non-cash transactions volumes trail that of China as shown in Table A2.1. In 2014, in terms of the number of non-cash transactions, India was about one-eighth that of China. Though India's position did improve from 2014, it nevertheless remained one-eighth that of China, reflecting a significant jump in non-cash use in China (so that India failed to catch up). In per-capita terms, the improvement in India was an impressive 350 per cent, nevertheless falling short of China's 426 per cent. It may be noted that, reflecting earlier reform in Brazil, the numbers and increases thereof had already stabilized there over the years considered.

Non-cash transactions have various forms. Table A2.2 reveals their percentage distribution and change during 2014–18. An examination of their distribution in 2018 reveals significant variations among the three

Table A2.1: Non-cash transactions, 2014–18

	Total No. (billion)			Increase (%)			Increase (%) per-capita		
	2014	2016	2018	2014–16	2016–18	2014–18	2014–16	2016–18	2014–18
Brazil	27.7	29.0	34.6	4.6	19.4	24.9	2.9	17.7	21.2
China	36.6	96.6	198.4	163.9	105.3	441.7	159.3	102.9	425.9
India	4.6	10.9	24.4	135.3	122.9	424.4	100.0	125.0	350.0

Source: Bank of International Settlements (Red Book Statistics), March 2021

Table A2.2: Mix (%) of non-cash transactions[1]

	Credit transfers[2]			Direct debits[3]			Cheques[4]			Cards[5] and e-money[6] payments		
	2014	**2016**	**2018**	**2014**	**2016**	**2018**	**2014**	**2016**	**2018**	**2014**	**2016**	**2018**
Brazil	36.0	34.3	31.4	20.0	18.4	18.6	4.3	3.0	1.8	39.8	44.3	48.2
China	7.0	8.2	4.6	7.1	1.5	0.3	1.6	0.3	0.1	84.3	90.0	95.0
India	31.4	35.3	48.7	5.0	3.3	2.2	25.8	11.0	4.6	37.9	50.3	44.5

Note: [1] Per cent of total cashless payments. [2] *Credit transfers* are payment instruments based on payment orders or possibly sequences of payment orders made for the purpose of placing funds at the disposal of the payee. Both the payment orders and the funds move from the payer's institution to the payee's institution, possibly via several other institutions as intermediaries and/or one or more payment systems. [3] *Direct debits* are payment instruments based on preauthorized debits, possibly recurrent, of the payer's account by the payee. [4] Cheques are payment instruments based on written orders from one party (the drawer) to another (the drawee, normally a bank) requiring the drawee to pay a specified sum on demand to the drawer or to a third party specified by the drawer. Cheques may be used for settling debts and withdrawing money from banks. Cheques include traveler's cheques and banker's drafts. [5] *Cards* are payment instruments based on a unique number that can be used to initiate a payment, cash withdrawal or cash deposit that is processed using/over a card scheme or – for withdrawals and deposits at the ATM – within the network operated by the issuer of the card. The number can be stored on a plastic card (one of the traditional meanings of the word 'card'), on another physical device (e.g., key tag, sticker, smartphone) or can be held virtually without a physical device. [6] *E-money* is prepaid value stored electronically, which represents a liability of the e-money issuer (a bank, an e-money institution or any other entity authorized or allowed to issue e-money in the local jurisdiction), and which is denominated in a currency backed by an authority. The aggregate does not include value of digital currencies as per the 2015 Committee on Payments and Market Infrastructures (CPMI) report 'Digital currencies'. For the purpose of this data collection, prepaid value stored electronically that is accepted only by the issuer (single-purpose) or by the issuer and a limited number of organizations/merchants, at a limited range of locations or for a limited number of purposes (limited uses) are not included under e-money.

Source: Bank of International Settlements (Red Book Statistics), March 2021

countries. India uses credit transfers and cheques more than Brazil or China while using credit cards less. Brazil uses the most direct debits compared to the others while China's use of credit cards and e-money payments is the highest, reflecting its low use of direct debits or cheques.

A comparison of the changes that occurred during 2014–18 reveals different trends. First, the use of cards and e-money payments in Brazil has overtaken those of cheques and transfers. In China, cards and e-money payments have grown and direct debits and cheques have become almost insignificant and, of course, there are low reported credit transfers. In India too, the use of cheques and direct debits reduced, while there was a significant increase in credit transfers and cards and e-money payments. It may perhaps be anticipated that both India and Brazil's future experience would also move in the direction of higher shares for cards and e-money payments.

Some may find it alarming at what pace India's cash use has been increasing compared to Brazil and China (see Table 2.2). What measures should India take? First, track for the next five years, its cash in circulation in terms of GDP, the objective being an observable decrease. Post demonetization, cash circulation dipped to 8.7 per cent of GDP in 2016 but, since then, it regained a rising trajectory until 2018. Second, track the number of non-cash transactions and whether their growth is approaching the gigantic leaps that China has achieved. Third, among non-cash components, are more Indians using net banking and increasing the use of credit transfers and direct debits. Banks should implement helpful programmes to educate even zero balance accountholders to use net banking. Without these changes, a salient ramification of any demonetization – to quickly move from cash to non-cash use – will remain unachieved.

APPENDIX 2.2

Macro-Economic Comparisons: Selected Economies

Table A2.3: Macro-economic indicators

Indicator	Brazil				China				India				
	2010	2016	2018	2019	2010	2016	2018	2019	1990	2010	2016	2018	2019
GDP growth (annual %)	7.5	-3.3	1.3	1.1	10.6	6.8	6.7	6.1	5.5	8.5	8.3	6.1	4.2
Exports of goods and services (% of GDP)	11	12	15	14	27	20	19	18	7	22	19	20	18
Imports of goods and services (% of GDP)	12	12	15	15	24	17	18	17	8	27	21	24	21
Gross capital formation (% of GDP)	22	15	15	15	47	43	44	43	29	40	30	32	30
Debt service (% of exports of goods, services and primary income)	18.4	51	33.1	53.1	3.0	6.9	8.2	9.6	33.0	6.8	17.3	11.4	9.0
Foreign direct investment (FDI), net inflows (US$ billions)	82.3	74.3	78.2	73.5	243.7	174.7	235.4	155.8	0.23	27.4	44.5	42.1	50.6
Military expenditure (% of GDP)	1.5	1.4	1.5	1.5	1.9	1.9	1.9	1.9	3.1	2.7	2.5	2.4	2.4

Source: World Development Indicators, 2020, World Bank (last updated on 16 December, 2020)

Table A2.4: Selected technology orientation

	Brazil				China					India			
Indicator													
	2010	**2016**	**2018**	**2019**	**2010**	**2016**	**2018**	**2019**	**1990**	**2010**	**2016**	**2018**	**2019**
Mobile cellular subscriptions (per 100 persons)	100.6	118.4	98.8	98.8	62.8	96.5	115.0	120.4	0	60.9	85.1	86.9	84.3
Individuals using the Internet (% of population)	40.7	60.9	67.5	67.5	34.3	53.2	54.3	54.3	0	7.5	22.0	34.5	34.5
High-technology exports (% of manufactured exports)	12	15	13	13	32	30	31	31	4	8	8	9	10

Source: World Development Indicators, 2020, World Bank (last updated on 16 December 2020)

Table A2.5: Consecutive administrations in India: performance on development indicators (2000–19)

Indicator	NDA-I		UPA-I		UPA-II		NDA-II		NDA-III
	2000	**2003**	**2004**	**2008**	**2009**	**2013**	**2014**	**2018**	**2019**
Macro-economic[1, 2]									
Inflation, GDP deflator (annual %)[3]	3.6	3.9	5.7	9.2	7.0	6.2	3.3	4.6	2.9
Agriculture, forestry and fishing, value added (% of GDP)	21.6	19.6	17.8	16.8	16.7	17.1	16.8	16.0	16.7
Industry (including construction), value added (% of GDP)	27.3	27.5	29.2	31.1	31.1	28.4	27.7	26.4	24.2
Exports of goods and services (% of GDP)	13.0	14.9	17.9	24.1	20.4	25.4	23.0	19.9	18.4
Imports of goods and services (% of GDP)	13.9	15.6	19.6	29.3	25.9	28.4	26.0	23.6	21.1
Gross capital formation (% of GDP)	26.7	29.5	36.1	37.9	40.1	34.0	34.3	31.7	29.7
Personal remittances, received (current US$) (millions)	12.9	21.0	18.8	50.0	49.2	70.0	70.4	78.8	83.3
Foreign direct investment, net inflows (BoP, current US$) (billions)	3.6	3.7	5.4	43.4	35.6	28.2	34.6	42.1	50.6
External debt stocks, total (DOD, current US$) (billions)[4]	101.1	118.9	123.6	227.1	256.3	427.2	457.5	521.0	560.0

Consecutive administrations in India: performance on development indicators (2000–19)

Indicator	NDA-I		UPA-I		UPA-II		NDA-II		NDA-III
	2000	**2003**	**2004**	**2008**	**2009**	**2013**	**2014**	**2018**	**2019**
Total debt service (% of exports of goods, services and primary income)[5]	17.1	29.2	14.5	9.7	6.0	8.1	18.6	11.4	9.0
Revenue, excluding grants (% of GDP)	11.7	11.9	12.1	12.8	11.4	12.6	11.6	13.1	..
Tax revenue (% of GDP)	8.8	9.1	9.6	11.0	9.8	11.0	10.0	12.0	
Military expenditure (% of GDP)	2.9	2.7	2.8	2.6	2.9	2.5	2.5	2.4	2.4
Mobile cellular subscriptions (per 100 persons)	0.3	3.0	4.6	28.9	43.1	69.2	72.9	86.9	84.3

Table A2.5: Consecutive administrations in India: performance on development indicators (2000–19) (continued)

Indicator	**NDA-I**		**UPA-I**		**UPA-II**		**NDA-II**		**NDA-III**
	2000	**2003**	**2004**	**2008**	**2009**	**2013**	**2014**	**2018**	**2019**
Individuals using the Internet (% of population)	0.5	1.7	2.0	4.4	5.1	15.1	21.0	34.5	34.5
Socio-economic indicators									
Population growth (annual %)	1.8	1.7	1.6	1.5	1.4	1.2	1.1	1.0	1.0
Life expectancy at birth, total (years)	62.5	63.7	64.1	65.8	66.2	67.9	68.3	69.4	..
Prevalence of undernourishment[6] (% of population)[7]	..	21.7	22.2	16.7	16.4	15.9	15.3	14.0	..
Immunization, measles (% of children ages 12–23 months)[8]	56.0	60.0	64.0	72.0	78.0	83.0	85.0	93.0	95.0

Consecutive administrations in India: performance on development indicators (2000–19)

Indicator	**NDA-I**		**UPA-I**		**UPA-II**		**NDA-II**		**NDA-III**
	2000	**2003**	**2004**	**2008**	**2009**	**2013**	**2014**	**2018**	**2019**
School enrolment, secondary (% gross)[9]	44.9	49.6	51.4	60.4	59.6	68.8	74.1	74.4	73.8
Urban population growth (annual %)	2.5	2.8	2.8	2.6	2.5	2.3	2.3	2.3	2.3
Forest area (sq km) (thousands)	653.9	667.8	672.5	689.6	693.7	703.3	705.0	..	..
Energy use (kg of oil equivalent per capita)[10]	417.3	424.3	439.7	501.6	544.6	605.8	636.6	..	..
CO2 emissions (metric tons per capita)	1.0	1.0	1.0	1.3	1.4	1.6	1.7	..	..
Electric power consumption (kWh per capita)	393.6	430.5	451.6	561.2	598.5	764.2	804.5	..	..
Statistical Capacity score (overall average)[11]	..	..	78.9	80.0	75.6	73.3	81.1	77.8	75.6
Poverty headcount ratio at $1.90 a day (2011 PPP)				56.4	50.6	47.6	39.9	32.8	22.5

(continued)

Table A2.5: Consecutive administrations in India: performance on development indicators (2000–19) (continued)

Note: [1] Going back in time, the 2020 WDI indicators report the decline in the poverty headcount ratio in the following manner. At $1.90 a day (2011 PPP), it was 39.9 per cent in 2004, 32.8 per cent in 2009, and 22.5 per cent in 2011. The first part of 2004 was NDA-ruled and, therefore, the statistic could be interpreted as such; 2009 and 2011 were both UPA years.

	1983	**1987**	**1993**	**2004**	**2009**	**2011**
Poverty headcount ratio at $1.90 a day (2011 PPP)	56.4	50.6	47.6	39.9	32.8	22.5

[2] Poverty headcount ratio at national poverty lines (% of population) was reported for 2004 (37.2) and 2009 (29.8); both were UPA years. [3] Inflation as measured by the annual growth rate of the GDP implicit deflator shows the rate of price change in the economy as a whole. The GDP implicit deflator is the ratio of GDP in current local currency to GDP in constant local currency. [4] Total external debt is debt owed to non-residents repayable in currency, goods, or services. Total external debt is the sum of public, publicly guaranteed, and private nonguaranteed long-term debt, use of IMF credit, and short-term debt. Short-term debt includes all debt having an original maturity of one year or less and interest in arrears on long-term debt. Data are in current U.S. dollars. [5] Total debt service to exports of goods, services and primary income. Total debt service is the sum of principal repayments and interest actually paid in currency, goods, or services on long-term debt, interest paid on short-term debt, and repayments (repurchases and charges) to the IMF. [6] Population below minimum level of dietary energy consumption (also referred to as prevalence of undernourishment) shows the percentage of the population whose food intake is insufficient to meet dietary energy requirements continuously. Data showing as 5 may signify a prevalence of undernourishment below 5%. [7] Prevalence of underweight, weight for age (% of children under 5) was available for 2014 (29.4). [8] Child immunization, measles, measures the percentage of children ages 12–23 months who received the measles vaccination before 12 months or at any time before the survey. A child is considered adequately immunized against measles after receiving one dose of vaccine. [9] Secondary education completes the provision of basic education that began at the primary level, and aims at laying the foundations for lifelong learning and human development, by offering more subject- or skill-oriented instruction using more specialized teachers. [10] Energy use refers to use of primary energy before transformation to other end-use fuels, which is equal to indigenous production plus imports and stock changes, minus exports and fuels supplied to ships and aircraft engaged in international transport. [11] The Statistical Capacity Indicator is a composite score assessing the capacity of a country's statistical system. It is based on a diagnostic framework assessing the following areas: methodology; data sources; and periodicity and timeliness. Countries are scored against 25 criteria in these areas, using publicly available information and/or country input. The overall statistical capacity score is then calculated as a simple average of all three area scores on a scale of 0–100.

Source: World Development Indicators, 2020, World Bank (last updated on 16 December, 2020)

APPENDIX 4.1

Selected Country Tables

Table A4.1: Selected countries: Human Development Index (HDI)[1]

HDI rank			Country	HDI Value			Life expectancy			Average school years			Per capita GNI ($)[3]		
2015	2017	2019[2]		2015	2017	2019	2015	2017	2019	2015	2017	2019	2015	2017	2019
1	1	1	Norway	0.95	0.95	0.96	81.9	82.1	82.4	12.5	12.8	12.9	64,683	65,732	66,494
10	13	17	US	0.92	0.92	0.93	78.9	78.9	78.9	13.3	13.4	13.4	59,559	61,019	63,826
16	14	13	UK	0.92	0.93	0.93	81.1	81.2	81.3	12.8	12.9	13.2	43,885	45,427	46,071
49	49	52	Russia	0.81	0.82	0.82	71.5	72.1	72.6	11.8	12.0	12.2	24,847	25,311	26,157
79	79	84	Brazil	0.76	0.76	0.77	75.0	75.5	75.9	7.6	7.8	8.0	14,775	14,248	14,263
90	86	85	China	0.74	0.75	0.76	75.9	76.5	76.9	7.7	7.8	8.1	12,644	14,333	16,057
119	113	114	S. Africa	0.70	0.71	0.71	62.6	63.5	64.1	10.1	10.2	10.2	12,528	12,322	12,129
131	130	131	India	0.62	0.64	0.65	68.6	69.2	69.7	6.2	6.5	6.5	5,391	6,119	6,681

Note: [1] 188 countries in 2015,189 countries in 2017 and 2019. [2] Ranking by HDI value for 2019, calculated using the recently revised data available in 2020. [3] Per capita GNI (constant 2017 PPP terms).

Source: Human Development Report, 2016, 2018 & 2020, UNDP

Table A4.2: Selected countries: changes in HDI

Country	Change in HDI rank		CHI[1]			IHDI[2]			HDI-IHDI (% loss)		
	2012–17	2014–19	2015	2017	2019	2015	2017	2019	2015	2017	2019
Norway	0	0	5.4	7.9	6.0	0.90	0.88	0.90	5.5	8.1	6.1
US	-5	-3	12.9	13.1	12.1	0.80	0.80	0.81	13.6	13.7	12.7
UK	5	0	7.8	9.1	7.9	0.85	0.84	0.86	8.0	9.4	8.2
Russia	3	1	9.6	9.3	10.0	0.73	0.74	0.74	9.8	9.5	10.2
Brazil	7	-2	25.0	23.2	24.4	0.56	0.58	0.57	25.5	23.9	25.5
China	7	12	–	14.2	15.7	–	0.64	0.64	–	14.5	16.0
S. Africa	6	-2	32.0	30.3	31.2	0.46	0.47	0.47	34.7	33.2	34.0
India	2	1	26.5	26.3	25.7	0.46	0.47	0.48	27.1	26.9	26.4

Note: [1] Coefficient of human inequality, which indicates the extent of inequality in a country. [2] Inequality-adjusted HDI.

Source: Human Development Report, 2016, 2018 and 2020

Table A4.3: Selected countries: Multi-dimensional Poverty (MDP)

Country	Number of poor in MDP (million)[1]		PMDP[2] (%)		Intensity of deprivation[3] (%)		MPI[4]		SMDP (Severe MDP) (%)		Inequality among the poor[5]
	2016	2018	2018	2020	2018	2020	2018	2020	2018	2020	2020
Brazil	7.9	8.0	3.8	3.8	42.5	42.5	0.016	0.016	0.9	0.9	0.008
China	54.2	55.5	4.0	3.9	41.4	41.4	0.017	0.016	0.3	0.3	0.005
India	369.2	377.5	27.5	27.9	43.9	43.9	0.121	0.123	8.6	8.8	0.014
South Africa	3.5	3.6	5.6	6.3	38.4	39.8	0.021	0.025	0.6	0.9	0.005

Note: [1] 2016 and 2018 values are reported in 2019 and 2020 MPI reports respectively. [2] Proportion of population in MDP. [3] Intensity is the average share of indicators in which poor people are deprived. [4] MPI = PMDP x Intensity (Range 0 to 1), reflecting both the share of people in poverty and the degree to which they are deprived. [5] Variance of individual deprivation scores of poor people. It is calculated by subtracting the deprivation score of each multidimensionally poor person from the average intensity, squaring the differences and dividing the sum of the weighted squares by the number of multidimensionally poor people.

Source: Global Multi-dimensional Poverty Index (MPI) Report 2020, joint project of Oxford Poverty & Human Development Initiative (OPHI) and UNDP

APPENDIX 5.1

Evidence on Inequality in the US

That slavery left an indelible mark on the US economy and society is without doubt. Its manifestation in the form of a continuation of inequality has been analysed by many authors. By the end of the 20th century, when economic growth slowed and inequality of income and wealth grew, whatever income gains there were, primarily benefited smaller slices of the population at the top.[1] As income and wealth distribution worsened, microeconomic aspects began to be analysed revealing how worsening distribution obstructed the economy and its economic mobility. Boushey (2019) reviewed this literature comprehensively. Chetty et al. (2017) found that fewer children from the middle class and at the bottom did better than their parents did, countering the achievements of the 1960s and 1970s. They estimated that 70 per cent of the decrease in absolute mobility would not have occurred had the inequality in income and wealth been kept in check. Clearly, for the US youth to move up, the gap between incomes at the top and the bottom has to narrow.

Economic inequality led to health inequality that, in turn, exacerbated differences in lifelong skills of people. Goldin and Katz (2010); Almond and Currie (2011); Currie and Thomas (1999) – demonstrated this in various ways. In the UK, 17,000 children born during one week in 1958 and tracked through adulthood, revealed that healthier ones passed school English and maths more easily; they were 4–5 per cent more able to have jobs, and received higher wages at age 33. Based on this, Currie and Hyson (1999) concluded that children's health at birth relates to health during life. Others related birth weight to the probability of graduating high school. Adult employment was also related to birth weight. Thus, child and family characteristics at school entry explained the number of

[1] Edlund and Kopczuk (2009) and others have shown that inequality of women (versus men) and of minorities (versus the majority) has worsened even more than the inequality of income itself.

years of education as well as other outcomes such as future employment. Epidemiologist David Barker pointed to mother's nutrition and health rather than only genetics or poor lifestyles as determinants of health disorders. These researchers have consistently taken the view that prenatal conditions had lifelong ramifications.

Education differences have had a dual directional relation with inequality, one feeding the other. Out of the 31 Organisation for Economic Co-operation and Development (OECD) member countries, the US ranks 20th in formal childcare, and 29th in preschool enrolment. An early 'controlled experiment' by a number of joint authors more than half a century ago, studied selected aspects of 123 African American children from low-income Michigan families. At age three to four, they were randomly assigned to, or excluded from, attending high quality pre-school. When they all reached around age 40 at the turn of the century, those who had attended pre-school, had attained higher school completion rates, college attendance, higher earnings, more stable housing and family relationships, and fewer arrests.[2]

The difference in education ultimately reflects different access to resources. Cooper and Stewart (2013) summarized research findings between 1988 and 2012 to conclude that poorer children performed poorly because they were poorer, implying that transferring money to poorer families would improve children's outcomes. This was established by Dahl and Lochner (2012) for children's performance in families that received transfers through the US's Earned Income Tax Credit programme.

Not only cash, but maternal nutrition, safe drinking water, pre-school services, school quality, neighbourhood safety, libraries, parks, zoos and museums – all have lasting effects on children. For this, feasibility to provide family care through paid parental leave ranks high, though the US lags behind Europe on this too. Ramey and Ramey (2010) argued that college educated parents spent more time with children to get them into competition for top college admissions. It was obvious that, otherwise, children would lose out in the competition.

Boushey pointed out that children and their impact on the future of the US economy could not be considered in a vacuum but as part of a holistic environment. She argued in favour of continually disaggregating economic growth by income groups as it occurred, in order to view the distribution effects of growth more clearly and, accordingly, take policy action to make it less concentrated.

---

[2] Today such controlled experiments would be considered unethical in advanced economies inasmuch as half the needy children were excluded from a good early education. It is curious that controlled experiments in rudimentary environments continue to be conducted by advanced economy researchers.

Boushey proposed a list of actions: (1) for every official updating of statistics on the growth of income and wealth, show how that growth had been distributed across income and wealth deciles. It may be added that this should be done for even fractions of the top decile since concentration is growing in some countries even within it. (2) Remove the hoarding of opportunity by the top cohorts which stops others from the right to equal opportunity and from contributing to growth or receiving benefit from it. (3) To achieve this, socio-economic policy must target society from early on through access to high quality child care, preschool, public schools of high quality, and public health. (4) Prioritize infrastructure investments that buttress them. (5) Regulate those who subvert fair processes and manipulate economic growth in their own favour. (6) Rein in monopoly power to free up the generation of more government revenue that could, in turn, be used for needed expenditures. (7) Boost the collective bargaining power of workers, and (8) discourage capital use in investments such as financial products that do not lead to real productive activity and, instead, exacerbate economic instability.

APPENDIX 8.1

Impact of Land Policy

There was a need to incorporate economic fundamentals in the legislation on land acquisition as proposed but that was lacking. Self-explanatory Figure A8.1 indicates how the price per unit of land supplied by farmers would be constrained reflective of government policy. It describes the agricultural land market in which government has entered with the objective of acquiring land on behalf of industry – public or private or in combination. S(L) is the supply curve of land which is a summation of distinct supply curves of individual farmers. While each farmer is likely to have a different valuation of his land asset and therefore possess a different price-to-supply relation, overall, the market sums up to S(L). Note that S(L) is upward sloping since more land will be offered in the market as a whole only as the price per unit of land increases.

On the other hand, the industrialist has a demand curve D(L) for land needed for his proposed project which reveals that he will tend to demand more land as its per unit price diminishes. However, he has a maximum per unit price, OF, which he will not venture to offer for the land he requires. It is important to point this out since governments, in particular some state governments, run to offer land at prices above which they tend to believe industry would not be attracted to invest.

If government did not intervene, then equilibrium in the market would occur at C, the demand–supply intersection, at a price of CL and the land exchanged would be OL. The problem is that this amount of land is insufficient for the project, the requirement being larger (OL). At this point, AB emerges as the measurement of mismatched prices, the suppliers wanting a price of AL per unit and the buyer offering only to pay BL per unit reflecting a mismatch in the demand and supply curves, AB at L. So, government intervenes to find ways to acquire OL amount of land, and usually at a per unit price of less than AL.

Figure A8.1: Supply–demand of land

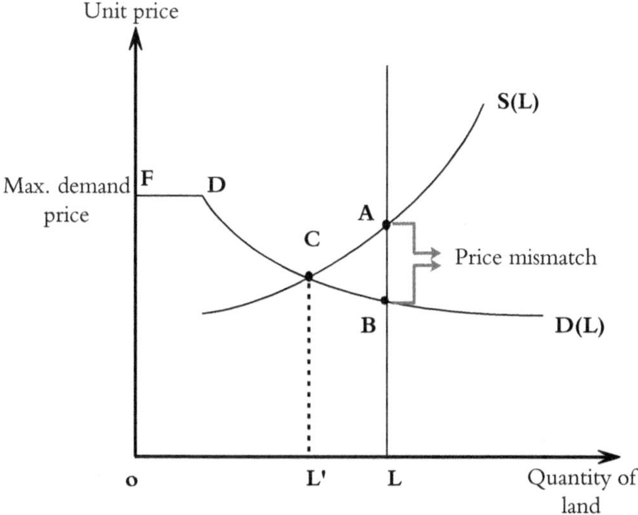

The issue is where, within the range AB, the government fixes the per unit price. Is it to be extracted from the supplier/farmer, the industrialist, or from the government budget. What is clear is that there is no economic justification for government to subsidize industry by indirectly taxing the farmer. Government's role should only be facilitation of the acquisition of land where this is not forthcoming due to the underlying intra-farmer variation in the composite S(L) curve. This the government could usefully achieve through variegated compensation of different farmers, while assuring that there is no transfer at the overall level from farmers to the industrialist.

The crux of the issue is the apprehension that public transfers do not work this way and invariably affect the farmer's or tribal's position adversely. Government's past economic practice is replete with examples, of which the 2006 Special Economic Zones (SEZ) Act or the 2015 Land Acquisition Act are just two.

Figure A8.2 demonstrates how a farmer or tribal's position may actually worsen using a box diagram. The initial points for industry and farmers are corner points A and B respectively. From here both would like to move, through a tatonnement process, towards the inside of the box where both would be better-off. Thus, both would prefer to move as close to preference ranking 4 (F_4 for farmers and I_4 for industry) as possible through acquisition or sale of land. For example, at D, both would gain, though industry would gain more than farmers (since industry would reach I_4 but farmers would languish at F_1).

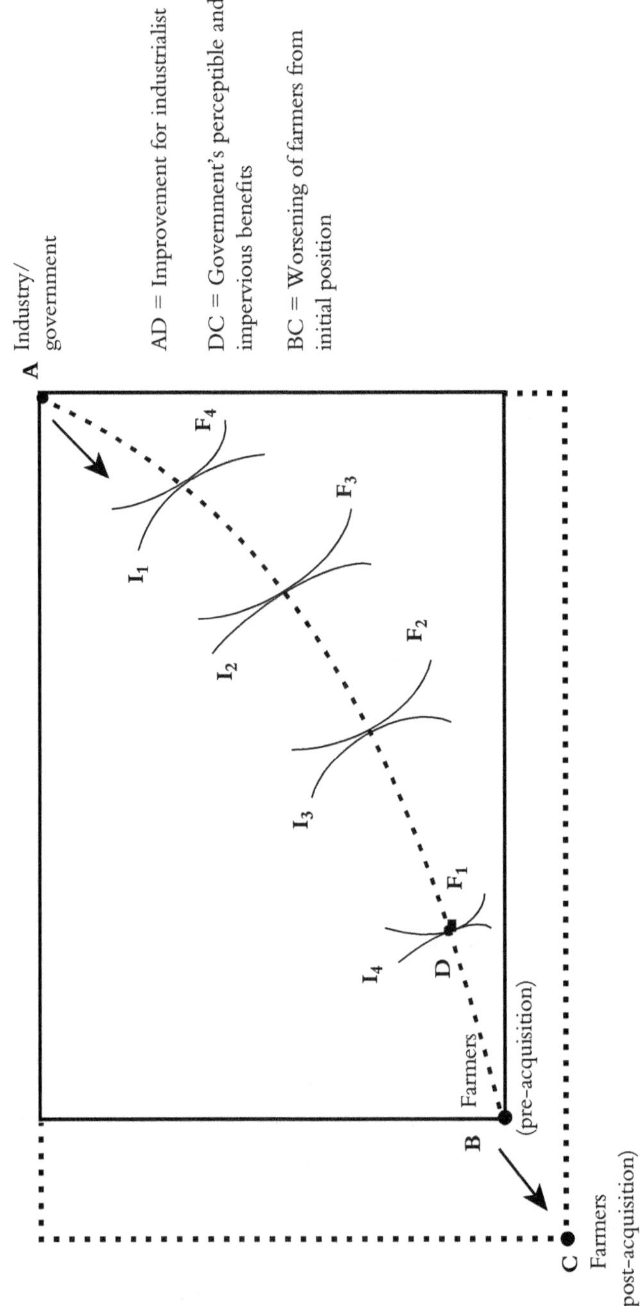

Figure A8.2: Farmer–industrialist trade-off

Indeed, recent history has convincingly demonstrated that farmers have receded from B, their initial position, appearing to move out of the box, to C, a worse-than-initial position. Figure A8.2 is drawn to show further that, instead of being a facilitator, government has bagged a benefit through receipts from leakage or unfulfilled promises of rehabilitation and resettlement, thus pushing farmers beneath even B, their initial position.

Remedial policy would have included the introduction of seriously designed and implemented – rather than routine, merely administrative, non-professional – Social Impact Assessment (SIA) 'in the public interest' before edifices such as the recent Acts. Bills[1] were rammed through parliament.[2] Indeed, the deleterious ramifications in the form of the social cost generated from months of mass action in 2020–21 by farmers and the heavy-handed corrective policies of government were for all to see from within and beyond the country's borders.

Figure A8.2 is illustrative of government policy repeatedly failing to ensure that a movement from B to C would be averted since it ignored the condition that the consent of 70 per cent of the affected communities would be garnered; those affected by the loss of land or associated livelihood would be protected; as well as the need for a Social Impact Assessment (SIA) 'in the public interest' related to the passing of the Act would be fulfilled.

1 Government of India Right to Fair Compensation and Transparency in Land Acquisition, Rehabilitation and Resettlement (Amendment) (LARR) Bill, 2015 sought to Amend the Act of 2013 (LARR Act, 2013) – The Farmers' Produce Trade and Commerce (Promotion and Facilitation) Act, 2020a; The Farmers (Empowerment and Protection) Agreement of Price Assurance and Farm Services Act, 2020b; and The Essential Commodities (Amendment) Act, 2020c.

2 The same lack slips into view in projects pertaining to national security and defence, rural infrastructure including electrification, affordable housing and housing for the poor, industrial corridors and infrastructure projects including ones under private-public partnership where ownership of land is with government.

APPENDIX 11.1

Impact of Asset Transfer on the Poor

Balboni et al. (2020) considered the impact of a small transfer of an asset in a study carried out in Bangladesh. Villager groups who were given one milch cow did significantly better in earning future incomes than did comparable groups who did not receive the asset. They used data from Bandiera et al. (2017)[1] pertaining to a region in Northern Bangladesh on 23,000 households living in 1,309 villages in the 13 poorest districts in the country. Of these households, over 6,000 were considered extremely poor; the lack of opportunity prevented 96 per cent of the sample villagers from undertaking presumably a preferred optimal occupation since access to opportunities depended on initial wealth.

The researchers used a transfer programme comprising the random allocation of an asset – milch cow – in 2007 that gave some of the poorest women in Bangladesh access to the same work opportunities as their wealthier counterparts in the same villages. The livestock was transferred jointly to a finite number of poor households versus those who did not receive such transfer. Monga, the selected region, was a famine-prone region which experienced irregular demand for casual wage labour mainly employed in agriculture and domestic service. They faced high grain prices, extreme poverty and food insecurity. The richer were usually self-employed and were found in livestock rearing and land cultivation. Productive assets set the rich and poor apart – the former possessing 94 times higher assets than the latter on average.

Exploiting variations in initial endowments, they concluded that, if a programme pushed individuals over a threshold level of initial assets, then they could get out of persistent poverty. In fact, transferees continued to

[1] It was based on data collected to evaluate BRAC's (an NGO) Targeting the Ultra-poor Programme.

acquire new assets on their own that, combined with own labour, generated further income, generating an accelerator perhaps. But if the threshold was not crossed, for example by those whose baseline assets were so low that the transfer could not heave them over the threshold, then they slid back, and were trapped back in poverty.[2] Thus a poverty trap did exist.

Another study by Bari et al. (2021) focused in Pakistan analysed the impact of loans tied to the hire-purchase of assets for business purposes. They worked through a major financial institution with a pool of borrowers who had completed previous loan cycles, and who wanted to expand their businesses by purchasing a fixed asset but were unable to do so due to their borrowing limit. The experiment offered a hire-purchase contract to finance a business asset worth four times a client's previous borrowing limit. They found large, persistent effects enabling the borrowers to run larger businesses, enjoy higher profits, and increase household consumption of food and finance children's education.

Banerjee and Duflo (2008) had, however, raised issue with the presumed underlying desire to expand a business in a beneficiary of an asset transfer. They questioned the presumption of empowerment generated through a new responsibility from a received asset. In a cross-country analysis, they found little evidence that the median poor entrepreneur tried to expand existing businesses; rather, it comprised more of a survival strategy instead, basically with the sole objective of battling to merely pull themselves out of poverty. According to the authors, after all, they already had to cope with the many challenges of living a life on very little money so that developing new business objectives appeared to be a far-fetched goal.

Banerjee and Dufflo's conclusions, therefore, appear to be in contraposition with those of Balboni, Bandiera, Bari, and others whose work came later. The latter's work provided impetus to policies oriented to the transfer of tangible and intangible assets to the very poor for business purposes with the objective of pulling them over the threshold of poverty through establishing small businesses and advancing their financial positions and, indeed, achieving a step up in household consumption.

---

2 They were about one-third of the sample and on average they lost 16 per cent of their asset value (inclusive of the transfer) by the fourth year. In contrast, those who did go past the threshold and accumulated additional assets, registered 4 per cent higher assets by the fourth year.

Index

References to tables appear in **bold** type. References to footnotes show both the page number and the note number (103n8).

B

D

E